Get the eBook FREE!

(PDF, ePub, Kindle, and liveBook all included)

We believe that once you buy a book from us, you should be able to read it in any format we have available. To get electronic versions of this book at no additional cost to you, purchase and then register this book at the Manning website.

Go to https://www.manning.com/freebook and follow the instructions to complete your pBook registration.

That's it!
Thanks from Manning!

Build a Career in Data Science

EMILY ROBINSON
AND JACQUELINE NOLIS

MANNING

SHELTER ISLAND

For online information and ordering of this and other Manning books, please visit
www.manning.com. The publisher offers discounts on this book when ordered in quantity.
For more information, please contact

  Special Sales Department
  Manning Publications Co.
  20 Baldwin Road
  PO Box 761
  Shelter Island, NY 11964
  Email: orders@manning.com

Manning Publications Co.
20 Baldwin Road
PO Box 761
Shelter Island, NY 11964

Development editor: Karen Miller
Review editor: Ivan Martinović
Production editor: Lori Weidert
Copy editor: Kathy Simpson
Proofreader: Melody Dolab
Typesetter: Dennis Dalinnik
Cover designer: Leslie Haimes

ISBN: 9781617296246
Printed in the United States of America

From Emily, to Michael,
and
From Jacqueline, to Heather, Amber, and Laura,
for the love and support you provided us throughout this journey.

brief contents

contents

preface

"How do I get your job?"

As veteran data scientists, we're constantly being asked this question. Sometimes, we're asked directly; at other times, people ask indirectly through questions about the decisions we've made in our careers to get where we are. Under the surface, the people asking the questions seem to have a constant struggle, because so few resources are available for finding out how to become or grow as a data scientist. Lots of data scientists are looking for help with their careers and often not finding clear answers.

Although we've written blog posts with tactical advice on how to handle specific moments in a data science job, we've struggled with the lack of a definitive text covering the end-to-end of starting and growing a data science career. This book was written to help these people—the thousands of people who hear about data science and machine learning but don't know where to start, as well as those who are already in the field and want to understand how to move up.

We were happy to get this chance to collaborate in creating this book. We both felt that our respective backgrounds and viewpoints complemented each other and created a better book for you. We are

- *Jacqueline Nolis*—I received a BS and MS in mathematics and a PhD in operations research. When I started working, the term *data science* didn't yet exist, and I had to figure out my career path at the same time that the field was defining itself. Now I'm a consultant, helping companies grow data science teams.
- *Emily Robinson*—I got my undergraduate degree in decision sciences and my master's in management. After attending a three-month data science bootcamp

in 2016, I started working in data science, specializing in A/B testing. Now I work as a senior data scientist at Warby Parker, tackling some of the company's biggest projects.

Throughout our careers, we've both built project portfolios and experienced the stress of adjusting to a new job. We've felt the sting of being rejected for jobs we wanted and the triumph of seeing our analyses positively affect the business. We've faced issues with a difficult business partner and benefited from a supportive mentor. Although these experiences taught us so much in our careers, to us the true value comes from sharing them with others.

This book is meant to be a guide to career questions in data science, following the path that a person will take in the career. We start with the beginning of the journey: how to get basic data science skills and understand what jobs are actually like. Then we go through getting a job and how to get settled in. We cover how to grow in the role and eventually how to transition up to management—or out to a new company. Our intention is for this book to be a resource that data scientists continue to go back to as they hit new milestones in their careers.

Because the focus on career is very important for this book, we chose to not focus deeply on the technical components of data science; we don't cover topics such as how to choose the hyperparameters of a model or the minute details of Python packages. In fact, this book doesn't include a single equation or line of code. We know that plenty of great books out there cover these topics; we wanted instead to discuss the often-overlooked but equally important nontechnical knowledge needed to succeed in data science.

We included many personal experiences from respected data scientists in this book. At the end of each chapter, you'll find an interview describing how a real, human data scientist personally handled dealing with the concepts that the chapter covers. We're extremely happy with the amazing, detailed, and vulnerable responses we got from all the data scientists we talked to. We feel that the examples they provide from their lives can teach much more than any broad statement we might write.

Another decision we made in writing this book was to make it opinionated. By that, we mean we intentionally chose to focus on the lessons we've learned as professional data scientists and by talking to others in the community. At times, we make statements not everyone might agree with, such as suggesting that you should always write a cover letter when applying for jobs. We felt that the benefit of providing viewpoints that we strongly believe are helpful to data scientists was more important than trying to write something that contained only objective truths.

We hope that you find this book to be a helpful guide as you progress in your data science career. We've written it to be the document we wish we had when we were aspiring and junior data scientists; we hope that you'll be glad to have it now.

acknowledgments

First and foremost, we'd like to thank our spouses, Michael Berkowitz and Heather Nolis. Without them, this book would not have been possible (and not just because Michael wrote the first draft of some of the sections despite being a bridge professional and not a data scientist, or because Heather evangelized half of the machine learning engineering content).

Next, we want to acknowledge the staff at Manning who guided us through this process, improved the book, and made it possible in the first place. Thank you especially to our editor, Karen Miller, who kept us on track and coordinated all the various moving parts.

Thank you to all the reviewers who read the manuscript at various points and provided invaluable detailed feedback: Brynjar Smári Bjarnason, Christian Thoudahl, Daniel Berecz, Domenico Nappo, Geoff Barto, Gustavo Gomes, Hagai Luger, James Ritter, Jeff Neumann, Jonathan Twaddell, Krzysztof Jędrzejewski, Malgorzata Rodacka, Mario Giesel, Narayana Lalitanand Surampudi, Ping Zhao, Riccardo Marotti, Richard Tobias, Sebastian Palma Mardones, Steve Sussman, Tony M. Dubitsky, and Yul Williams. Thank you as well to our friends and family members who read the book and offered their own suggestions: Elin Farnell, Amanda Liston, Christian Roy, Jonathan Goodman, and Eric Robinson. Your contributions helped shape this book and made it as helpful to our readers as possible.

Finally, we want to thank all of our end-of-chapter interviewees: Robert Chang, Randy Au, Julia Silge, David Robinson, Jesse Mostipak, Kristen Kehrer, Ryan Williams, Brooke Watson Madubuonwu, Jarvis Miller, Hilary Parker, Heather Nolis, Sade Snowden-

Akintunde, Michelle Keim, Renee Teate, Amanda Casari, and Angela Bassa. Additionally, we're grateful for those who contributed to sidebars throughout the book and suggested interview questions for the appendix: Vicki Boykis, Rodrigo Fuentealba Cartes, Gustavo Coelho, Emily Bartha, Trey Causey, Elin Farnell, Jeff Allen, Elizabeth Hunter, Sam Barrows, Reshama Shaikh, Gabriela de Queiroz, Rob Stamm, Alex Hayes, Ludamila Janda, Ayanthi G., Allan Butler, Heather Nolis, Jeroen Janssens, Emily Spahn, Tereza Iofciu, Bertil Hatt, Ryan Williams, Peter Baldridge, and Hlynur Hallgrímsson. All these people provided valuable perspectives, and together, they know much more than we ever could.

about this book

Build a Career in Data Science was written to help you enter the field of data science and grow your career in it. It walks you through the role of a data scientist, how to get the skills you need, and the steps to getting a data science job. After you have a job, this book helps you understand how to mature in the role and eventually become a larger part of the data science community, as well as a senior data scientist. After reading this book, you should be confident about how to advance your career.

Who should read this book

This book is for people who have not yet entered the field of data science but are considering it, as well as people who are in the first few years of the role. Aspiring data scientists will learn the skills they need to become data scientists, and junior data scientists will learn how to become more senior. Many of the topics in the book, such as interviewing and negotiating an offer, are worthwhile resources to come back to throughout any data science career.

How this book is organized: a roadmap

This book is broken into four parts, arranged in the chronological order of a data science career. Part 1 of the book, Getting started with data science, covers what data science is and what skills it requires:

- Chapter 1 introduces the role of a data scientist and the different types of jobs that share that title.

- Chapter 2 presents five example companies that have data scientists and shows how the culture and type of each company affects the data science positions.
- Chapter 3 lays out the different paths a person can take to get the skills needed to be a data scientist.
- Chapter 4 describes how to create and share projects to build a data science portfolio.

Part 2 of the book, Finding your data science job, explains the entire job search process for data science positions:

- Chapter 5 walks through the search for open positions and how to find the ones worth investing in.
- Chapter 6 explains how to create a cover letter and résumé and then adjust them for each job you apply for.
- Chapter 7 provides details on the interview process and what to expect from it.
- Chapter 8 is about what to do after you receive an offer, focusing on how to negotiate it.

Part 3 of the book, Settling into data science, covers the basics of the early months of a data science job:

- Chapter 9 lays out what to expect in the first few months of a data science job and shows you how to make the most of them.
- Chapter 10 walks through the process of making analyses, which are core components of most data science roles.
- Chapter 11 focuses on putting machine learning models into production, which is necessary in more engineering-based positions.
- Chapter 12 explains how to communicate with stakeholders—a task that data scientists have to do more than most other technical roles.

Part 4 of the book, Growing in your data science role, covers topics for more seasoned data scientists who are looking to continue to advance their careers:

- Chapter 13 describes how to handle failed data science projects.
- Chapter 14 shows you how to become part of the larger data science community through activities such as speaking and contributing to open source.
- Chapter 15 is a guide to the difficult task of leaving a data science position.
- Chapter 16 ends the book with the roles data scientists can get as they move up the corporate ladder.

Finally, we have an appendix of more than 30 interview questions, example answers, and notes on what the question is trying to assess and what makes a good answer.

People who haven't been data scientists before should start at the beginning of the book, whereas people who already are in the field may begin with a later chapter to guide them in a challenge they're currently facing. Although the chapters are ordered to flow like a data science career, they can be read out of order according to readers' needs.

The chapters end with interviews of data scientists in various industries who discuss how the topic of the chapter has shown up in their career. The interviewees were selected due to their contributions to the field of data science and the interesting journeys they followed as they became data scientists.

liveBook discussion forum

Purchase of *Build a Career in Data Science* includes free access to a private web forum run by Manning Publications where you can make comments about the book, ask technical questions, and receive help from the author and from other users. To access the forum, go to https://livebook.manning.com/#!/book/build-a-career-in-data-science/discussion. You can also learn more about Manning's forums and the rules of conduct at https://livebook.manning.com/#!/discussion.

Manning's commitment to our readers is to provide a venue where a meaningful dialogue between individual readers and between readers and the author can take place. It is not a commitment to any specific amount of participation on the part of the author, whose contribution to the forum remains voluntary (and unpaid). We suggest you try asking the author some challenging questions lest their interest stray! The forum and the archives of previous discussions will be accessible from the publisher's website as long as the book is in print.

about the authors

Emily Robinson

WRITTEN BY JACQUELINE NOLIS

Emily Robinson is a brilliant senior data scientist at Warby Parker and previously worked at DataCamp and Etsy.

I first met Emily at Data Day Texas 2018, when she was one of the few people who attended my talk on data science in industry. At the end of my speech, she shot her hand up and asked a great question. To my surprise, an hour later we had swapped; I was watching her calmly and casually give a great presentation while I was eagerly waiting to raise my hand and ask her a question. That day, I knew she was a hard-working

ABOUT THE AUTHORS

xxv

and clever data scientist. A few months later, when it came time for me to find someone to co-author a book, she was at the top of my list. When I sent her the email asking whether she would be interested, I figured that there was a good chance she would say no; she was probably out of my league.

Working with Emily on this book has been a joy. She is deeply thoughtful about the struggles of junior data scientists and has the ability to clearly understand what is important. She is constantly getting her work done and somehow also is able to squeeze out extra blog posts while doing it. Now having seen her at more conferences and social events, I've watched as she's talked to many data scientists and made all of them feel comfortable and welcome. She's also an expert in A/B testing and experimentation, but it's clear that this just happens to be the area she's working in at the moment; she could pick up any other part of data science and be an expert in that if she wanted to.

My only disappointment is that I'm writing these words about her at the end of creating the book, and with us finishing, someone besides me will have the next opportunity to collaborate with her.

Jacqueline Nolis

WRITTEN BY EMILY ROBINSON

Whenever someone asks me whether I would recommend writing a book, I always say, "Only if you do it with a co-author." But that's not actually the full picture. It should be "Only if you do it with a co-author who is as fun, warm, generous, smart, experienced, and caring as Jacqueline." I'm not sure what it's like working with a "normal" co-author, because Jacqueline has always been amazing, and I feel incredibly lucky to have gotten to work with her on this project.

It would be easy for someone as accomplished as Jacqueline to be intimidating. She has a PhD in industrial engineering, got $100,000 for winning the third season of the reality television show *King of the Nerds*, was a director of analytics, and started her own successful consulting firm. She's spoken at conferences across the country and is regularly asked back by her alma mater to advise math undergraduates (her major) on careers. When she spoke at an online conference, the compliments about her presentation flooded the chat, such as "the best so far," "excellent presentation," "really helpful," and "great, dynamic presentation." But Jacqueline never makes anyone feel inferior or bad for not knowing something; rather, she loves making difficult concepts accessible, such as in her great presentation called "Deep learning isn't hard, I promise."

Her personal life is equally impressive: she has a wonderfully vibrant house in Seattle with her wife, son, two dogs, and three cats. I'm hoping that she might also one day adopt a certain co-author to fill out the very few empty spaces. She and her wife, Heather, have even given a presentation to a packed audience of 1,000 people eager to hear about how they used R to deploy machine learning models to production at T-Mobile. They also possibly have the best meet-cute story of all time: they met on the aforementioned show *King of the Nerds*, where Heather was also a competitor.

I'm very thankful to Jacqueline, who could have earned much more money for much less aggravation by doing anything other than writing this book with me. It is my hope that our work encourages aspiring and junior data scientists to become contributors to our community who are as great as Jacqueline is.

about the cover illustration

Part 1
Getting started
with data science

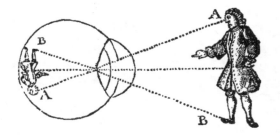

If you do a Google search for *how to become a data scientist,* you'll likely be confronted with a laundry list of skills, from statistical modeling to programming in Python through communicating effectively and making presentations. One job description might describe a role that's close to a statistician's, whereas another employer is looking for someone who has a master's degree in computer science. When you look for ways to gain those skills, you'll find options ranging from going back to school for a master's degree to doing a bootcamp to starting to do data analysis in your current job. Put together, all these combinations of paths can feel insurmountable, especially to people who aren't yet certain that they even want to be data scientists.

The good news is that there isn't a single data scientist who has all these skills. Data scientists share a foundation of knowledge, but they each have their own specialties, to the point that many couldn't swap jobs. The first part of this book is designed to help you understand what all these types of data scientists are and how to make the best decisions to start your career. By the end of this part, you should be prepared with the skills and understanding to start your job search.

Chapter 1 covers the basics of data science, including the skills you need for the job and the different types of data scientists. Chapter 2 goes into detail about the role of a data scientist at five types of companies to help you better understand what the job will be like. Chapter 3 covers the paths to getting the skills required for being a data scientist and the advantages and disadvantages of each. Finally, Chapter 4 covers how to create a portfolio of data science projects to get hands-on experience doing data science and create a portfolio to show to potential employers.

1

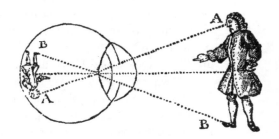

What is data science?

This chapter covers
- The three main areas of data science
- The different types of data science jobs

"The sexiest job of the 21st century." "The best job in America." Data scientist, a title that didn't even exist before 2008, is now the position employers can't hire enough of and job seekers strive to become. There's good reason for the hype: data science is a hugely growing field, with a median base salary of more than $100,000 in the United States in 2019 (http://mng.bz/XpMp). At a good company, data scientists enjoy a lot of autonomy and are constantly learning new things. They use their skills to solve significant problems, such as working with doctors to analyze drug trials, helping a sports team pick its new draftees, or redesigning the pricing model for a widget business. Finally, as we discuss in chapter 3, there's no one way to become a data scientist. People come from all backgrounds, so you're not limited based on what you chose to study as an undergraduate.

But not all data science jobs are perfect. Both companies and job seekers can have unrealistic expectations. Companies new to data science may think that one person can solve all their problems with data, for example. When a data scientist is finally hired, they can be faced with a never-ending to-do list of requests. They might be tasked with immediately implementing a machine learning system when no work has been done to prepare or clean the data. There may be no one to mentor or guide them, or even empathize with the problems they face. We'll discuss these issues in more depth in chapters 5 and 7, where we'll help you avoid joining companies that are likely to be a bad fit for a new data scientist, and in chapter 9, where we'll advise you on what to do if you end up in a negative situation.

On the other side, job seekers may think that there will never be a dull moment in their new career. They may expect that stakeholders will follow their recommendations routinely, that data engineers can fix any data quality issues immediately, and that they'll get the fastest computing resources available to implement their models. In reality, data scientists spend a lot of time cleaning and preparing data, as well as managing the expectations and priorities of other teams. Projects won't always work out. Senior management may make unrealistic promises to clients about what your data science models can deliver. A person's main job may be to work with an archaic data system that's impossible to automate and requires hours of mind-numbing work each week just to clean up the data. Data scientists may notice lots of statistical or technical mistakes in legacy analyses that have real consequences, but no one is interested, and they're so overloaded with work that they have no time to try to fix them. Or a data scientist may be asked to prepare reports that support what senior management has already decided, so they may worry about being fired if they give an independent answer.

This book is here to guide you through the process of becoming a data scientist and developing your career. We want to ensure that you, the reader, get all the great parts of being a data scientist and avoid most of the pitfalls. Maybe you're working in an adjacent field, such as marketing analytics, and wondering how to make the switch. Or maybe you're already a data scientist, but you're looking for a new job and don't think you approached your first job search well. Or you want to further your career by speaking at conferences, contributing to open source, or becoming an independent consultant. Whatever your level, we're confident that you'll find this book helpful.

In the first four chapters, we cover the main opportunities for gaining data science skills and building a portfolio to get around the paradox of needing experience to get experience. Part 2 shows how to write a cover letter and resume that will get you an interview and how to build your network to get a referral. We cover negotiation strategies that research has shown will get you the best offer possible.

When you're in a data science job, you'll be writing analyses, working with stakeholders, and maybe even putting a model into production. Part 3 helps you understand what all those processes look like and how to set yourself up for success. In part 4, you'll find strategies for picking yourself back up when a project inevitably fails. And when you're ready, we're here to guide you through the decision of where to take your career: advancing to management, continuing to be an individual contributor, or even striking out as an independent consultant.

Before you begin that journey, though, you need to be clear on what data scientists are and what work they do. Data science is a broad field that covers many types of work, and the better you understand the differences between those areas, the better you can grow in them.

1.1 What is data science?

Data science is the practice of using data to try to understand and solve real-world problems. This concept isn't exactly new; people have been analyzing sales figures and trends since the invention of the zero. In the past decade, however, we have gained access to exponentially more data than existed before. The advent of computers has assisted in the generation of all that data, but computing is also our only way to process the mounds of information. With computer code, a data scientist can transform or aggregate data, run statistical analyses, or train machine learning models. The output of this code may be a report or dashboard for human consumption, or it could be a machine learning model that will be deployed to run continuously.

If a retail company is having trouble deciding where to put a new store, for example, it may call in a data scientist to do an analysis. The data scientist could look at the historical data of locations where online orders are shipped to understand where customer demand is. They may also combine that customer location data with demographic and income information for those localities from census records. With these datasets, they could find the optimal place for the new store and create a Microsoft PowerPoint presentation to present their recommendation to the company's vice president of retail operations.

In another situation, that same retail company may want to increase online order sizes by recommending items to customers while they shop. A data scientist could load the historical web order data and create a machine learning model that, given a set of items currently in the cart, predicts the best item to recommend to the shopper. After creating that model, the data scientist would work with the company's engineering team so that every time a customer is shopping, the new machine learning model serves up the recommended items.

When many people start looking into data science, one challenge they face is being overwhelmed by the amount of things they need to learn, such as coding (but which language?), statistics (but which methods are most important in practice, and which are largely academic?), machine learning (but how is machine learning different from statistics or AI?), and the domain knowledge of whatever industry they want to work in (but what if you don't know where you want to work?). In addition, they need to learn business skills such as effectively communicating results to audiences ranging from other data scientists to the CEO. This anxiety can be exacerbated by job postings that ask for a PhD, multiple years of data science experience, and expertise in a laundry list of statistical and programming methods. How can you possibly learn all these skills? Which ones should you start with? What are the basics?

If you've looked into the different areas of data science, you may be familiar with Drew Conway's popular data science Venn diagram. In Conway's opinion (at the time of the diagram's creation), data science fell into the intersection of math and statistical knowledge, expertise in a domain, and hacking skills (that is, coding). This image is often used as the cornerstone of defining what a data scientist is. From our perspective, the components of data science are slightly different from what he proposed (figure 1.1).

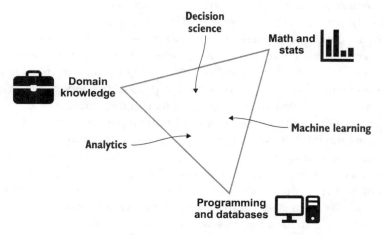

Figure 1.1 **The skills that combine to make data science and how they combine to make different roles**

We've changed Conway's original Venn diagram to a triangle because it's not that you either have a skill or you don't; it's that you may possess it to a different extent from others in the field. Although it's true that all three skills are fundamental and that you need to have each to a degree, you don't need to be an expert in all of them. We put within the triangle different types of data science specialties. These specialties don't always map one-to-one with job titles, and even when they do, different companies sometimes call them different things.

So what does each of these components mean?

1.1.1 *Mathematics/statistics*

At the basic level, mathematics and statistics knowledge is data literacy. We break down that literacy into three levels of knowledge:

- *That techniques exist*—If you don't know that something is possible, you can't use it. If a data scientist was trying to group similar customers, knowing that statistical methods (called *clustering*) can do this would be the first step.
- *How to apply the techniques*—Although a data scientist may know about many techniques, they also need to be able to understand the complexities of applying them—not only how to write code to apply the methods, but also how to configure them. If the data scientist wants to use a method such as *k*-means clustering to group the customers, they would need to understand how to do *k*-means

clustering in a programming language such as R or Python. They would also need to understand how to adjust the parameters of the method, for example, by choosing how many groups to create.

■ *How to choose which techniques to try*—Because so many possible techniques can be used in data science, it's important for the data scientist to be able to quickly assess whether a technique would work well. In our customer grouping example, even after the data scientist focuses on clustering, they have to consider dozens of different methods and algorithms. Rather than trying each method, they need to be able to rule out methods quickly and focus on just a few.

These sorts of skills are used constantly within a data science role. To consider a different example, suppose that you work at an e-commerce company. Your business partner might be interested in what countries have the highest average order value. If you have the data available, this question is easy to answer. But rather than simply presenting this information and letting your customer draw their own conclusions, you could dig deeper. If you have one order from country A for $100, and a thousand orders from country B that average $75, it is correct that country A has the higher average order value. But would you be confident in saying that this means your business partner should definitely invest in advertising in country A to increase the number of orders? Probably not. You have only one data point for country A, and maybe it's an outlier. If country A had 500 orders instead, you might use a statistical test to see whether the order value was significantly different, meaning that if there really was no difference between A and B on this measure, you'd be unlikely to see the difference you did. In this one paragraph-long example, many different assessments were made on what approaches were sensible, what should be considered, and what results were deemed to be unimportant.

1.1.2 Databases/programming

Programming and databases refer to the ability to pull data from company databases and to write clean, efficient, maintainable code. These skills are in many ways similar to what a software developer has to know, except that data scientists have to write code that does open-ended analysis rather than produces a predefined output. Each company's data stack is unique, so no one set of technical skills is required for a data scientist. But broadly, you'll need to know how to get data from a database and how to clean, manipulate, summarize, visualize, and share data.

In most data science jobs, R or Python is the main language. R is a programming language that has its roots in statistics, so it's generally strongest for statistical analysis and modeling, visualization, and generating reports with results. Python is a programming language that started as a general software development language and has become extremely popular in data science. Python is known for being better than R at working with large datasets, doing machine learning, and powering real-time algorithms (such as Amazon's recommendation engines). But thanks to the work of many contributors, the two languages' capabilities are now at near parity. Data scientists are successfully using R to make machine learning models that are run millions of times a week, and they're also making clean, presentable statistical analyses in Python.

R and Python are the most popular languages for data science for a couple of reasons:

- They're free and open source, meaning that many people, not just one company or one group, contribute code that you can use. They have many packages or *libraries* (sets of code) for doing data collection, manipulation, visualization, statistical analysis, and machine learning.
- Importantly, because each language has such a large following, it's easy for data scientists to find help when they run into problems. Although some companies still use SAS, SPSS, STATA, MATLAB, or other paid programs, many of them are starting to move to R or Python instead.

Although most data science analysis is done in R or Python, you'll often need to work with a database to get the data. This is where the language SQL comes in. SQL is the programming language that most databases use to manipulate data within them or to extract it. Consider a data scientist who wants to analyze the hundreds of millions of records of customer orders in a company to forecast how orders per day will change over time. First, they would likely write a SQL query to get the number of orders each day. Then they would take those daily order counts and run a statistical forecast in R or Python. For this reason, SQL is extremely popular in the data science community, and it's difficult to get too far without knowing it.

Another core skill is using *version control*—a method of keeping track of how code changes over time. Version control lets you store your files; revert them to a previous time; and see who changed what file, how, and when. This skill is extremely important for data science and software engineering because if someone accidentally changes a file that breaks your code, you want the ability to revert or see what changed.

Git is by far the most commonly used system for version control and is often used in conjunction with GitHub, a web-based hosting service for Git. Git allows you to save (*commit*) your changes, as well as see the whole history of the project and how it changed with each commit. If two people are working on the same file separately, Git makes sure that no one's work is ever accidentally deleted or overwritten. At many companies, especially those with strong engineering teams, you'll need to use Git if you want to share your code or put something into production.

Can you be a data scientist without programming?

It's possible to do a lot of data work using only Excel, Tableau, or other business intelligence tools that have graphical interfaces. Although you're not writing code, these tools claim to have much of the same functionality as languages such as R or Python, and many data scientist do use them sometimes. But can they be a complete data science toolkit? We say no. Practically, very few companies have a data science team where you wouldn't need to program. But even if that weren't the case, programming has advantages over using these tools.

The first advantage of programming is reproducibility. When you write code instead of using point-and-click software, you're able to rerun it whenever your data changes, whether that's every day or in six months. This advantage also ties into version control: instead of renaming your file every time your code changes, you can keep one file but see its entire history.

The second advantage is flexibility. If Tableau doesn't have a type of graph available, for example, you won't be able to create it. But with programming, you can write your own code to make something that the creators and maintainers of a tool never thought of.

The third and final advantage of open source languages such as Python and R is community contribution. Thousands of people create *packages*, and publish them openly on GitHub and/or CRAN (for R) and pip (for Python). You can download this code and use it for your own problems. You're not reliant on one company or group of people to add features.

1.1.3   *Business understanding*

> *Any sufficiently advanced technology is indistinguishable from magic.*
>
> Arthur C. Clarke

Businesses have, to put it mildly, varying understanding of how data science works. Often, management just wants something done and turns to its data science unicorns to make that thing happen. A core skill in data science is knowing how to translate a business situation into a data question, find the data answer, and finally deliver the business answer. A businessperson might ask, for example, "Why are our customers leaving?" But there's no "why-are-customers-leaving" Python package that you can import—it's up to you to deduce how to answer that question with data.

Business understanding is where your data science ideals meet the practicalities of the real world. It's not enough to want a specific piece of information without knowing how the data is stored and updated at your specific company. If your company is a subscription service, where does the data live? If someone changes their subscription, what happens? Does that subscriber's row get updated, or is another row added to the table? Do you need to work around any errors or inconsistencies in the data? If you don't know the answers to these questions, you won't be able to give an accurate answer to a basic question like "How many subscribers did we have on March 2, 2019?"

Business understanding also helps you know what questions to ask. Being asked "What should we do next?" by a stakeholder is a little like being asked "Why do we not have more money?" This type of question begs more questions. Developing an understanding of the core business (as well as the personalities involved) can help you parse the situation better. You might follow up with "Which product line are you looking for guidance regarding?" or "Would you like to see more participation from a certain sector of our audience?"

Another part of business understanding is developing general business skills, such as being able to tailor your presentations and reports to different audiences. Sometimes, you'll be discussing a better methodology with a room full of statistics PhDs, and sometimes, you'll be in front of a vice president who hasn't taken a math class in 20 years. You need to inform your audience without either talking down or overcomplicating.

Finally, as you become more senior, part of your job is to identify where the business could benefit from data science. If you've wanted to build a prediction system for your company but have never had management support, becoming part of the management team can help solve that problem. A senior data scientist will be on the lookout for places to implement machine learning, as they know its limitations and capabilities, as well as which kinds of tasks would benefit from automation.

Will data science disappear?

Underlying the question about whether data science will be around in a decade or two are two main concerns: that the job will become automated and that data science is overhyped and the job-market bubble will pop.

It's true that certain parts of the data science pipeline can be automated. Automated Machine Learning (AutoML) can compare the performance of different models and perform certain parts of data preparation (such as scaling variables). But these tasks are just a small part of the data science process. You'll often need to create the data yourself, for example; it's very rare to have perfectly clean data waiting for you. Also, creating the data usually involves talking with other people, such as user experience researchers or engineers, who will conduct the survey or log the user actions that can drive your analysis.

Regarding the possibility of a pop in a job-market bubble, a good comparison is software engineering in the 1980s. As computers grew cheaper, faster, and more common, there were concerns that soon a computer could do everything and that there would be no need for programmers. But the opposite thing happened, and now there are more than 1.2 million software engineers in the United States (http://mng.bz/MOPo). Although titles such as webmaster did disappear, more people than ever are working on website development, maintenance, and improvement.

We believe that there will be more specialization within data science, which may lead to the disappearance of the general title data scientist, but many companies are still in the early stages of learning how to leverage data science and there's plenty of work left to do.

1.2 *Different types of data science jobs*

You can mix and match the three core skills of data science (covered in section 1.1) into several jobs, all of which have some justification for having the title data scientist. From our perspective, these skills get mixed together in three main ways: analytics, machine learning, and decision science. Each of those areas serves a different purpose for the company and fundamentally delivers a different thing.

When looking for data science jobs, you should pay less attention to the job titles and more to the job descriptions and what you're asked in the interviews. Look at the backgrounds of people in data science roles, such as what previous jobs they held and what their degrees are. You may find that people who work in similar-sounding jobs have totally different titles or that people who have the same data scientist title do totally different things. As we talk in this book about different types of data science jobs, remember that the actual titles used at companies may vary.

1.2.1 Analytics

An *analyst* takes data and puts it in front of the right people. After a company sets its yearly goals, you might put those goals in a dashboard so that management can track progress every week. You could also build in features that allow managers to easily break down the numbers by country or product type. This work involves a lot of data cleaning and preparation but generally less work to interpret the data. Although you should be able to spot and fix data quality issues, the primary person who makes decisions with this data is the business partner. Thus, the job of an analyst is to take data from within the company, format and arrange it effectively, and deliver that data to others.

Because the analyst's role doesn't involve a lot of statistics and machine learning, some people and companies would consider this role to be outside the field of data science. But much of the work, such as devising meaningful visualizations and deciding on particular data transformations, requires the same skills used in the other types of data science roles. An analyst might be given a task such as "Create an automated dashboard that shows how our number of subscribers is changing over time and lets us filter the data to just subscribers of specific products or in specific geographical regions." The analyst would have to find the appropriate data within the company, figure out how to transform the data appropriately (such as by changing it from daily to weekly new subscriptions), and then create a meaningful set of dashboards that are visually compelling and automatically update each day without errors.

Short rule: an analyst creates *dashboards and reports that deliver data.*

1.2.2 Machine learning

A *machine learning engineer* develops machine learning models and puts them into production, where they run continuously. They may optimize the ranking algorithm for the search results of an e-commerce site, create a recommendation system, or monitor a model in production to make sure that its performance hasn't degraded since it was deployed. A machine learning engineer spends less time on things like creating visualizations that will convince people of something and more time doing the programming work of data science.

A big difference between this role and other types of data science positions is that the work output is primarily for machine consumption. You might create machine learning models that get turned into application programming interfaces (APIs) for other machines, for example. In many ways, you'll be closer to a software developer than to other data science roles. Although it's good for any data scientist to follow best coding practices, as a machine learning engineer, you must do so. Your code must be performant, tested, and written so that other people will be able to work with it. For this reason, many machine learning engineers come from a computer science background.

In a machine learning engineer role, a person may be asked to create a machine learning model that can—in real time—predict the probability that a customer on the website will actually finish their order. The machine learning engineer would have to find historical data in the company, train a machine learning model on it, turn that model into an API, and then deploy the API so that the website can run the model. If that model stops working for some reason, the machine learning engineer will be called to fix it.

Short rule: a machine learning engineer creates *models that get run continuously*.

1.2.3 *Decision science*

A *decision scientist* turns a company's raw data into information that helps the company make decisions. This work relies on having deep understanding of different mathematical and statistical methods and familiarity with business decision-making. Furthermore, decision scientists have to be able to make compelling visualizations and tables so that the nontechnical people they talk to will understand their analysis. Although a decision scientist does plenty of programming, their work generally gets run only once to make a particular analysis, so they can get away with having code that's inefficient or difficult to maintain.

A decision scientist must understand the needs of the other people within the company and figure out how to generate constructive information. A marketing director, for example, might ask a decision scientist to help them decide which types of products should be highlighted in the company's holiday gift guide. The decision scientist might investigate what products have sold well without being featured in the gift guide, talk to the user research team about conducting a survey, and use principles of behavioral science to do an analysis to come up with the optimal items to suggest. The result is likely to be a PowerPoint presentation or report to be shared with product managers, vice presidents, and other businesspeople.

A decision scientist often uses their knowledge of statistics to help the company make decisions under uncertainty. A decision scientist could be responsible for running their company's experimentation analytics system, for example. Many companies run online experiments, or A/B tests, to measure whether a change is effective. This change could be as simple as adding a new button or as complicated as changing the ranking system of search results or completely redesigning a page. During an A/B test, visitors are randomly assigned to one of two or more conditions, such as half to the old version of the home page, which is the *control*, and half to the new version, which is the *treatment*. Then visitors' actions after they enter the experiment are compared to see whether those in the treatment have a higher rate of performing desirable actions, such as buying products.

Because of randomness, it's rare for the metrics in the control and treatment to be exactly the same. Suppose that you flipped two coins, and that one turned up heads 52 times out of 100 and one 49 times out of 100. Would you conclude that the first coin is more likely to turn up heads? Of course not! But a business partner might look at an experiment, see that the conversion rate is 5.4 percent in the control and 5.6 percent in the treatment, and declare the treatment to be a success. The decision scientist is there to help interpret the data, enforce best practices for designing experiments, and more.

Short rule: a decision scientist creates analyses that produce *recommendations.*

1.2.4 *Related jobs*

Although the three areas discussed in the preceding sections are the main types of data science positions, you may see a few other distinct roles that fall outside those categories. We list those jobs here, because it's good to understand the positions that are out there and because you may need to collaborate with colleagues in these positions. That said, if you're interested in one of these roles, the material in this book may be less relevant to you.

BUSINESS INTELLIGENCE ANALYST

A *business intelligence analyst* does work similar to that of an analyst, but they generally use less statistical and programming expertise. Their tool of choice may be Excel instead of Python, and they may not ever make statistical models. Although their job function is similar to that of an analyst, they create less-sophisticated output because of the limitations of their tools and techniques.

If you want to do machine learning or programming, or to apply statistical methods, a business intelligence analyst position could be a very frustrating role, because it won't help you gain new skills. Also, these jobs usually pay less than data science jobs and are considered to be less prestigious. But a business intelligence analyst job can be a good entry point to becoming a data scientist, especially if you haven't worked with data in a business setting before. If you want to start as a business intelligence analyst and grow into becoming a data scientist, look for positions in which you can learn some skills you may not have, such as programming in R or Python.

DATA ENGINEER

A *data engineer* focuses on keeping data maintained in databases and ensuring that people can get the data they need. They don't run reports, make analyses, or develop models; instead, they keep the data neatly stored and formatted in well-structured databases so that other people can do those things. A data engineer may be tasked with maintaining all the customer records in a large-scale cloud database and adding new tables to that database as requested.

Data engineers are pretty different from data scientists, and they're even more rare and in demand. A data engineer may help build the data backend components of a company's internal experimentation system and update the data processing flow when the jobs start taking too long. Other data engineers develop and monitor batch and streaming environments, managing data from collection to processing to data storage.

If you're interested in data engineering, you'll need strong computer science skills; many data engineers are former software engineers.

RESEARCH SCIENTIST

A *research scientist* develops and implements new tools, algorithms, and methodologies, often to be used by other data scientists within the company. These types of positions almost always require PhDs, usually in computer science, statistics, quantitative social science, or a related field. Research scientists may spend weeks researching and trying out methods to increase the power of online experiments, getting 1% more accuracy on image recognition in self-driving cars, or building a new deep learning algorithm. They may even spend time writing research papers that may rarely be used within the company but that help raise the prestige of the company and (ideally) advance the field. Because these positions require very specific backgrounds, we don't focus on them in this book.

1.3   *Choosing your path*

In chapter 3, we cover some options for obtaining data science skills, the benefits and drawbacks of each option, and some suggestions for choosing among them. At this point, it's good to start reflecting on the area of data science you want to specialize in. Where do you already have experience? We've seen data scientists who are former engineers, psychology professors, marketing managers, statistics students, and social workers. A lot of times, the knowledge you've gained in other jobs and academic areas can help you be a better data scientist. If you're already in data science, it's helpful to reflect now on which part of the triangle you're in. Are you happy with it? Do you want to switch to a different type of data science job? Transitioning is often available.

Vicki Boykis: Can anyone become a data scientist?

With all the optimism (and big potential salaries listed in news articles) around data science, it's easy to see why it presents attractive career opportunities, particularly as the range and scope of data science job titles continues to expand. But as a new entrant to the field, it's important to have a realistic, nuanced view of where the data science market is heading for the next couple years and adjust accordingly.

There's a couple of trends impacting the data science field today. First, data science as a field has been around for ten years, and as such, has moved through the early stages of the hype cycle: mass media hype, early adoption, and consolidation. It's been overhyped, talked about in the media, adopted by Silicon Valley companies and beyond, and we're now at the point of high-growth adoption across larger companies and the standardization of data science workflow toolsets like Spark and AutoML.

Second, as a result, there is an oversupply of new data scientists, who've come from bootcamps, newly-established data science programs in universities, or online courses. The number of candidates for any given data science position, particularly at the entry level, has grown from 20 or so per slot to 100 or more. It's not uncommon anymore to see 500 resumes per open position.

Third, the standardization of toolsets and the ready supply of labor, as well as the demand for people who have more experience in the field, has meant a shift in the way data science titles are distributed and a creation of a hierarchy of data science jobs and descriptions. For example, in some companies "data scientist" may mean creating models, but in some it means mostly running SQL analyses, the equivalent of what the data analyst title used to be.

This means several things for those looking to get into data science as newcomers. First and most importantly, they may find the job market to be extremely competitive and crowded, especially for those who are new to the industry in general (like college graduates), or those making the transition from other industries, and competing with thousands of candidates just like them. Second, they may be applying for jobs that are not truly reflective of data science as it's portrayed in blog posts and the popular press—solely writing and implementing algorithms.

Given these trends, it's important to understand that it may be hard to initially differentiate yourself from the other resumes on the pile to get into the final round of interviews. Though the strategies you read in this book may seem like a lot of work, they will help you stand out, which is needed in this new, competitive data science environment.

1.4   *Interview with Robert Chang, data scientist at Airbnb*

Robert Chang is a data scientist at Airbnb, where he works on the Airbnb Plus product. He previously worked at Twitter, where he worked on the Growth team, doing product analytics, creating data pipelines, running experiments, and creating models. You can find his blog posts on data engineering, his advice for new and aspiring data scientists, and his work at Airbnb and Twitter at https://medium.com/@rchang.

What was your first data science journey?

My first job was as a data scientist at *The Washington Post*. Back in 2012, I was ready to leave academia and go into industry, but I didn't know what I wanted to do. I hoped to be a data visualization scientist, having been impressed by work at *The New York Times*. When I went to my school's career fair and saw that *The Washington Post* was hiring, naïve as I was, I just assumed they must be doing similar things to *The New York Times*. I applied and got the job, not doing any more due diligence.

If you were to ask for an example of how not to start your data science career, I definitely would volunteer myself! I got the job hoping to do either data visualization or modeling, but I realized very quickly my job was more that of a data engineer. A lot of my work was building ETL (extract transform load) pipelines, rerunning SQL scripts, and trying to make sure reports ran so we could report top-level metrics to executives. This was very painful at the time; I realized what I wanted to do was not aligned with what the company really needed and eventually left the job.

But in my subsequent years at Twitter and Airbnb, I realized I was seeing the norm and not the exception. When you're building out the data capabilities, you have to build it layer upon layer. Monica Rogati has written a famous blog post on the hierarchy of data science needs, which is extremely spot-on (http://mng.bz/ad0o). But at the time, I was too new to appreciate how real, live data science work was done.

What should people look for in a data science job?

If you're looking for a data science position, you should focus on the state of data infrastructure of the company. If you join a company where there's just a bunch of raw data that's not stored in a data warehouse, it will probably take you months or sometimes even years to get to a point where you can do interesting analytics, experimentation, or machine learning. If that's not something you expect to do, you will have a fundamental misalignment between the stage of the company and how you want to contribute to the organization.

To assess this, you can ask questions like "Do you have a data infrastructure team? How long have they been around? What is the data stack? Do you have a data engineering team? How do they work with data scientists? When you're building out a new product, do you have a process for instrumenting the logs, building out the data tables, and putting them into your data warehouse?" If those things aren't there, you will be part of the team that is responsible for building that, and you should expect to be spending quite a lot of time on that.

The second thing to look for is the people. There are three kinds of people you should be paying attention to. Assuming you don't want to be the first data scientist, you want to join a data science organization where there is an experienced leader. An experienced leader knows how to build and maintain a good infrastructure and workflow for data scientists to be productive. Second, look for a manager who is supportive of continuous learning. Lastly, it's super important, especially when you're new to work, to work with a tech lead or senior data scientist who is very hands-on. For your day-to-day work, that's the person who helps you the most.

What skills do you need to be a data scientist?

I think it depends on what kind of job you're looking for and what bar the employer sets. Top-tier companies in general have a high bar, sometimes unreasonably high, because there are a lot of people trying to join the company. They're generally looking for unicorns—someone who has data wrangling skills with R or Python as well as experience building ETL pipelines, data engineering, experiment design, and building models and putting them into production. That puts a lot of pressure on the candidates! While those are all skills you can eventually learn and may be useful for whatever problems that you're solving, I don't think they're necessary to get into data science.

If you know R or Python and a little bit of SQL, you're already in a pretty good position to get into data science. If you can plan out your career by learning more things up front, that's always helpful, but I don't think that's a requirement. It's more important to have a love for learning. If you're trying to get hired by top tech companies, you need a little more, but that's more for signaling effect than for what you really need on the job. It's helpful to make the distinction between the core skills you need to start your career in data science and others that are nice to have if you want to get into a competitive, brand-name company.

Summary

- The data science skill set varies across people and positions. Although some knowledge is fundamental, data scientists don't need to be experts in every relevant field.
- Data science jobs have different areas of focus: putting the right, cleaned data in front of stakeholders (analytics); putting machine learning models into production (machine learning); and using data to make a decision (decision science).

2

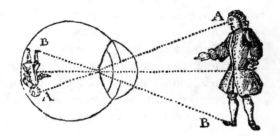

Data science companies

This chapter covers

- Types of companies hiring data scientists
- The pros and cons of each company type
- The tech stacks you may see at different jobs

As discussed in chapter 1, data science is a wide field with lots of different roles: research scientist, machine learning engineer, business intelligence analyst, and more. Although the work you do as a data scientist depends on your role, it is equally influenced by the company where you're working. Big company versus small, tech versus traditional industry, and young versus established can influence project focus, supporting technology, and team culture. By understanding a few archetypes of companies, you'll be better prepared when you're looking at places to work, either for your first data science job or your nth one.

The aim of this chapter is to give you an understanding of what some typical companies are like to work at each day. We're going to present five fictional companies that hire data scientists. None of these companies are real, but all are based on research and our own work experiences, and they illustrate basic principles that can be broadly applied. Although no two companies are exactly alike, knowing these five archetypes should help you assess prospective employers.

Even though these stereotypes are based on what we've seen as trends in these industries, they're certainly not gospel. You may find a company that totally breaks the mold of what we say here—or a specific team in the company that's unlike the company itself.

Although the companies in this chapter are fake, all the blurbs you'll see are by real data scientists working at real companies!

2.1 MTC: Massive Tech Company

- Similar to: Google, Facebook, and Microsoft
- Company age: 20 years
- Employees: 80,000

MTC is a tech company with a massive footprint, selling cloud services, consumer productivity software such as a text editor, server hardware, and countless one-off business solutions. The company has amassed a large fortune and uses it to fund unusual research and development (R&D) projects such as self-driving scooters and virtual reality (VR) technology. Their R&D makes the news, but most members of the technical workforce are engineers who make incremental improvements in their existing products, add more features, improve the user interface, and launch new versions.

2.1.1 Your team: One of many in MTC

MTC has nearly a thousand data scientists spread across the company. These data scientists are largely grouped into teams, each supporting a different product or division, or individually placed within a non-data science team to fully support it. There are, for example, VR headset data scientists on one team, marketing data scientists on a second team, and VR-headset marketing data scientists on a third team, while the VR-headset supply chain team has their own data scientist too.

If you were a member of one of those data science teams, when you joined, you would have been onboarded quickly. Large organizations hire new people every day, so the company should have standard processes for getting you a laptop and access to data, as well as training you on how to use any special tools. On the team, you'd be tasked with doing data science for your particular area of focus. That area could include creating reports and charts that executives could use to justify funding projects. It could also be building machine learning models that would be handed off to software developers to put into production.

Your team is likely to be large and full of experienced people. Because MTC is a large, successful tech company, it has the broad footprint to draw in many good recruits to hire. Your team will be large, so people within it may be working on nearly unrelated tasks; one person could be doing an exploratory analysis for a director in R, for example, and another could be building a machine learning model in Python for a sister team. The size of the team is a blessing and a curse: you have a large body of expert data scientists to discuss ideas with, but most of them probably don't have familiarity with the particular tasks you are working on. Also, there is an established hierarchy on your team. The people with the more senior positions tend to be listened to more because they have more experience in the field and more experience with dealing with different departments at MTC.

The work your team does is likely a healthy balance of keeping the company running, such as making monthly reports and providing quarterly machine learning model updates, as well as doing new projects, such as creating a forecast that has never been done before. The team's manager has to balance the flood of requests for data science work from other teams, which help those teams in the short term, with the desire to do innovative but unrequested work that may provide long-term benefits. With MTC's large cash stores, the company can afford to do a lot more innovation and R&D than other companies, a fact that trickles down into willingness to try interesting new data science projects.

2.1.2 *The tech: Advanced, but siloed across the company*

MTC is a massive organization, and with organizations of this size, it's impossible to avoid using different types of technology throughout the company. One department may store order and customer data in a Microsoft SQL Server database; a different department may keep records in Apache Hive. Worse, not only is the technology to store data disjointed, but also, the data itself may be. One department may keep customer records indexed by phone number; a different department may use email addresses to index customers.

Most MTC-size companies have their own homemade technology stacks. Thus, as a data scientist at MTC, you have to learn the specific ways to query and use data that are particular to MTC. Learning these specialized tools is great for getting you more access within MTC, but the knowledge you gain can't be transferred to other companies.

As a data scientist, you will likely use several possible tools. Because MTC is so big, it has plenty of support for major languages such as R and Python, which many people use. Some teams may also use paid languages such as SAS or SPSS, but this situation is a bit rarer. If you want to use an unusual language that you enjoy but that few other people use, such as Haskell, you may or may not be able to, depending on your manager.

The machine learning stack varies dramatically depending on what part of the company you are in. Some teams use microservices and containers to deploy models efficiently, whereas others have antiquated production systems. The diversity in tech stack for deploying software makes it difficult to connect to other teams' APIs; there is no one central location for learning about and understanding what is going on.

2.1.3 The pros and cons of MTC

Being a data scientist at MTC means having an impressive job at an impressive company. Because MTC is a tech company, people know what a data scientist is and what helpful things you can do. Having a universal understanding of your role makes the job a lot easier. The high number of data scientists in the company means that you have a large support network you can rely on if you are struggling, as well as smooth processes for joining the company and gaining access to required resources. You'll rarely find yourself stuck and on your own.

Having lots of data scientists around you comes with cons as well. The tech stack is complex and difficult to navigate because so many people have built it up in so many ways. An analysis you've been asked to re-create may be written in a language you don't know by a person who's no longer around. It'll be harder to stand out and be noticed because there are so many other data scientists around you. And you may find it difficult to find an interesting project to work on because so many of the obvious projects have already been started by other people.

Because MTC is an established company, working there gives you more job security. There is always the risk of layoffs, but working for MTC isn't like working for a startup, where funding could dry up at any moment. Also, at large companies, managers lean more toward finding a new team for someone to work on rather than firing them; firing opens all sorts of legal complications that require thorough backup support for the termination decision.

Something that's both a pro and con of MTC is that people serve in many specialized roles within the company. Data engineers, data architects, data scientists, market researchers, and more all perform different roles that relate to data science, which means you'll have lots of people to pass work off to. You have a low chance of being forced to create your own database, for example. This situation is great for passing off work outside your expertise, but it also means that you can't stretch your skills.

Another con of MTC is the bureaucracy. In a large company, getting approvals for things like new technology, trips to conferences, and starting projects can require going far up the chain of command. Worse, the project you've been working on for years could be canceled because two executives are fighting, and your project is collateral damage.

MTC is a great company for data scientists who are looking to help solve big problems by using cutting-edge techniques—both decision scientists who want to do analyses and machine learning engineers who want to build and deploy models. Large companies have lots of problems to solve and a budget that allows for trying new things. You may not be able to make big decisions yourself, but you'll know that you've contributed.

MTC is a poor choice for a data scientist who wants to be the decision-maker and call the shots. The large company has established methods, protocols, and structures that you have to follow.

2.2 HandbagLOVE: The established retailer

Handbag LOVE

- Similar to: Payless, Bed Bath & Beyond, and Best Buy
- Company age: 45 years
- Size: 15,000 employees (10,000 in retail stores, 5,000 in corporate)

HandbagLOVE is a retail chain with 250 locations across the United States, all selling purses and clutches. The company has been around for a long time and is filled with experts on how to lay out a store and improve the customer experience. The company has been slow to adopt new technology, taking plenty of time before getting its first website and its first app.

Recently, HandbagLOVE has seen its sales drop, as Amazon and other online retailers have eaten away at its market share. Knowing that the writing is on the wall, HandbagLOVE has been looking to improve via technology, investing in an online app and an Amazon Alexa skill, and trying to use the value of its data. HandbagLOVE has had financial analysts employed for many years calculating high-level aggregate statistics on its orders and customers, but only recently has the company considered hiring data scientists to help them understand customer behavior better.

The newly formed data science team was built on a base of financial analysts who previously made Excel reports on performance metrics for the company. As Handbag-LOVE supplemented these people with trained data scientists, the team started to provide more-sophisticated products: monthly statistical forecasts on customer growth in R, interactive dashboards that allow executives to understand sales better, and a customer segmentation that buckets customers into helpful groups for marketing.

Although the team has made machine learning models to power the new reports and analyses, HandbagLOVE is far from deploying machine learning models into continuously running production. Any product recommendations on its website and app are powered by third-party machine learning products rather than having been built within the company. There is talk on the data science team about changing this situation, but no one knows how many years away that is.

2.2.1 Your team: A small group struggling to grow

The team leans heavily toward data scientists who can do reporting rather than being trained in machine learning because machine learning is so new. When members of the team have needed modern statistical and machine learning methods, they've had to teach themselves because no one around already knew them. This self-teaching is great in that people get to learn new techniques that are interesting to them. The downside is that some of the technical methods used may be inefficient or even wrong because there are no experts to check the work.

HandbagLOVE has laid out general paths for data scientists to progress into senior roles. Unfortunately, these career paths aren't specific to data science; they're high-level goals copied and pasted from other positions, such as software development, because no one really knows what the metrics should be. To progress in your career, you have to convince your manager that you're ready, and with luck, your manager can get approval to promote you. On the plus side, if the team ends up growing, you'll quickly become a senior person on the team.

Because the data science team provides reports and models for departments throughout the company (such as marketing, supply chain, and customer care), the members of the data science team are well known. This fact has given the team a great deal of respect within the company, and in turn, the data science team has a lot of camaraderie within it. The combination of the size of the team and the level of influence within the company allows data scientists to have far more influence than they would in other companies. It's not unusual for someone on the data science team to meet with top-level executives and contribute to the conversation.

2.2.2 Your tech: A legacy stack that's starting to change

A common phrase you hear when talking about technology at HandbagLOVE is "Well, that's how it's always been." Order and customer data are stored in an Oracle database that's directly connected to the cash register technology and hasn't changed in 20 years. The system has been pushed well past its limits and has had many modifications bolted on. All that being said, the system still works. Other data is collected and stored in the central database as well: data collected from the website, data from the customer care calls, and data from promotions and marketing emails. All these servers live on the premises (*on-prem*), not in the cloud, and an IT team keeps them maintained.

By having all the data stored in one large server, you have the freedom to connect and join the data however you want. And although your queries sometimes take forever or overload the system, usually you can find a workaround to get you something usable. The vast majority of analyses are done on your laptop. If you need a more powerful computer to train a model, getting it is a hassle. The company doesn't have a machine learning tech stack because it doesn't have any in-house machine learning.

2.2.3 The pros and cons of HandbagLOVE

By being at HandbagLOVE, you have a lot of influence and ability to do what you think is wise. You can go from proposing making a customer lifetime value model, building it, and using it within the company without having to persuade too many people to let you run with your idea. This freedom, which is due to a combination of the size of the company and the newness of data science, is very rewarding; you're incredibly empowered to do what you think is best. The downside of this power is that you don't have many people to call on for help. You're responsible for finding a way to make things work or dealing with the fallout when things don't work.

The tech stack is antiquated, and you'll have to spend a lot of time making work-arounds for it, which is not a great use of time. You may want to use a newer technology for storing data or running models, but you won't have the technical support to do it. If you're not able to set up any new technology entirely by yourself, you'll just have to get by without using it.

A data scientist's salary won't be as high as it would be at bigger companies, especially tech ones. HandbagLOVE just doesn't have the cash available to pay high data science paychecks. Besides, the company doesn't need the best of the best anyway—just people who can do the basics. That being said, the salary won't be terrible; it'll certainly be well above what most people at the company make with similar years of experience.

HandbagLOVE is a good company to work at for data scientists who are excited to have the freedom to do what they think is right but perhaps aren't interested in using the most state-of-the-art methods. If you're comfortable using standard statistical methods and making more mundane reporting, HandbagLOVE should be a comfortable place to grow your career. If you're really interested only in using start-of-the-art machine learning methods, you won't find many projects to do at HandbagLOVE; neither will you find many people there who know anything about what you're talking about.

2.3   *Seg-Metra: The early-stage startup*

- Similar to: a thousand failed startups you haven't heard of
- Company age: 3 years
- Size: 50 employees

Seg-Metra is a young company that sells a product that helps client companies optimize their website by customizing for unique segments of customers. Seg-Metra sells its product to businesses, not consumers. Early in its brief history, Seg-Metra got a few big-name clients to start using the tool, which helped the company get more funding from venture capitalists. Now, with millions of dollars at hand, the company is looking to scale in size quickly and improve the product.

The biggest improvement that the founders have been pitching to investors is adding basic machine learning methods to the product. This improvement was pitched to investors as "cutting-edge AI." With this new funding in hand, the founders are looking for machine learning engineers to build what was pitched. They also need decision scientists to start reporting on the use of the tool, allowing the company to better understand what improvements to make in the product.

2.3.1 *Your team (what team?)*

Depending on when a data scientist gets hired, they may very well be the first data scientist in the company. If they're not the first, they'll be among the first few data science hires and likely report to the one who was hired first. Due to the newness of the team, there will be few to no protocols—no established programming languages, best practices, ways of storing code, or formal meetings.

Any direction will come from that first data scientist hire. The culture of the team will likely be set by their benevolence. If that person is open to group discussion and trust of the other team members, the data science team as a whole will decide things such as what language to use. If that person is controlling and not open to listening, they will make these decisions themselves.

Such an unstructured environment can create immense camaraderie. The whole data science team works hard, struggles to get new technologies, methods, and tools working, and can form deep bonds and friendships. Alternatively, those who have power could inflict immense emotional abuse on those who don't have power, and because the company is so small, there is little accountability. Regardless of exactly how Seg-Metra's growth shakes out, the data scientists at this early-stage company are in for a bumpy and wild ride.

The work of the team can be fascinating or frustrating, depending on the day. Oftentimes, data scientists are doing analyses for the first time ever, such as making the first attempt to use customer purchase data to segment customers or deploying the first neural network to production. These first-time analyses and engineering tasks are exciting because they're uncharted territory within the company, and the data scientists get to be the pioneers. On other days, the work can be grueling, such as when a demo has to be ready for an investor and the model still isn't converging the day before. Even if the company has data, the infrastructure may be so disorganized that the data can't feasibly be used. Although the work is chaotic, all these tasks mean that the data scientists learn lots of skills very quickly while working at Seg-Metra.

2.3.2 *The tech: Cutting-edge technology that's taped together*

By being a young company, Seg-Metra isn't constrained by having to maintain old legacy technology. Seg-Metra also wants to impress its investors, which is a lot easier to do when your technology stack is impressive. Thus, Seg-Metra is powered by the most recent and greatest methods of software development, data storage and collection, and analysis and reporting. Data is stored in an assortment of modern cloud technologies, and nothing is done on-prem. The data scientists connect directly to these databases and build machine learning neural network models on large Amazon Web Services (AWS) virtual machine instances with GPU processing. These models are deployed by means of modern software engineering methods.

At first glance, the tech stack is certainly impressive. But the company is so young and growing so fast that issues continually arise with the different technologies working together. When the data scientists suddenly notice missing data in the cloud storage, they have to wait for the overworked data engineer to fix it (and that's if they're lucky enough to have a data engineer). It would be great if Seg-Metra had a dedicated development operations (DevOps) team to help keep everything running, but so far, the budget has been spent elsewhere. Further, the technology was installed so quickly that even though the company is young, it would be difficult to monitor it all.

2.3.3 *Pros and cons of Seg-Metra*

As a growing startup, Seg-Metra has a lot of appeal. The growth of the company is providing all sorts of interesting data science work and an environment in which data scientists are forced to learn quickly. These sorts of positions can teach skills that jump-start a career in data science—skills like working under deadlines with limited constraints, communicating effectively with non-data scientists, and knowing when to pursue a project or to decide that it's not worthwhile. Especially early in a career, developing these skills can make you much more attractive as an employee than people who have worked only at larger companies.

Another pro of working at Seg-Metra is that you get to work with the latest technologies. Using the latest tech should make your job more enjoyable: presumably, the new technologies coming out are better than the old technologies. By learning the latest tech, you should also have a more impressive résumé for future jobs. Companies looking to use newer technology will want you to help guide the way.

Although the pay is not as competitive as at larger companies, especially tech companies, the job does provide stock options that have the potential to be enormously valuable. If the company eventually goes public or gets sold, those options could be worth hundreds of thousands of dollars or more. Unfortunately, the odds of that happening are somewhere between getting elected to city council and getting elected to the U.S. Congress. So this fact is a pro only if you enjoy gambling.

One con of working at Seg-Metra is that you have to work very hard. Having 50- to 60-hour work weeks is not uncommon, and the company expects everyone to contribute everything they can. In the eyes of the company, if everyone isn't working together, the company won't succeed, so are you really going to be the one person to use all their vacation time in a year? This environment can be hugely toxic, ripe for abuse and a lot of employee burnout.

The company is volatile, relying on finding new clients and help from investors to stay afloat, giving Seg-Metra the con of low job security. It's possible that in any year, the company could decide to lay off people or go under entirely. These changes can happen without warning. Job insecurity is especially difficult for people who have families, which causes the demographics of the company to skew younger. A young workforce can also be a con if you want to work with a more diverse, experienced team.

Overall, working at Seg-Metra provides a great opportunity to work with interesting technology, learn a lot quickly, and have a small chance of making a ton of money. But doing so requires an immense amount of work and potentially a toxic environment. So this company is best for data scientists who are looking to gain experience and then move on.

Rodrigo Fuentealba Cartes, lead data scientist at a small government consulting company

The company I work at provides analytics, data science, and mobile solutions for governmental institutions, armed and law enforcement forces, and some private customers. I am the lead data scientist, and I am the only one in charge of data science projects in the entire company. We don't have data engineers, data wranglers, or any other data science roles there because the department is relatively new. Instead, we have database administrators, software developers, and systems integrators, and I double as a system/software architect and open source developer. That might look odd and definitely puts a strain on me, but it works surprisingly well.

One strange story from my job: I was working in a project that involved using historical information from many environmental variables, such as daily weather conditions. There was a lack of critically needed data because an area of study didn't have weather stations installed. The project was in jeopardy, and the customer decided to shut the project down in a week if their people could not find the information.

I decided to fly to the area and interview some fishermen, and I asked how they knew that it was safe to sail. They said they usually sent a ship that transmitted the weather conditions over the radio. I visited a radio station, and they had handwritten transcripts of communications since 1974. I implemented an algorithm that could recognize handwritten notes and extract meaningful information, and then implemented a natural language processing pipeline that could analyze the strings. Thanks to going out to the field and finding this unusual data, the project was saved.

Gustavo Coelho, data science lead at a small startup

I have been working for the last 11 months in a relatively new startup which focuses on applying AI to HR management. We predict future performance of candidates or their likelihood of being hired by a certain company. Those predictions are aimed at helping speed up the hiring process. We rely heavily on bias mitigation in our models. It's a small company; we have 11 people; and the data science team makes up five of them, including me. The whole of the company is dedicated to helping the data science team deliver the trained models into production.

Working at a small startup gives me the chance to learn new concepts and apply them every day. I love thinking about the best way to set up our data science processes so we can scale and give more freedom to our data scientists to focus on data science. HR is not a tech-savvy field, so more than half of the project length is spent explaining the solution to our clients and helping them get comfortable with the new concepts. And then when we finally get the go-ahead, there is also a lot of time spent coordinating with the client's IT department to integrate into our data pipeline.

2.4   *Videory: The late-stage, successful tech startup*

- Similar to: Lyft, Twitter, and Airbnb
- Company age: 8 years
- Size: 2,000 people

Videory is a late-stage, successful tech startup that runs a video-based social network. Users can upload 20-second videos and share them with the public. The company has just gone public, and everyone is ecstatic about it. Videory isn't close to the size of MTC, but it's doing well as a social network and growing the customer base each year. It's data-savvy and has probably had data analysts or scientists for a few years now or even since the start. The data scientists on the team are very busy doing analyses and reporting to support the business, as well as creating machine learning models to help pair people with artists to commission work.

2.4.1   *The team: Specialized but with room to move around*

Videory is still at the point where you can gather all the data scientists in an extra-large conference room. Given the size of the company, the team may be organized in a centralized model. Every data science person reports to a data science manager, and all are in a single large department of the organization. The central data science team helps other groups throughout the company, but ultimately, the team sets its own priorities.

Some data scientists are even working on internal long-term academic research projects that have no immediate benefits.

There's specialization among the data science team at Videory, given the size of the company. There's also some delineation among people who do the heavy machine learning, statistics, or analytics. Videory is small enough that it's possible to switch between these groups over time. The data scientists usually have some interaction—such as training sessions, monthly meetings, and a shared Slack channel—that you wouldn't find at companies like MTC, which are too big for everyone to talk together. The subteams are likely to use different tools, and a group of people with PhDs publish academic papers and do more theoretical work.

2.4.2   *The tech: Trying to avoid getting bogged down by legacy code*

Videory has a lot of legacy code and technology, and probably at least a few tools that were developed internally. The company is likely trying to keep up with tech developments, and it plans to switch over to a new system or supplement the existing ones with new technologies. As in most companies, a data scientist will almost definitely query a SQL database to get data. The company probably has some business intelligence tools as well, because there are a lot of non-data science consumers.

As a data scientist at Videory, you'll definitely get to learn something new. All these companies have big data and systems to deal with it. SQL won't be enough; the company needs to process billions of events every month. You may be able to try Hadoop or Spark when you need to pull out some custom data that's not stored in the SQL database, however.

The data science is typically done in R or Python, with plenty of experts available to provide assistance if things prove to be difficult. The machine learning is deployed through modern software development practices such as using microservices. Because the company is well known as a successful startup, lots of talented people work there, using their cutting-edge approaches.

2.4.3   *The pros and cons of Videory*

Videory can be a good size for data scientists; enough other data scientists are around to provide mentorship and support, but the team is still small enough that you can get to know everyone. Data science is recognized on the company level as being important, which means that your work can get recognition from vice presidents and maybe even the C suite (CEO, CTO, and so on.). You'll have data engineers to support your work. The data pipelines may get slow sometimes or even break, but you won't be responsible for fixing them.

In an organization of more than 1,000 people, you'll need to deal with inevitable political issues. You may be pressured to generate numbers that match what people want to hear (and can tell their bosses in order to get a bonus) or face unrealistic expectations about how fast something can be developed. You can also end up working on things that the business doesn't really need because your manager asked you to.

Sometimes, you'll end up feeling that you've had no direction or your time was wasted. While it won't change as much as at an early-stage startup, the organization will still change a lot; what's a priority one quarter can be totally ignored the next.

Although other data scientists at Videory will be more knowledgeable than you on most data science topics, you might quickly become the expert on a specific one, such as time series analysis. This situation can be great if you like mentoring and teaching others, especially if your work supports taking time to learn more about your particular field of expertise by reading papers or taking courses. But it can be hard when you feel that no one can check your work or push you to learn new things. You'll always have more to learn, but what you learn may not be in the area you want to focus on.

Overall, Videory provides a nice blend of some of the benefits of the other archetypes. It's large enough that there are people around to provide help and assistance when needed, but not so large that requests get stuck in bureaucratic madness or departments overlap in scope. Data scientists who work at the company get plenty of chances to learn, but due to the specialization of roles, they don't get the opportunity to try everything. This company is a great place for data scientists who are looking for a safe bet that provides chances to grow, but not an overwhelming number of chances.

Emily Bartha, the first data scientist at a midsize startup

I work at a midsize startup that has a product focused on insurance. As the first data scientist, I get to help define our strategy around using data and introducing machine learning into our product. I sit on the data team in the company, so I work very closely with data engineers, as well as our data product manager.

A day in my life at work starts with morning standup with the data team. We talk about what we have planned for the day and any blockers or dependencies. I spend a lot of time digging through data: visualizing, creating reports, and investigating quality issues or quirks in the data. I spend a lot of time on documentation too. When I code, I use GitHub, like the rest of the engineering team, and have team members review my code (and I review theirs). I also spend a good chunk of the day in meetings or side-of-desk collaboration with members of my team.

Having worked at bigger companies in the past, I love working at a small company! There is a lot of freedom to take initiative here. If you have an idea and want to work to make it a reality, no one will get in your way. Look for a company that has already made an investment in data engineering. When I arrived, there were already several data engineers and a strategy for instrumentation, data collection, and storage. When you work at a small company, things are constantly changing and priorities are shifting, which makes it important to be adaptable. People who enjoy diving deep on a project and working on it for months may not enjoy working at a startup, because it often requires developing solutions that are good enough and moving on to the next thing.

2.5 *Global Aerospace Dynamics: The giant government contractor*

> # GLOBAL AEROSPACE DYNAMICS

- Similar to: Boeing, Raytheon, and Lockheed Martin
- Company age: 50 years
- Size: 150,000 people

Global Aerospace Dynamics (GAD) is a huge and rich company, bringing in tens of billions of dollars in revenue each year through various government contracts. The company develops everything from fighter jets and missiles to intelligent traffic-light systems. The company is spread across the country through various divisions, most of which don't talk to one another. GAD has been around for decades, and many people who work there have been there for decades too.

GAD has been slow on the uptake when it comes to data science. Most of the engineering divisions have been collecting data, but they struggle to understand how it can be used in their very regimented existing processes. Because of the nature of the work, code needs to be extremely unlikely to have bugs and ruthlessly tested, so the idea of implementing a machine learning model, which has limited predictability when live, is dicey at best. In general, the pace of work at the company is slow; the tech-world motto "Move fast and break things" is the polar opposite of the mentality at GAD.

With the number of articles on artificial intelligence, the rise of machine learning, and the need to use data to transform a business, the executives of GAD are ready to start hiring data scientists. Data scientists are showing up on teams throughout the organization, performing tasks such as analyzing engineering data for better reporting, building machine learning models to put into products, and working as service providers to help GAD customers troubleshoot problems.

2.5.1 *The team: A data scientist in a sea of engineers*

Although their roles depends on where in GAD they are and what project they're working on, the average data scientist is a single person on a team of engineers. At best, there may be two or three data scientists on your team. The data scientist has the job of supporting the engineers with analysis, model building, and product delivery. Most of the engineers on the team have only a very loose understanding of data science; they remember regressions from college but don't know the basics of collecting data or feature engineering, the difficulties of validating a model, or how models get deployed. You'll have few resources to help you when things go wrong, but because so few people understand your job, no one else might notice that things are going wrong.

Many of the engineers on the team will have been with the company for ten or more years, so they'll have plenty of institutional knowledge. They'll also be more likely to have the mindset "We've been doing things this way since I've been here, so why should we change?" That attitude will make it more difficult for ideas proposed by data scientists to be implemented. The slower nature of the defense industry means that people tend to work less hard than in other places; people clock in for 40 hours a week, but casually slipping down below that total isn't unusual. At other companies, you can be overwhelmed by having too many tasks, whereas at GAD, the stress comes from not having enough work to do and being bored.

Promotions and raises are extremely formulaic, because managers must follow rules to reduce bias (and thus be less likely to get GAD sued) and also because that's how things have been done for decades. Getting raises and promotions largely has to do with how many years you've worked at the company. Being an extremely hard worker may make your next promotion come a year earlier or earn you a somewhat higher bonus, but there's little chance that a junior data scientist will rise quickly to become a lead data scientist. The flip side is that employees rarely get fired.

2.5.2   *The tech: Old, hardened, and on security lockdown*

Although the technology stack varies greatly between groups in GAD, it all tends to be relatively old, on-prem instead of in the cloud, and covered in security protocols. Because the data involved covers topics like fighter-jet performance, it's essential for the company that the data isn't leaked. Further, the company needs legal accountability for any technology it uses in case something goes wrong, so open source tends to be frowned upon. Whereas Microsoft SQL Server is more expensive than PostGRES SQL, for example, GAD is happy to pay Microsoft the extra money, knowing that if there's a security bug, they can call Microsoft to deal with it.

In practice, this setup looks like data being stored in SQL Server databases run by an IT team that's extremely stingy about who has access to what. The data scientists are allowed to access the data, but they have to run Python on special servers that have limited internet access so that any libraries don't secretly send data to foreign countries. If the data scientists want to use special open source software, there's little chance that IT and security will approve it, which makes it much more difficult for the data scientists to work.

If code needs to be deployed to production systems, it tends to be deployed in traditional ways. GAD is just beginning to adopt modern methods of putting machine learning code into production.

2.5.3   *The pros and cons of GAD*

The pros of working at GAD are that the data science jobs are slow, comfortable, and secure. The less rigorous pace of the job means that you're more likely to have energy left over when you get home for the evening. You'll often find yourself with free time when you're working, which you can spend reading data science blogs and articles without anyone complaining. The fact that few other people know the basics of data science means that you'll have fewer people questioning you. And because GAD is a massive organization that's worried about legal liabilities, you'd have to really underperform to get fired.

The downsides of working at GAD are that you're less likely to learn new skills than you would be at other companies. You'll likely be assigned to a single project for years, so the technologies and tools used for that project will quickly become mundane. Worse, the skills you *do* learn will be for outdated technology that isn't transferrable to other institutions. And although you won't get fired easily, you also won't get promoted easily.

GAD is a great place to work if you find a team doing projects that you find enjoyable and you don't want work to be your life. Many people work for GAD for decades because it's comfortable, and they're happy with being comfortable. But if you demand challenges to keep you going, GAD might not be a good fit.

> ### Nathan Moore, data analytics manager for a utilities company
>
> The company I work at provides and sells power for hundreds of thousands of people, and the company is partially owned by the government. The company itself has around 1,000 employees spread across many different functions. My job involves investigating and prototyping new data sources and working with the database specialists to clean and document current data sources. We've got a bunch of legacy systems and new initiatives happening, so there's always something to do.
>
> At the moment, a day in the life involves meetings, reviewing specifications for ETL, trying out a new machine learning technique I found on Twitter, giving feedback on reporting, learning to use JIRA and Confluence, and answering many emails. In the past I've been involved in model development and assessment, data analysis when some overnight processing fails, and submissions to government on an industrywide review of the sector.
>
> We're large enough that we've got a good team of analysts to work on a variety of projects, from day-to-day reporting to large customer segmentation projects. I've had lots of opportunities to move around in the business and have worked here for 11 years. But since we have billions of dollars of assets, risk aversion is high within the company, and pace of change is a little bit slow. We have a large-enough IT department that can support everyday functions, but any significant project, like the systems upgrade, means resources are scarce for any nonpriority improvements. Everything needs to be justified and budget set aside, and there is plenty of politics to navigate.

2.6 *Putting it all together*

When you're looking at companies to work for, you'll find that many of them are similar to these companies in various ways. As you go through job applications and interviews, it can be helpful to try to understand the strengths and weaknesses of working at these companies (table 2.1).

Table 2.1 A summary of companies that hire data scientists

Criteria	MTC Massive tech	HandbagLOVE Retailer	Seg-Metra Startup	Videory Mid-tech	GAD Defense
Bureaucracy	Lots	Little	None	Some	Lots
Tech stack	Complex	Old	Fragile	Mixed	Ancient
Freedom	Little	Lots	TONS	Lots	None
Salary	Amazing	Decent	Poor	Great	Decent
Job security	Great	Decent	Poor	Decent	Great
Chances to learn	Lots	Some	Lots	Lots	Few

2.7 Interview with Randy Au, quantitative user experience researcher at Google

Randy Au works on the Google Cloud team. Having worked in data science with a focus on human behavior for more than a decade, he blogs about how to think about working at startups and different types of companies at https://medium.com/@randy_au.

Are there big differences between large and small companies?

Yes. Usually, it's more organizational and structural. There are points in a company where culture changes because of the scale. At a 10-person startup, everyone does everything because everyone's wearing all the hats. Meanwhile, around 20 people, things start specializing. You start getting three- or four-person teams dedicated to specific things. People can think harder about certain things, and you don't have to learn everything about a company. At around 80 to 100 people, the existing teams don't scale anymore. Then there's a lot more process around things. You don't know everyone in the company anymore. You don't know what everyone's up to, and so there's a lot more overhead to reach common understanding. Beyond that, after about 150 to 200 people, it's impossible to know what's going on around the company, so the bureaucracy has to exist. Then you go to Google, which is 100,000 people. There, you have no idea what most of the company is doing.

The smaller the company, the more likely you're going to interact with everyone in the company. At a 40-person company, I would have the CEO sitting at my desk as we're both exploring a dataset together. That will never happen in Google. But are you okay with the situation that happens in a lot of startups where you're building an F1 car and you're driving it at the same time, and everyone's arguing whether you should have a steering wheel? When you're the data person at a small company, the methods don't really matter as much; you're just trying to squeeze all the data and get some insights out of it. It's okay to not be as rigorous so you can make decisions more quickly.

Are there differences based on the industry of the company?

Some industries have historically had math or data people. An insurance company has actuaries, for example. Those people have been around for a hundred years, and they really know their stats. If an insurance company is going to bring in data scientists, they come with a slightly different view on it. They already have this built-in structure for extremely talented stats people. They're going to be filling a gap somewhere else: there's going to be a gap in their big data or in optimizing their website or something.

Finance also has a long tradition of having quants. I remember failing a quant finance interview once because they did a code test. But as a data scientist, I just make sure my code is functional and gives the correct answer; I don't think too hard about performance until it becomes a problem. Their coding test literally tested you on performance and dinged you points for not being performant automatically. I was like, "Oh, yeah, you guys are in finance. I get it."

I think if you talk to everyone who's doing data science work, the vast but silent majority are people who are doing this kind of grunt work that's not sexy at all. I got a ridiculous amount of responses to the article I wrote about data science at startups that were people saying, "Yeah, this is my life." This is not what people talk about when they talk about data science. It's not the sexy "Here's a new shiny algorithm I applied from this arXiv paper." I don't think I've applied anything in an arXiv paper in the 12 years I've worked. I'm still using regression because regression really works! I think that is the reality of it.

You're going to be cleaning up your data; I don't think there's anyone even at the Facebooks and the Googles who doesn't have to clean data. It might be slightly easier to clean up your data because there's structure around it. But no, you're going to have to clean up your data. It's a fact of life.

What's your final piece of advice for beginning data scientists?

Know your data. This does take a long time—six months to a year or more if it's a complicated system. But your data quality is the foundation of your universe. If you don't know your data, you're going to make a really bizarre statement about something that your data just can't let you say. Some people will say, "Oh, I have the number of unique cookies visiting my website, and that's equal to the number of unique people." But that's not true. What about those people who are using multiple devices or browsers?

To really know your data, you need to make friends with the people with domain knowledge. When I was doing financial reports, I made friends with the finance people so I could learn the conventions accounting has about how they name things and the order of how things are subtracted. Maybe you got 50 million pages from this one IP, and someone else will realize that's IBM. You won't know all this stuff, but someone probably will.

Summary

- Many types of companies hire data scientists.
- Data science jobs vary, largely based on each company's industry, size, history, and team culture.
- It's important to understand what kind of company you're considering.

3

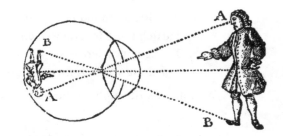

Getting the skills

This chapter covers

- Different ways to learn data science
- Understanding what makes a good academic program or bootcamp
- Choosing the route that's best for you

Now that you've decided to become a data scientist, you need to acquire the skills! Fear not: wondering how to learn the skills of a data scientist is one of the universal parts of becoming a data scientist. There are many ways to do it, from watching YouTube videos to getting a degree, and lots of people will tell you that the way they did it is the only correct path. Worse, it's easy to feel overwhelmed by the amount you have to learn, such as algorithms, programming languages, and statistical methods—and then you throw in the different business domains. Just thinking about it can be emotionally draining.

The good news is that there are only four main methods to get the skills you need. Each method has its advantages and drawbacks, but when you lay them out, it usually becomes clear which is the right approach for you. By the end of this chapter, you should understand the different methods, and after some reflection, you should be able to decide on the best route for your situation. You can do this!

The four methods of getting data science skills in this chapter are

- Earning a graduate degree in data science or a related field
- Participating in a data science bootcamp (an 8- to 15-week crash course)
- Doing data science work in your current job
- Teaching yourself through online courses and data science books

We will walk through all these methods in this chapter.

What if you haven't graduated from college?

Most of this chapter assumes that you've graduated from college, most likely with a technical degree. If you don't meet that criterion, don't worry; most of the chapter still applies, but you need to make a few adjustments when reading it.

If you haven't graduated from college, you'll likely want to get an undergraduate degree before following the steps in the chapter. Your best bet is a related technical degree that teaches you some data science skills, such as mathematics, statistics, or computer science. If you choose one of these majors, try to use any flexible credit requirements to fill gaps in your data science skill set. Some schools now offer data science undergraduate degrees, which should make you extremely well suited to get a job after college. After finishing your degree, you should be able to get a data science job straight out of school (especially if you follow the guidance in parts 1 and 2 of this book). You can also choose to follow the additional steps listed in this chapter, such as teaching yourself extra data science skills or doing data science work on your first job.

If you've graduated from college with a nontechnical degree, this chapter's guidelines still hold. It might be an extra-good idea to get a data science graduate degree, however, because the longer time period of study will give you more time to get up to speed on your technical skills. You may be inclined to get a second, technical undergraduate degree, but avoid this method at all costs. Getting a second degree is extremely expensive and time-consuming; besides, you can gain that knowledge in other ways.

3.1   *Earning a data science degree*

Many colleges offer graduate degrees in data science, with programs covering a mixture of topics in computer science, statistics, and business. Because these programs are master's degree programs, they generally take two years and cost $70,000 USD or more. As with most graduate programs, you can choose to go through the program more slowly while having a job and/or potentially take the classes as online courses. Although many schools offer an actual data science degree, depending on your interests, you may choose instead to get a degree in computer science, statistics, business analytics, operations research, or something very close to data science.

The good thing about a data science degree is that it's exhaustive; due to the length of the program and the amount of time you spend in it, you should have all the knowledge needed to get started as a junior data scientist. Through coursework and projects, you'll get experience using statistics and machine learning methods, as well as hands-on programming. If you come into the program without much programming experience, you should be able to pick it up on the way (although you may have to take an extra course or two).

Graduate degrees in data science have a few downsides:

- They are extremely expensive, both in terms of the cost of tuition and the opportunity cost from not earning income and gaining direct work experience while you're a full-time student.

  Graduate programs are an order of magnitude more expensive than the other options in both money and in time. Spending years studying before you feel ready to switch careers is a huge amount of time in your life, and if you decide partway through that you don't want to be a data scientist, you can't get that money or time back.

- If you come from a background that's related to data science, such as software development, or have substantial undergraduate coursework in the field, a graduate program will teach you a lot of stuff you already know. That means that in a long program, you may get only a small amount of useful new information—a huge drawback that can make the program frustrating to you.

- These programs are taught by academic professors. Most academic professors have spent their whole career in academia, making the material they teach often quite different from what people use in industry. A particularly disengaged professor may use old languages such as SPSS, for example, or won't understand modern tools such as version control. This situation is especially common in degree programs outside data science. Some universities bring in people from industry to teach courses, but these people may not know much about teaching. It's difficult to tell how much of a program uses modern techniques until you're in it. During the application process, try to find opportunities to talk to current or former students to get a feeling for the program and how useful it is for a career.

3.1.1 Choosing the school

As you start searching for graduate data science programs, you may be quickly overwhelmed by the number of options. Worse, you may find your mailbox full of flyers for different programs, and you may get annoying calls from recruiters. Depending on how much work you want to do, you should likely apply to somewhere between three and ten of these programs. Apply to too few, and it's possible that you won't get into any; apply to too many, and you'll find yourself devoting excessive time (and application fees) to graduate applications.

To decide which schools to apply to, consider these metrics:

- *Whether you'll be happy with the location and lifestyle [very important]*—You'll likely be looking at graduate programs all across the country, but what your life looks like outside school will be quite different if you go to a school in Los Angeles versus upstate New York. If the climate, proximity to friends, or cost of living don't work for you, it doesn't matter how good the program is, because you'll be unhappy in it.

- *What topics the program's coursework covers [important]*—Because data science is so new, universities may have dramatically different coursework. This situation is especially complicated by which department the program lives in; a computer science–based data science program is going to focus on methods and algorithms, for example, whereas a business-school program will focus more on applications and rely on case studies. Check whether the course material covers weaknesses in your skill set (refer to chapter 1).

- *How much project work the program has [important]*—The more project work a program involves, the more you'll learn about how data science works in practice and the better prepared you'll be for industry. (Projects are covered in depth in chapter 4.) Significant projects are also great for putting on your résumé, which can help you get an internship during the graduate program or get that first job later.

- *Where graduates end up [important]*—Often, a school provides statistics on where students go after they graduate, such as what percentage end up in academia or at Fortune 500 companies. These statistics can be informative, but schools show metrics that make them look best, even if those metrics are misleading (which is ironic, because understanding what constitutes a misleading statistic is a skill you'll learn as a data scientist). If possible, try reaching out to some of the program alumni through LinkedIn to get an unbiased perspective on how graduates fare. Especially if you want to work at a large corporation, you can research what companies recruit directly at that school. You can still apply for a job if those companies don't recruit, but your job application may be given less consideration.

- *Funding [rare but very important]*—In rare circumstances, schools offer funding for master's degree students, paying for your coursework and sometimes adding a stipend if you're a teaching assistant for a class. If you're offered a stipend, we highly recommend that you take it; not having to pay for your degree and getting a salary to boot is financially a much better option than paying the bills yourself. If the funding involves teaching, you'll also have the benefit of being forced to learn how to communicate with a roomful of people, which will be helpful in your data science career. The downside is that teaching takes lots of time, which will distract you from your studies.

- *How closely the program is connected with businesses in the area [medium-important]*—If the school does a lot of work with local companies, especially tech ones, the school is connected with the community. That connection will make it easier to get an internship or a job, and will give you more interesting materials during classes. It also lowers the chance of having professors who are out of touch with the methods used outside academia.

- *Admission requirements [not very important]*—Some schools require you to have taken certain courses to be admitted. Most programs require you to have taken some mathematics courses, such as linear algebra, as well as some programming courses, such as an introduction to Java. If you're missing one or two of the required courses, you may be able to get the requirement waived or take make-up courses when you're in the program. If you don't have any of the prerequisites, or if the school requires a specific undergraduate degree (such as computer science), the program may not be a good fit for you.

- *Prestige of the school [not at all important]*—Unless you get accepted to an extremely prestigious school, such as Stanford or Massachusetts Institute of Technology, employers won't care how well known the school is. Prestige matters mainly if you're looking to go into academia instead of industry, but in that case, you should be getting a PhD and not a master's degree (and also reading a different book from this one). Prestige is useful only for the strong alumni networks that these schools provide.

- *Your advisor [very important, but . . .]*—If the graduate program you're considering has a thesis or dissertation component, you'll have an advisor from the school guiding you through it. Having an advisor with a similar work style and area of interest to you, along with not being an abusive person, will easily make the difference between succeeding in the program and failing in it. Unfortunately, it's very difficult to know before going to a school which advisor you'll pair with, never mind what their personality is like. So although this point is extremely important, you can do only so much to make decisions based on it. If, however, the program is entirely coursework-based or has only a capstone project, an advisor won't matter much.

When coming up with your list of schools, try making a spreadsheet that lists how the different schools fare in each metric. But when you have all the data, you may find it hard to rank the schools objectively. How can you really say whether a school in a city you'd hate to live in but that is well connected to industry is better or worse than a school in a city you'd love that has no project work? We recommend that you let go of the idea of finding the objective "best." Instead, group the schools into "love," "like," and "okay," and then only apply to your loves and likes.

Online graduate programs

More and more schools are offering online graduate programs, making it possible to learn everything you need to know without having to walk onto a college campus. The obvious benefit of this program is that taking courses online is dramatically more convenient than having to spend hours each week going to a university. Also, online programs don't have nearly the stigma as they did at their inception, so you shouldn't worry whether employees will view your degree as being legitimate. The downside is that it is much more difficult to stay engaged with the program and the material if you're doing everything online. It'll be harder to interact with your professors when you have questions, and it'll be easier to half pay attention and not do your homework. In a sense, the convenience of an online program can also be its downfall: you don't have as much incentive to stick with it. If you think that you have the ability to stay committed and focused in an online program, it can be a great choice; just beware of the risks.

3.1.2 *Getting into an academic program*

To get into an academic program, you need to apply. If you're familiar with applying to graduate programs, the application process for data science master's degrees is similar to the rest. The first step is writing your application. Schools typically announce in the fall how to apply, including deadlines and materials needed. Graduate-school applications usually require the following:

- *A one- to two-page letter of intent* describing why you're a good fit for the program. In this letter, focus as much as possible on why you would make a good contribution to the program. Things such as having experience in some skills required by data science or examples of related work you've done are extremely useful. Try to avoid making cliché statements such as "I have been interested in data science ever since I was a child." Lots of resources on writing good graduate-school essays are available, and your undergraduate school may also have a department to help with this task.

- *A transcript* from your undergraduate school to show that you have the necessary prerequisites for the program. Your school's website should have instructions on how to get this transcript, but keep in mind that it usually costs money and takes a week or more to be delivered. Don't leave this task till the last minute!

- *Graduate Record Examination (GRE) scores* that meet some minimum level in verbal skills and math. The mathematics GRE should in theory be easy for anyone going into a data science program, because the math is the foundation of data science. However, many people haven't seen tricky math questions since high school, so it's a really good idea to study. The verbal test can be harder and may require substantial study. The GREs require you go to a special location and can be a pain to schedule, so be proactive, and try to take the exam early. If English isn't your native language, you'll probably need to get a minimum score on the Test of English as a Foreign Language (TOEFL) or International English Language Testing System (IELTS).

- *Three letters of recommendation* stating why you would be good for this graduate program. These letters can be from professors you've had or people such as your boss if your job is tangentially related to data science. Ideally, the writers should be able to talk about why you would be a good data scientist, so they should have seen you perform well. Try to avoid college professors who can say only "This person got an A in my class" and employers who can't say much about your work in a technical environment. If you're an undergraduate student who's reading this book, now may be a good time to get to know your professors better by going to office hours, attending seminars, and joining academic clubs.

These materials take time to pull together, and if you are applying to many schools at the same time, compiling them can end up being a full-time job. Most applications are due between December and February, and you hear back around February or March.

If you get accepted, you have until April to decide whether you want to be in the program. When your acceptances come in, don't worry too much about which school is the "best"—just choose one where you think you'll be happy!

3.1.3 *Summarizing academic degrees*

Putting it all together, graduate programs in data science are a good fit for people who want an extensive education and can afford it. Those people may be coming from a field in which they haven't done much programming or technical work, such as marketing. A graduate program would allow them to learn all the components of data science at a pace that makes the transition reasonable.

Graduate programs are *not* good for people who already have many of the required skills; the programs are much too long and too expensive to be worthwhile. Also, the teachers aren't industry experts, so the little new knowledge they impart may not even be very relevant. You may need to get industry experience from internships during your graduate program to augment the degree itself.

If you're thinking that you need extensive training before you could be a data scientist, go for it; start looking for graduate schools you like. If you feel that getting more education is going to be a lot of work, and that there's got to be an easier way, consider the options in the next few sections.

Do I need a PhD to get a data science job?

Probably not.

PhDs are degrees that take many years to obtain and that focus on training students to become professors. You have to spend years doing research to find a new method or solution to a problem that's very slightly better than a previous one. You publish to academic journals and move state-of-the-art research forward in an extremely specific area. But as chapters 1 and 2 have shown, little work that a data scientist does is like academic research. A data scientist cares much less about finding an elegant, state-of-the-art solution and much more about quickly finding something that's good enough.

A fair number of data science job posts require a PhD. But the skills acquired in a PhD program are rarely what's needed for the job; usually, the PhD requirement is a signal from the company that the position is considered to be prestigious. The material you can learn from a master's or undergraduate degree program will suit you fine for the vast majority of data science jobs.

Also, getting a PhD incurs huge opportunity cost. If it takes seven years to graduate, you could have been working at a company for seven years instead, getting better at data science and making far more money.

You could go get a PhD and then be a data scientist, but don't let anyone tell you that you need this degree.

3.2   *Going through a bootcamp*

A *bootcamp* is an 8- to 15-week intensive course put on by companies such as Metis and Galvanize. During the bootcamp, you spend more than eight hours every day learning data science skills, listening to industry speakers, and working on projects. At the end of the course, you'll usually present a capstone project to a room full of people from companies that are looking to hire data scientists. Ideally, your presentation will get you an interview and then a job.

Bootcamps teach you an incredible amount in a very short time, which means that they can be great for people who have most of the skills needed for data science but need a bit more. Consider someone who has been working as a neuroscientist and has done programming as part of their work. A data science bootcamp could teach them topics such as logistic regressions and SQL databases. With their science background plus those basics, they should be ready to get a data science job. Sometimes, the best part of a bootcamp isn't the knowledge itself, but the confidence you get from the program that you can actually do the work.

3.2.1   *What you learn*

A good bootcamp has a syllabus that is highly optimized to teach you exactly what you need to know to get a data science job—and nothing more. The program goes beyond just technical skills, including opportunities to work on projects and network with people. The following sections offer more details on what you should expect a bootcamp to cover.

SKILLS

Bootcamps are great supplements to existing education. By doing a bootcamp, you'll be able to get a data science job quickly, without spending two years in a program (as you would if you were to seek a master's degree). This fact might be especially attractive if you already have a master's degree in a non-data science field. The skills you typically get in a bootcamp are

- *Introductory statistics*—This skill includes methods of making predictions with data such as linear and logistic regressions, as well as testing methods you could use on the job, such as t-tests. Due to the very limited time range, you won't get very deep into why these methods work, but you'll learn a lot about how to use them.
- *Machine learning methods*—The program will cover machine learning algorithms such as random forests and support vector machines, as well as show you how to use them by splitting data into training and testing groups and by using cross-validation. You may learn algorithms for specific cases such as natural language processing or search engines. If none of those words makes sense to you, you could be a good fit for a bootcamp!
- *Intermediate programming in R or Python*—You'll learn the basics of how data is stored in data frames and how to manipulate it by summarizing, filtering, and

plotting data. You'll learn how to use the statistical and machine learning methods within the chosen program. Although you may learn R or Python, you probably won't learn both, so you may have to learn the other after you finish the bootcamp if you need it for your first job.

- *Real-world use cases*—You'll learn not only the algorithms, but also where people use them—using a logistic regression to predict when a customer will stop subscribing to a product, for example, or using a clustering algorithm to segment customers for a marketing campaign. This knowledge is extremely useful for getting a job, and questions about use cases often show up in interviews.

PROJECTS

Bootcamps have a highly project-based curriculum. Instead of listening to lectures for eight hours a day, you'll spend most of your time working on projects that can best help you understand data science and get you started with your own data science portfolio (the subject of chapter 4). That's a huge advantage over academia, because your skills will be aligned with what you need to succeed in industry, which is often similar to project-based work.

In a project, you first collect data. You could collect that data by using a web API that a company has created to pull its data, scraping websites to collect the information from them, or using existing public datasets from places such as government websites. Next, you'll load the data into R or Python, write scripts to manipulate the data, and run machine learning models on it. Then you'll use the results to create a presentation or report.

None of those steps in the project requires a bootcamp. In fact, chapter 4 of this book is entirely about how you can do data science projects on your own. That being said, having a project as part of a bootcamp means that you'll have instructors guiding you and helping you if things go wrong. It's difficult to stay motivated if you're working alone and easy to get stuck if you don't have a person to call for help.

A NETWORK

Lots of people go from bootcamps to successful careers at places like Google and Facebook. The bootcamps keep alumni networks that you can use to get your foot in the door at those companies. The bootcamp may bring in data science speakers during the program, as well as people from industry to view your final presentations. All these people can serve as connections to help you get a job at their companies. Having points of entry to companies with data science positions can make all the difference when it comes to finding a job, so it's worth stressing this perk of bootcamps.

In addition to meeting people during the course, you can use tools such as LinkedIn to contact alumni from your bootcamp. These people may be able to help you find a job at their companies or at least point you in the direction of a company that would be a good fit.

For all these connections, you have to be proactive, which may mean talking to speakers after they present and sending messages on social networks to people you haven't talked to before. This process can be scary, especially if you aren't especially comfortable with social interaction with strangers, but it's necessary to get the most value out of the bootcamp. Check out chapter 6 for tips on writing an effective networking request.

3.2.2 Cost

One significant downside to a bootcamp compared with self-teaching is the cost: the tuition is generally around $15,000 to $20,000. Although you may be able to get scholarships to cover part of the tuition, you also have to consider the opportunity cost of not being able to work full-time (and likely even part-time) during the program. Moreover, you'll probably be on the job market for several months after your bootcamp. You won't be able to apply during the bootcamp because you'll be too busy and won't have learned the skills yet, and even a successful data science job application process can take months from application to starting date. Altogether, you could end up being unemployed for six to nine months because of the bootcamp. If you're able to teach yourself data science in your free time or learn on the job, you can keep working and not paying tuition, which can save you tens of thousands of dollars.

3.2.3 Choosing a program

Depending on where you live, you likely have only a few options for bootcamps. If you want to do an in-person bootcamp, even a large city probably has only a handful of programs. If you don't live in a large city and want to do a bootcamp, you may have to move to a large city temporarily, which can add to the cost of the program and make it a greater upheaval.

Alternatively, online bootcamps for data science are available. Be careful, however: as with graduate programs, one of the benefits of in-person bootcamps is that you'll have people around you to motivate you and keep you focused. If you take an online course, you lose that benefit, which can make an online bootcamp a $20,000 version of the same courses you could get through free or cheap open online courses.

In choosing among the bootcamps in your area, consider checking out their classrooms, talking to some of the instructors, and seeing where you feel most comfortable. But beware: in both academia and bootcamps, lots of people are looking to make a quick buck on people who want to become data scientists. If you aren't careful, you could end up completing a program that won't help you get a job at all and will leave you with tens of thousands of dollars' worth of debt. For bootcamps, it's extremely important to talk to alumni. Do you see successful graduates on LinkedIn? If so, talk to those people to find out how they feel about their experience. If you can't find people on LinkedIn who went through the program, that fact is a huge red flag.

3.2.4 *Summarizing data science bootcamps*

Bootcamps can be great programs for people who want to switch careers and already know some of the basics of data science. They can also be useful for people who are just leaving school and want to have a few data science projects in their portfolio while they're in the job market. Bootcamps are not designed to take you from 0 to 60, though; most of them have competitive admissions requirements, and you need to have a background in the fundamentals of programming and statistics to get in and then get the most out of the program.

3.3 *Getting data science work within your company*

You may find yourself in a data-science-adjacent job. An unusual, but often very effective method of learning data science is to start doing more and more data science work as part of your current job. Maybe you're a businessperson who adds a business spin to data science reports and could start adding your own graphs. Or maybe you work in finance, making spreadsheets that you could move into R or Python.

Consider a hypothetical Amber, a person who has been working for several years in the market research department, running surveys on customers and using a market-research graphical user interface (GUI) to aggregate the survey results. Amber has a background in sociology and did a small amount of programming during their under-grad years. They frequently work with the data science department, passing along survey data and helping the data scientists understand it so that they can use it in models. Over time, Amber starts to do a bit of work for the data science team—a bit of feature extraction in R here, a bit of creating visualizations there. Soon, the data science team is relying more and more on Amber. During this time, they're really improving the team members' programming and data science skills. After a year, they join the data science team full-time, leaving market research behind.

Trying to do some data science in your current job is a great method because it's low-risk and has built-in motivation. You aren't trying to do an expensive bootcamp or degree program that you have to quit your job for; you're just trying to add a little data science work where you can. And the fact that you're doing data science in your own job is motivating because the work you'll do is valuable to others. Over time, you can do more data science work until eventually, it's all you do, as opposed to taking an educational program and then suddenly switching jobs.

Former market researcher and now data scientist Amber had several things going for them:

- They had existing relationships with the data science department which provided mentorship.
- They understood the basics of programming and data visualization.
- They were motivated enough to learn data science techniques within their job.
- The data science department was able to provide small projects that they could tackle, and over time, these projects grew, enabling Amber to become a data scientist.

When you're trying to do more data science work in your company, look for places where you can find small data science projects and people to help you with them. Something as simple as creating a report or automating an existing one can teach you a lot about data science.

One important note if you're taking this path: never become a burden for someone else. Direct burdens might be very obvious, such as repeatedly asking people to create cleaned datasets for you, or less obvious, such as continually asking someone to review work you've done. You can also create an accidental burden by adding new tools to your team. If you're in finance, and everyone uses Microsoft Excel except you (you now use R), you've just made managing your team more complicated. Even the action of asking someone for work you can do is a burden, because then they need to find something for you to do. Just be careful as you learn these skills that you aren't creating issues for other people.

Two conversation perspectives

What you say: "I'm happy to help in any way I can; just let me know how! Thanks!"

What you think they hear: "I'm a person who is eager to work for you. You can hand me that exciting but simple project you've held on to for so long, and I will do it for you!"

What they actually hear: "Hi! I want to be helpful, but I have no idea what your needs are. I also don't know what my skills are relative to your workload, so good luck finding a task for me to do. Also, if you do somehow find a task that's perfect for me, you'll probably have to review it a bunch of times before it's good. All this work will take away from your already-minimal available hours. Thanks!"

To make this path work, you need to employ a few key strategies:

- *Be proactive*—The more you can do work before people ask for it, the more you'll become more independent and less of a burden. The data science team may have a task, such as labeling data or making a simple report, that's time-intensive and uninteresting. You can offer to help with that work. Be careful about just diving in and doing it yourself, though: you may end up doing the task in a way that doesn't provide any value but provides the team the opportunity to redo your work. If you can get the task started and then get other people's input, however, it's possible you can save the team a lot of time.

- *Pick off new skills one at a time*—Don't try to learn everything about data science all at once. Find a single skill that you want to learn through work and then learn it. You may want to learn how to make reports with R, for example, because the data science team does that all the time. By finding a small project to help the team with, you can pick up the skill and add it to your tool belt. From there, you can learn a different data science skill.

- *Be clear about your intentions*—It'll be pretty obvious fairly quickly that you're trying to pick up extra work to learn to be a data scientist. If you're proactive and let the data science team know that you're interested in learning more, the team will be able to plan to have you help. Also, the team members will be more understanding about your inexperience, because they were new and learning once too.

- *Avoid being pushy*—Helping a person become a data scientist is an immense amount of work, and often, data science teams are already overworked. If you find that the team doesn't have the time or bandwidth to help you, don't take it personally. Although it's okay to check in occasionally if you think the team's been out of touch, if you're too persistent with your requests, the team will quickly become uncomfortable. Members will view you as being less a potential resource and more a nuisance.

> **When opportunities aren't there**
>
> You may find yourself in a situation where there are no opportunities for using data science in your current role. It's possible that the constraints of your job prevent you from using R or Python, or trying to implement data science techniques. In these situations, you may have to take drastic measures. Quitting your job to do a bootcamp or graduate degree is risky but effective for getting you out of your current role and into data science. You could also try teaching yourself in your free time, but that method has tons of drawbacks (see section 3.4). Another option is trying to find a new job in your field that would allow you to learn more in that position. But there's no guarantee that when you got to the new job, you'd get the flexibility you were promised.
>
> None of these options are easy, but unfortunately, that's the reality of the situation. It's going to take work to get into a data science position, but the effort might well be worth it.

3.3.1 Summarizing learning on the job

Learning on the job can be an effective way to become a data scientist, provided that you have a job in which you can apply data science skills and people around who can mentor you. If those things align, this route is a great one, but for many, these things are not in place. If you think this route is viable for you, we highly recommend taking it. Jobs don't often allow for learning on the job, so take the opportunity if you have it.

3.4 Teaching yourself

An enormous number of books cover data science (such as, uh, this one), as well as many online courses. These books and sites promise to teach you the basics of data science as well as the in-depth technical skills through a medium (and at a price point) that is practical. These courses and books—as well as all the data science blogs, tutorials, and Stack Overflow answers—can provide enough of a grounding that people can teach themselves data science.

These self-driven learning materials are great for picking up individual skills. If you want to understand how to do deep learning, for example, a book can be a great way to do it. Or if you want to get the basics of R and Python, you can take an online course to get started.

Teaching yourself data science entirely through self-driven online courses and books is just like teaching yourself to play an instrument through YouTube videos or learning anything else without a teacher: the value of this method is mostly a function of your perseverance. Learning new skills can take hundreds or thousands of hours. It's really hard to put thousands of hours into data science when the best TikTok compilations are one tab over. It's also hard to know where to start. If you want to learn everything in data science, who is to say which book you should read first (such as, uh, this one)?

Learning on your own means that you don't have a teacher or role model. By not having a teacher of whom you can ask questions, as you would in an academic program or bootcamp, you won't have a ready ability to understand when you're doing something wrong or know what to do next. The time spent being directionless or going down an incorrect path is a hurdle to understanding the material. The best way to counteract the lack of a teacher is to find a community of people where you can ask questions. One great example is the TidyTuesday program (https://github.com/rfordatascience/tidytuesday), started by Thomas Mock; every Tuesday, aspiring and practicing data scientists use R to tackle a data science problem.

If you do decide to go down the self-driven route, it's important to have some constructive work to do. Reading books and watching videos is great, but you learn far more from doing your own data science work and learning from that work. To put it a different way, reading books about bicycles can be educational, but you'll never learn to ride a bicycle without actually getting on one. Make sure to find a project that you want to do, such as taking a dataset and finding interesting results from it, creating a machine learning model and API, or using a neural network to generate text. In chapter 4, we go into far more detail on these sorts of projects. For other methods of learning data science, the projects can be about building a portfolio, but for self-driven learning, the projects are critical to learning.

3.4.1   *Summarizing self-teaching*

Learning on your own is hard—possible, but hard. You need to be able to figure out the order in which you want to learn things, keep yourself motivated enough to learn the skills, and do it all without having a mentor or teacher to help you. You'll also have a more difficult time displaying your qualifications on a résumé than if you used other methods. This method is our least-recommended way to become a data scientist because of how many things can go wrong and the number of people who don't succeed in staying focused. If you want to pick up a single skill or technology, taking this route can be more feasible, but learning everything you need to be a data scientist is a hard route.

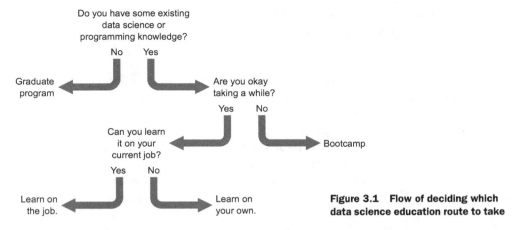

Figure 3.1 **Flow of deciding which data science education route to take**

3.5 *Making the choice*

How do you choose among these four very different avenues to data science? The process is different for everyone, but we propose answering three questions (figure 3.1):

1. *Do you already have some data science knowledge?* Specifically, have you programmed in at least one programming language beyond light coursework? Do you know how to query data from a SQL database? Do you know what things like linear regressions are?
   a. If your answer is "No, I've got a lot to learn," you're probably best suited for an academic program such as a master's degree. This program will teach you all these topics over a long-enough time period that they'll really settle in.
   b. If your answer is "Yes, I know this stuff," move on to question 2.

2. *Are you comfortable with taking a year or more to gain the necessary data science skills rather than incurring the costs of being unemployed for six to nine months to get a data science job more quickly?* It's difficult to learn new skills quickly when you're focused solely on learning; it's even harder to do so while working at a full-time job. Are you okay with the path's taking longer so you can keep working full-time?
   a. If your answer is "No, I've gotta go fast," take a bootcamp. In three months, you'll know a ton of data science and will be ready to embark on your search for a new job, which could take three to six months longer.
   b. If your answer is "Yes, I want to take my time," move on to question 3.

3. *Can you learn data science in your current job?* Can you do data science things within your current role, such as make an analysis, store some data in SQL, or try using R or Python? Is there a team that could mentor you or give you some small tasks?
   a. If your answer is "Yes, I can learn at work," try doing that, and use your job as a springboard to data science.
   b. If your answer is "No, my job has no opportunities," it's time to hit the books and online courses.

Although these questions should provide you a starting point, you don't have to make one final decision. You can start by reading books independently, and if you find that you want to go faster, switch to a bootcamp. You can also get a master's degree in the evening while trying to do data science in your current job. There isn't one perfect answer; what matters is finding an approach that works for you, If something isn't working, change it until it does.

When you've chosen your route, it's time to follow it! Enroll in that master's degree program, join that bootcamp, or buy those books and start reading. For the purposes of this book, we'll assume that time passes and you've succeeded in learning the fundamental skills you need to be a data scientist. In the next few chapters, you'll use those skills to create a data science portfolio that can help you get your first data science job.

3.6   *Interview with Julia Silge, data scientist and software engineer at RStudio*

Julia Silge is known for her popular blog posts on data science, along with the tidytext package that she and David Robinson developed, which is a cornerstone of NLP in R and has been downloaded more than 700,000 times. She and Robinson also coauthored the book *Text Mining with R: A Tidy Approach* (O'Reilly). Julia worked for several years as a data scientist at Stack Overflow, and now develops open source machine learning tools at RStudio.

Before becoming a data scientist, you worked in academia; how have the skills learned there helped you as a data scientist?

When I was doing research as an academic, some of my days were spent collecting real-world data. That experience taught me to think about the process the data is created by. In that case, it was created by a physical process that I could touch. I could actually see things that contributed to why the data was messy or why we didn't get a data point in a particular night. I see direct parallels to my work for several years at a tech company that dealt with web data; there was some process that generated that data, and I had to think carefully about how we recorded that data and how that process could go well or wrong. That experience with real-world data informs my approach to developing machine learning tools now.

Another set of skills I learned before being a data scientist was communicating and teaching. I was a college professor for a number of years, and I also have had roles where I have dealt with customers. In those roles, I practiced the skill of having a concept and trying to transfer that knowledge or understanding to another person. I strongly believe that's a part of most data scientists' role. If we train some model or do some statistical analysis, the value of it is small compared to when we are able to take that same model or analysis and explain what it means, how it works, or how to implement it in the broader context.

When deciding to become a data scientist, what did you use to pick up new skills?

I certainly think academic programs, bootcamps, and online materials are all great options for different people in different situations. Given that I already had a PhD, I didn't want to go back to school and spend more money. I will admit that I applied to a couple of bootcamps, and they took a pass on me! When I was deciding to make this career transition into data science, what I perceived was that I could do that job, but I needed to demonstrate to other people that I could. I also needed to update my machine learning knowledge and some of the techniques because when I was in grad school, modern machine learning had not really entered astrophysics.

I went the route of online courses and embracing a lot of self-directed study. I joke around that I took every MOOC (massive open online course) that existed: it was a *lot*. I took about six months where I was slightly underemployed in the job I had, and I just hit the online courses really hard. I had been out of school for a long time, and I had been excited about the material. I hadn't been doing even data analysis for a while, so getting back into data analysis was really exciting!

Did you know going into data science what kind of work you wanted to be doing?

When I looked at my options ahead of time and saw what people were doing, like how people talked about *analyze* versus *build* data science, I absolutely saw myself as an analyze person. I saw myself less of an engineer and more of a scientist—a person who works to understand things and answer questions but not so much build things. And that has been where my career started. I was the only data scientist at Stack Overflow for most of my time there, and I was on a team with very talented, knowledgeable data engineers. Being the only data scientist, my job was a bit of both data analysis and model building. Now, working on open source tools, I have "software engineer" in my title and I am spending more energy building than analyzing.

What would you recommend to people looking to get the skills to be a data scientist?

One thing that I would strongly emphasize is that you need to demonstrate that you can do this job. That can look different for different people. It's still a young-enough field that people aren't sure what it means to be a data scientist and who can be one; it's still very undefined. There is still a lot of uncertainty in what this role means, and the positions are highly paid enough that the perceived risk to a company hiring wrong is very high, so companies are very risk-averse. Companies need to be sure that the candidate can do that job. Some ways I've seen people demonstrate that they can do the job is through open source contributions, speaking at local meetups on projects they've done, and developing a portfolio of projects on a blog or GitHub profile. For me, I took all the MOOCs and things I needed to learn, and started a blog about all of these projects. What I pictured to myself was that these projects and blog posts would be something that we could talk about in a job interview.

Summary

- Four proven paths to learn the skills to be a data scientist are academic programs, bootcamps, picking the skills up in your current job, and teaching yourself on the side.
- Each of these methods has trade-offs in terms of the materials taught, the time it takes, and the level of self-motivation required.
- To choose a path for yourself, take time to reflect on what skills you already have, where your strengths lie, and what resources you have.

4

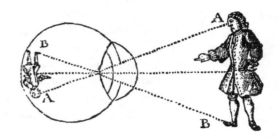

Building a portfolio

This chapter covers

- Creating a compelling data science project
- Starting a blog
- Full walkthroughs of example projects

You've now finished a bootcamp, a degree program, a set of online courses, or a series of data projects in your current job. Congratulations—you're ready to get a data scientist job! Right?

Well, maybe. Part 2 of this book is all about how to find, apply for, and get a data science position, and you can certainly start this process now. But another step can really help you be successful: building a portfolio. A *portfolio* is a set of data science projects that you can show to people so they can see what kind of data science work you can do.

A strong portfolio has two main parts: GitHub repositories (*repos* for short) and a blog. A GitHub repo hosts the code for a project, and the blog shows off your communication skills and the non-code part of your data science work. Most people don't want to read through thousands of lines of code (your repo); they want a quick explanation of what you did and why it's important (your blog). And who knows—you might even get data scientists from around the world reading your blog, depending on the topic. As we discuss in the second part of this chapter, you don't have to just blog about analyses you did or models you built; you could also explain a statistical technique, write a tutorial for a text analysis method, or even share career advice (such as how you picked your degree program).

This isn't to say that you need to have a blog or GitHub repos filled with projects to be a successful data scientist. In fact, the majority of data scientists don't, and people get jobs without a portfolio all the time. But creating a portfolio is a great way to help you stand out and to practice your data science skills and get better. We hope that it's fun, too!

This chapter walks you through the process of building a good portfolio. The first part is about doing a data science project and organizing it on GitHub. The second part goes over best practices for starting and sharing your blog so that you get the most value out of the work you've done. Then we walk you through two real projects we've done so that you can see the process end to end.

4.1   Creating a project

A data science project starts with two things: a dataset that's interesting and a question to ask about it. You could take government census data, for example, and ask "How are the demographics across the country changing over time?" The combination of question and data is the kernel of the project (figure 4.1), and with those two things, you can start doing data science.

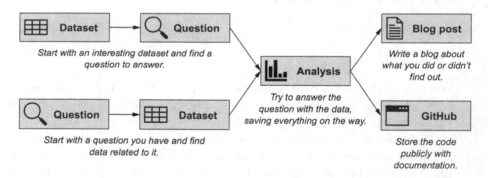

Figure 4.1   The flow of creating a data science project

4.1.1   Finding the data and asking a question

When you're thinking about what data you want to use, the most important thing is finding data that's interesting to you. Why do you want to use this data? Your choice of data is a way to show off your personality or the domain knowledge you have from your previous career or studies. If you're in fashion, for example, you can look at articles about Fashion Week and see how styles have changed in the past 20 years. If you're an enthusiastic runner, you can show how your runs have changed over time and maybe look to see whether your running time is related to the weather.

Something you shouldn't do is use the Titanic dataset, MNIST, or any other popular beginning datasets. It's not that these learning experiences aren't good; they can be, but you're probably not going to find anything novel that would surprise and intrigue employers or teach them more about you.

Sometimes, you let a question lead you to your dataset. You may be curious, for example, about how the gender distribution of college majors has changed over time and whether that change is related to median earnings after graduation. Then you'd take to Google and try to find the best source of that data.

But maybe you don't have a burning question that you've just been waiting to have data science skills to answer. In this case, you can start by browsing datasets and seeing whether you can come up with any interesting questions. Here are a few suggestions for where you might start:

- *Kaggle.com*—Kaggle started as a website for data science competitions. Companies post a dataset and a question, and usually offer a prize for the best answer. Because the questions entail machine learning models that try to predict something, such as whether someone would default on a loan or how much a house would sell for, users can compare models based on their performance on a holdout test set and get a performance metric for each one. Kaggle also has discussion forums and "kernels" in which people share their code so you can learn how others approached the dataset. As a result, Kaggle has thousands of datasets with accompanying questions and examples of how other people analyzed them.

  The biggest benefit of Kaggle is also its biggest drawback: by handing you a (generally cleaned) dataset and problem, it's done a lot of the work for you. You also have thousands of people tackling the same problem, so it's difficult to make a unique contribution. One way to use Kaggle is to take a dataset but pose a different question or do an exploratory analysis. But generally, we think that Kaggle is best for learning by tackling a project and then seeing how you performed compared with others, thus learning from what their models did, rather than as a piece of your portfolio.

- *Datasets in the news*—Recently, many news companies have started making their data public. FiveThirtyEight.com, for example, a website that focuses on opinion-poll analysis, politics, economics, and sports blogging, publishes data it can use for articles and even links to the raw data directly from the article website. Although these datasets often require manual cleaning, the fact that they're in the news means that an obvious question is probably associated with them.

- *APIs*—APIs (application programming interfaces) are developer tools that allow you to access data directly from companies. You know how you can type in a URL and get to a website? APIs are like URLs, but instead of a website, you get data. Some examples of companies with helpful APIs are *The New York Times* and Yelp, which let you pull their articles and reviews, respectively. Some APIs even have R or Python packages that specifically make it easier to work with them. rtweet for R, for example, lets you pull Twitter data quickly so that you can find tweets with a specific hashtag, what the trending topics in Kyoto are, or what tweets Stephen King is favoriting. Keep in mind that there are limitations and terms of service to how you can use these APIs. Right now, for example, Yelp limits you to 5,000 calls a day, so you won't be able to pull all reviews ever. APIs are great for providing extremely robust, organized data from many sources.

- *Government open data*—A lot of government data is available online. You can use census data, employment data, the general social survey, and tons of local government data such as New York City's 911 calls or traffic counts. Sometimes, you can download this data directly as a CSV file; at other times, you need to use an API. You can even submit Freedom of Information Act requests to government agencies to get data that isn't publicly listed. Government information is great because it's often detailed and deals with unusual subjects, such as data on the registered pet names of every animal in Seattle. The downside of government information is that it often isn't well formatted, such as tables stored within PDF files.

- *Your own data*—There are many places where you can download data about yourself; social media websites and email services are two big ones. But if you use apps to keep track of your physical activity, reading list, budget, sleep, or anything else, you can usually download that data as well. Maybe you could build a chatbot based on your emails with your spouse. Or you could look at the most common words you use in your tweets and how those words have changed over time. Perhaps you could track your caffeine intake and exercise for a month to see whether you can predict how much and well you sleep. The advantage of using your own data is that your project is guaranteed to be unique: no one else will have looked at that data before!

- *Web scraping*—Web scraping is a way to extract data from websites that don't have an API, essentially by automating visiting web pages and copying the data. You could create a program to search a movie website for a list of 100 actors, load their actor profiles, copy the lists of movies they're in, and put that data in a spreadsheet. You do have to be careful, though: scraping a website can be against the website's terms of use, and you could be banned. You can check the robots.txt file of a website to find out what is allowed. You also want to be nice to websites: if you hit a site too many times, you can bring it down. But assuming that the terms of service allow it and you build in time between your hits, scraping can be a great way to get unique data.

What makes a side project interesting? Our recommendation is to pick an exploratory analysis in which any result will probably teach the reader something or demonstrate your skills. You might create an interactive map of 311 calls in Seattle, color-coded by category; this map clearly demonstrates your visualization skills and shows that you can write about the patterns that emerge. On the other hand, if you try to predict the stock market, you likely won't be able to, and it's hard for an employer to assess your skills if you have a negative outcome.

Another tip is to see what comes up when you Google your question. If the first results are newspaper articles or blog posts that answer exactly the question you were asking, you may want to rethink your approach. Sometimes, you can expand on someone else's analysis or bring in other data to add another layer to the analysis, but you may need to start the process over.

4.1.2 *Choosing a direction*

Building a portfolio doesn't need to be a huge time commitment. The perfect is definitely the enemy of the good here. Something is better than nothing; employers are first and foremost looking for evidence that you can code and communicate about data. You may be worried that people will look and laugh at your code or say, "Wow, we thought this person might be okay, but look at their terrible code!" It's very unlikely that this will happen. One reason is that employers tailor their expectations to seniority level: you won't be expected to code like a computer science major if you're a beginning data scientist. Generally, the bigger worry is that you can't code at all.

It's also good to think about the areas of data science we covered in chapter 1. Do you want to specialize in visualization? Make an interactive graph using D3. Do you want to do natural language processing? Use text data. Machine learning? Predict something.

Use your project to force yourself to learn something new. Doing this kind of hands-on analysis will show you the holes in your knowledge. When data you're really interested in is on the web, you'll learn web scraping. If you think that a particular graph looks ugly, you'll learn how to make better visualizations. If you're self-studying, doing a project is a nice way to overcome the paralysis of not knowing what to learn next.

A common problem with self-motivated projects is overscoping. *Overscoping* is wanting to do everything or keep adding more stuff as you go. You can always keep improving/editing/supplementing, but then you never finish. One strategy is to think like Hollywood and create sequels. You should set yourself a question and answer it, but if you think you may want to revisit it later, you can end your research with a question or topic for further investigation (or even "To be continued . . .?", if you must).

Another problem is not being able to pivot. Sometimes, the data you wanted isn't available. Or there's not enough of it. Or you're not able to clean it. These situations are frustrating, and it can be easy to give up at this point. But it's worth trying to figure out how you can salvage the project. Have you already done enough work to write a blog post tutorial, maybe on how you collected the data? Employers look for people who learn from their mistakes and aren't afraid to admit them. Just showing what went wrong so that others might avoid the same fate is still valuable.

4.1.3   *Filling out a GitHub README*

Maybe you're in a bootcamp or a degree program in which you're already doing your own projects. You've even committed your code to GitHub. Is that enough?

Nope! A minimal requirement for a useful GitHub repository is filling out the README file. You have a couple of questions to answer:

- *What is the project?* What data does it use? What question is it answering? What was the output: A model, a machine learning system, a dashboard, or a report?
- *How is the repository organized?* This question implies, of course, that the repo is in fact organized in some manner! There are lots of different systems, but a basic one is dividing your script into parts: getting (if relevant) your data, cleaning it, exploring it, and the final analysis. This way, people know where to go depending on what they're interested in. It also suggests that you'll keep your work organized when you go to work for a company. A company doesn't want to risk hiring you and then, when it's time to hand off a project, you give someone an uncommented, 5,000-line script that may be impossible for them to figure out and use. Good project management also helps the you of the future: if you want to reuse part of the code later, you'll know where to go.

But although doing a project and making it publicly available in a documented GitHub repo is good, it's very hard to look at code and understand why it's important. After you do a project, the next step is writing a blog post, which lets people know why what you did was cool and interesting. No one cares about pet_name_analysis.R, but everyone cares about "I used R to find the silliest pet names!"

4.2   *Starting a blog*

Blogs allow you to show off your thinking and projects, but they can also offer a non-technical view of your work. We know, we know—you just learned all this great technical stuff! You want to show it off! But being a data scientist almost always entails communicating your results to a lay audience, and a blog will give you experience translating your data science process into business language.

4.2.1   *Potential topics*

Suppose that you've created a blog. Are people really going to be interested in your projects? You don't even have a data scientist title yet; how can you teach anyone anything?

Something good to remember is that you are best positioned to teach the people a few steps behind you. Right after you've learned a concept, such as using continuous integration for your package or making a TensorFlow model, you still understand the misconceptions and frustrations you've had. Years later, it's hard to put yourself in that beginner's mindset. Have you ever had a teacher who was clearly very smart and yet couldn't communicate concepts at all? You didn't doubt that they knew the topic, but they couldn't break it down for you and seemed to be frustrated that you didn't just get it right away.

Try thinking of your audience as the you of six months ago. What have you learned since then? What resources do you wish had been available? This exercise is also great for celebrating your progress. With so much to learn in data science, it's easy to feel that you've never done enough; pausing to see what you've accomplished is nice.

You can group data science blog posts into four categories:

- *Code-heavy tutorials*—Tutorials show your readers how to do things like web scraping or deep learning in Python. Your readers will generally be other aspiring or practicing data scientists. Although we call the tutorials *code-heavy*, you'll usually still want there to be as many lines of text as code, if not more. Code generally isn't self-explanatory; you need to walk a reader through what each part does, why you'd want to do it, and what the results are.

- *Theory-heavy tutorials*—These tutorials teach your readers a statistical or mathematical concept, such as what empirical Bayes is or how principal component analysis works. They may have some equations or simulations. As with code-heavy tutorials, your audience is usually other data scientists, but you should write so that anyone who has some mathematics background can follow along. Theory-heavy tutorials are especially good for demonstrating your communication skills; there's a stereotype that many technical people, especially if they have PhD degrees, can't explain concepts well.

- *A fun project you did*—As we hope that we convinced you in section 4.1, you don't need to work only on groundbreaking medical image recognition. You can also find out which of the *Twilight* movies used only words from Shakespeare's *The Tempest*. Julia Silge, for example, whom we interviewed in chapter 3, used neural networks to generate text that sounds like Jane Austen. These blog posts can focus more on the results or the process, depending on what the most interesting part of your project was.

- *Writing up your experience*—You don't have to just blog about tutorials or your data science projects. You can talk about your experience at a data science meetup or conference: what talks you found interesting, advice for people going to their first one, or some resources that the speakers shared. This type of post can be helpful to people who are considering attending the same event the following year or who can't attend conferences for logistical or financial reasons. Again, these types of blog posts give potential employers insight into how you think and communicate.

4.2.2 Logistics

But where should you put your interesting writing? For a blog, you have two main options:

- *Make your own website.* If you work in R, we suggest using the package blogdown, which lets you create a website for a blog using R code (wild, right?). If you use Python, Hugo and Jekyll are two options, both of which let you create static blog websites and come with a bunch of themes that other people have built, letting you write blog posts in markdown. We suggest that you don't worry much about your theme and style; just pick one you like. Nothing is worse than not writing blog posts because you got too distracted by changing the blog's appearance. Simple is probably best; it can be a pain to change your theme, so it's better not to pick one you may get sick of in six months.

- *Using Medium or another blogging platform.* Medium is a free, online publishing platform. The company generally doesn't write content; instead, it hosts content for hundreds of thousands of authors. Medium and sites like it are good options if you want to start quickly, because you don't have to worry about hosting or starting a website; all you do is click "New Post," start writing, and publish. You can also get more traffic when people search the blogging site for terms such as *data science* or *Python*. But one concern is that you're at the platform's mercy. If the company changes its business model and puts everything behind a paywall, for example, you can't do anything to keep your blog posts free. You also don't get to create a real biography section or add other content, such as a page with links to talks you've given.

One common question people have about blogging is how often they need to post and how long those posts should be. These things are definitely personal choices. We've seen people who have micro blogs, publishing short posts multiple times a week. Other people go months between posts and publish longer articles. There are some limitations; you do want to make sure that your posts don't start to resemble *Ulysses*. If your post is very long, you can split it into parts. But you want to show that you can communicate concisely, as that's one of the core data science skills. Executives and even your manager probably don't want or need to hear all the false starts you had or the 20 different things you tried. Although you may choose to include a brief summary of your false starts, you need to get to the point and your final path quickly. One exception, though, is if your final method is going to surprise readers. If you didn't use the most popular library for a problem, for example, you may want to explain that you didn't because you found that the library didn't work.

What if you're worried that no one will read your blog and that all your work will be for nothing? Well, one reason to have a blog anyway is that it helps your job applications. You can put links to your blog posts on your résumé when you reference data science projects and even show them to people in interviews, especially if the posts have nice interactive visualizations or dashboards. It's not important to have hundreds or thousands of readers. It can be nice if you get claps on Medium or if you're featured in a data science company's newsletter, but it's more important to have an audience that will read, value, and engage with the material than to have high metrics.

That's not to say there's nothing you can do to build readership. For one thing, you should advertise yourself; although it's a cliché, having a #brand is useful for building a network in the long term. Even if something seems to be simple, it's probably new to a bunch of practicing data scientists just because the field is so big. People at the companies you want to work for may even read your stuff! Twitter is a good place to start; you can share the news when you release a post and use the appropriate hashtags to get wider readership.

But your blog is valuable even if no one (besides your partner and pet) reads it. Writing a blog post is good practice; it forces you to structure your thoughts. Just like teaching in person, it also helps you realize when you don't know something as well as you thought you did.

4.3 Working on example projects

In this section, we walk you through two example projects, from the initial idea through the analysis to a final public artifact. We'll use real projects that the authors of this book did: creating a web application for data science freelancers to find the best-fit jobs and learning neural networks by training one on a dataset of banned license plates.

4.3.1 Data science freelancers

Emily Robinson

THE QUESTION

When I was an aspiring data scientist, I became interested in one way some data scientists make extra money: freelancing. *Freelancing* is doing projects for someone you're not employed by, whether that's another person or a large company. These projects range from a few hours to months of full-time work. You can find many freelancing jobs posted on freelancing websites like UpWork, but because data science is a very broad field, jobs in that category could be anything from web development to an analysis in Excel to natural language processing on terabytes of data. I decided to see whether I could help freelancers wade through thousands of jobs to find the ones that are the best fit for them.

THE ANALYSIS

To gather the data, I used UpWork's API to pull currently available jobs and the profiles of everyone in the Data Science and Analytics category. I ended up with 93,000 freelancers and 3,000 jobs. Although the API made it relatively easy to access the data (as I didn't have to do web scraping), I still had to make functions to do hundreds of API calls, handle when those API calls failed, and then transform the data so I could use it. But the advantage of this process was that because the data wasn't readily available, there weren't hundreds of other people working on the same project, as there would have been if I'd used data from a Kaggle competition.

After I got the data in good shape, I did some exploratory analysis. I looked at how education levels and country affected how much freelancers earned. I also made a correlation graph of the skills that freelancers listed, which showed the different types of freelancers: web developers (PHP, jQuery, HTML, and CSS), finance and accounting (financial accounting, bookkeeping, and financial analysis), and data gathering (data entry, lead generation, data mining, and web scraping), along with the "traditional" data science skill set (Python, machine learning, statistics, and data analysis).

Finally, I created a similarity score between profile text and the job text, and combined that score with the overlap in skills (both freelancers and jobs listed skills) to create a matching score for a freelancer and a job.

THE FINAL PRODUCT

In this case, I didn't end up writing a blog post. Instead, I made an interactive web application in which someone could enter their profile text, skills, and requirements for jobs (such as a minimum feedback score for the job poster and how long the job would take), and the available jobs would be filtered to meet those requirements and sorted by how well they fit the user.

I didn't let the perfect be the enemy of the good here; there are plenty of ways I could have made the project better. I pulled the jobs only once, and because I did this project four years ago, the application still works, but none of those jobs are available anymore. To make the application valuable over the long term, I'd need to pull jobs nightly and update the listings. I also could have made a more sophisticated matching algorithm, sped up the initial loading time of the app, and made the appearance fancier. But despite these limitations, the project met a few important goals. It showed that I could take a project and allow people to interact with it rather than be limited to static analyses that lived on my laptop. It had a real-world use case: helping freelancers find jobs. And it took me through the full data science project cycle: gathering the data, cleaning it, running exploratory analyses, and producing a final output.

4.3.2 *Training a neural network on offensive license plates*

Jacqueline Nolis

THE QUESTION

As I grew as a data scientist, I was always frustrated when I saw hilarious blog posts in which people trained neural networks to generate things like new band names, new Pokémon, and weird cooking recipes. I thought these projects were great, but I didn't know how to make them myself! One day, I remembered that I had heard of a dataset of all the custom license plates that were rejected by the state of Arizona for being too offensive. If I could get that dataset, it would be perfect for finally learning how to make neural networks—I could make my own offensive license plates (figure 4.2)!

Figure 4.2 Sample output of the offensive license plate generator neural network

THE ANALYSIS

After submitting a public records request to the Arizona Department of Transportation, I got a list of thousands of offensive license plates. I didn't know anything about neural networks, so after receiving the data, I started scouring the internet for blog posts describing how to make one. As primarily an R user, I was happy to find the Keras package by RStudio for making neural networks in R.

I loaded the data into R and then checked out the RStudio Keras package example for generating text with neural networks. I modified the code to work with license-plate data; the RStudio example was for generating sequences of long text, but I wanted to train on seven-character license plates. This meant creating multiple training data points for my model from each license plate (one data point to predict each character in the license plate).

Next, I trained the neural network model, although it didn't work at first. After putting the project down for a month, I came back and realized that my data wasn't being processed quite right. When I fixed this problem, the results that the neural network generated were fantastic. Ultimately, even though I didn't change the RStudio example much, by the end, I felt much more confident in creating and using neural networks.

THE FINAL PRODUCT

I wrote a blog post about the project that walks through how I got the data, the act of processing it to be ready for the neural network, and how I modified the RStudio example code to work for me. The blog post was very much an "I'm new at neural networks, and here is what I learned" style of post; I didn't pretend that I already knew how all this worked. As part of the blog post, I made an image that took the text output of my neural model and made it look like Arizona license plates. I also put the code on GitHub.

Since I wrote that blog post and made my code available, numerous other people have modified it to make their own funny neural networks. What I learned from this goofy project eventually helped me to make high-impact machine learning models for important consulting engagements. Just because the original work isn't serious doesn't mean that there isn't value in it!

4.4 *Interview with David Robinson, data scientist*

David Robinson is the co-author (with Julia Silge) of the tidytext package in R and the O'Reilly book *Text Mining with R*. He's also the author of the self-published e-book *Introduction to Empirical Bayes: Examples from Baseball Statistics* and the R packages broom and fuzzyjoin. He holds a PhD in quantitative and computational biology from Princeton University. Robinson writes about statistics, data analysis, education, and programming in R on his popular blog: varianceexplained.org.

How did you start blogging?

I first started blogging when I was applying for jobs near the end of my PhD, as I realized that I didn't have a lot out on the internet that showed my skills in programming or statistics. When I launched my blog, I remember having the distinct fear that once I wrote the couple of posts I had ready, I would run out of ideas. But I was surprised to find that I kept coming up with new things I wanted to write about: datasets I wanted to analyze, opinions I wanted to share, and methods I wanted to teach. I've been blogging moderately consistently for four years since then.

Are there any specific opportunities you have gotten from public work?

I did get my first job from something I wrote publicly online. Stack Overflow approached me based on an answer I'd written on Stack Overflow's statistics site. I'd written that answer years ago, but some engineers there found it and were impressed by it. That experience really led me to have a strong belief in producing public artifacts, because sometimes benefits will show up months or years down the line and lead to opportunities I never would have expected.

Are there people you think would especially benefit from doing public work?

People whose résumés might not show their data science skills and who don't have a typical background, like having a PhD or experience as a data analyst, would particularly benefit from public work. When I'm evaluating a candidate, if they don't have those kinds of credentials, it's hard to say if they'll be able to do the job. But my favorite way to evaluate a candidate is to read an analysis they've done online. If I can look at some graphs someone created, how they explained the story, and how they dug into the data, I can start to understand whether they're a good fit for the role.

How has your view on the value of public work changed over time?

The way I used to view projects is that you made steady progress as you kept working on something. In graduate school, an idea wasn't very worthwhile, but then it became some code, a draft, a finished draft, and finally a published paper. I thought that along the way, my work was getting slowly more valuable.

Since then, I've realized I was thinking about it completely wrong. Anything that is still on your computer, however complete it is, is worthless. If it's not out there in the world, it's been wasted so far, and anything that's out in the world is much more valuable. What made me realize this is a few papers I developed in graduate school that I never published. I put a lot of work into them, but I kept feeling they weren't quite ready. Years later, I've forgotten what's in them, I can't find them, and they haven't added anything to the world. If along the way I'd written a couple of blog posts, sent a couple of tweets, and maybe made a really simple open source package, all of those would have added value along the way.

How do you come up with ideas for your data analysis posts?

I've built up a habit that every time I see a dataset, I'll download it and take a quick look at it, running a few lines of code to get a sense of the data. This helps you build up a little of data science taste, working on enough projects that you get a feel for what pieces of data are going to yield an interesting bit of writing and which might be worth giving up on.

My advice is that whenever you see the opportunity to analyze data, even if it's not in your current job or you think it might not be interesting to you, take a quick look and see what you can find in just a few minutes. Pick a dataset, decide on a set amount of time, do all the analyses that you can, and then publish it. It might not be a fully polished post, and you might not find everything you're hoping to find and answer all the questions you wanted to answer. But by setting a goal of one dataset becoming one post, you can start getting into this habit.

What's your final piece of advice for aspiring and junior data scientists?

Don't get stressed about keeping up with the cutting edge of the field. It's tempting when you start working in data science and machine learning to think you should start working with deep learning or other advanced methods. But remember that those methods were developed to solve some of the most difficult problems in the field. Those aren't necessarily the problems that you're going to face as a data scientist, especially early in your career. You should start by getting very comfortable transforming and visualizing data; programming with a wide variety of packages; and using statistical techniques like hypothesis tests, classification, and regression. It's worth understanding these concepts and getting good at applying them before you start worrying about concepts at the cutting edge.

Summary

- Having a portfolio of data science projects shared in a GitHub repo and a blog can help you get a job.
- There are many places to find good datasets for a side project; the most important thing is to choose something that's interesting to you and a little bit unusual.
- You don't have to blog only about your side projects; you can also share tutorials or your experience with a bootcamp, conference, or online course.

Chapters 1–4 resources

Books

Practical Data Science with R, 2nd ed., by Nina Zumel and John Mount (Manning Publications)

This book is an introduction to data science that uses R as the primary tool. It's a great supplement to the book you're currently holding because it goes much deeper into the technical components of the job. It works through taking datasets, thinking about the questions you can ask of them and how to do so, and then interpreting the results.

Doing Data Science: Straight Talk from the Frontline, by Cathy O'Neil and Rachel Schutt (O'Reilly Publications)

Another introduction to data science, this book is a mixture of theory and application. It takes a broad view of the field and tries to approach it from multiple angles rather than being a set of case studies.

R for Everyone, 2nd ed., by Jared Lander, and *Pandas for Everyone,* by Daniel Chen (Addison-Wesley Data and Analytics)

R for Everyone and *Pandas for Everyone* are two books from the Addison-Wesley Data and Analytics Series. They cover using R and Python (via pandas) from basic functions to advanced analytics and data science problem-solving. For people who feel that they need help in learning either of these topics, these books are great resources.

Think Like a Data Scientist: Tackle the Data Science Process Step-by-Step, by Brian Godset (Manning Publications)

Think Like a Data Scientist is an introductory data science book structured around how data science work is actually done. The book walks through defining the problem and creating the plan, solving data science problems, and then presenting your findings to others. This book is best for people who understand the technical basics of data science but are new to working on a long-term project.

Getting What You Came For: The Smart Student's Guide to Earning an M.A. or a Ph.D., by Robert L. Peters (Farrar, Straus and Giroux)

If you've decided to go to graduate school to get a master's or PhD degree, you're in for a long, grueling journey. Understanding how to get through exams and qualifications, persevering through research, and finishing quickly are all things that are not taught directly to you. Although this book is fairly old, the lessons it teaches about how to succeed still apply to grad school today.

Bird by Bird: Some Instructions on Writing and Life, by Anne Lamott (Anchor)

Bird by Bird is a guide to writing, but it's also a great guide for life. The title comes from something Anne Lamott's father said to her brother when he was freaking out about doing a report on birds he'd had three months to do but had left to the last night: "Bird by bird, buddy. Just take it bird by bird." If you've been struggling with perfectionism or figuring out what you can write about, this book may be the one for you.

Blog posts

Bootcamp rankings, by Switchup.org

https://www.switchup.org/rankings/best-data-science-bootcamps

Switchup provides a listing of the top 20 bootcamps based on student reviews. Although you may want to take the reviews and orderings with a grain of salt, this blog is still a solid starting point for choosing which bootcamps to apply to.

What's the Difference between Data Science, Machine Learning, and Artificial Intelligence?, by David Robinson

http://varianceexplained.org/r/ds-ml-ai

If you're confused about what is data science versus machine learning versus artificial intelligence, this post offers one helpful way to distinguish among them. Although there's no universally agreed-upon definitions, we like this taxonomy in which data science produces insights, machine learning produces predictions, and artificial intelligence produces actions.

What You Need to Know before Considering a PhD, by Rachel Thomas

https://www.fast.ai/2018/08/27/grad-school

If you're thinking that you need a PhD to be a data scientist, read this blog first. Thomas lays out the significant costs of getting a PhD (in terms of both potential mental health costs and career opportunity costs) and debunks the myth that you need a PhD to do cutting-edge research in deep learning.

Thinking of Blogging about Data Science? Here Are Some Tips and Possible Benefits, by Derrick Mwiti

http://mng.bz/gVEx

If chapter 4 didn't convince you of the benefits of blogging, maybe this post will. Mwiti also offers some great tips on making your posts engaging, including using bullet points and new datasets.

How to Build a Data Science Portfolio, by Michael Galarnyk

http://mng.bz/eDWP

This is an excellent, detailed post on how to make a data science portfolio. Galarnyk shows not only what types of projects to include (and not include) in a portfolio, but also how to incorporate them into your résumé and share them.

Part 2
Finding your
data science job

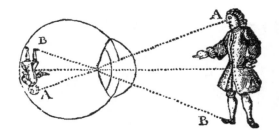

Now that you're equipped to get a data science job, it's time to do it. This part of the book covers everything you need to know to conduct a successful job search, starting with finding open positions and ending with negotiating and accepting a job offer. The job-hunt process in data science has some unique quirks because of the nature of the field. We'll prepare you for parsing the many job postings that mean *data scientist* and what companies are looking for in a take-home case study. Although this part is especially useful if you haven't had a data science job before, the material can still be useful as a refresher for junior and senior data scientists.

Chapter 5 covers searching for data science positions and how to handle the dizzying array of job postings. Chapter 6 teaches you how to create a strong data science résumé and cover letter, providing examples to base your material on and the principles behind them. Chapter 7 is all about what to expect from and how to prepare for the data science job interview, from the initial phone screen to the final on-site meeting. Chapter 8 walks through what to say when you receive an offer from a company, including how to decide whether to accept it and why and how to negotiate.

5

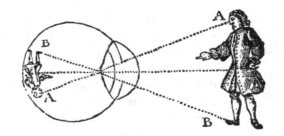

The search: Identifying the right job for you

This chapter covers

- Finding open jobs that might be a good fit
- Decoding job descriptions to understand what the roles are really like
- Picking the jobs to apply for

You've got the skills, and you've got the portfolio; all you're missing is the data science job! You should expect the job search process to take some time, though. Even successful job applications usually take at least a month from applying to getting an offer, and more commonly several months. But by laying out some best practices in this chapter, we hope to make the process as painless as possible.

In this chapter, we focus on how to look for data science jobs. First, we cover all the places where you can find jobs, making sure that you won't unknowingly narrow your options. Then we show you how to decode these descriptions to find out what skills you actually need (spoiler: not all of them) and what the jobs might be like. Finally, we show you how to choose the ones you're best suited for, using the knowledge you've gained about data science skills and company archetypes in the first four chapters.

5.1   *Finding jobs*

Before worrying about crafting the "perfect" résumé and cover letter, you need to know where to send them! Job boards such as LinkedIn, Indeed, and Glassdoor are good places to start your search. It's worth looking at more than one website, because not all companies will post on each one. If you're part of an underrepresented group in tech, you should also look for job sites that specifically target you, such as POCIT and Tech Ladies, which are for people of color and women in technology, respectively. The type of job you're applying for may also influence where you look; for example, there are job boards for specific types of companies, such as start-ups (AngelList) and technology (Dice).

Make sure to browse widely. As discussed in chapter 1, data science jobs go by many names other than data scientist. Different companies use different names for similar roles, and some are even changing what their titles mean, so all the people who were data analysts one year might be data scientists the next, with no change in responsibility!

Some examples of titles you might encounter (figure 5.1) are

- *Data analyst*—This position is often a junior position and can be a great way to start in the field if you don't have a science, technology, engineering, or mathematics (STEM) degree and haven't done any data analysis for a company before. As we discuss later in section 5.1.1, you do want to be extra careful with a data analyst position to make sure that the role will involve programming and statistics or machine learning.

- *Quantitative, product, research, or other types of analysts*—These roles have even more diversity than data analysts in terms of your responsibilities. You may be doing exactly the same type of work as data scientists at other companies, or you may be spending your days with legacy Microsoft Excel spreadsheets.

- *Machine learning engineer*—As implied by the title, these jobs focus on the machine learning part of data science and usually require a strong engineering background. If you have a degree in computer science or have been working as a software engineer, this role could be a great one for you.

- *Research scientist*—These positions often require a PhD, though there might be some negotiation room if you have a master's in computer science, statistics, or a closely related field.

Data analyst	**Product analyst**	**ML engineer**	**Research scientist**
entry level	*job varies*	*software-focused*	*theoretical*
Analyze data and create reports	Focus on one part of the company	Build ML models to power the business	Research-focused job; requires advanced degree

Figure 5.1   Some job titles that don't include "data science" that you may find when searching

When you're starting your search, try searching for simply *data* on one of these job boards and spending an hour reading job posts. This work will give you a better idea of what industries are represented in your area and what types of positions are open. You'll pick up on patterns that will let you skim new listings more quickly. Finding jobs that are a good match for you, rather than all the jobs that are available, will narrow the field to a manageable number. Don't worry too much about a job's title; use the description to evaluate fit.

Be extremely cautious about thinking of job-hunting as a numbers game. If you're looking in a big tech city like New York or San Francisco or in multiple cities, you'll find hundreds of jobs listed. Checking job boards can quickly become an obsession because it's an easy way to feel productive ("I read 70 job descriptions today!"). And just like using Twitter and Facebook, checking constantly for updates can be addictive. Checking more than every three to five days generally doesn't add value. Checking only once a month could mean that you miss out on a good opportunity, but no company fills a position (that's actually open) within two days of posting it on a job board.

If you're interested in specific companies, check out the careers pages on their websites. Just as you should search for multiple job titles, check different departments. Some companies may put data science in finance, engineering, or other departments, so if you don't check there, you won't find them.

> **NEW GRADUATES** When you're searching for jobs, look for positions specifically titled "New Grad," "Junior," "Associate," and "Entry-Level." Also look at your career center for help, and go to any job fairs on campus.

5.1.1 Decoding descriptions

When you start reading job descriptions, data science job postings may seem to fall into one of two categories:

- *A business intelligence analyst position*—In this type of role, you'll use business intelligence tools such as Excel and Tableau, maybe with a little SQL, but generally, you won't code. If you want to grow your coding skills, machine learning toolbox, or statistics and data engineering knowledge, these jobs are not a good fit.
- *A unicorn*—At the other end of the extreme, you have a job listing asking for someone with a PhD in computer science who's also worked as a data scientist for more than five years; is an expert on cutting-edge statistics, deep learning, and communicating with business partners; and has experience with a huge range of responsibilities, from doing production-level machine learning to creating dashboards to running A/B tests. These types of job descriptions usually mean that the company doesn't know what it's looking for, and it expects a data scientist to solve all its problems without any support.

Don't worry, though: we promise there are more than these two types of jobs. A better way of thinking about these jobs is in terms of experience. Is the company looking for someone to build a department of their own and has no data pipeline infrastructure in place? Or is it looking for a fifth member for its currently productive data science team, hoping that this new person contributes immediately but not expecting them to be an expert on data manipulation, business communication, and software development all at the same time? To do this, you need to take a job description and figure out what the employer is actually looking for. Suppose that you're looking at cat-adoption listings and that the cat Honeydew Melon is described as "liking to ask about your day." You'd need realize that this description actually means she'll constantly meow for attention, which could be bad for your home.

In job descriptions, some famous phrases to look out for include "Work hard and play hard," meaning that you'll need to work long hours and be expected to attend informal company events (such as going to bars), and "Self-starter and independent," meaning that you won't get a lot of support. By knowing how to read between the lines, you can make sure that you apply for the right jobs.

The first thing to keep in mind is that job descriptions are generally wish lists with some flexibility. If you meet 60 percent of the requirements (perhaps you're a year short of the required work experience or haven't worked with one component of the company's tech stack) but are otherwise a good fit, you should still apply for the job. Definitely don't worry too much about plusses or "nice to haves." Additionally, the requirement for years of work experience is just a proxy for the necessary skills; if you coded in grad school, that experience could count. That being said, applying to a post for a senior data scientist that requires five years of work experience as a data scientist, proficiency in Spark and Hadoop, and experience deploying machine learning models into production probably isn't the best use of your time if you're an aspiring data scientist coming from marketing; the company is looking for a different level of experience and qualifications.

DEGREE REQUIREMENTS   Many data scientist jobs list a degree in a "quantitative discipline" (fields such as statistics, engineering, computer science, or economics) as a requirement. If you don't have one of those degrees, can you still apply for these jobs? Generally, yes. We discuss this topic in more depth in chapter 6, but if you took classes in those areas (including at a bootcamp or online), you can emphasize that education. If you followed the advice in chapter 4 by building a portfolio and writing blog posts, you can show those projects to employers as evidence that you can do the work.

One complication in data science postings is that different words may mean the same thing. Machine learning and statistics are infamous for this. One company may ask for experience in regression or classification and another for experience in supervised learning, but overall, these terms are equivalent. The same goes for A/B testing, online experimentation, and randomized control trials. If you're not familiar with a term, Google it; you may find you've done the work under a different name! If you haven't worked with a specific technology that's referenced in the posting, see whether you've done something similar. If the listing cites Amazon Web Services (AWS), for example, and you've worked with Microsoft Azure or Google Cloud, you have the skill of working with cloud computing services.

The other benefit of knowing how to decode a job description is the ability to detect red flags (section 5.1.2). No company is going to straight-up say that it's bad to work for. The earlier you recognize a likely bad work situation, the better, so you'll want to start looking for any warning signs in the job description.

5.1.2 Watching for red flags

Finding a job is a two-way street. During this process, you may feel that companies have all the power and that you need to prove you're deserving. But you—yes, you—can also be selective. Ending up in a toxic workplace or a mind-numbingly boring job is a really hard situation. Although you won't always be able to tell whether this will be the case just from a job description, you can watch out for a few warning signs:

- *No description*—The first warning sign is no description of the company or job itself—just a list of requirements. Those organizations have forgotten that hiring is a two-sided process and aren't thinking about you. Or they may be buying into the data science hype and just want to have data scientists without setting anything up so that they can work productively.
- *Extensive, broad requirements*—A second warning sign is the aforementioned unicorn description (section 5.1.1). Even though that example is extreme, you should be wary of any job description that describes two or three of the job types (decision science, analytics, and machine learning) as primary responsibilities. Although it's normal to be expected to have base competency in each role, no person is going to be able to fill all those roles at an expert level. Even if someone could, they wouldn't have time to do everything.
- *Mismatches*—Finally, look for mismatches between the requirements and the description of the position. Is the employer asking for experience in deep learning, but the job functions are making dashboards, communicating with stakeholders, and running experiments? If so, the company may just want someone who can use the hottest tool or who's a "prestigious" data scientist with a Stanford PhD in artificial intelligence, when actually, they can't use that specialized knowledge.

5.1.3 Setting your expectations

Although you should have standards for a potential job, you don't want to demand perfection. Aspiring data scientists sometimes see their path broken down this way: "Steps 1-98: Learn Python, R, deep learning, Bayesian statistics, cloud computing, A/B testing, D3. Step 99: Get a data science job. Step 100: Profit." This example is an exaggeration, but part of the data science hype is idealization of what it's like to work in the field. After all, data scientist is "the best job in America" (http://mng.bz/pyA2), with a six-figure paycheck and high job satisfaction. You might imagine getting to spend every day on the most interesting problems in the field with the smartest colleagues. The data you need will always be accessible and cleaned, and any issues you face will be solved immediately by a team of engineers. Your job will be exactly as described, and you'll never have to do the parts of data science that interest you least.

Unfortunately, this scenario is a fantasy. Just as we hope that part 1 of this book convinced you that you don't need to know everything before getting into the field, companies aren't going to be perfect unicorns either. There's a reason why this book doesn't end with you getting a data science job. Although becoming a data scientist is a great accomplishment and you should be proud, data science is a field in which you'll always be learning. Models will fail, workplace politics will scrap the work you've been doing for the past month, or you'll spend weeks working with engineers and product managers to collect the data you need.

It's especially easy to idealize companies that are well-known, either generally or for data science. Maybe you went to a talk, and one of the company's employees blew you away. Maybe you've been following that person's blog for months and know that they're on the cutting edge of the field. Maybe you read an article saying that the company has nap pods, gourmet meals, and lots of friendly office dogs. But whatever attracted you likely has interested other aspiring data scientists as well; most of these companies get hundreds of applications for an open position and can set the bar higher than needed to do the job. In any case, the work you read about may be in a totally different division, and the position that's open actually may be uninteresting.

Even with realistic expectations, you likely won't end up in your dream job for your first data science role. It's easier to transition within your field or to bring data science into your current role; even if you're looking to leave your domain eventually, you may need to start by moving to a position in which you can leverage your other skills. That doesn't mean you shouldn't have certain requirements and preferences, but you'll want to have some flexibility. It's very normal to switch jobs in tech even after a year or two, so you're not signing yourself up for the next 15 years. But you can't know exactly what you want before you're even in the field, and you'll learn even from bad jobs, so don't stress too much.

5.1.4   Attending meetups

Though job boards are a common way to find open positions, they're usually not the most effective places to apply. As we discuss in chapter 6, submitting your application cold online often has a very low response rate. According to a survey by Kaggle in 2017 (https://www.kaggle.com/surveys/2017), the two most common ways that people who are already employed as data scientists look for and get jobs is through recruiters and friends, family members, and colleagues. A great way to build that network is by going to meetups.

Meetups generally are in-person meetings held on weekday evenings. There usually is a speaker, panel, or series of speakers presenting on a topic that's relevant to the event. Meetups should be free or have only a nominal fee, which sometimes goes toward food. Some meetups may have only 20 people; others may fill a room with 300. Some have meetings every month; others meet only a few times a year. Some encourage members to stay in the space afterward to talk or meet at a nearby bar; others focus on the talk itself. Some have very specific focuses, such as advanced natural language processing in Python; others may offer an introduction to time series one month and advanced deep learning models the next. It's worth trying a few meetups to see what you enjoy most. The topic is important, but you want to find a place where you feel welcome and enjoy talking with the other attendees. Almost all meetups have accounts on https://www.meetup.com, so you can search for data science, machine learning, Python, R, or analytics to find relevant meetups in your area.

Many data science meetups have time at the beginning for people to announce whether they're hiring. Go up and talk to these people; recruitment is part of their job, and even if their current openings aren't a good fit, they may be able to give you good advice or suggest other places to look.

You may also meet another attendee who works in the company or subindustry you're interested in. You can ask whether they have time for an informational interview so that you can learn more about the field. An informational interview isn't (or, rather, shouldn't be) a passive-aggressive way of looking for a referral; instead, it's a great way to get a look inside a company and get advice from someone who's in the field. Although we talk in chapter 6 about the advantages of being referred for a job, we don't recommend asking people you've just met to refer you. That's a strong ask for someone they don't know, and no one likes feeling that they're being used. If someone tells you about an opening at their company and says they can refer you, that's a great bonus, but you'll gain a lot from doing informational interviews even if they don't.

Attending meetups is also great for other reasons. For one, they allow you to find like-minded people who are local. If you've moved to a new city or just graduated from college, you may feel like a stranger in your town. Going to meetups is a great chance to develop your career and build your social circle. You can take advantage of meetups to network or build some contacts who may be able to help you with anything from specific data science questions to job-hunting recommendations or general mentorship. Also, whereas some meetups post recordings of their talks online, others don't, so attending in person is the only way to hear that talk.

Unfortunately, meetups can have a few drawbacks. It can be daunting to join a meetup of only a few people, all of whom are experienced and/or know one another. Impostor syndrome can definitely creep in, but you should fight through it, as there are few more welcoming spaces than a good meetup. Finally, although meetups offer a great chance to see the local data science scene, they can be insular or lack diversity, depending on how welcoming the organizers are and how connected the particular meetup is to a diverse community.

5.1.5 *Using social media*

If you don't live in or near a city, there may not be any data science meetups near you. In this case, Twitter and LinkedIn are great places to start building your network. When you follow a few well-known data scientists, you frequently find more people to follow as you see who gets retweeted or mentioned a lot. You can also start making a name for yourself.

We like to use Twitter in a few ways:

- *Sharing work*—When you've written a great blog post, you want people to see it! It's totally normal to self-promote by linking to your work with a short description.
- *Sharing other people's work*—Have you read something great? Had a package save you hours of frustration? Seen a slide in a talk that was particularly helpful? If so, help other people reach enlightenment too. In chapter 6, we discuss one of the best ways to reach out to someone: mention how you've benefitted from their work. Tagging the creator in your post is a great way to get on their radar in a positive way. If you're sharing a talk, check whether the conference or meetup has a hashtag; using that hashtag in your tweet is a great way to give it more visibility.
- *Asking for help*—Is there a problem you've been stuck on that you (and Google) haven't been able to solve? It's likely that someone else out there has faced the same issue. Depending on the type of problem, there may be specific forums or websites where you can ask questions, or you can put out a general call by using a relevant hashtag.
- *Sharing tips*—Not everything warrants making a blog post, but if you have a quick tip, share it. The topic may feel like something that "everyone" knows, but remember: people who are just getting started don't know everything. Even people who have used a certain language for years may not know about a new way to do something.

If you're able to be public about your job search, you can also post on social media that you're looking and ask whether anyone has any leads. Even though you may not have a strong data science network yet, you may have friends, former classmates, and colleagues who might know about positions within their companies. This approach generally works better on social media platforms where people who are connected to data science tend to congregate, such as LinkedIn or Twitter, but even social media networks such as Facebook may have connections with opportunities.

It's common early in your career to feel that you have no network yet; networks seem to be held by people who already have data science jobs! The solution is to network not only when you're looking for a job, but also long before that. The more you can get out of your comfort zone and talk to the people around you at conferences, meetups, academic institutions, barbecues, and the like, the more prepared you'll be the next time you look for a job.

Keeping the pipeline full

A common mistake in job-searching is to pin your hopes on one opportunity and not keep applying and interviewing elsewhere. But what happens if that opportunity falls through? You don't want to have to start the job search process again from zero. You want to have multiple opportunities in each stage: applications you've sent out, human-resources screens, take-home case studies, and in-person interviews. Don't consider the process to be over until you've accepted an offer in writing.

Having multiple opportunities also helps you deal with rejection. Rejection is almost inevitable when you're job-searching, and it's hard not to take it personally or as an indication of your worth. In some cases, you may not even be notified that you're rejected; you just never hear back from the company. But many reasons why you might not have gotten the job are out of your control. The company may have closed the position without hiring anyone, went with an internal candidate, or accepted someone when you were still early in the process. Rejection hurts, especially from a company you were really excited about, and you should take a little time to process your feelings. But having other options will help keep you motivated and making progress.

Finally, having multiple potential options makes it easier for you to reject a job. Maybe you got through the HR screen and case study, only to find that there are no data engineers around; the data science team is only a few people, even though the company is large; or what the company is looking for is very different from what it advertised. Although you shouldn't wait for the perfect data science role (as no such thing exists), you probably have a few non-negotiable requirements, and it's much easier to stick to those requirements if you see that they can be fulfilled in other jobs.

5.2 Deciding which jobs to apply for

By now, you should have a list of at least a dozen jobs you're somewhat interested in and could be a good fit for. Do you apply for all of them immediately?

Well, some people do apply for dozens or even hundreds of jobs. They're trying to play the odds, figuring that if there's a 10% chance of getting a response to any given job, applying to as many companies as possible will give them the most responses. But they're operating under a fallacy: if you have a finite amount of energy and time, spreading it across 100 applications instead of 10 makes each one weaker. We talk in chapter 6 about how to tailor your applications to each position, but that's possible only if you're selective about where you apply. It's pretty much impossible to do that for 50 companies.

R AND PYTHON   Should you apply for a job if the company asks for Python and you know R, or vice versa? Although knowing one language certainly makes it easier to pick up the other one, you'll already be learning a lot at your first data scientist job: working with stakeholders, internal politics, statistics, the datasets, and so on. Even if you could get the job, learning a new language on top of everything else can be difficult. Thus, we generally recommend applying only for jobs that use your main language. If knowing one of those languages is a plus, but the other one isn't required, you probably want to be wary; this job description could mean that you won't actually be coding. Finally, some jobs ask for both languages. You also want to be a little wary here; usually, this requirement means that people use either language, not that everyone knows both, which can make collaborating difficult. This type of job can work out, but be sure to ask during your interviews what the split between languages is. If you would be one of only two people using Python on the team of 20, improving your programming skills is going to be hard.

You'll want to return to what you learned in the first two chapters about the types of data science companies and of data science work. Do you want to try all the different parts of data science, tuning a recommendation system one month and creating a lifetime-value model the next? If so, you'll probably want to work for a company that started doing data science recently, as more mature companies will have specialized roles. On the other hand, big tech companies also have legions of data engineers, so getting routine data is fast and easy.

Some of this will be obvious from the basic facts about the company; a 10-person startup, for example, isn't going to have a mature data science system. But how can you find out more?

First, see whether the company has a data science blog. Usually only tech companies have this type of blog, but reading these posts is invaluable for learning about what work the data scientists actually do. Your positive thoughts about specific posts on a company's blog are also great to include in your cover letter for that company (covered in chapter 6). If you've never heard of a company, spend some time on its website. When you know what the company does and how it makes money, you can start making guesses about what kind of data science work it needs. Finally, if you're really interested in a company, see whether any of the company's data scientists have a blog in which they talk about their work or have given talks about it.

When reading about a company, remember to think about what's generally important to you. Does the ability to work from home sometimes matter? What about the number of vacation days? If you want to go to conferences, does the company offer a travel budget and time off to attend? Also, reading what the company says about itself can tell you its values. Does it talk about foosball, beer in the office, and catered dinners? That company is likely to be full of young employees. Or does it emphasize flexible work hours or family leave? That company is more likely to be friendly to parents. In chapter 8, we discuss how you can negotiate much more than salary, but at this stage, you can at least see whether a company advertises benefits that align with your priorities.

Now that you have a manageable list of potential jobs, it's time to apply! In chapter 6, we walk you through creating a great résumé and cover letter, including how to tailor them for each position.

5.3 *Interview with Jesse Mostipak, developer advocate at Kaggle*

Jesse Mostipak comes from a background in molecular biology and worked as a public-school teacher before falling in love with not-for-profit data science. At the time of this interview, she was managing director of data science at Teaching Trust. You can find her writing about not-for-profit data science, advice on learning R, and other topics on her website, https://www.jessemaegan.com.

What recommendations do you have for starting a job search?

Think about how attached you are to the data scientist title. If you decide to not concern yourself with what you're called and to instead focus on the work that you're doing, you'll have a lot more flexibility in finding jobs. Some non-data-scientist keywords to search for are *analysis, analyst,* and *data.* While you'll have more to filter through, you may find a title like "research and evaluation" where you're qualified for that position but never would have come across it if you were just looking for data scientist.

When looking at jobs, focus on what you want to do as a data scientist. For me, I don't get a lot of pleasure from calculating the return on investment from website clicks. I asked myself, "What causes do I care about? Which organizations are aligned with that?" I cared a lot about the Girl Scouts, and they happened to be looking for an analyst position, so I was able to move in and do that. The same thing happened with Teaching Trust when I wanted to move more into education.

How can you build your network?

When I was making the transition to data science, I did a lot of things that failed for a very long time. I was the person who was reposting on Twitter every data science article that I saw, putting out 20 posts a day that had no engagement. You should think about who you want to meet, why, what value you bring to that relationship, and what's authentic to you. Think about branding yourself, not necessarily in a stringent way, but making sure how you show up online and in social media spaces is authentic to you. For me, I realized I couldn't be a perfect data scientist and wait to be on social media until I know everything in data science, because that was going to be never. I decided instead that I would talk about the things that I'm learning and be transparent about the process, and that's how I built my network.

What do you do if you don't feel confident applying to data science jobs?

If you're developing skills, can do some analyses in Python or R, and have the basics under control, you should focus on how you can get comfortable taking risks and failing. You have to fail a lot as a data scientist. If you are worried about taking a risk and failing in the job application process, what's going to happen when you take a risk on a model and the model doesn't work out? You need to embrace the idea of ambiguity and iteration. You have to apply and try; you're going to get rejected from jobs, but that's normal! I get rejected from jobs on a regular basis; it's just part of the experience.

What would you say to someone who thinks "I don't meet the full list of any job's required qualifications?"

Some research suggests that certain groups of people especially feel they need to be 100% qualified, whereas other groups say "I meet 25%? I'm applying!" Wrangle that confidence of the 25%-qualified, and go for it. But you may also be getting tripped up in decoding the language of the job description. For example, let's say there's a discrete skill listed, such as 10 years working with SQL databases. You might think "I don't have that; I have seven years working with Microsoft Access." But I would say that's still a transferable skill. It's on you as the applicant to tell yourself "I may not have this exact skill, but I have one that's a lot like it. I need to take a look at SQL, see how transferable my skill is, and tell this company the amazing things I've accomplished with Microsoft Access and that they should hire me because I know I can do this with SQL and then some."

What's your final piece of advice to aspiring data scientists?

You need to develop your communication skills and your ability to roll with it. You should be able to communicate across all levels of your organization in a way that respects the expertise of the people you're talking to and also shows you exist to make their lives easier.

By *rolling with it*, I mean being able to say something like "That's not the way I would approach that problem or this project, but I can see where you're coming from. Let's try it that way and maybe I can modify it in this way." You also need to be flexible, because people are still just figuring out data science. Organizations want data scientists, but then they don't know what to do with them. You serve at the pleasure of your organization; if their needs have changed, you need to evolve and adapt to best meet those needs.

Finally, know that your job description might change. You have to be able to say, "This isn't what I thought I would be doing, but how can I make this work for me?" You can't say, "I am the best at neural networks, but I'm not doing neural networks, so obviously, this job is crap." You need to know that any position that you take is going to change and evolve as the needs of the company do.

Summary

- Search for general terms like *data* on job boards, and focus on the descriptions, not the titles.
- Don't worry about meeting 100% of the qualifications listed.
- Remember the job-search process is a two-way street. Look out for red flags, and think about what kind of data science you want to do.

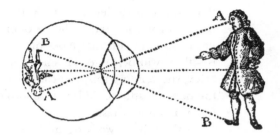

6

The application:
Résumés and cover letters

This chapter covers
- Writing a compelling résumé and cover letter
- Tailoring your application to each position

You've got a list of open jobs you're interested in; now it's time to let the employers know you exist! Pretty much every job will require you to submit a résumé: a glorified list of your skills and experience. Most jobs also ask for a cover letter: a one-page letter describing why you should be considered for the job. It would be easy to jot down your previous jobs quickly and write a boilerplate letter saying that you're interested in the company, but in this situation, putting in more effort can be the deciding factor in whether you make it to an interview.

In this chapter, we start with making sure that your base résumé and cover letter are as effective as possible, covering best practices and common mistakes to avoid. Then we show you how to take that "master" résumé and cover letter and refine them for each job. Finally, we show you how networking can help get your carefully crafted application into the hands of a hiring manager instead of into an overflowing pile of résumés.

NOTE The only goal of a résumé is to convince a person who's barely skimming your résumé that you are worth interviewing.

The key theme throughout this chapter is that you need to convince a person quickly that you're qualified for the position. Company recruiters often get hundreds of résumés for each data science opening. Furthermore, because data science encompasses so many distinct types of jobs, the range of skills of people who apply for the positions will be huge. This act reinforces the notion that your materials have to say "Hey, you reading this, you can stop skimming this massive pile, because you've found the person with the skills you're looking for." But being able to show that you're qualified isn't an easy task.

Although networking and personalizing your application take time, they yield much better results than spending just an hour writing a basic cover letter and résumé and then applying for dozens of jobs with one click. You'll be more likely to get an interview, as you'll have matched your application to the company's requirements. And when you reach the interview (the topic of chapter 7), you'll be able to give a great answer to the common question "Why are you interested in this role?"

6.1   *Résumé: The basics*

The goal of your résumé isn't to get you the job; it's to get you an interview. Recruiters who run the interview process get in trouble if they bring in people who clearly don't meet the qualifications for the job, and they're praised when the people fit the qualifications well. Your résumé needs to show the reader that you meet the requirements for the position so that the recruiter is comfortable moving you on in the process.

That goal is very different from creating a catalog of every experience you had, which unfortunately is a goal of many inexperienced résumé writers. Although you do want to avoid having gaps on your résumé by leaving off recent jobs, you can spend less time on those that aren't related to data science. And even if you have a lot of data science experience, you should still focus on highlighting the most relevant jobs. If you have a multipage résumé, most recruiters won't have time to read all of it; neither will they be able to tell which parts to read. No one will tell you "Well, we would have hired you, but you didn't put your lifeguarding job in high school on your résumé, so we couldn't."

There'll be plenty of time later in the interview process to go through your jobs, education, and data science projects in depth. For now, you want to focus on what's most relevant for meeting the qualifications of the position you're applying for. During the rest of the process, you'll focus on your great qualities that will help you stand out from the other applicants, but for the first step, it's good to focus on fitting into the hiring manager or recruiter's expectations.

With that in mind, we'll walk through the basic structure of a résumé, how to create good content within that structure, and how to think about the many résumé rules that get thrown around. Plenty of this content could apply to any technical position in industry, but we'll focus as much as possible on what is unique about data science. We've also made an example résumé for you to use as a guide (figure 6.1).

SARA JONES

San Francisco, CA · 534-241-6264
sarajones@gmail.com · linkedin.com/in/sarajones · sarajones.github.io · github.com/sarajones

EXPERIENCE

JUNE 2019 – PRESENT, SAN FRANCISCO, CA
DATA SCIENCE FELLOW, AWESOME BOOTCAMP
- Built a web application in Python that recommends the best New York City neighborhood to live in based on someone's budget, lifestyle preferences, and work
- Analyzed 2,200 New York Times business articles (obtained via API) using natural language processing (TFIDF and NMF), visualizing how topics changed over time

AUGUST 2017 – JUNE 2019, SAN FRANCISCO, CA
INVESTMENT CONSULTANT, BIGCO
- Created a forecasting model in Python that boosted quarterly revenue by 10%
- Automated generating weekly market and industry trend reports

SEPTEMBER 2016 – JUNE 2017, NEW ORLEANS, LA
INTRODUCTION TO STATISTICS TEACHING ASSISTANT, COOL UNIVERSITY
- Led weekly review sessions of sixty students, earning a 4.86/5 rating in evaluations
- Created and open-sourced study guides that have been downloaded over 1,500 times

JUNE 2016 – AUGUST 2016, NEW ORLEANS, LA
ECONOMICS RESEARCH ASSISTANT, COOL UNIVERSITY
- Conducted an in-person experiment on decision-making with 200 participants, using cluster analysis to analyze the results in Python
- Published the resulting paper in the Journal of Awesome Economics

EDUCATION

JUNE 2017, NEW ORLEANS, LA
BA ECONOMICS, STATISTICS MINOR COOL UNIVERSITY
GPA 3.65/4.0
Relevant Coursework: Linear Algebra, Introduction to Regression and Statistical Computing, Experimental Design, Econometrics, Elements of Algorithms and Computation

SKILLS

- Python
- SQL
- Machine learning
- Git

- Pandas
- Seaborn
- Scikit-learn
- NumPy

Figure 6.1   Example résumé for an aspiring data scientist

6.1.1   *Structure*

In this section, we walk through each section of the example résumé, going into more detail about what you want to include.

SECTION: CONTACT INFORMATION

SARA JONES

San Francisco, CA · 534-241-6264

sarajones@gmail.com · linkedin.com/in/sarajones · sarajones.github.io · github.com/sarajones

Including your contact information is necessary so that the recruiter can contact you! You need to include your first and last name, phone number, and email at a minimum. Beyond that, you can put links to places where they can find more information about you, including social media profiles such as LinkedIn, online code bases such as GitHub, and personal websites and blogs. To figure out what to add, ask yourself this question: "If someone clicks it, would they think more highly of me?" A link to your project portfolio from chapter 4, for example, is a fantastic thing to include. But a link to a GitHub profile that's empty save for a clone of a tutorial project is not. If you have any data science work that's publicly available, try to figure out a way to show it here.

Generally, you also want to include the city and state you live in, which will let the recruiter know that you're nearby and can commute to the job or that you'd need to relocate if you got the job. Some companies are hesitant to relocate new hires because of the expense, so if you don't live nearby and don't want to bite that bullet, you could potentially leave your location off.

If your legal name doesn't match the name you commonly go by, you can use your common name. Farther along in the process, you'll need to let the company know what your legal name is for things such as background checks, but you aren't required to use your legal name when applying.

Finally, don't use an email address that's potentially offensive (i_hate_python @gmail.com, for example) or something that might expire (such as a school email address).

SECTION: EXPERIENCE

JUNE 2019 – PRESENT, SAN FRANCISCO, CA
DATA SCIENCE FELLOW, AWESOME BOOTCAMP

- Built a web application in Python that recommends the best New York City neighborhood to live in based on someone's budget, lifestyle preferences, and work
- Analyzed 2,200 New York Times business articles (obtained via API) using natural language processing (TFIDF and NMF), visualizing how topics changed over time

This section is where you show that you're qualified for the job through previous jobs, internships, or bootcamps you've done. If your past jobs are related to data science, such as software engineering, that's great: spend a fair amount of your résumé on them. If a job isn't related to data science, such as being an art history professor, you should still list the jobs, but don't spend much time on them. For each position you've held, list the company name, the month and year of your start and end, your job title, and at least one bullet point (two or three for the most relevant jobs) describing what you did. If you're a new or recent graduate, you can include internships and research jobs in college.

This section should be the largest in your résumé and could potentially take up half the space available. It's also often the most important, because it's the first place recruiters will look to see whether you have data science experience that could be related to the job they're hiring for. Due to the importance of getting this section right, we'll go in depth into how to create the best content for it in section 6.1.2.

SECTION: EDUCATION

EDUCATION

JUNE 2017, NEW ORLEANS, LA
BA ECONOMICS, STATISTICS MINOR COOL UNIVERSITY
GPA 3.65/4.0
Relevant Coursework: Linear Algebra, Introduction to Regression and Statistical Computing,
Experimental Design, Econometrics, Elements of Algorithms and Computation

In this section, you list your educational experiences, ideally to show that you have a set of skills that would be useful for the data science job. If you went to school past high school, even if you didn't get a degree, list your school(s), dates (same format as your work experience), and your area of study. If this job will be your first one out of school, and your grade-point average is high (above 3.3) you can list it; otherwise, leave it off. If you're a recent graduate, and you took statistics, mathematics, or computer science, or any other classes that involved them (such as social science research methods or engineering), you can list those classes.

Recruiters will be very interested to see whether you have an area of study that's relevant to data science, such as a degree in data science, statistics, computer science, or math. They'll also be interested to see the level of your degree. Because many data science topics aren't covered until graduate levels of programs, having a graduate degree will help. Recruiters generally won't care about what school you went to unless it's extremely famous or prestigious, and even then, this credential won't matter if you're more than a few years out of school. It's nice for recruiters to see any boot-camps, certificates, or online programs, though, because they show that you've furthered your education.

Although the education section of your résumé can give valuable information to the recruiter, you can't really improve the section by doing anything less than going out and getting an additional degree or certificate, which we covered in chapter 3.

SKILLS

- Python
- SQL
- Machine learning
- Git

- Pandas
- Seaborn
- Scikit-learn
- NumPy

This section is where you can explicitly list all the relevant skills you have to contribute in a data science setting. Ideally, a recruiter will see this section and nod while saying "Yes, good," because you'll have skills listed that are relevant to the job. On data science résumés, there are two types of skills to list in this section:

- *Programming/database skills*—These skills can be programming languages such as Python and SQL, frameworks and environments such as .NET or JVM, tools such as Tableau and Excel, or ecosystems such as Azure and Amazon Web Services (AWS).
- *Data science methods*—The second type is data science methods such as regressions and neural networks. Because you can list so many possible methods, try to focus on a key few that together show that you have the essentials and a few special skills. Something such as "regressions, clustering methods, neural networks, survey analysis," for example, shows that you have the basics and depth.

Try not to list more than seven or eight skills to avoid overwhelming people, and don't list skills that have no chance of being relevant for the job (such as an obscure academic programming language from your time in graduate school).

List only the skills that you'd be comfortable using on the job, not a language you haven't touched in five years and don't want to pick up again. If something is on your résumé, it's fair game for a recruiter to ask about it. If the data science job postings that you've viewed request certain skills—skills that you have—make sure to list them! That information is exactly what recruiters look for.

We recommend that you don't use star ratings, numbers, or other methods to try to indicate how strong you are in each skill. For one thing, ratings don't mean anything: anyone could rate themselves 5/5. If you give yourself all perfect scores, hiring managers may think that you're not honest or good at self-reflection; if you give yourself lower scores, they may doubt your abilities. Also, it's not clear what you consider each level to be. Does 5/5 mean that you think you're one of the best in the world, that you know how to do an advanced task, or that you're better at certain skills than your co-workers? If a hiring manager does want you to self-assess your level of different skills, they'll ask you in an interview.

Don't list soft skills such as critical thinking and interpersonal skills; although they're crucial to being a successful data scientist, putting them on your résumé is meaningless, because anyone can do that. If you do want to highlight your skills in these areas, talk about how you used them in specific instances within the experience section of your résumé. Also, you don't need to list basic skills that anyone who applies would be expected to have, such as working with Microsoft Office Suite.

SECTION: DATA SCIENCE PROJECTS (OPTIONAL)

If you've done data science projects outside work, you can create a section for those projects. This section is great for candidates who have less work experience but have done projects on the side or in a school or bootcamp. You're basically telling the recruiter this: "Although I may not have much relevant work experience, that doesn't matter, because I've still done the full data science process."

For each project, you'll need a title, descriptions of what you did and how you did it, and the results. In fact, the data science projects should look as though they're jobs in structure and content, so everything in section 6.1.2 on generating content applies to them too. Ideally, you'll have a link to a blog post or at least to a GitHub repository that has an informative README file. Data science is a technical field in which it's unusually easy just to show the work you did, and this section is a great place to do that. If you have enough relevant work experience, you can skip this section but still talk about projects in your interviews.

SECTION: PUBLICATIONS (OPTIONAL)

If you published papers that are related to data science in a master's or PhD program, you should include them. If you published papers in other fields, even quantitative ones such as physics or computational biology, you can include them, but only briefly. Because they are not directly related to data science, the person reading them won't get much out of the publications except that you worked hard enough to get published. You can list the relevant work you did during your research in the experience section, such as "created an algorithm to analyze millions of RNA sequences per minute." But publication in a journal that the hiring manager has never heard of, even if it's a prestigious one in your field, won't go too far on its own.

OTHER SECTIONS

You can add other sections, such as Honors and Awards if you've won Kaggle competitions or received a scholarship or fellowship, but they aren't necessary. You don't need to include references; speaking to your references will come later in the process, and you can share that information if you progress that far. Objective statements usually aren't needed and are redundant, given the other information in your résumé. The phrase "data scientist experienced in Python looking for a position to develop A/B testing and modeling skills," for example, isn't going to make a recruiter more excited!

PUTTING IT TOGETHER

Generally, you put your contact information at the top, followed by the next-most-important section. If you're in school or just graduated, you probably need to put your education at the top; if you don't have relevant work or education, put your data science projects at the top; otherwise, put your work experience there. Within your work and education sections, list your experiences in reverse chronological order, from most recent to least.

We've seen lots of effective formats for data science résumés. In this field, you have a bit from freedom in your design; there's nothing close to a standard format. Despite that freedom, you always want to focus on making your résumé easy to scan quickly. Because recruiters spend so little time looking at your résumé, you don't want them to spend that time trying to figure out how to find your most recent job. Don't make your design distract from your content; consider how others will view it. Some good practices include

- Clear headers for sections so that it's easy to jump between them
- More whitespace to make reading the content easier
- Bold important words, such as the titles you've held at each company

If ideas such as whitespace and headers are overwhelming, stick to a résumé template you found online, or consult a design specialist.

Generally, you want to limit your résumé to a single page. This practice serves two purposes: given the brief skim your résumé will get, you want to make sure that the recruiter spends that time on the information you think is most valuable, and it shows that you can communicate concisely and understand what parts of your experience are most important to share. If a person submits a 17-page résumé (which we've seen), it strongly suggests that they have no idea what in their past makes them a good candidate and that they feel entitled to other people's time to read it.

Finally, make sure that you're consistent throughout your résumé. If you abbreviate month names in your education section, abbreviate them in your work experience section too. Although you can use different fonts and sizes for headings and body text, don't switch up the format from bullet point to bullet point. Use past tense for previous positions and present tense for a current one. These things show that you pay attention to the small details and (again) help readers process your content quickly, as they won't be distracted by font or style changes. A single inconsistency is unlikely to cost you an interview, but sometimes, details make all the difference.

PROOFREADING   It's essential to proofread your résumé! A few typos or grammatical mistakes may lead your application to the (metaphorical) trash bin. Why so harsh? When recruiters are sifting through hundreds of résumés, two kinds stand out: those that are clearly exceptional (rare) and those that are easy to eliminate. The latter kind need some rules of thumb, and in addition to résumés that clearly don't meet the requirements, résumés with typos are an easy reason to eliminate an applicant. Data science jobs require paying attention to detail and checking your work; if you can't do that when putting your best foot forward in an application, what does that fact suggest about your work? In addition to using the spell-check feature in your word processor, have at least one other person read your application carefully.

6.1.2 *Deeper into the experience section: generating content*

We hope that coming up with the dates and titles of your work and education history is easy enough. But how do you come up with those punchy bullet points to describe your work experience (or data science projects)?

The common mistake people make on their résumés is to create just a list of their job duties, such as "Generated reports for executives using SQL and Tableau" or "Taught calculus to three sections of 30 students." There are two problems with this approach: it states only what you were responsible for, not what you accomplished or how you did it, and it may not be framed in a way that's relevant to data science. For the previous two examples, you could describe the same work as "Automated the generation of sales forecasts reports for executives using Tableau and SQL, saving four hours of work each week" or "Taught calculus to 90 students, earning an average of 9.5/10 in student evaluations, with 85 percent of students getting a 4 or 5 on the BC Calculus AP Exam."

As much as you can, you want to explain your experience in terms of skills that are transferrable to data science. Even if you haven't worked in data science or analytics, was there any data that you did work with? Hiring managers are willing to consider experience outside data science roles as still relevant, but you have to explain why they should. If any of your work can conceivably be related to taking data and understanding it, you should put enormous effort into creating a concise story about what you did. Did you analyze 100GB of star data for an astrophysics PhD? Did you manage 30 Excel files to plan staffing for a bakery? Lots of activities involve using data to understand a problem.

Have you used tools such as Google Analytics, Excel, or Survey Monkey? Even if those tools may not be the ones the job is asking for, working with data of any type is relevant. What communication skills did you use? Did you explain technical or niche concepts, maybe in PhD research talks or to other parts of the business? If coming up with transferrable skills is difficult, don't worry; the rest of the advice on writing better bullet points will still help. But if you haven't done so already, you should think about how your education or side projects can demonstrate data science skills, especially if your work experience can't.

For the least-relevant positions that you held a few years ago, it's okay to have just one bullet point. But you generally don't want to leave a job off your résumé if it will leave a gap of more than a few months. If you've been in the workforce for a while and had a lot of jobs, it's okay to list only the three or four most recent.

You might be finding that this process is a lot easier for the job you're currently in than the one you had five years ago. One good practice is to keep a list of your accomplishments and the major projects you've worked on. When you're in a job each day, making incremental progress, you can forget how impressive the whole is when you step back. People know that your résumé isn't an exhaustive list, so they won't think "It took her 15 months to build an automated system for tracking and scoring sales leads that saved their sales team more than 20 hours of manual work a week." They'll think "Wow, we need a system like that!"

In general, bullet points can fall into two categories. The first is big accomplishments, such as "Created a dashboard to monitor all running experiments and conduct power calculations." The second category is average or totals, such as "Implemented and analyzed more than 60 experiments, resulting in more than $30 million in additional revenue."

In either case, each bullet point should start with a verb and (ideally) be quantifiable. Rather than say, "I made presentations for clients," write "Created more than 20 presentations for Fortune 500 executives." It's even better if you can quantify the impact you had. Writing "Ran 20 A/B tests on email campaigns, resulting in a 35% increase in click rate and 5% increase in attributed sales overall" is much more powerful than "Ran 20 A/B tests on email campaigns."

6.2 *Cover letters: The basics*

Although the purpose of a résumé is to give hiring managers relevant facts about your work experience and education, the purpose of the cover letter is to help them understand who you are as a person. Your cover letter is where you can explain how you've researched the company and highlight why you're a great fit. If your résumé doesn't show a linear path, a cover letter can pull everything together and explain how the pieces fit to make you a great candidate for this job. Even just showing that you know what the company is, that you've read its About web page, or that you've used its product (if it's available for individuals) goes a long way. Your cover letter is your best tool to help hiring managers understand things that don't fit well in bullet lists.

Unlike a résumé, a cover letter may be optional. But if a company has a place to submit one, do so; some companies will eliminate candidates if they haven't written one. It's not uncommon for companies to give a specific thing for you to write about, such as your favorite supervised learning technique. This request usually is made to check whether people have read and followed the request of the job description instead of sending a generic cover letter everywhere. You definitely want to let the company know that you can follow instructions.

Knowing that a cover letter is to help the company better understand who you are, a common mistake we see in cover letters is focusing on what the company can do for you. Don't say, "This would be a great step for my career." A hiring manager's job is not to help as many careers as possible; it's to hire people who can help the company. Show them how you can do that. Even if this job would be your first data science job, what relevant experience do you have? What record of achieving results (even if they're not related to data science) can you share so that it's clear you work hard and accomplish goals? Don't undercut yourself; try to think broadly about how you can make yourself appealing to the company.

Like your résumé, your cover letter should be short; three-quarters to one page is usually the rule. Focus on your strengths. If the job description lists four skills, and you excel in two, talk about those two! Don't feel that you have to make excuses for skills that you lack.

Figure 6.2 shows an example cover letter.

SARA JONES

New York, NY · 534-241-6264
sarajones@gmail.com · linkedin.com/in/sarajones · sarajones.github.io · github.com/sarajones

---

GREETING

Dear Jared,

INTRODUCTORY PARAGRAPH

I am writing to express my strong interest in applying for the Data Scientist position at Awesome Company. I've enjoyed reading Awesome Company's data science blog since it started 8 months ago. The post on using topic modeling to automatically generate tags for your support articles was immensely helpful in one of my own projects to classify articles in the New York Times business section.

1-2 PARAGRAPHS OF DATA SCIENCE WORK EXAMPLES

I recently graduated from Awesome Bootcamp, a full-time, 3-month Data Science immersive. At Awesome Bootcamp, I designed, implemented, and delivered data science projects in Python involving data acquisition, data wrangling, machine learning, and data visualization. For my final project, I gathered 3,000 neighborhood reviews and ratings from Neighborhood Company. By using natural language processing on the reviews and available listings from Real Estate Company's API, I built a recommendation system that will match you to a neighborhood based on your budget, preferences, and a free-text description of your ideal neighborhood. You can try it out here: myawesomewebapp.com.

Prior to Awesome Bootcamp, I was an Investment Consultant at BigCo. When I joined, my team of six was all using Excel. While exceeding my targets, I began automating common tasks in Python, such as generating a weekly market and industry trends report, saving the team hours each week. I then developed a tailored curriculum to teach them Python. The initiative was so successful the company asked me to develop a full 2-day workshop and flew me out to three other offices to teach it, reaching over 70 consultants.

CLOSING PARAGRAPH

I am confident that my expertise in Python, academic training in Economics and Statistics, and experience delivering business results would make me a great fit for the Data Science team. Thank you for your consideration.

SIGNOFF

Sincerely,
Sara Jones

Figure 6.2 An example cover letter with highlights showing the different components

6.2.1 Structure

Cover letters have a less-well-defined set of rules than résumés. That being said, here's a good general structure you can follow:

- *Greeting*—Ideally, find out who the hiring manager or recruiter for the position is. The first place to look is the job description itself; that person's name might be listed. Even if all that's listed is an email address, you can probably figure out who the recruiter is with some online searching. Otherwise, check LinkedIn and the company website to see whether one of them identifies the team leader.

Even if you end up aiming too high—maybe the vice president of the department who will be your skip level (manager's manager)—you've still shown that you did your research. Finally, if you can't find a name, address your letter to Dear *Department Name hiring manager* (such as *"Dear Data Analytics hiring manager)."* Don't say "Dear Sir or Madam"; that phrase is archaic and generic.

- *Introductory paragraph*—Introduce yourself, name the position you're interested in, and briefly explain why you're excited about the company and role. If the company has a data science blog, or if any of its data scientists have given talks or written blog posts on their work, this paragraph is a great place to mention that you've watched or read those. Connect what you learned from those presentations with why you're excited about the position or company.

- *One to two paragraphs of examples of data science work*—Connect your previous accomplishments with this role. Add details to something you discussed in your résumé and go in depth on one role or side project, giving specific examples. Follow the "Show, don't tell" principle; instead of writing that you're a "detail-oriented, organized problem-solver," provide an example of being this kind of person at work.

- *Closing paragraph*—Thank the recruiter for their time and consideration. Sum up your qualifications by explaining why you'd be a good fit for the position.

- *Signoff*—"Sincerely," "Best," and "Thank you for your consideration" are all good closings. Avoid writing anything too casual or overly friendly, such as "Cheers" or "Warmest regards."

6.3   *Tailoring*

The previous two sections lay out general rules for writing an effective cover letter and résumé. But the best way to differentiate yourself from other candidates is to tailor those documents to the position you're applying for.

The first person who screens your data science résumé isn't likely to be the manager for a position; it may not even be a human! At larger companies, applicant tracking systems automatically screen résumés for keywords, surfacing those that contain those words. Such a system may not recognize "linear modeling" as meeting the requirement for experience in "regression." A human reader may not, either; a human-resources person may have been given nothing besides the job description and instructions to find promising candidates. You don't want to risk a recruiter's not understanding that your project using "k-nearest neighbors" means that you have experience in clustering analysis or that *NLP* is the acronym for *natural language processing*. You want someone to be able to look back and forth between your résumé and the job description easily, finding exact matches for the requirements in your experience. Although you don't want to overload your résumé with tech jargon, you do want to use the keywords (such as *R* or *Python*) a few times to help the résumé make it through these screens.

We recommend that you have a "master" résumé and cover letter you can pull from rather than starting from scratch each time. This approach is especially helpful if you're applying for different types of positions. If some jobs emphasize machine learning and others exploratory analyses, it's much easier if you have bullet points and related key terms ready to go. Your master résumé and cover letter can be longer than one page, but make sure that the résumé and cover letter you submit are always less than a page.

Tailoring your application to the position doesn't mean that you need to have one bullet point or skill for every single requirement. As we discussed in chapter 5, job descriptions are generally wish lists; try to figure out which ones list the core skills for the job. Sometimes, companies helpfully divide skills and experience into "requirements" and "nice-to-haves," but even if they don't, you may be able to tell which is which from the description of the job responsibilities. Although companies would love to get someone who gets a check-plus on everything, most won't be holding out for it.

One exception is big tech firms and well-known, fast-growing startups. These companies get a lot of candidates and are looking for reasons to reject people. They're very worried about false positives, meaning hiring someone who is bad or even just average. They don't really care about false negatives—not hiring someone who is great—because they have lots of great people in the pipeline. For these companies, you usually do have to meet 90% of the requirements, if not 100%.

6.4 *Referrals*

Company websites and job boards all have a place where you can apply, sometimes with a click of a button if you've saved your résumé on the job board. Unfortunately, because it's so easy to apply this way, your résumé often ends up in a pile of hundreds or even thousands of similar cold applications. That's why we recommend not applying this way until you've exhausted other options. Reading job postings is a great way to get a feel for what kind of jobs are available, but the best way to get your foot in the door is to have someone hold it open for you.

You want to try to use the hidden back door to most companies: referrals. A *referral* means a current employee recommending someone for a position, usually by submitting that person's application and information through a special system. Many companies offer referral bonuses, paying employees a couple thousand dollars if they refer someone who gets and accepts a job offer. Companies like people who are referred because they come pre-vetted: someone who already works at the company and (presumably) is doing well thinks that this person would be a good fit. Even if someone doesn't formally refer you, being able to write in your cover letter "I discussed this position with [Star Employee X]" and have that person tell the hiring manager to look out for your résumé are huge benefits.

How do you find people who can refer you? Start by looking at LinkedIn to see whether you know anyone who works at a company you're interested in. Even if you haven't spoken to that person in a while, it's perfectly fine to reach out with a polite message. Next, look for people who previously worked at the same company or went to the same school as you. You're more likely to get a response to a cold message if you mention something you have in common. Finally, look for people who are second-degree contacts to see who you have in common. If you're on good terms with any of your mutual connections, reach out to that person to see if they'd be willing to introduce you.

If you're reaching out to a data scientist, take some time to learn about what they do. Do they have a blog, Twitter account, or GitHub repo where they've shared their work? Mark Meloon, a data scientist at ServiceNow, wrote in his blog post "Climbing the relationship ladder to get a data science job" (http://mng.bz/O95o) that the most effective messages are ones that combine a compliment about the content he's published with a request to ask some more questions. This way, you'll also avoid asking about things they've already publicly talked about and can focus on getting advice that you couldn't find elsewhere.

Remember that it's not only people in data science who can help you. Although other data scientists are best positioned to tell you what it's like to work at their company, people in any position can refer you. If someone you know works at a company you want to apply to, reach out to them! At the very least, they can still offer you insight into the company culture.

Crafting an effective message

In his blog post "Do you have time for a quick chat?" (http://mng.bz/YeaK), Trey Causey, a senior data science manager at Indeed.com, outlines some suggestions for effectively reaching out to someone you don't know to talk about your project, job search, or career choice. By following these guidelines, you'll be much more likely to get a response, have a productive meeting, and build a good foundation for a continuing relationship:

- Have an agenda for what you want to discuss, and include it in your email.
- Suggest a few times (including an ending time 30 minutes later) and a location near the person's workplace.
- Buy their lunch or coffee.
- Get there early.
- Have specific questions and goals for your conversation based on the agenda you sent. Don't just ask for "any advice you can give me."
- Keep track of the time, and let them know when you've used all the time you asked for; if they want to keep talking, they will.
- Thank them, and follow up on anything you talked about.

Here's how Trey pulls that all together into a sample message:

"Hi, Trey. I read your blog post on data science interviews and was hoping I could buy you a coffee at Storyville in Pike Place this week to ask you a few questions about your post.

I'm currently interviewing, and the part about whiteboard coding was really interesting to me. I'd love to hear your thoughts on how to improve whiteboard coding questions and answers, as well as share some of my own experiences with these types of questions.

Could you spare 30 minutes sometime—say, Tuesday or Wednesday of next week? Thanks for writing the post!"

6.5 Interview with Kristen Kehrer, data science instructor and course creator

Kristen Kehrer is a data science instructor at University of California—Berkeley Extension, faculty member at Emeritus Institute of Management, and founder of Data Moves Me, LLC. Data Moves Me helps data science teams communicate machine learning model results to stakeholders so that the business can make decisions confidently. She holds an MS in applied statistics and is a co-author of the upcoming book *Mothers of Data Science* (self-published).

How many times would you estimate you've edited your résumé?

Oh, a million! I come from a blue-collar family, where my dad was a firefighter and my mom stayed at home, so I was never taught how to write a great résumé for industry. But I did okay by asking others for help when I was getting out of grad school. I also have always been the type to keep track of any new project I work on or anything interesting that I could add to my résumé. I wasn't one of those people who'd go for two years without updating my résumé. More recently, my old company paid for a career coach when they laid me off. I got to learn all about résumé best practices and how to effectively position myself to land a great job.

I absolutely advise people to update their résumé often. Especially if you've been working at the same place for a while, it is very difficult to try and think about all the relevant things that you could add to your résumé. For example, I co-authored a couple posters in the healthcare industry that won awards. That's not relevant to every position I apply for, but if I am applying to a position in healthcare, I'd want to be able to reference that research. If I didn't keep track of it, I would not be able to remember who my co-authors were or what the title of the poster was.

What are common mistakes you see people make?

So many things! One is the four-page résumé that still has that they were a swimming coach. Another is not realizing that the applicant tracking systems don't parse certain things well. If people have icons or charts on their résumé, that's going to come through as a blob on a lot of the older automated systems and may end up with you being automatically rejected. I also don't like when people put, say, three stars for Python, because you're not giving people any context, and whichever skill you're putting two stars for, you're saying that you're not good at that thing.

Do you tailor your résumé to the position you're applying to?

I'm not obsessive about it. But almost all medium to large companies now use an applicant tracking system, and you want to be able to rank high in terms of matching keywords. If I saw things on a particular job description that matched things that I've done, but were maybe worded slightly differently, I'd just edit a couple words to match the verbiage that they're using on their job description.

What strategies do you recommend for describing jobs on a résumé?

I tell people to optimize their résumé for the job they want, not the job they have. You don't need to make a list of all the things that you've ever done. Instead, think about what you've done that you can reposition for data science. For example, if you're a math teacher, you've been explaining technical or mathematical material to a non-technical audience. Or maybe you worked on a project where, even though it wasn't in analytics, you had to work cross-functionally across multiple teams. Overall, you want to be able to show that you're able to solve problems, self-manage, communicate well, and achieve results. Finally, you can use side projects to highlight your technical chops and the initiative that you're taking.

What's your final piece of advice for aspiring data scientists?

You need to start applying to data science jobs. Too many people just keeping taking online courses because they think they need to know a million things to become a data scientist, but the fact is, you're going to start a job, and you're still going to have more to learn. Even ten years in, I still have more to learn. By applying, you'll get feedback from the market. If nobody responds to your résumé, maybe it's that you're not positioning yourself well, or maybe it's that you don't quite have the skills. Gather some feedback from a few people and then choose an area to focus on, such as being able to automate processes in Python. Work on that, add it to your résumé, and apply to more. You need to apply, get responses, and iterate and move forward until you get a job.

Summary

- Your résumé isn't an exhaustive list of everything you've ever done. You need it to get you an interview, not the job, so focus on matching it closely to the job description.
- Cover letters let you show why you're interested in an organization and how your experience positions you to make a valuable contribution.
- Talking to people who currently work at a company, especially if they're data scientists, is the best way to get insight into specifics about openings and company culture.

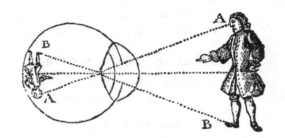

7

The interview: What to expect and how to handle it

This chapter covers

- What interviewers are looking for
- Common types of interview questions
- Proper etiquette when communicating with a company

If you stop to consider the process of an interview, you might realize just how tricky it is: somehow, you need to show total strangers that you'd be good in a role you know about only from a few paragraphs in a job posting. In the interview, you may be asked technical questions at all levels about different technologies—some of which you may not have used before. Further, during the interview you'll need to learn enough about the company to be able to decide whether you'd *want* to work there. You have to do all of these things in only a few hours, all while acting professional and proper. It's enough to give you some serious anxiety sweats.

The good news is that with the right preparation and mindset, data science interviews can be taken from panic-attack-inducing to manageable, tolerable, and maybe even an enjoyable experience.

In this chapter, we walk you through what interviewers are looking for and how to adjust your thinking to align with their needs. We discuss technical and nontechnical questions, as well as a data science case study. Finally, we go through how to behave and what questions you should be asking interviewers. With this information, you should be well prepared for what lies ahead.

7.1   *What do companies want?*

When employees of a company are interviewing candidates for an open position, they're looking for one crucial person:

Someone who can do the job.

This is the only type of person they're looking for. Companies aren't looking for the person who gets the most interview questions right or who has the most degrees or years of experience. They only want someone who can do the work that needs to be done and help the team move forward with its goals.

But what does it take to do a job? Well, a few things:

- *Having the necessary skills*—The necessary skills can be both technical and nontechnical. On the technical side, you need to understand the skills we cover in chapter 1: some combination of math and statistics, as well as databases and programming. On the nontechnical side, you need general business acumen, as well as skills such as project management, people management, visual design, and any number of other skills that are relevant to the role.
- *Being reasonable to work with*—If you say something offensive, act defensive, or have any number of other character flaws that would make it difficult for other people to interact or collaborate with you, a company won't want to hire you. This means that during the interview (and always, actually), you'll want to be agreeable, compassionate, and positive. This doesn't mean that your interviewer should want to grab a beer with you. It just means that the people on your future team need to see you as being someone they want to work with.
- *Being able to get things done*—It's not enough to have the skills to do the job; you have to be able to use them! You need to be able to find solutions to problems on the job and implement those solutions. Data science has lots of places where a person can get stuck, such as figuring out messy data, thinking through the problem, trying different models, and tidying a result. A person who can overcome each of those challenges will be much better at doing the job than someone who sits around waiting for help without asking for it. People who try to make everything perfect have trouble with this part as well: never being able to call your work done means that you can never put the work to use.

Knowing that those three things are what companies look for in candidates, you're ready to jump into the interview process. As we walk through the process of how the interview works and the questions that often come up, we'll frame our discussion in terms of those three ideas.

7.1.1 The interview process

Although the exact process of a job interview varies by company, interviews tend to follow a basic pattern. This pattern is designed to maximize the amount of information a company learns about the candidate while minimizing the amount of time it takes for people within the company to run the interview. The people who do interviews are typically busy, have many interviews to facilitate, and want to allow for fair comparisons between candidates, so the process is streamlined and consistent. Here is a basic outline of what to expect in an interview process (figure 7.1):

1 *An initial phone screening*—This screening typically is a 30-minute (or sometimes 60-minute) phone interview with a technical recruiter: a person who has lots of experience in screening candidates and knows technical terms but doesn't do technical work themselves. From the company's perspective, the goal of this interview is to check whether you have any chance of being qualified for the job. The recruiter wants to screen out people who clearly wouldn't be a good fit, such as people who aren't remotely qualified (don't have the required skills) or who sound abrasive or mean (and won't work well with others). On the technical side, the interviewer is checking whether you potentially have the minimum skills needed, not that you're the best at them. They're much more likely to ask "Have you used linear regressions before?" than "How do you compute the maximum likelihood estimate for a gamma distribution?" After the first phone interview, the company occasionally requires another phone interview with a more-technical screener. If the initial phone screening goes well, within a few weeks, you'll have . . .

2 *An on-site interview*—This interview is often two to six hours long and makes up the main part of the interview process. During this visit, you'll get to see where you'd work and meet the people you'd work with. This interview gives the company time to ask more-probing questions about your background, your skills, and your hopes and dreams as a data scientist. You'll be interviewed by multiple people during the visit, each asking questions on different topics, some technical and some nontechnical. The goal of this interview is to ensure (via technical questions) that you have the necessary skills and (via behavioral questions and

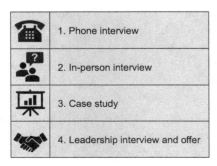

	1. Phone interview
	2. In-person interview
	3. Case study
	4. Leadership interview and offer

Figure 7.1   The four steps of the interview process

how you conduct yourself) that you're reasonable to work with. If this interview goes well, it's time for . . .

3 *A case study*—You'll get a description of a real-world problem and data related to it. You'll be given time on-site or at home over the weekend to analyze the data, try to solve the problem, and create a report about it. Then you'll present your report to the hiring team. This exercise shows the team that you have the necessary skills (through how good your report is) and that you can get things done (through how much you were able to do in the report). Not all companies require this step; sometimes, they replace it with a presentation about your past work. If your case study report goes well, you'll have . . .

4 *A final leadership interview and offer*—This interview is with the senior manager, director, or some other leader of the team. The purpose is for the leader to give their approval of your fit for the position and the team. If the leadership interview even happens in the first place, it means that the data science team thought you were a good fit, so it's rare for this interview to overrule that approval. Note that this interview often happens right after the case study, but it could happen at the beginning or end of the first on-site interview. Assuming that it goes well, you'll get an offer in less than two weeks!

When the process involves all these steps, you usually get an offer letter somewhere between three weeks and two months after you submitted your resume. As you can see, each part of the interview process is designed to achieve a different goal for the company.

In the following sections, we dive into each part of this process, showing you how to showcase your skills and capabilities in each setting.

7.2   Step 1: The initial phone screen interview

Your first interaction with the company will likely be a 30-minute phone call with a recruiter. It's important to make a good first impression. Depending on the size of the company, however, the person you'll be talking to is likely to be unrelated to the data science team you'd be working on, so y*our goal is to show the company that you could do this job, not necessarily that you're the best person for the job.*

Why? The person you'll be talking to during this phone interview has the job of filtering out the unqualified candidates. When the recruiter talks to a candidate, they're trying to assess whether it's worthwhile for someone on the data science team to talk to the candidate. Lots of times, people apply to jobs they don't have the skills for (or lie about having the required skills), so the recruiter wants to prevent them from moving onward. As a candidate, your goal is to get the recruiter to understand that you're at least minimally qualified for the position.

The recruiter is likely to ask you these sorts of questions:

- *Tell me about yourself.*—(This isn't technically a question, but it's treated as one.) The recruiter is asking you to give a one- or two-minute overview of your background. They want to hear you describe experiences that relate to the job at hand. If you're applying for a decision science position, for example, they'll want to hear about your academic background and any jobs or projects in which you did an analysis. It's important for your answer to fall into the one- to two-minute range. If your answer is less than a minute long, you'll seem like you don't have enough going on, and if it's more than two minutes, you'll seem like you don't know how to summarize a story.

- *What sorts of technologies are you familiar with?*—The recruiter is checking whether you have the technical experience to do the job. Beyond this specific question, you should expect to be asked questions about your familiarity with math and statistics, databases and programming, and the business domain (refer to chapter 1). You'll also want to mention any technologies you know that are related to the position or were mentioned in the job posting. If you don't have exactly what the job posting asked for (such as Python instead of R), that's okay; just be open and honest about that fact. If you happen to know more of the tech stack that the company uses, perhaps from having talked to people who work there, try to frame your answer around that fact.

- *What makes you interested in this position?*—The recruiter is trying to understand what drew you to the company in the first place. A particularly well-thought-out answer shows that you do your homework and can get things done. Answering "I just clicked 'Apply' on every data science job on LinkedIn" would show that you have poor judgment. Don't overthink questions such as these; just demonstrate that you know what the company does and have a genuine interest in the role. As much as possible, try to connect the role with your background and interests.

Although the recruiter will ask you questions about yourself and your background, this call is also a time for you to gain better understanding of the position itself. The recruiter should spend at least 10 minutes talking about the role and the team you're interviewing for. During this time, ask questions so that you can be sure you'll want the job and so that you can demonstrate a sincere interest in the role. These questions can include topics such as travel, the company's culture, how the team is changing, the team's priorities, and why the role opened in the first place.

It's possible that during the call, the recruiter will try to understand your salary expectations, either directly ("What are you expecting for a salary?") or indirectly ("How much do you currently make?"). To put this approach in a positive light, the recruiter is making sure that the company can afford to meet your salary expectations so as to not waste time interviewing someone who wouldn't take what the company can offer. In a negative light, the recruiter may be trying to lock you into a salary lower than what the company could offer because you're giving them information about your expectations. As much as possible, avoid discussing salary until you're farther along in the process. Chapter 8 covers salary negotiations.

During the call, make sure to ask what the next step in the process is and what the timeline is. The recruiter should say something like "We would bring you in for an interview next, and we should know in a week whether that will happen or not." "What are the next steps?" is a totally normal and fine thing to ask. Don't ask the recruiter directly whether you're going to move on to the next interview. That question will put them on the spot and possibly make them feel uncomfortable—and they likely don't have the authority to make the decision anyway.

If the phone interview goes well, you'll be asked to move on to an on-site interview.

7.3   Step 2: The on-site interview

This step is the heart of the interview process. The company invited you on-site to do an interview and booked it for multiple hours. You took a day off work and put on some nicer-than-normal clothing, and you're heading out.

> ### What to wear to the interview
>
> One aspect of interviews that's often discussed and debated is what to wear to it. For data science positions, this question is complicated by the fact that jobs can fall in all sorts of industries, each with its own culture and dress code. What's completely appropriate for one interview may be totally inappropriate for the next.
>
> Your best bet is to ask your recruiter when scheduling the interview what people wear to interviews, as well as what the general company dress code is. The recruiter wants you to succeed and shouldn't lead you astray. Otherwise, try to talk to someone who works at that company or a similar company. If all else fails, assume that bureaucratic industries (finance, defense, health care, and so on) have strict dress codes, whereas young companies or tech companies (startups, massive tech companies) have loose dress codes. Avoid extremes (sandals, shorts, cocktail dresses, top hats); wear something you feel comfortable in.

The goal of this interview is to help the company understand whether you'd be able to do the job it's hiring for—and whether you'd do it well. Depending on the company and position, anywhere from three to ten people may be coming in for an interview, each with their own strengths and weaknesses. The company wants to find the person who'd be the best fit—or the first person interviewed who'd be pretty good at the job.

Throughout the interview, reinforce the idea that you can do the job well. This concept is different from being the smartest candidate, the candidate with the most years of experience, or the candidate who has used the most types of technology. Instead, you want to be a candidate who has a healthy balance of being reasonable to work with, has enough skills to do the work, and can get things done.

What will happen during these multiple hours of interviews? An on-site interview usually includes the following:

- *A tour of the workplace and an introduction to the team*—The company wants you to understand what working there would be like and potentially impress you with free beverages and snacks (if available). This part takes less than 15 minutes, but it's good to get a decent look around to see whether you'd be happy working there. Are the work spaces calm and easy to work in? Do the people look reasonably happy and friendly? Are the laptops eight years old? While you're walking around on this tour, you'll often be making small talk with someone from the company. Watch out! This conversation is part of the interview; if you come off as unpleasant or mean, you may miss out on the job offer. Shoot for coming off as nice, but most important, be your authentic self (unless your authentic self is a jerk).

- *One or more technical interviews*—This part can take anywhere from 30 minutes to multiple hours, depending on how rigorous the company is. You'll be asked questions on many topics and may need to do work on a whiteboard or computer. (We go into more detail about these questions later in section 7.4.1 and the appendix.) The point of this interview isn't for the interviewer to understand the deepest topics you know or whether you can solve the trickiest problems. The point is to see whether you have the minimally necessary skills to do the job, so your objective is to show that you have what's needed.
- *One or more behavioral interviews*—The point of behavioral interviews is to understand how well you get along with others and how well you get things done. You'll be asked a lot of questions about your experiences, including how you dealt with difficult situations and how you make sure that projects come to fruition. You may be asked very general job questions such as "Tell me about a time you dealt with a difficult co-worker" to more data-science-specific queries such as "How do you deal with a data science project in which the model fails?" These questions won't necessarily have right or wrong answers; they'll be open to interpretation by the interviewer.

TIP Before the day of your on-site interview, you can ask the recruiter or hiring manager what the interview will be like. At minimum, they should give you a schedule showing who you'll be talking to and what topics they'll be covering. If you ask, they may be able to give you some specific details about what to expect during the technical and behavioral parts of the interview. This information will help you arrive prepared.

Going through an on-site interview is emotionally taxing. You'll have to switch quickly from thinking about technical topics to questions about yourself and your dreams, all while presenting yourself in a professional and friendly way. Depending on the size of the company, one or many people may be interviewing you, and you'll want to make a good impression on each of them. One of the best ways to manage nerves during an interview is to remember that the interviewers are people too and that they want you to perform well just as much as you do. They're your allies, not your adversaries.

In the following sections, we dive deeper into different parts of the interview. This section of the chapter goes into different parts of the on-site interview, but check out the appendix for a detailed list of interview questions and example answers, and details on how to think about the questions.

7.3.1   *The technical interview*

For many data scientists, a technical interview is the most frightening part of the whole interview process. It's easy to imagine yourself stuck in front of a whiteboard being asked a question you have no idea how to answer and knowing that you won't get the job. (Just writing that sentence induced anxiety in the authors!)

To best understand how to handle the technical interview, you need to reframe how you think about it. If you've read chapter 4 of this book and created a data science portfolio, you've already passed the technical interview. The point of this interview is to see whether you have the skills necessary to be a data scientist and, by definition, have those skills because you've done data science! If during an interview, you find yourself being judged for not being able to answer a tricky question, that's a sign that the interviewer is doing a bad job, not you. You have the necessary skills, you have experience under your belt, and this part of the interview is designed for you to express those facts. If the interview doesn't allow you to do so, that's not your fault.

In this process, you try to show the interviewer that *you have the skills needed for the job*. Showing that you have a set of skills is a very different activity from answering every question you're asked perfectly. A person can give exactly the answers an interviewer wants to hear and still do poorly on the interview, or they can give incorrect answers and do well. Consider two answers to an interview question:

Interviewer: What is k-fold cross validation?

Answer A: You randomly partition the data into k even groups and use it as test data for k models.

Answer B: You randomly draw a sample of data and use it as test data for a model k times. Then you take the average of the models and use it. This method is really a method for handling overfitting because you have a bunch of models that all have different training data. I used this method on the main project in my portfolio where I predicted house prices.

Technically, answer A is correct and answer B is not (that's cross validation, but not technically k-fold because the data wasn't split into even groups). That being said, answer A gave the interviewer no information except that the interviewee knew the definition, although answer B showed that the candidate knew the term, knew why it was used, and had practical experience with it. This example illustrates why it's so important that, during an interview, you think about how to convey the fact that you have the skills.

Specifically, you can do a few things in your data science technical interview to convey to the interviewer that you have these skills:

- *Explain your thinking*—As much as possible, don't just give an answer; also explain why you got the answer. Giving an explanation shows the interviewer how you think about the subject and can show that you're on the right track even if you didn't give the right answer. One word of caution: although repeating the question aloud may feel helpful (such as "Hmm . . . would a linear regression work here?"), some interviewers may take this behavior as a sign that you don't know much. Practice answering questions directly, and practice how you frame your thought process from the start.

- *Reference your experiences*—By talking about projects or work you've done, you're repeatedly grounding the conversation in your real-world practical skills. This approach can make an ambiguous answer more credible and concrete, or just provide an alternative topic of conversation if your answer is a little off the mark. You have to take this approach in moderation, however; if you spend too much time talking about your past instead of talking about the question at hand, you may seem to be avoiding the issue.

- *Be open and honest if you don't know an answer*—It's totally possible (and normal!) not to know the answer to every question in the interview. Try to be up-front and explain what you *do* know about the answer. If, for example, you're asked "What is a semi join?" and you don't know the answer, you could say something like "I haven't heard of that kind of join before, but I suspect that it might be related to an inner join." Being open about what you don't know is better than confidently being incorrect; interviewers are often wary of people who don't know what they don't know.

TIP When answering interview questions, your instinct might be to answer as quickly as possible. Try to fight that instinct; it's much better to wait to give a strong answer than to give a weak one quickly. With the stress of an interview, it's hard to slow your speech rate, so practice answering questions beforehand to get more comfortable.

The following are the general types of questions you'll get in the technical interview. Again, check out the appendix for example interview questions and answers.

- *Math and statistics*—These questions test how well you understand the academic topics that are a necessary foundation for a data science job. They include
  - *Machine learning*—This topic includes knowledge of different machine learning algorithms (*k*-means, linear regression, random forest, principal components analysis, support vector machines), different methods of using machine learning algorithms (cross-validation, boosting), and general expertise in using them in practice (such as when certain algorithms tend to fail).
  - *Statistics*—You may be asked purely statistical questions, especially if your work is in an area that answers them, such as experimentation. These questions can include statistical tests (such as t-tests), definitions of terms (such as ANOVA and *p*-value), and questions about probability distributions (such as finding the expected value of an exponential random variable).
  - *Combinatorics*—This field of mathematics covers all things related to counting. Logical problems in this field include questions like "If a bag has six different-colored marbles in it, how many combinations are there if you pull

two out without replacement?" These questions have little to do with the job of a data scientist, but interviewers sometimes believe that the answers provide insight into your problem-solving skills.

- *Databases and programming*—These questions test how effective you would be in the computer-based parts of a data science job. They include
  - *SQL*—In almost any data science interview, you'll be asked questions about querying databases in SQL. This knowledge is needed for most jobs, and being familiar with SQL indicates that you should be able to get started in your new role quickly. Expect to be asked questions about how to write SQL queries for sample data. You may be given a table of student grades in multiple classes, for example, and asked to find the names of the best-scoring students in each class.
  - *R/Python*—Depending on the company, you may be asked to answer general programming questions by writing pseudocode or to solve particular questions by using R or Python (whichever language the company uses). Don't worry if you know R and the company uses Python (or the reverse); usually, companies are willing to hire and train in the new language on the job because a lot of knowledge is transferrable. Expect to be asked a question that involves writing code (such as "How would you filter a table in R/Python to include only the rows above the 75th percentile of a score column?").
- *Business domain expertise*—These questions are highly dependent on the company you're applying to. They're used to see how familiar you are with the type of work the company does. Although you could pick up this knowledge on the job, the company would rather you already have it. Here are some sample questions used in different industries:
  - *E-commerce company*—What is the click-through rate of an email? How does it compare with open rate, and how should they be thought of differently?
  - *Logistics*—How do you optimize production queues? What are some things to think about when running a factory?
  - *Not-for-profit*—How should a not-for-profit organization try to measure donor growth? How could you tell whether too many donors aren't renewing?
- *Tricky logic problems*—Beyond problems that are related to data science, you may get general brain-teaser questions in your interview. These questions have the reported purpose of trying to test your intelligence and ability to think on your feet. In practice, the questions don't do anything of the sort. Google did a massive study (http://mng.bz/G4PR) and found that these sorts of questions had no ability to predict how a candidate would do on the job; they only served to make the interviewer feel smart. These questions tend to be like "How many shampoo bottles are there in all the hotels in the United States?" You can often Google to see whether large companies use these types of questions (and which ones).

It's hard to say exactly which of these questions you'll be asked and how much time you'll be able to spend on them; these factors are highly dependent on the company and the person interviewing you. Try your best to remain calm and confident as you work through the questions, even if you're unable to answer some of them. If the interviewer is talking to you as you give a partial answer, they may be thinking that you're doing well and may be willing to point you in the right direction. Often, the questions are designed to cover so many topics that no data scientist could answer all of them, so by design, you'll have some that you won't be able to answer.

Interviewing the interviewer

Each time you meet a new person during the on-site interview, they'll end their part with "Do you have any questions for me?" This question is one of your only opportunities to get candid information about the job, so use the time wisely! You can find out more about the technology used and the work, as well as how the team functions. Your questions show that you have a sincere interest in the company, so it's worth thinking of questions in advance. Here are some examples:

- *"What technologies do you use, and how do you train new hires on them?"* This question is great if the interview hasn't gone into detail about the technology stack. The answer will give you insight into whether the company has formal training processes or hopes that employees will pick up the knowledge on their own.
- *"Who is our team's stakeholder, and what's the relationship with them like?"* You're asking who is going to be calling the shots on the work. If the relationship is poor, you may end up being a slave to the stakeholder's demands, even if that goes against your judgment.
- *"How do you do quality control on data science work?"* Because the team doesn't want to put out work with errors, there should be some checks in their process. In practice, many data science teams have no checks, and they blame the creator of the work when things go wrong. That kind of workplace is toxic and one to avoid!

7.3.2 *The behavioral interview*

The behavioral interview is designed to test your interpersonal skills and give the data scientists on the team a better understanding of who you are and what your background is. Although technical questions are bunched into one or two blocks of time, the behavioral questions may appear throughout the whole on-site interview: in a one-hour session with a human-resources representative, a ten-minute window of closing questions from a technical interviewer, or even small talk with one employee while you wait for another to arrive. So be ready to answer behavioral questions at any time.

Here are a few example interview questions that you should expect to be asked. You can find more behaviorial questions and answers in section A.4 of the appendix:

- *"Tell me about yourself."* This "question" shows up during the phone screening and can show up every time you talk to a new person. Again, try to give a one- to two-minute summary, but this time, tailor it to the person you're talking with.

- *"What's a project you've worked on, and what did you learn from it?"* This question is intended to show whether you can look at a project in your history and be introspective about it. Have you processed what went well and what didn't?

- *"What is your greatest weakness?"* This question is infuriating because it seems that from a game-theory perspective, you want to give an answer that shows as little weakness as possible. In practice, what the interview is trying to do is check whether you understand your own limitations and have areas that you're actively trying to improve.

Notice that all these questions are very open-ended and have no right or wrong answers. But there are ways of expressing yourself that can dramatically improve the way your answers are received.

For most of these questions, especially ones that ask about your experiences, your answers should follow a general framework:

1 Explain the question in your own words to show that you understood it.
2 Explain an experience in which that situation occurred, focusing on why the problem existed.
3 Describe the action you took to resolve the problem, as well as the result.
4 Give a summary of what you learned.

Consider this request: "Tell me about a time you delivered something to a stakeholder, and you got a negative result." A response could be something like "So you're asking about a time I disappointed someone with my work [*1. explaining the question back*]? That happened on my last job, where I had to do a report on customer growth. Our team was juggling a lot of different requests, so I didn't have much time to focus on a request from one director. When I handed over a report that I spent only a day on, that director was very disappointed with it [*2. describing the problem*]. First, I apologized for not meeting her expectations; then I worked with her to see how we could reduce the scope of the request and still meet her needs [*3. providing a solution*]. From this experience, I learned it's best to let someone know early if you can't meet their request so that you can come to a mutually agreeable solution [*4. what you learned*]."

A nice thing about behavioral-interview questions is that they're all similar, so you can plan answers in advance! If you have three or four stories that cover working in a challenging situation, handling difficult teammates, and managing failure, you can draw on those stories for most interview questions. This approach is much less stressful than trying to think up a story and improvise on the fly. If you have time, you can practice telling these career tales out loud to a friend to learn how to structure them best.

In almost every interview, you'll be asked to describe a past project, so it's worthwhile to be well prepared. The ideal project for a story covers the points listed in this section: it was a challenging situation in which you overcame adversity, especially difficult teammates, and then found a solution. Ideally, the story will fit into the four-step answer style, too.

That being said, it's often difficult to find a story about a project that has every interesting twist and turn in it, especially if you're an aspiring data scientist. If you find yourself lacking an answer, try telling a simple story about a project in your portfolio. Even an answer like "I thought it would be interesting to analyze an unusual dataset, so I obtained it, cleaned it, and found an interesting result I blogged about" shows the interviewer that you can work through the task of doing an analysis.

The best technique for answering behavioral questions is something that many people have explored. You can think about methods down to the level of the exact wording to use and the seconds to spend on each answer. That being said, most of the techniques aren't specific to data science, so you can easily go deeper by reading general books and articles about interviewing. We offer recommendations in the resources section that follows chapter 8.

7.4   *Step 3: The case study*

If you did well on the on-site interview, you'll be asked to complete a case study: a small project that shows the company how well you do data science in practice. Someone on the data science team will you give a dataset, a vague problem to solve with it, and a set time period to solve it in. You might be asked to solve the problem during the on-site interview, with an hour or two to work, or you may be given a longer period, such as a weekend, so that you can do the work at home. You'll generally be allowed to use the programming languages or tools you're most familiar with, although it's possible that the company will limit you to the tools it uses. When your time has elapsed, you'll share your results in a short presentation to or discussion with a group of people from the data science team. Here are some example case studies:

- Given data on promotional emails sent by a company and data on orders placed, determine which of the email campaigns did best and how the company should market differently in the future.
- Given the text of 20,000 tweets in which the company was mentioned, group the tweets into topics that you think would be useful to the marketing team.
- An expensive A/B test was run on the company website, but halfway through, the data stopped being collected consistently. Take the experiment data and see whether any value can be derived from it.

Notice that in each example case study, the objective isn't a direct data science question. Questions such as "Which campaign did best?" make sense in a business context, but there isn't a "Which campaign did best?" algorithm that you can apply. These case studies are useful as interviewing tools because they require you to go from the very beginning of a problem all the way to a solution.

That said, exactly what is the company looking to see in a good case study? They want to know the following things:

- *Can you take a vague, open-ended problem and figure out some methods of solving it?* It's entirely possible that you won't solve the problem, but as long as you make an attempt in a reasonable direction, you're showing that you have the technical skills and can get things done.

- *Can you work with messy real-world data?* The data you'll be given will likely require filtering, creating joins, feature engineering, and handling missing elements. By giving you a complex dataset, the company is giving you the kind of work that you'd be doing on the job.
- *Can you structure an analysis?* The company wants to know whether you look at the data in a methodical, well-thought-out way or investigate things that don't relate to the task at hand.
- *Can you produce a useful report?* You'll have to create a presentation about your work and possibly documents such as Jupyter Notebooks or R markdown reports. The company wants to know whether you can make something that's useful to the business and structure a useful narrative.

The good news is that the skills and techniques needed for great case studies are the exact same ones that you need for good portfolio projects: taking data and a vague question and producing an output. It's even better if you made a blog post; that mimics creating a presentation for an interview case study!

You'll want to take into account a few minor differences between a portfolio project and a case-study problem:

- In a case study, you have a limited amount of time to do the analysis. This time can be set by the calendar, as in one week from the day you get the materials, or set by the hours worked, as in no more than 12 hours of time spent. That short amount of time means that you'll want to be strategic about where you spend your hours. In general, the data cleaning and preparation steps take much longer than data scientists expect. Just getting tables to join together, filtering malformed characters out of strings, and loading the data into a development environment can take a lot of time, and typically, that part of the work won't be impressive to the company. Try not to get overly focused on preparing the data the best way possible if it means having too little time to do an analysis.
- Another difference with case studies is that you're judged on your presentation of results, so you want to have a well-polished presentation with really interesting results. The act of creating a presentation can feel both uninteresting and less important than doing the analysis itself, however, so many data scientists put off creating the presentation until the very end. Putting the presentation off until the end is bad because you may run out of time, or you may find that the analysis isn't as interesting as you hoped when you don't have time to make changes. As much as possible, start working on the presentation early, and build it as you progress in your analysis.
- One final difference with a case study is that you have an extremely specific audience: the small number of people you're presenting to. With a portfolio

project, you don't really know who will look at it, but with a case study, you can hypertarget your analysis. If possible, when you're first given the case study, ask who the audience of the case study presentation will be. If the audience members are all data scientists, you can make your presentation more technical, such as including details of the machine learning methods you used and why you chose them. If the audience is business stakeholders, try to go light on the technical components, and focus more heavily on how your findings would affect business decisions. If the audience is a mix of data scientists and business stakeholders, try to include enough of each kind of details so that if one member of the group dominates the discussion, you have enough to placate them.

The presentation itself is usually about 20 to 30 minutes of presenting your findings, with 10 to 15 minutes of questions from the audience about your approach and findings. It's a good idea to practice your presentation and plan what you want to say during each part of it. Practicing also helps you keep to the allotted time; you don't want to talk for only 5 minutes or for 50 minutes straight. During the question-and-answer section, you'll be peppered with questions on all sorts of topics. You may go from answering a question about a parameter in your model straight to a question about the business effect of what you found. A good practice is to take a moment to think about the question before answering so that you can get your bearings and think through your response. In the event that you don't have an answer you're confident about, it's generally best to give some version of "I'm not sure, but . . ." and then offer some ideas on how you could find the answer. If possible, add the relevant context that you do know.

7.5 *Step 4: The final interview*

When the case study is over, likely during the same trip to the office as your case study, you'll have one last interview. This interview will be with a person who makes the final call, such as the manager of the data science team or the director of engineering. Depending on how the company runs the interview process, this person may be prepared with information about how you performed in the earlier parts of the process, or they may know nothing about it. The objective of this interview is for that final person to greenlight your hiring.

It's hard to know what questions you'll be asked during the final interview, because they depend heavily on the person who'll be interviewing you. A technical person may focus on your technical experience and what skills you have, whereas a businessperson may ask you about your problem-solving approaches. Regardless of the type of person who does the interviewing, you should definitely expect questions that are the same style as those in the behavioral interview, such as "How do you handle difficult situations and deal with problems?" For these questions, being open, honest, and sincere will go a long way.

Following up

After each part of the interview process, you may be inclined to contact people from the company in one form or another. Following up can show gratitude to the people you've met, as well as give you more information about how the process is unfolding. If you do this task poorly, however, reaching out can come off as abrasive or desperate and may jeopardize your chances of getting the job. You can use any of three methods to follow up, depending where you are in the process:

- *Before anyone from the company has contacted you*—If you've sent your application but haven't heard back, don't follow up. The lack of response is a sign that the company isn't interested.
- *After contact but before you've met anyone in person*—After the phone interview, you should follow up only if you're unsure of your status in the process. You can follow up with one email only if it's past the time when the company said the next step would happen. In that case, simply ask for a status update.
- *After in-person contact*—You can (but in no way need to or necessarily should) email a brief thank-you note to the people who interviewed you. If you don't hear back from them when they said you would, you can also email the recruiter, asking for an update.

7.6 *The offer*

If all goes well, within a week or two of your final interview, you'll get a call from someone at the company letting you know that the company is going to extend you an offer. Congratulations!

In chapter 8, we go into much more detail about what makes a good offer, how to compare offers for different data science jobs, and how to ask a company to improve its offer.

Unfortunately, it's also possible to be disappointed; you may not get an offer from the company. After taking a moment to grieve the loss of the potential job, you can view this situation as an opportunity to learn what areas you can improve in for your next interview. If you made it only to the initial phone screening, that's probably a sign that your base qualifications weren't a fit for the particular role. In that case, you should consider adjusting the jobs you apply for. If you made it to the on-site interview or case study, but no farther, there's likely a specific reason why you weren't a good fit for the company or role; try to deduce whether there's something you could focus on for the next interview. If you made it through the final interviews but didn't get the job, that usually means you were well suited to the position, but someone else happened to be a slightly better fit. In this case, there isn't much to do but continue to apply for similar roles. You shouldn't reach out to the company to ask why you weren't hired; you're unlikely to get an honest answer, and the question will be viewed as being unprofessional.

7.7   Interview with Ryan Williams, senior decision scientist at Starbucks

Ryan Williams recently transitioned from being a manager of data science at a marketing and sales consulting firm, where he ran the data science interview process. Now at Starbucks, he helps inform decision-making for the Starbucks Rewards program as part of the company's analytics and insights team. He has a bachelor's degree from the University of Washington, where he dual-majored in statistics and economics. Before he joined Starbucks, his career focused on the consulting industry.

What are the things you need to do to knock an interview out of the park?

The big thing in general is just preparation. There's a whole skill set that goes into interviewing that is very specific to interviewing. A lot of people think they can just walk into an interview and their experience is naturally going to shine through. I have felt that myself, and I've seen other people come into interviews with that mindset. But with questions such as "Tell us about a time you had trouble communicating," unless you've really prepared, you can babble and talk in circles. There's really a skill set that you need in interviewing, and the way to prepare for that is to read up on the typical questions you're going to face. No matter where you're interviewing, you're going to face some behavioral questions, you're going to face some technical questions, and you're going to face some business-case questions.

So know the common behavioral questions. Know the types of technical questions people are going to ask, and understand the business-case-type questions. Unless you're prepared in the right ways to demonstrate your experience, you're not necessarily going to get that opportunity in an interview.

How do you handle the times where you don't know the answer?

One case that I remember is that I was interviewing at one of the bigger tech companies, and they asked lots of harder and harder stats questions. It got to the point where they asked me something that was super-academic. I think it was that given a certain probability distribution function, how would you use its moment generating function to find the kurtosis of the distribution? I was likely well . . . that's something maybe I could have answered in college, but I definitely can't now.

That being said, when I gave my answer, the interviewer was clearly disappointed. I could go on a whole rant about it, but I wasn't happy because I feel like that was the type of question that's really more trivia than something that demonstrates my thinking. Having a job is about resourcefulness in your ability to solve things you don't know. It's not about your ability to come into a room knowing everything you need to know already.

What should you do if you get a negative response to your answer?

There's the emotional component where you're going to be unhappy with the fact that you were unable to answer the question, but you have to not let that tank the interview for you. It's natural to keep thinking about what you could have done to get that problem right instead of what you could do to answer the next question. But you really have to just be able to move on and stay sharp about the questions that you're going to get in the future.

I would say if you are running into questions like that, you need to be interviewing the company too. They're asking you a lot of questions, but you should be using the types of questions they're asking you to infer whether this is actually a company you want to work for. For me, a company that thinks that it's super-important for a data scientist to be able to derive a moment generating function three times to get the kurtosis is not necessarily the type of environment that I feel is going to be best for me to work in.

What has running interviews taught you about being an interviewee?

I am a lot more thoughtful about the types of questions I'm being asked when I'm being interviewed and also the types of questions that I'm asking in an interview. Before I ever interviewed people myself, I took the interview questions at face value. Being interviewed felt like taking a test because the interviewer is asking a question and I thought I only needed to answer it right. I wasn't evaluating the types of questions being asked, which now I'm a lot more conscious of. Is this interviewer asking me questions that are a lot of trivia? Do they want me to whiteboard a lot of programming problems? Do they care about the things I care about in that data science role?

Summary

- The interviewing process is similar across most companies for data science.
- For on-site interviews, expect technical and behavioral questions.
- Be prepared to do a data science case study.
- Take time to prepare for and practice answers to common interview subjects.
- Know what you want to learn about the company and role during your interview.

8

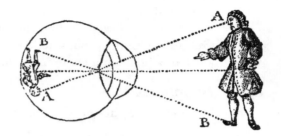

The offer: Knowing what to accept

This chapter covers

- Handling the initial offer
- Negotiating your offer effectively
- Choosing between two "good" options

Congratulations! You've got a data science job offer. This is a big accomplishment, and you should definitely take a little time to savor it. You've done a lot of work over the past months or even years to get to this point.

This chapter will help you respond to and decide on the offers you receive. Even though you're probably really excited, you *should not* immediately say "Yes! When can I start?" when you get an offer. All data science jobs are not created equal. You've been selective in where you've applied, but you may have found out things in the interview that raised concerns. Or you have a benefit that's a hard requirement for you, such as good health insurance for your family, and you need to look over the offer details. Even if you're sure that you want to take an offer, you still shouldn't say yes immediately: you want to negotiate! The time when you have an offer but haven't accepted it yet is the time when you have the most power. Now that this employer has finally found someone it's excited about (you!), the company wants to close you. Recruiting is very expensive; it takes up a lot of time for

119

human resources and the data science team to evaluate applicants and interview them, and every week without the new hire is a week in which the company doesn't benefit from the work of that (hypothetical) person. Use this opportunity to ask for what's important to you, whether that's a higher salary, working from home once a week, or a higher budget for attending conferences.

8.1   The process

In general, the offer process goes something like this:

1 *The company tells you that an offer is coming.* It wants you to know about the offer as soon as possible so that you don't accept an offer from a different company first.

2 *The company makes the offer.* By email or phone call (followed by an email), the company lets you know the details on salary, start date, and other things that are necessary for your decision. It usually also gives you a date by which you have to accept or decline the offer.

3 *You give an initial response.* As discussed in section 8.2, unless you're absolutely sure that you don't want to take the job, we recommend that you express your enthusiasm and ask for a few days to a week to think about the offer rather than say yes immediately. When you have your next conversation with the company, you'll begin the negotiation process (section 8.3).

4 *Negotiate for the best offer you can get.* You may get an answer immediately when you negotiate, but often, the company will need some time to let you know whether it can give you a better offer.

5 *Decide whether the offer is good enough for you, and give them your final decision.*

8.2   Receiving the offer

The call or email you receive that extends you an offer is usually from the hiring manager, recruiter, or human resources person you've been working with. Whoever you deal with at this point, however, your response should be the same.

Start by saying how happy and excited you are about the offer. If you sound unenthusiastic about working there, the company is going to get worried that even if you take the offer, you won't stay there long and won't be contributing your best work.

WHEN YOU'RE VERY DISAPPOINTED   Although we generally recommend waiting to start negotiating until you have all the details in writing and have had a few days to think, if you're very disappointed in the offer, you'll probably want to start discussing that fact. Suppose that the salary is 25% less than you expected. You could start by saying something like this: "Thank you so much. I'm really excited about this opportunity and the work I'd be doing at company Z. But I want to be honest that the salary is a fair amount lower than I was expecting. I know that in New York City, the market rate for someone such as myself with a master's degree and five years of experience is in the range of X to Y. What can we do to get the offer more aligned with that range?"

You could also use a higher competing offer or a higher current salary as a reason for asking for more. Reserve this tactic for use when the salary would make you turn down the job immediately, not for a job you'd take but want to negotiate 5% more salary. Getting 20% more may be impossible, no matter how good a negotiator or candidate you are, and it's better to find that out earlier rather than later.

The company should tell you that you'll be getting the details in an email, and if not, you should request it. This request serves two purposes:

- You get to sit down and take time to read everything and consider the whole package, without frantically taking notes during a phone call and trying to decipher your handwriting later.
- You should never consider the offer to be official until it's in writing. Most of the time, you won't have a problem, but you don't want to have a misunderstanding over the phone and think that you accepted a certain salary and benefits package, and find out later that this isn't the case.

When you receive the offer, it should include your title, salary, any options or stock units offered, and the benefits package. If it doesn't include the details you need, such as the full explanation of health insurance benefits, you can ask for that as well.

Finally, you should have a specified time window in which to accept the offer. The time window should be at least a week; if it's less than that, ask for a week. The best thing to do is be confident and say, "I need a few days to consider this." If you're unable to be that solid in your convictions, this is a great time to discuss the situation with someone else, such as a partner, family member, or lucky goldfish. It helps to have an external decision-maker and constraint. That way, the recruiter or manager knows they can't just pressure you on the spot.

Sometimes, companies give you an "exploding" offer, which means that you have to respond in less than a week; otherwise, the offer will be rescinded. The deadline should never be as soon as needing to respond in that initial phone call, but it might be just 24 hours later. Usually, you can push the deadline back by saying something like "I know we both want this to be a great fit. Choosing my next company is a big decision, and I need a week to consider it carefully." In the worst-case scenario, a company will refuse, for some reason, to wait for you to fully evaluate the offer. If you find yourself in this situation, that's a huge red flag. A company that isn't willing to respect your needs in this area is a company that won't respect your needs in other areas. By giving you a small time window, the company knows that it's pressuring you to act quickly, which causes more anxiety and may lead you to make a bad decision. Although many people are applying for data science jobs, companies are still struggling to find people who are good fits, so a company that treats applicants that way has something strange happening in it.

If you're interviewing with other companies, let those companies know that you received an offer and when you need to respond. If you're in the final round of interviews, those companies may be able to speed up the process so that they can get you an offer before you need to decide on your current offer. It's totally normal to update other companies when you receive another offer; they'll appreciate it. When you reach out to them, reiterate how excited you are about them and the work you'd do there. Some companies may not be able to do anything, but at least you'll have given them a chance. Again, because companies often struggle to find data scientists to hire, if they find someone they like, they generally can move quickly.

8.3   Negotiation

A lot of people hate negotiating a job offer. One reason is that it's perceived as being strictly a zero-sum game: if you gain, they lose. Another reason is that it feels selfish and greedy, especially if the offer is better than your current job. It's easy to look at a situation and not feel that you deserve more money than a company initially offers and that you're lucky to have any offer at all. But when you're in this position, you owe it to yourself to do your best to maximize your offer.

You—yes, you—are the person who's best suited for this job. We all face impostor syndrome, but the company sees in you what it wants for this job. As we mentioned at the beginning of the chapter, at this moment, you're in your strongest position to negotiate. And companies expect you to negotiate! You want to be prepared. An appropriate salary isn't related to what you made before or what the company may initially offer; instead, it depends on what companies are offering for people with your skill set. Make sure that you get paid as much as your peers, that the total compensation matches your expectations, and that you get the benefits that are most important to you. You have a chance to make 5% of your salary in a five-minute phone call; you can handle the discomfort for that long.

The need to negotiate is especially strong in data science, which has a massive disparity in salaries. Because the field is so new, and because many types of roles fall into data science, there aren't clear standards for what people make. Two people who have the same skill set can have wildly different salaries when one person calls himself a data scientist and the other calls herself a machine learning engineer. These differences in salary get compounded as people move to new, higher-paying jobs. At this point, there's little correlation between the amount a person is making and that person's qualifications and abilities.

8.3.1   What is negotiable?

The first thing many people think of when negotiating a job offer is salary. Before you reach the final rounds of interviews, you should research the salaries not just for data scientists in general, but also for that industry, the city the company is located in, and the particular company if it already has data scientists. Although the offer may be a big salary jump, remember that you want to be paid similarly to your peers at your new company. You are not obligated to let the company know your current salary during the interview process, and in some cities and states, it is illegal for companies to ask. If you go on Glassdoor and find that the average data scientist makes twice as much as you do, that's great.

During the interview process, if you're asked what you currently make or what your salary expectations are, try to avoid giving an answer, as you may risk getting a lower offer because the company will know it can meet your expectations. You can try answering "Right now, I'm more focused on finding a position that will be a good fit with my skills and experience. I'm sure if we find a mutual fit, we can come to an agreement on an overall compensation package." If the person keeps pressing you, such as by saying they need to know to make sure you won't expect something out of the offered range, you can reply, "I understand that you want to make sure my expectations match your compensation band. What is your range for the position?" You could also say, "I'd need to ask a few more questions [of the hiring manager/senior data scientist/any person you'll have in the interview flow to whom you're not talking right now] to get a better idea of what the position entails before I can provide a realistic expectation." If the person refuses to give a range and won't move forward if you don't give a number, that's a bad sign. If you absolutely need to give an answer because you love the company and have tried deflecting multiple times, say something like this: "Although I'm certainly flexible, depending on the overall package, I know from my research that $X to $Y is standard for someone with my experience and education."

Caitlin Hudon: On impostor syndrome

Making big career changes is a time when many people—even experienced, senior data scientists!—feel pangs of impostor syndrome. *Impostor syndrome* is the feeling of doubt about your accomplishments and worry about being exposed as a fraud. Salary negotiation in particular is tricky: it's a high-stakes situation and a literal exercise in determining your worth. Your feelings about your worth will almost certainly play into your decision-making, so it's important to combat feelings of impostor syndrome so that you can be objective and assertive about all that you bring to the table.

Impostor syndrome is especially common in data science. Depending on whom you ask, a data scientist is some combination of an analyst/statistician/engineer/machine learning pro/visualizer/database specialist/business expert, each of which is a deep position in its own right. It's also a constantly expanding field where there can be a lot of pressure to stay on top of new technologies. So when we boil it down, we have people from a variety of backgrounds coming to a new field with many applications whose boundaries aren't clearly defined (thus causing inevitable gaps in their knowledge of that field as a whole) and where technology is changing faster than a single person can keep up with. If this feels like a lot for a single person to contend with, that's because it is!

This brings us to my approach to combating impostor syndrome, which is to focus on my unique experience and how it makes me unique, rather than to compare myself to an impossible-to-achieve data scientist ideal. To get there, I've accepted that I will never be able to learn everything there is to know in data science—I will never know

(continued)

every algorithm, every technology, every cool package, or even every language—and that's okay. (The great thing about being in such a diverse, growing field is that nobody will know all of these things—and that's okay too!)

Furthermore, you and I know things and have experience that others don't. The knowledge and experience you have both overlaps with others and also sets you apart from others, but is not a subset of others. Focus on your own unique experience. You've had to earn it, after all, and it's important to remember that it sets you apart from other data scientists.

When you're in the midst of salary negotiations, if you find yourself up against your own impostor syndrome, take a minute to think about all of the skills that you've learned, the problems you've solved, and all of the great assets you'd be bringing to your future team. Your experience is valuable, and you should be paid fairly for it. Don't be afraid to ask for what you deserve.

You shouldn't feel bad for asking to be paid what you think is reasonable. What you think is reasonable shouldn't be defined by what you've made before—only what you want to make in the new position. Companies frequently offer a lower amount, anticipating that you'll negotiate up to what they expect to pay a new hire, so it's very common to get at least a 5% increase.

But you can negotiate much more than salary. First, there are other direct monetary benefits, such as a signing bonus, moving allowance, and stock. A signing bonus is easier for the company to give than the same amount of salary increase, as it's a onetime thing. The same goes for a moving allowance; if you'll be moving, ask about the company's relocation policy. If the company is a big one, there's likely a standard relocation package, and it may even work with a particular moving company to help. Even small companies may be able to give you something; you won't necessarily find out unless you ask.

But you can go even broader than that. Go back to what you thought about in the job-search process. What's important to you? Some things are hard to negotiate; the healthcare options and 401(k) match, for example, are often set by human resources and are standard for everyone in a role. You want to consider these things earlier in the process when choosing where to apply and interview. For non-startup companies, you can usually find employee reviews on Glassdoor that include information about the benefits package. But there are lots of things you can ask for now, such as

- A flexible or remote work schedule
- An earlier review (six months versus a year), which could get you a raise faster
- Educational benefits
- A budget for going to conferences

When you do this, keep in mind the organization's restrictions. Not-for-profit organizations, for example, are unlikely to have much room to negotiate salary, but they might be flexible on hours or vacation. A company whose data team is already distributed is more likely to let you work from home a few days per month than a company where everyone is in the same office. Ensure that what you're asking for is in writing and honored. You don't want to negotiate an early review and never get it when you arrive on the job. Also keep in mind that these sorts of nonsalary negotiations are likely to make adjustments only on the margins. If the salary is far below what you want, there's no way that these changes could make the offer acceptable.

8.3.2 *How much you can negotiate*

Your best negotiation lever is a competing offer. A competing offer lets a company know that there's a market for your services at a higher price and that you have another place to go. If you find yourself with two offers, it's best to make statements like this: "I'd much rather work with you, but company ABC is offering me this much more. Can you match that?" Don't lie; if you try to say that to both companies, it could easily come back to haunt you.

Another piece of leverage you have is your current job. Most companies know that you won't want to take a pay cut. If you're relatively happy or have better benefits at your company, use that leverage. Even if the offer has a higher salary, remember to calculate the value you get from your benefits as well. Suppose that your current employer offers a 3% 401(k) match and the offering company offers none. That match effectively raises your salary by 3% versus what the new company is offering. Or maybe your company pays your full health insurance premiums, whereas at the offering company you'd need to pay $200 a month for health insurance for your family. This fact can be especially helpful if you're transitioning to data science from a lower-paying field, so your salary will increase a lot, but you'll be losing a benefit that you get at your current job. You can bring these points up as reasons why you're asking for a higher salary.

When placing a value on your skills, consider how uniquely your background suits your new job. You don't necessarily have to be an experienced data scientist. It would be great if you were one of the three people to earn a PhD in artificial intelligence at Stanford this year. But suppose that your offer is to be a data scientist who helps sales and that you used to be in sales. Having that domain knowledge is a huge advantage that even more experienced data scientists may not be able to bring to the position. The more it seems like the position was designed for you when you saw the job posting, the more leverage you're likely to have.

Sometimes, it can be difficult to recognize the full picture of a job offer. If you'd need to move, for example, you should consider moving costs and also changes in the cost of living. A $90,000 salary in Houston will go a lot farther than a $95,000 salary in New York City. Tally up all the extra benefits. Things such as a good health-care plan or 401(k) match can be worth thousands or tens of thousands of dollars. In general, don't lose sight of the forest for the salary tree.

If you've negotiated and get everything you asked for, the company expects you to accept! You should start the negotiating process only if you'll take the offer when all your conditions are met. Otherwise, why bother? One reason could be that you have another offer you really want to take, and the better this offer is, the more you can negotiate that one. This tactic is extremely risky, however, and you want to be careful about possibly burning bridges. Even if you never work at the company that you use as leverage, the employees who interviewed you or made your offer may remember.

It's very, very rare for a company to pull an offer because you negotiated. If it does, that's a sign that you definitely don't want to work there. It's totally normal to negotiate respectfully; rejecting a candidate for that reason is a huge red flag. Take it as a bad situation avoided.

A brief primer on RSUs, options, and employee stock purchase plans

This sidebar is intentionally called a "brief primer," not an "exhaustive overview." We highly recommend doing more research on whatever is contained in your offer letter.

Generally, all the following items vest over a four-year period with a one-year cliff. *One-year cliff* means that if you leave the company before one year, you get nothing. Instead, you get the one year's worth all at once at your one-year anniversary. After that, they will generally vest every quarter or month for the following three years:

- *Restricted Stock Units (RSUs)*—You'll see a dollar amount of RSUs given to you in an offer. If you take the price of the stock at the time of your offer and divide the monetary amount by it, you'll get the number of shares over time as they vest. If the shares go up in value, your compensation goes up. When the shares vest, you'll get them as stock at that time; your company usually holds back some amount for taxes in the form of shares.

  Suppose that you get an offer of $40,000, vesting over four years with a one-year cliff. Right now, the stock is trading at $100 a share, so you'll get 100 shares after one year and 25 shares each quarter afterward. After you work there for one year, you'll get 65 shares (35 held back for taxes). At that point, you can do whatever you want with your shares as long as you comply with company rules. (Usually, you can sell stock only during certain periods, for example.) If you're working for a private company, the vesting works the same way, but you generally won't be able to sell your shares until the company goes public or gets acquired.

- *Stock options*—Options give you the "option" to buy a certain amount of stock at a specified exercise price, which is generally the fair market value of the shares at the time the option is granted. If the stock later trades way above that price, that's great news; if you can buy some stock for $10 a share and it's trading at $30, you'll make an instant $20 if you just buy and sell the shares right away! If the stock doesn't trade above the exercise price, though, it's worthless; you don't want to exercise an option to buy a stock for $10 if you could buy it in the market for $5.

  Options are really great for early employees at a company that gets big, but they can also be like lottery tickets. As long as your company stays private, the options have limited value, and even if the company goes public, the stock may end up trading below your option value. Unlike RSUs, which are generally going to be worth something, options may never be worth any money.

- *Employee stock purchase plans (ESOPs)*—These plans allow you to buy company stock at a discount. You contribute to the plan through payroll deduction and then reach a purchase date at which your money is used to buy shares of the company. These plans offer two benefits:
  - The discount on stock price, which may be as much as 15%.
  - A lookback provision. If the price has gone up between the beginning of the offering period and the purchase date, you'll get to pay the lower price.

  Suppose that at the beginning of the offering period, the company's stock is worth $10. You contribute $9,000 over a year and then reach the purchase date. At a discount rate of 10 percent, you get to buy 1,000 shares ($9,000/$9). If the stock price is now $20, those 1,000 shares are worth $20,000, meaning that you could sell them and get $11,000 in profit!

8.4   *Negotiation tactics*

Now that we've gone over the big picture, we'll walk through some specific negotiation tips:

- *Remember to start by showing that you're thankful and excited.* We hope that you're both! You want the company to feel that you're on its side and that you're working together to get a solution. Not feeling that you're working together is a red flag against working there.
- *Be prepared.* Before the phone call, prepare notes about exactly what you're looking to change in the offer and what total compensation you'd like. In the heat of the moment, it's extremely easy to blurt out a lower number than you wanted to make the other person happy in that moment. Having notes helps you avoid this situation.
- *Listen to what the person at the other end is telling you.* If they stress that they don't negotiate salary, but compensation is important to you, ask about more options or a signing bonus. Try to work with them to find a solution rather than being immobile in your position. Although negotiating can feel like a zero-sum game, it doesn't have to be! Something very important to you may not be as important to the company, for example, so it's easy for the company to give. Remember that the company wants you to be set up for success and happy in your role.
- *Don't seem like you're focused only on money* (even if you are). This attitude can come off badly. You want to show that you're motivated by the work you'll be doing, the mission of the company, and your new colleagues. Seeming like you're in it only for the money can leave a bad taste in the recruiter's mouth, and they're more likely to worry that you'll jump at a chance to leave for a higher salary.
- *Try to keep a communal focus.* Instead of saying "I really need more options," for example, say "I'm really excited about the long-term growth prospects of your

company and how I can help you succeed. That's why I'm interested in being even more invested by having some additional options."

- *Package your desires together instead of going point by point.* That way, the recruiter will get the full picture of what you want instead of feeling that every time the two of you settle an issue, another one might turn up. That being said, you can hold back the substitutes you're willing to accept. You might ask for a higher salary, more options, and the ability to work from home one day a week, but if the company can't do the salary, you can ask about a signing bonus instead. If possible, also list the importance of each item to you.
- *Avoid self-deprecation.* You read the part earlier in this chapter about how great you are? Read it again. Don't undercut yourself by saying something like "I know I haven't worked as a data scientist before" or "I know I don't have a PhD, but. . . ." You have exactly what the company is looking for, or it wouldn't have made you an offer!

You can find a lot more advice and research on how to negotiate effectively in many articles and books, and we've shared some of our favorites in the appendix.

> **NEGOTIATING AS A WOMAN**   For a while, the common research theory was that "Women don't ask." That theory was one proposed reason why women are paid less than men: it holds that women don't negotiate job offers or ask for raises. Recent research, however, has shown that at least in some areas, women do negotiate as much as men; they're just less likely to be successful. Unfortunately, some bias exists. Some of the tactics we discuss in this section, such as having a communal focus (using *we* instead of *I*, for example), are especially beneficial to women.

8.5   *How to choose between two "good" job offers*

Receiving two (or more!) good offers is a great problem to have! But you still have to make a choice. Having multiple offers won't always lead to this problem, of course. Sometimes, you prefer one job so much more that the decision is easy. But what do you do if that's not the case?

The first step is to go back to section 8.3. Negotiate! If you really like one company better than the other but there's some deal-breaker for you, see whether the company can change that situation. Be honest about what you're looking for. As discussed earlier, that competing offer is great leverage to have and makes it more likely to get what you're looking for.

Next, you can ask to meet again with the hiring manager or potential co-workers to gather more information. Maybe you didn't ask about the average number of meetings a week, how many teams you'd be working with, how requests are prioritized, or anything else that would be helpful to assess whether this company is a place where you'd enjoy working.

When you're looking at an offer, consider the long term. You may have a short-term concern: if you have high student debt or will be starting a family soon, you may want to take the best-paying offer so you can start paying down your debt or saving money. But if you're fortunate enough to be able to think beyond immediate financial concerns, you want to focus on maximizing long-term potential. What kind of work would you be doing at each company? If one job will give you training that enables you to move up two steps at your next post and the other will have you doing things you learned on your first day at bootcamp, you shouldn't jump at the latter offer just because the company has a better vacation package. Remember that salaries in data science can jump from one position to the next by as much as 30 to 40 percent. If your résumé is a little sparse, and this job is a good chance to put a prestigious name on it, you might take a job at a slightly lower salary for a year or two.

Finally, don't be afraid to let smaller factors influence you. Does one job involve a shorter commute or a more spacious office? If both companies meet your minimum criteria and are similar when it comes to your most important deciding factors, you can start considering the smaller factors.

In situations such as this one, considering multiple life choices may be reasonable. Do you take the exciting but risky startup job or stick to your reasonable government-contractor job? Do you take the offer that has you managing people or continue to work as an independent contributor?

Often, you have no objective way to decide which route is better. You can't tell whether the new job would be a good fit until you actually take the offer. You can't know whether you'll like managing until you become a manager. This is an infuriating fact of life.

If you find yourself struggling with these decisions, it may help to reflect on the fact that you can only do the best you can with the information you have. You can't expect yourself to see the future. If you make a decision and ultimately are unhappy with the outcome, you can move on from it. You can quit a job, move back after changing cities, or go back to being an independent contributor. Life is complicated, and you can learn a lot even from paths that don't lead to the outcomes you want.

When you do make a decision, turn down any other offers with grace. It's the polite thing to do, and the data science world is small. You don't want to reject an offer by saying "I can't believe you gave me that lowball offer; you're a terrible company and completely unethical" and then find that the person you yelled at is the hiring manager for your dream job five years later.

8.6 *Interview with Brooke Watson Madubuonwu, senior data scientist at the ACLU*

Brooke Watson Madubuonwu is a senior data scientist at the American Civil Liberties Union (ACLU), where she provides quantitative support for litigation and advocacy teams on issues related to civil rights. She has a master's degree in epidemiology and previously worked as a research scientist.

What should you consider besides salary when you're considering an offer?

It helps to know your priorities before going into that process. It's easy to compare salary, but you also want to compare the day-to-day or month-to-month experience of working at each place. I tend to think about the aspects of the job in three categories: lifestyle, learning, and values.

Lifestyle is about the day-to-day way that the job interacts with other parts of your life. Where will I live? Can I work remotely? Will I be working evenings and weekends? Will I get to travel? Will I have to travel? What health care, child care, and retirement investment options are available to me? Do I have the flexibility I need to care for my family? That's the lifestyle bucket.

There's also the learning bucket. Am I going to grow in this role? What systems are in place to ensure that I'm growing? Am I excited to learn from my boss and from the team?

Finally, I think about the values and mission of the company or organization and the specific team. Do this organization and this team work toward something that aligns with my values? Does the team value inclusion? Is this a product or a team that I want to continue to build? Each of those three buckets can have different levels of importance at different times.

I've negotiated for a title change before in a previous role, and you can negotiate for things such as education and conference resources, work-from-home days, travel support, or equity. Data science is a vast field that's always advancing, so I think it's also important to protect time in your day to continue developing your skills.

What are some ways you prepare to negotiate?

In the past, I've been very uncomfortable talking about my own value and advocating for my worth. That's something that I have been trying to unlearn throughout my career. What can be really helpful is having allies in your corner. Have a close friend practice the negotiation with you and have them take your part. Many people, myself included, find it much easier to advocate for our friends than for ourselves. Listening to the way someone else describes your strengths and your needs can be very motivating, and it really helps to put yourself in that mindset. Ask yourself, "How would I talk about someone I love, who I knew was a great fit for this role, and who I wanted to succeed?" That's how you should talk about yourself.

What do you do if you have one offer but are still waiting on another one?

If you've been through all, or most, of the interview process with a company you're waiting for, it usually doesn't hurt to mention to them that you have another offer. You can also usually buy more time with the offering employer by asking for a week or two to review the details and discuss the offer with your family. Negotiating further, asking detailed questions about benefits, and asking to speak with team members about the work or culture are all actions you can take to serve the dual purpose of collecting more information about the role and buying more time.

But if you're still very early in the interview process at another company, you may not be able to speed it up, and you have to compare the offer on the table to your current situation. If you have just graduated or are between jobs, you may not have the financial luxury of waiting. But if you are currently employed and still not interested by the offer on the table, it may be worth it to you to remain in your current role until you find a better fit. My first data science offer wasn't a great fit, and though I was very keen to transition into the field, it was worth waiting for a better match.

What's your final piece of advice for aspiring and junior data scientists?

I would advise aspiring and junior data scientists to keep an open mind about titles. I think the data scientist title has this allure for people, especially for those coming up in data science majors, which didn't exist when I was in college. They can feel if they don't get a job as a data scientist right when they graduate, they've failed. But the day-to-day functions of a data scientist might exist in a data analyst, a researcher, or one of many other kinds of roles, which can be a really great proving ground for you to hone your skills. I built my coding chops as a research assistant, and later as a research scientist, for years before anyone called me a data scientist, and the work was just as engaging and interesting. Even data-entry work as an undergrad has shaped my thinking about the way data collection decisions inform the analytical possibilities. No job is too small if you're willing to learn as you go.

Summary

- Don't accept an offer immediately: get the details in writing, and ask for some time to look the offer over.
- Negotiate, negotiate, negotiate! You can ask for a higher salary or other monetary benefits, but don't forget about things like a flexible work schedule and a conference budget.
- When you're weighing two good offers, remember to consider the long-term potential of each, not just the initial salary.

Chapter 5–8 resources

Books

I Will Teach You to be Rich, 2nd ed., by Ramit Sethi (Workman Publishing Company)

This franchise is a blog, a book, videos, and several other media, and they're all helpful for getting a job. Sethi has amazing resources on how to think through an interview and give answers that will be well-received. These resources also have tools for salary negotiation, asking for a raise, and other tricky conversations that can happen when you advocate for yourself.

What Color Is Your Parachute? 2020: A Practical Manual for Job-Hunters and Career-Changers, by Richard N. Bolles (Ten Speed Press)

This book is the book for finding a new job. Much like chapters 5–8 of this book, it covers understanding what you want in a job, doing a search, making a résumé, interviewing, and negotiating. The book gives you a good view of how to think broadly about finding a job, although nothing in it is specific to technical jobs (never mind data science jobs).

Cracking the Coding Interview, by Gayle Laakmann McDowell (CareerCup)

Cracking the Coding Interview is a book devoted to helping software engineers get jobs, including almost 200 interview questions and answers. Although many of the questions aren't relevant to data science, plenty of them are, especially if you're looking for a job such as machine learning engineer that's heavily coding-based.

Blog posts and courses

"Advice on applying to data science jobs," by Jason Goodman

http://mng.bz/POlv

This is a great blog post about the lessons learned from applying for data science jobs and finding out how they're generalized. This post covers many of the concepts that are in chapters 5–8, but with his personal perspective about how he felt during the process.

"How to write a cover letter: The all-time best tips," by the Muse Editor

http://mng.bz/Jzja

Although chapter 6 provides guidance on writing a cover letter, it's nice to have multiple perspectives. This blog post covers topics that aren't in that chapter, such as how to not worry about bragging.

"Up-level your résumé," by Kristen Kehrer

https://datamovesme.com/course_description/up-level-your-resume

Our chapter 6 interviewee created this paid course to help aspiring data scientists optimize their résumés and cover letters for getting past applicant-tracking systems (aka robot screeners) and recruiters. If you haven't been getting many first-round interviews, this course may be for you.

"How to quantify your resume bullets (when you don't work with numbers)," by Lily Zhang

https://www.themuse.com/advice/how-to-quantify-your-resume-bullets-when-you-dont-work-with-numbers

If you're struggling with our advice on how to make your résumé experience bullet points quantitative, this post can help. It covers three ways to quantify your experience: range, frequency, and scale.

"How women can get what they want in a negotiation," by Suzanne de Janasz and Beth Cabrera

https://hbr.org/2018/08/how-women-can-get-what-they-want-in-a-negotiation

This blog post in the *Harvard Business Review* covers how women can overcome the inherent biases against them when negotiating salaries and job offers. This topic is a valuable one for women to think about, because the value of negotiating more effectively compounds over the course of a career.

"Ten rules for negotiating a job offer," by Haseeb Qureshi

https://haseebq.com/my-ten-rules-for-negotiating-a-job-offer

This blog post goes in depth on how to negotiate a job offer successfully. When you're at that phase of applying for a job, having the right information can mean a difference of thousands of dollars, so check this post out as you approach this stage.

Part 3
Settling into data science

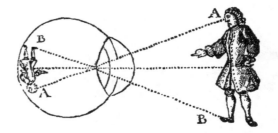

Starting your first data science job is quite an accomplishment, but it's only the beginning of your data science career. Working at a company as a data scientist is quite different from doing data science as a hobby or as part of a course. You may need to pick up all sorts of other concepts, from corporate etiquette to the proper way to put code into production. The huge difference between your expectation of what the role will be like and what the work truly is like can be a shock. This part of the book aims to provide a comforting cushion to soften that jolt. By reading this part, you'll know what to expect in a data science job and be better prepared to excel in it.

Chapter 9 is about the first months on the job, from the first few days, when you may feel totally lost, through settling in as you learn more about the role, your co-workers, and the data. Chapter 10 provides a guide to creating good analyses (a large part of most data science roles) by making and executing a plan at the start. Chapter 11 discusses taking machine learning models and putting them into production, introducing concepts such as unit testing that are essential for more engineering-based data science roles. Chapter 12 is a deep dive into the extremely relevant task of working with stakeholders, which is often the part of a data science job that people struggle with most.

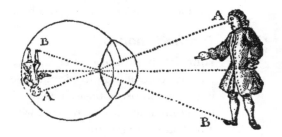

9

The first months on the job

This chapter covers

- What to expect in your first few weeks as a data scientist
- How to become productive by building relationships and asking questions
- What to do if you're in a bad work environment

In this chapter, we're going to walk you through what to expect in your first few months and how to use them to set yourself up for success. These months will have an outsize impact on how the job goes; this is your chance to set up a system and support network that will allow you to be successful. Although each data science job is different, some broad patterns and principles apply to any job.

When you start working, you'll instinctively want to get as much done as possible. Fight that instinct. You need to be sure that you're not just accomplishing tasks, but doing them in the right way. When you're starting a job is the easiest time to ask questions about how something should be done, because you aren't expected to know the processes at your new company. Managers occasionally forget that you don't have the institutional knowledge that your predecessor may have had, so you might get tasked with something that doesn't make sense to you. You might be able to fake your way through the first few tasks, but you'll be much better served by asking questions early and finding out how to approach your work process.

9.1   *The first month*

Your first month at one company will look really different from your first month at another type of organization. Large and small companies will approach your onboarding from almost opposite perspectives. Figure 9.1 compares what you might expect at two companies: a massive one with tons of data scientists and one with no or barely any data science team. (In chapter 2, these examples would be MTC and Seg-Metra, respectively.) These two examples highlight the ends of a spectrum, but the company you're working for will likely fall in between.

Onboarding at a   Onboarding at a
large organization   small company

Figure 9.1   Onboarding at a large organization is like going through a factory line, while a small company is more ad hoc. (Twitter Emojis from the Twemoji project)

9.1.1   *Onboarding at a large organization: A well-oiled machine*

You're one of dozens of people starting this week. You got an email the week before telling you where to go, when to arrive, and what you need to bring. Now you begin a formal, multiday onboarding process with people from different departments. You're issued your laptop and go through the process of setting it up. You listen to presentations about the company culture, human resources policies, and how the company is organized. Everything runs like clockwork; the company has onboarded thousands of employees before.

On the data science side, you'll get help setting up your coding environment. There's likely to be a checklist or extensive documentation on everything you need to do to get access to the data. There's also a central repository of old reports and documentation of the data for you to read and absorb. No one is expecting you to deliver much right away; although your co-workers are excited to have you join the team, they know that you'll need time to adjust. You'll be expected to take a few weeks to go through all the training and get your access approved for the systems. You may be frustrated that it's taking so long to feel productive, but a slow start is natural in this environment.

If you're given a list of to-dos or an assignment, you should take it seriously, but worry more about the process than the result. Established data science teams often have their own idiosyncrasies that you'll need to adopt. It's not just good to ask questions at this stage; it's essential to your ability to perform your job later. The first few months are your chance to see what's been done before you and learn about the rhythm of your peers.

9.1.2 *Onboarding at a small company: What onboarding?*

"Oh, you're starting today?" If you're joining a small startup, don't be surprised if not everything is ready, including your laptop. You may be left on your own to figure out how to access the data. When you do get in, it may turn out that the data isn't well optimized for your job and that a SQL query on a small table of 100,000 rows takes six minutes to run. Onboarding sessions for learning about the company may not happen for weeks, if there even are any, because not enough people may be starting in a given week for it to make sense to run those sessions frequently.

There are no data science standards to speak of. No one will tell you what programming language to use or how to approach and structure an analysis. You will, however, be asked to start getting results quickly. Unlike at a large organization, you don't have to worry about not being productive; you'll be asked to do that right away. You do have to worry a lot more that you're accidentally doing something wrong and no one will tell you, finding out a few months later that your (incorrect) work is already being relied upon. That's why it's still imperative to ask questions and work to get a foothold before you no longer have the fallback position of being new. Going from crisis to crisis will cause you to burn out quickly, so work to build your own processes that will allow you to be successful in the long run.

9.1.3 *Understanding and setting expectations*

One of the most important things you can do in your first weeks is have a meeting with your manager to discuss priorities. This meeting is important because it gives you knowledge about what you're supposed to be working toward in your job. In some data science jobs, the priority is to provide analyses to a specific set of stakeholders to help grow a particular part of the business. In other data science jobs, the goal is to make high-performing models for the website. And in some jobs, both or neither of these goals may apply.

You may feel that you should already know the job expectations from the job posting and interview process. Although this is sometimes true, a lot can change between the interview process and the start of the job. The interviewers may not be on the same time frame as you, or the organization may have changed before you joined. By talking to your manager as early as possible, you'll get the most up-to-date information and have time to spend discussing it.

Ideally, your manager has a vision of what you'll be doing but is open to your priorities and strengths. Together, you want to define what success means in your job. Generally, your success is tied to making your team and/or manager successful; if the members of the data science team aren't all working broadly toward the same objective, it can be difficult to support one another. To define your own success, you need to understand what problems the team is trying to solve and how performance is evaluated. Will you be helping to generate more revenue by working on experiments to increase conversion, or will you be making a machine learning model to help customer service agents predict a customer's concerns, with the goal of decreasing average time spent per request?

Performance goals usually do *not* mean "Make a machine learning model with 99% accuracy" or "Use the newest statistical model in your analysis." These tools help you solve a problem; they're not the goal itself. If your models and analyses deal with problems that people don't care about, they're pretty much useless. Thinking that developing the highest-performing models is the goal is a common misconception among people entering their first data science jobs. It makes sense that this misconception is common, because many academic research and educational courses cover the many methods of making accurate models. Ultimately, however, for most data science jobs, having highly accurate models isn't enough to be successful. Things such as the model's usefulness, level of insight, and maintainability are often more important. (Chapters 10 and 11 discuss these ideas in more detail.)

You can't know when you start a new job what the expectations are in terms of job responsibilities. Some companies value teamwork; you may be expected to work on several projects at the same time but drop your work on a moment's notice to help a colleague. Other companies ask that you have deliverables on a regular basis, and it's OK to ignore emails or Slack messages to finish your project. The way to find out whether you're meeting expectations is to have regular meetings with your direct supervisor. In most companies, you'll have a weekly one-on-one so that you can discuss what you're working on or any issues you have. These meetings exist so that you can find out whether you're spending your time on the tasks that matter to your boss. Why should you guess what is wanted when you can get explicit feedback? Thinking in shorter-term blocks will help you be sure that you're on the right track when the larger performance reviews come along.

Setting yourself up for success

Unless you're at a very small company, there'll be a formal performance review process, so be sure to ask about what that process entails and when it will happen. One common practice is to have a review every six months, with salary increases and promotions potentially following. Many companies do this review as a 360 process, in which you get direct feedback not just from your manager, but also from your peers. If this is the case, find out whether you'll choose the peers or whether your manager chooses them, so you can understand who your most important stakeholders are.

More established data science teams may have a matrix that shows what areas you're evaluated on and what's expected for each area at different levels of seniority. One area could be technical expertise, for example. A junior data scientist may be expected to have only foundational knowledge and show that they're learning; a mid-level data scientist may have one area of expertise; and a senior data scientist may be the company's go-to person for a whole area, such as A/B testing or writing big data jobs. If a matrix doesn't exist, see whether you can come up with a few areas with your manager.

Regardless of the system, make a plan with your manager to have a review after your first three months if that's not common practice. This review will help you make sure you're on the same page as your manager, give updates, and plan the rest of your first six months and year.

The point of defining success is not that you already need to be excelling in every area during your first months. In fact, most companies won't do a formal performance evaluation of someone who's been there for less than six months, because much of that time has been spent on-ramping. Rather, defining success is about making sure as you learn about your role and begin work that you do so with the big picture in mind.

9.1.4 *Knowing your data*

You do need to learn about the data science part as well, of course. If your company has been doing data science for a while, a great place to start is reading reports that employees have written. Reports will tell you not only what types of data your company keeps (and give you key insights), but also the tone and style of how you should communicate your results. Much of a data scientist's job is conveying information to nontechnical peers, and by reading reports, you'll have a sense of just how nontechnical those peers are. See how simplified or complex the writers make certain concepts, and you'll be less likely to over- or underexplain when it comes time to write your own reports.

Then you'll need to learn where the data lives and get access to it. Getting this access includes knowing what table contains the data you want and maybe also what data system has it. Perhaps the most frequently accessed data lives in a SQL database, but the event data from two years ago lives in HDFS (Hadoop Distributed File System), which you need to use another language to access.

Take a broad look at the data you're going to be working with on a regular basis, but go in with an open mind. Some tables have documentation (either packaged with the data or in a report about the data) that explains potential quality issues or quirkiness. Read those documents first, as they'll keep you from investigating "mysteries" that later turn out to have been solved. Then take a look at a few rows and summary statistics. This information can help you avoid "gotchas," in which you find out that some subscriptions start in the future or that a column often has missing values. When you find surprises that aren't documented, the best way to figure them out is usually to talk to the expert on that table. That person may be a data scientist, if your company is large enough, or someone who collected the data. You might find out that the surprise is a true issue that needs fixing, or it might turn out to be what's expected. Subscriptions that start in the future, for example, could be those that have been paused and set to restart on that date. Or the coupons for last year's New Year promo that you find used in May of this year may have been used in May because the support team issued them.

Some companies are better than others about having data that was created for testing separate from real data, although others merge the data without a second thought. In the latter case, you want to ask around whether you should exclude certain orders or activity generated by test accounts or special business partnerships. Similarly, some datasets include users with radically different behavior. American Airlines, for example, once offered a lifetime pass that included a companion fare. One of the people with the pass used the companion fare for strangers, pets, or his violin and might fly multiple times a day. Although you may not have anyone so extreme, it's not uncommon for newer businesses to offer deals that later look silly (such as 10 years of access for $100) and may need to be accounted for in your analysis.

Throughout this process of investigating the data, you're figuring out what kind of overall shape your data is in. If you're at a smaller company, you may find that you need to work with engineers to collect more data before the overall data can be useful. If you're at a larger company, you'll be deciphering dozens of tables to see whether what you want exists. Maybe you're looking for tables with a column called Order across 12 databases. Ideally, there should be well-documented, well-maintained tables for the core business metric, such as transactions or subscriptions. But that's likely not to be the case for other, less-important datasets, and you should try to learn more if you're going to focus on one of the less-documented areas.

Make sure that you learn how the data got to you. If you're working with something such as website data, it'll likely flow through multiple systems to get from the website to the database you can use. Each of these systems likely changes the data in some way. When data collection suddenly stops, you want to know where to try to find the problem (rather than panic about it). But some places have data that people input manually, such as doctors in a hospital or survey results. In these situations, you have to worry less about pipelines and much more about understanding the many attributes of the data and potential places where a human entered it incorrectly. Pretty much anywhere you go, you'll have to deal with some data dirtiness.

As you go along, try writing down any "gotchas" in the data and making a map of where everything lives. It's difficult to remember these sorts of facts over the course of a job, and many companies don't have a great system for documentation or data discovery. Just as commenting code helps your future self and others understand its purpose, documenting data provides enormous dividends. Although keeping this documentation locally on your laptop is OK, the best thing to do is store it somewhere that everyone in the company can access. You'll be helping future new hires and even current data scientists at the company who aren't familiar with that specific area.

Elin Farnell: Thoughts on the transition from academia to industry

After eight years as a mathematician in academia, I started considering a move to industry when I recognized that certain aspects of my work that I valued most were central to data science positions in industry. Two of my research projects were collaborations with an engineering company under grants for the Department of Defense and Department of Energy. What I loved about these projects was that our research group got to tackle interesting mathematical questions, while knowing that what we were developing would be used to address a problem in the real world. I also appreciated the opportunity to learn new mathematical content in order to solve the problem and to collaborate with an interdisciplinary team. In my recent move from academia to industry, certain aspects of my new career path stood out for their contrast to my previous experience:

- *The breadth–depth trade-off*—In academia, a top priority, especially for early-career researchers, is often to establish a research program centered on a deep, narrow subfield. In industry, on the other hand, the goal is generally to solve a wide range of problems, which means learning about and utilizing a broad set of tools from across your field. Both settings can be rewarding in different ways. The extent to which this breadth–depth trade-off is manifested varies depending on institution and research area in academia, or team and project focus in industry. Where your personal preferences fit on the breadth–depth spectrum should help you assess various job opportunities.
- *Autonomy*—Academia offers significant autonomy in terms of what research projects you choose to focus on. In industry, it's expected that you will solve the problems your employer wants you to solve (usually with significant flexibility in terms of how you go about solving it). As I noted in the intro paragraph, the upside to this top-down problem definition is that it comes with the knowledge that what you're working on will have a positive impact in the real world. It should also be noted that there are mechanisms for increased autonomy in industry; many positions have the flexibility for data scientists to propose new areas for future work, and internal or external grant work can open up time and resources for new projects as well.
- *Work–life balance*—My sense from most people who have worked in both worlds and my personal experience so far is that work–life balance tends to be better in industry. In academia, it is generally quite difficult to set boundaries, and it is natural to take work home with you every night and weekend. Although work outside of the standard hours is also common in industry, it's more driven by deadlines and tends to go in phases. The work–life balance you find is extremely dependent on the culture at the particular institution or company, and also on how you personally engage in and contribute to that culture. I've known people in both settings who have found it difficult to manage, and I've known people in both who have successfully found a healthy balance.

9.2   *Becoming productive*

Eventually, you should be making your manager look good and lightening their workload, but in the beginning, you will make it harder, and that's expected. It takes longer than you think to get fully productive. It's normal to feel frustrated during this time, but remember that you're dealing with a lot of cognitive load from being in a new environment. You're trying to pick up on the (likely unspoken) norms about how long people take for lunch, what the working hours are, what forms of communication to use, whether everyone closes their laptop when they walk away from the desk, and more. On top of that, you have a whole data system to get to know.

It's important to stress that it's an easy mistake to make to assume that you have to prove yourself quickly and early, such as "I need to do everything faster, or else they'll wonder why they hired me." This is a case of impostor syndrome (chapter 8). Unless you're in a truly dysfunctional company, it'll expect some ramp-up time. Instead of proving yourself quickly, focus on positioning yourself to deliver value over the longer term (within months, not weeks). Early on, you're going to be asking more of the company ("Can I get access to this? Why is this query so slow?") than you're giving back (in the form of reports, analyses, and models).

That being said, you can still deliver some value early. Focus on simple and entirely descriptive questions, such as "What is the distribution of our client sizes?" or "What percentage of our users are active each week?" In the process, you'll familiarize yourself with the company's data and also find some of the snags and traps that are waiting. During your check-ins with your manager, show off some of your in-progress work so that you can see whether you're headed in the right direction. It's frustrating to put in a lot of time and find yourself answering the wrong question, using a methodology that your boss hates, or that you're using the wrong data source.

Focusing on simpler questions also keeps you from embarrassing yourself by giving an incorrect conclusion because you're trying to answer a complicated question without learning all the details of the data first. This situation can be challenging, because if your stakeholders are new to data science, their first question might be something like "Can you predict which sales deals will close?" or "How can we maximize user retention?" But as we'll talk about in chapter 12, one of your jobs as a data scientist is to dig into the business question to find the data question behind it. If people don't know or have misconceptions about basic facts (such as what percentage of users make a second purchase or how many people click ads), they won't be asking the right questions.

Two strategies can help you become productive more quickly: asking questions and building relationships. Asking questions helps you understand the details of your job more quickly. Building relationships allows you to understand the context of your role in the organization.

9.2.1 *Asking questions*

One of the biggest things that can hold you back in your career is being afraid to ask questions or say "I don't know." As we've said before, data science is such a big field that no one knows everything or even 20% of it! And there's no way you could know all the intricacies of your company's data. Your manager would much rather you ask questions and take up a few minutes of someone's time than be stuck spinning your wheels for days. A helpful question can be anything from a technical question (such as "What statistical test do we use for detecting a change in revenue in an A/B test?") to a business question (such as "Which team is responsible for this product?").

That being said, all questions are not created equal. Here are some suggestions for asking better questions:

- *Try to learn from observation about the question culture at the company.* Do people ask questions in person, on a Slack channel, in forums, or by email? Getting the channel right means that you're less likely to bother someone. You also can ask your manager the meta-question of how to ask questions.

- *It's good to show that you've been proactive.* You might say "I researched this and found these three things" or "This sounds like X. Is it?" By having done some research yourself, you may be able to answer the question on your own, and you'll be able to ask questions with a better understanding of the concept.

- *Don't ask questions when you can find the answers quickly on your own.* Unless the topic comes up while you're working with someone or discussing an issue, you want to avoid asking questions that are answered in the first Stack Overflow result on Google (such as "What's the difference between a vector and a list in R?").

- *Find the experts and be thoughtful about their time.* Although some of your questions will be general, you might also have deeply technical questions. Finding out who are the experts on various statistical or programming methods is important, as those people are generally the ones you need to get answers from. You don't want to be a burden on this type of person (or anyone), so if you realize that you have many questions for a particular person, try to schedule a meeting with them. People are much less likely to feel put-upon if they have a few time-boxed meetings rather than face questions every few minutes. It can also help to ask that person's style. Some people within the company have the role of supporting others, but if that person is also required to have deliverables, see whether they have a calendar that blocks out certain times where they aren't reachable, and respect those times.

- *Avoid voicing criticisms veiled as questions,* such as "Why do you code this request this way instead of the clearly better way I learned in undergrad?" Try to genuinely understand why things are done the way they are. If the company has been around for a while, there's a lot of technical debt. If a large company has physical servers, for example, moving that data to the cloud is more than a half-year of work for dozens of engineers. When people ask "Why don't we just do X? It's so easy and would save us a lot of time," they often assume that other people don't understand the problem or feel that it's urgent. But the reason they're not doing X may be because of things you have no idea about, such as legal constraints.

- *Team up with someone else.* A great way to learn is to pair with people. Instead of just asking questions and getting answers, you can see how people found those answers. For a technical question, pairing with someone is also a way to see their coding environment and learn new techniques. Even if your question is about how to get data, you can learn what table that data is in, how they knew which table, and maybe some coding tricks. Your eventual goal is to be able to answer as many questions yourself as possible by knowing where to look.

- *Make a list.* Finally, if you have questions that don't need an immediate response, try to keep a list of things that might be useful to know, such as how often the data refreshes, the size limit for queries, and how far back certain data goes on the local server. Then go over these items in a block with your mentor or manager. This approach prevents you from interrupting someone over and over, which can become a bother if you're not careful.

9.2.2   *Building relationships*

An important part of feeling comfortable in your new work environment is building a support network. Some people do this more easily than others, but you want to make sure that you engage in some nontechnical talk with people. In most cases, this means setting up meetings with people you've never talked to before to get to know them and their work. This time isn't wasted; it allows both you and your co-workers to feel more comfortable relying on one another if you know more than names and job titles.

Approaching someone you don't know can be daunting, but you can use your questions as a way to start a conversation with someone. People like being helpful and feeling knowledgeable, so don't be afraid to use questions as an in as long as you're polite and friendly in your queries. When you know a few people, even the largest offices feel less intimidating. It's also normal to message people you'll be working closely with to ask whether you can set up a 30-minute meeting to get to know each other. If you work in a large office, ask your manager to make a list of people you should get to know.

In an office of any size, it's good to find out who to go to for specific questions. One person might be the company's best at SQL, and someone else might be in charge of the experimentation system. It's very helpful to know who to turn to when you face a technical hurdle, and that person usually isn't your manager. You also want to at least introduce yourself to your skip-level boss—not so you can tattle on your boss, but because making yourself known to the person will make it easier when they have to discuss you with your boss.

Similarly, you should try to meet all the stakeholders you'll be working with. If the data science team is fewer than ten people, try to meet with all of them individually. If you'll be working with data engineers or other data people, talk with them. These meetings can be informal, but it's important for you not to exist solely as an email signature. Even if you mostly work remotely, try to use a video conferencing system so that people can see your face.

Do a lot of listening, both in official meetings and during social opportunities such as lunch. Meet people who work in data-adjacent areas (which could be everything from engineering to finance to sales operations to marketing analytics), and hear how they currently do their jobs. Don't rush in with a statement like "I could do that better" or make commitments early, such as "We'll build you a machine learning platform to do that." Simply focus on collecting information and thoughts. And don't forget that everything doesn't always need to be about work. It's nice to get to know people on a personal level, whether by asking about their weekend plans, favorite TV shows, or hobbies.

One last word to the wise: befriend the office manager. Office managers control a lot of the things that can make your day better: snacks, the lunch order, what type of hand lotion is in the bathroom, and so on. They also have one of the hardest and most thankless jobs around, so make sure that they feel appreciated.

Mentorship and sponsorship

"Find a mentor" is one of the most common pieces of career advice, but it can be frustratingly inactionable. It's true that having a *mentor*—someone who offers you career advice—can help you solve thorny issues and make better decisions. But unlike learning programming or improving your communication skills, the process of getting a mentor doesn't involve classes you can take or books you can read. So how do you find one?

Fortunately, mentorship doesn't necessarily need to be a long-term relationship. Angela Bassa (whom we interview in chapter 16) put together a list of people who were willing to answer questions and mentor data science newcomers at datahelpers.org. A mentor may not be someone you can call about every career dilemma you face, but you could find one to help with a specific problem you're having, such as practicing behavioral interviews or making your first R package.

One type of person can have even more influence on your career: a sponsor. A *sponsor* is someone who gives people opportunities, whether by funding their project, advocating for their promotion, introducing them to important people, or making sure that they get assigned to the types of challenging projects that can help them grow. Even more than for a mentor, you need to show a sponsor that you'll do a good job with the opportunity they're offering. If someone recommends you to speak at a conference, for example, and you never respond to the organizer or give a clearly unprepared talk, your behavior reflects poorly on the recommender. You don't have to have done the same thing before, but if you can show that you did something similar (such as gave a meetup talk), and if you're responsive and polite in your communications with a sponsor, you can build their confidence that you'll do the job well.

(continued)

If you want someone to be a long-term mentor or sponsor, keep them updated on how you've followed their advice or taken advantage of the opportunity they helped you with. Many people are mentors and sponsors because they want to help people, and it's gratifying for them to hear how you've benefited. And if you never communicate with them except when you need something, they may feel that you're just using them, which no one wants.

A lot of articles about sponsorship and mentorship are about finding those people at your company, which is especially important if you work for a large organization. But it's common for data scientists to change jobs every few years, and the data science community has enough small subpockets that you can start building a positive reputation and find sponsors and mentors outside of your company who will stay with you through multiple jobs.

9.3   *If you're the first data scientist*

Everything up to this point of the chapter applies to the first few months of any data scientist position, but being the first data scientist in an organization provides its own unique set of challenges. Given how new the field is and how many small companies lack data scientists, being the first one isn't uncommon. For those reasons, as the first data scientist in a company, you should be especially prepared when you begin.

When you start your new position, there'll be absolutely no precedents. No one has decided yet whether to use Python, R, or some other programming language. No one has figured out how to manage the work. Should software development practices such as agile be used to decide what to work on, or should you do whatever you feel like that day? How should the code be managed? Should a GitHub professional license be bought or a Microsoft TFS server used, or can you keep all the files in your My Documents folder on your laptop without backups?

Because there are no precedents, everything you do will implicitly become a precedent. If you happen to enjoy doing your work in the obscure programming language F#, for example, you're forcing the next data scientist to learn F#. It's in your best interest to make decisions that will benefit whatever the team looks like down the line, which may mean using a more common programming language than the one that's your favorite. This approach has to be balanced with the fact that focusing too much on the future can cause serious harm to the present. If you spent three months setting up a beautiful pipeline for sharing reports with other data scientists automatically, but the second data scientist isn't hired for five years, that work was a waste. Every day, either directly or indirectly, you'll be making decisions that have large consequences.

Besides having to figure out the role on your own, you have to sell data science to the rest of the organization. Because the company hasn't had data scientists before, most people won't understand why you're around. The faster people get your role, the more likely they are to want to work with you and keep a data scientist around. These conversations are also about managing expectations. As we've discussed before, some people think that data science is basically magic and that their first data scientist can immediately solve some of the company's biggest problems. You'll need to set realistic expectations about (a) what data science is capable of and (b) how quickly those goals can be reached. Therefore, your job will require you to continually explain data science in general to people, as well as what in particular you can do to help the business. Sitting quietly in a corner working on models for months is possibly OK if you're the 20th data scientist on a team, but you certainly can't do that as the first.

Although being the first data scientist is a lot more work and a lot riskier than other positions, it also has great payoffs. By making the technical decisions, you get to choose things that are more in line with what you want. By selling data science to the organization, you get to be better known and more influential. And as the data science team grows, you're in line to be the head of it, which can be great for career growth.

9.4   *When the job isn't what was promised*

Entering a data science job and finding that it's nowhere near what you expected can be crushing. After months of work, you've finally broken into the field, and now you might have to go out and start all over again. Worse, you may worry that leaving quickly will look terrible on your résumé. Does that mean you have to put in a year? Managing a bad environment and deciding whether to leave is challenging. In the following sections, we cover two main categories of problems: the work is terrible, and the work environment is toxic. Although there's no silver bullet to solve these problems, we'll walk through some potential mitigation strategies.

9.4.1   *The work is terrible*

First, take a hard look at your expectations. Is the problem something along the lines of "All my data isn't cleaned! I spent two days just on data prep! The data engineers don't fix everything immediately!" Those problems are going to be part of every data science role. Even data scientists at the biggest companies with hundreds of engineers have these problems; there's so much data that it's impossible for it all to be perfectly vetted. Although the core tables should be clean and well-documented, you'll likely encounter data in your subareas that you need to improve or work with others to collect.

One way to check how realistic your expectations are is to check them with other data scientists. If you graduated with a related degree or a bootcamp, ask your peers or people in the alumni network what they think of the data environment you're working in. If you don't know many data scientists yet, try to go to meetups or join online communities if you're in a small town or rural area. (We covered this topic in depth in chapter 5.) If other data scientists at your company had previous data science jobs, see whether they can give you an idea of how this one compares.

Another situation may be that the work is tedious and boring. The job you got hired to do might have been forecasting, for example, but in practice, all you do is press the rerun button on someone else's existing forecasting model once a month. In that case, see whether you can carve out some side projects in the organization or automate some processes. If the work is boring but not time-consuming, take the opportunity to do things that are related to data science. Continue to build your data science portfolio with side projects, write blog posts, or take online courses. These tactics will help position you for your next role.

Finally, you can learn even from bad jobs. Is there any way you can tailor your job so that you'll do more things from which you can learn? What areas can you improve upon? Maybe your peers won't help you learn how to write better code, but can you learn about what mistakes are easy to make in building a data science team? It's very likely that there are some smart and well-meaning people in your company, so what happened to make the work bad? By learning what you don't like, you'll know what to watch out for in your next job search and be better prepared to avoid mistakes if you ever start your own data science team.

9.4.2   *The work environment is toxic*

Section 9.4.1 discusses a bad but manageable situation. But what if your work is really toxic? What if your manager and stakeholders have completely unrealistic expectations and threaten to fire you because you're not making progress in predicting lifetime value when they have no data for it? Or you get penalized when your answers don't meet the company's expectations? Companies that are new to data science may expect you to sprinkle your data science fairy dust to solve the company's core problems. They may tell you "Build a model to tell whether text is written well"—a problem that no one in the field has even come close to solving. In this case, you need to adjust the company's expectations or risk feeling like a constant underperformer. Speaking up for yourself in this circumstance is difficult, but there are usually reasonable and smart people working at any company. If they say, "If you were a better data scientist, you would be able to do this," that's a huge red flag. Even if a much more experienced data scientist could tackle the problem, the company should have recognized that fact when it was designing and hiring for the role.

Maybe the problem is that people and teams aren't collaborating. Instead of seeing where they can help, teams may be trying to sabotage one another. They focus only on how they can get ahead, and they may even see having success at the company as a zero-sum game: if you or your team is doing well, theirs is losing. Besides creating an unhealthy environment, this situation often leads to a lot of wasted work, as you may end up duplicating someone else's project because they wouldn't share their data or learning with you.

The problem may have nothing to do with the data science part at all; the environment may be sexist, racist, homophobic, or otherwise hostile. There's no reason why you should feel uncomfortable going to work every day. Even if you're not getting openly hostile harassment, being talked over in meetings, being addressed by incorrect pronouns, or being asked "But where are you *really* from?" all add up.

Unfortunately, solving these types of problems usually requires the involvement of top leadership and active engagement from everyone else. But the fact that the workplace is toxic often indicates that leadership is nonexistent or even actively contributing to the problem. If the problem is rooted in one bad person, ideally, others will recognize that fact, and the person will be removed. But if the problem is widespread, it may be close to impossible to change, and trying to change it as a junior employee is a quick recipe for burnout. In these situations, you want to think carefully about whether you need to leave.

9.4.3 Deciding to leave

Deciding whether it's right to leave your job is an extremely personal decision. Although no one can give you a simple flow chart that will make the decision painless and easy, we can offer some questions to think about to guide your decision:

- Do you have enough savings, a partner with a second income who can support you, or family members whom you can ask for a loan if you leave without having another job?
- Is your job affecting your health or life outside work?
- If the issue is the work, have you talked with your manager about the issues and tried to resolve them?
- Is it possible to switch teams or roles—if not now, within a few months?

If the answers to these questions make you feel that you need to leave, one option is to start looking for other jobs immediately. But you may worry about how having a short job stint on your résumé will look or how you'd explain it to interviewers. If you've been on the job for only a few weeks, and you came to it directly from your last job, consider getting in touch with your previous manager. It's likely that your position hasn't been filled yet, and if you left on a good note, you may be able to go back.

If you're looking for a new job, here are a few tips on talking about your short stint during your interview:

- *Wait for the interviewer to bring up the subject.* Don't feel that you need to talk about it proactively; it may not be a concern, especially because the company is clearly interested. (You've reached the interview stage!)
- *Find some positive experience and learning from the job you can talk about.* Those experiences and lessons may be a project you worked on, exposure to the industry, or guidance from a senior leader.
- *When asked why you left so soon, keep it short and neutral.* You're in a difficult situation because you want to be honest about why you left and about how it wasn't through any fault of your own, but if you're too open and honest, the interviewer may unfairly perceive you as difficult to work with. Thus, your best bet is to give a vague "The requirements of my job weren't what I expected, and I wasn't able to use my skills and expertise to benefit the company" and leave it at that. If you've learned something about the type of work environment you want, share it. Maybe you were the first data scientist at a company, and you realized that you want to be a part of a larger team.

If you've decided to leave, check out chapter 15 for information on how to do so gracefully, including searching for a new job while you're working full-time and leaving on a good note.

But maybe you can't leave because your visa is tied to your workplace or the company is the only one doing data science in your small town. If that's your situation, here are some tips:

- *Remember that you are not your job.* You don't have to take responsibility for poor decisions that the company makes. Unless you're in a leadership position, you likely have little control over what the company does.
- *Try to keep yourself healthy.* Don't sacrifice sleep, exercise, and time with friends and family members.
- *Talk to someone.* Maybe that person is a partner, a friend, or a therapist. They may have advice to give, but just listening to you will help.
- *Think about reporting personal harassment.* If you're being harassed by a specific person, consider reporting them to your human resources department. Make sure that you document your reporting. Don't drop by human resources in person; send emails and get emails back so that you have a record of the process. Eventually, you may want to point out certain things that were said to you, and having a written record will be helpful. If the company does nothing, you can file a claim with the Equal Employment Opportunity Commission if you're in the United States. Unfortunately, reporting harassment is not without risk: although it's illegal to do so, companies have retaliated against employees for reporting by stalling their career growth or even firing them. Even if you don't want to report harassment, consider keeping documentation of any harassment you experience in case you decide to report it later.
- *See whether you can think outside the box about leaving the company.* Maybe you feel that you can't leave because the only options available to you are going to a less-prestigious company, getting a lower title, or temporarily depleting your savings. But don't underestimate the negative effects of staying in a toxic environment: if you can make a short-term sacrifice to leave, leaving will likely be worthwhile in the long term.

We hope that you'll never be in this type of situation, but it's handy to have a little "Break glass in case of emergency" information somewhere. Keep in mind that switching jobs in the data science field is common (as we discuss further in chapter 15), so there's no career reason to stay in a workplace that makes you uncomfortable.

9.5   *Interview with Jarvis Miller, data scientist at Spotify*

Jarvis Miller works as a data scientist in the Personalization Mission at Spotify, focusing on improving the listening experience for each user. When this interview was conducted, he was working as a data scientist at BuzzFeed. He graduated in 2018 with a master's degree in statistics.

What were some things that surprised you in your first data science job?

Two things that surprised me were how much I could improve as a writer and how I needed to explain my data science contribution to the business without using jargon. I had this idea that because stakeholders had been working with data scientists, they have learned to understand the language, and thus, I didn't really have to change the way I explained things. I realized that that's absolutely not the case, and I can't simply say, "I ran a logistic regression on this data to classify . . ." On the being-a-better-writer side, I've begun to flesh out the story when I write a report; improve my data storytelling abilities; and explain things in a way to where product managers, designers, and stakeholders who aren't in tech at all can understand what I'm saying.

I came from academia, where I felt it was all about whether you found the result at the end of the day; it didn't matter whether you started working right before the deadline or if you planned way ahead. In industry, you have a big overall goal, but you figure out how to break it down into versions. You get the first version working, ship it, learn about whether it's doing well or not, and maybe improve it in a future quarter. I was used to going until it is done. But here, I had to learn how to prioritize parts of a project and then wrap it up. I learned to document what I had done and what there is to do in the next version; and then make it shareable, whether that's by putting a report into a shared folder or making an app so people can use my work and see what it's supposed to do.

What are some issues you faced?

Speaking out was something I really struggled with. When I started, I was doing an isolated project, and the person I reported to was in New York, and I was in LA. If I was confused, I didn't know whether I should message them immediately or save it for our meeting. I knew I didn't want to be derailed by something that was blocking my work, but I wasn't even sure when something was a blocker. I think this is a common problem for data scientists, especially for those in marginalized groups or who switched from a different field. They may feel like because they're new or not experts, they can't express displeasure or voice an opinion. If I could go back, I would have a conversation sooner about how I'm feeling isolated and how I'm not sure how communication works at this company.

Can you tell us about one of your first projects?

One of them was to revamp our A/B testing platform, which was a very broad problem. I started by getting a list of people to talk with about what they did at BuzzFeed, how they worked, and how A/B testing fit into that workflow. We then discussed the specific tool: what did they dislike and why, and what was their workflow when using it? Unfortunately, this led to the issue of taking on too much. A lot of people had multiple suggestions, and I gave them all equal weight, which ended up with 50 big things that I needed to do. But my manager asked me to break those suggestions up into the must-haves and the nice-to-haves, including the reasons why these were prioritized the way they were. He suggested listing the overall goal of the project and giving ideas weights based on their contribution towards the goal and how long they would take.

What would be your biggest piece of advice for the first few months?

Remember that you've been hired for a reason: they respect your point of view, and they think they can help you learn and that they can learn from you. If you have an opinion, try and let someone know. If you hate speaking in a big group, maybe message one person, run it through with them, and bounce ideas back and forth before you express it in front of the larger group.

This doesn't just apply for the technical side of the job. For me, in the first few minutes of my one-on-one with my manager, I don't want to immediately jump into what I've done. I want to have a few minutes to have a casual conversion to destress and clear my mind. I know that this helps my productivity, and my company wants me to be productive, so I should let them know. Your opinion is valued, and it's worth sharing, especially if it's about how you like to be treated or how you can be most productive and flourish in this role, because they don't know you like you know yourself, and your being productive will benefit everyone.

Summary

- Don't worry about becoming fully productive right away. Instead, focus on building relationships, tools, and your understanding of the data, which will make you productive in the long term.
- If you're in a bad work situation, try to work to get control to mitigate the impact on your health and career.

10

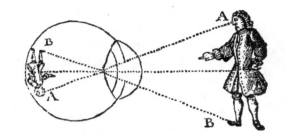

Making an effective analysis

This chapter covers

- Planning an analysis
- Thinking through code, data, and project structure
- Delivering the analysis to the client

This chapter is written in the context of data scientists who focus on decision science and analytics—people who use data to provide ideas and suggestions to the business. Although machine learning engineers also have to do analysis before building and deploying models, some of the content around stakeholder management with pretty visualizations is less relevant. If you're a machine learning engineer and you're reading this book, don't worry; this chapter is still plenty relevant to you, and you'll love chapter 11, which covers deploying models into production.

The backbone of many data science jobs is making *analyses*: brief documents that use data to try to explain a business situation or solve a business problem. Modern companies are built on reporting and analyses. People who make decisions aren't comfortable doing so without data to back up their choices, and data scientists are some of the best people to find meaning in the data. Analyses are also important for building machine learning tools, because before a machine learning model can be built, the context of the dataset needs to be understood. Crafting an analysis that can take the vast amount of company data and convert it into a concise result that clarifies the matter at hand is extremely difficult and practically an art. How can a person be expected to take tables with millions of records on historical information, each with complexities and nuances within them, and turn that into a definitive "Yes, the data says this idea is good"? The act of figuring out what is meaningful mathematically, what the business cares about, and how to bridge the gap between the two is not something you should expect to know how to do naturally.

In this chapter, we'll go through the basics of how to build an analysis so that you understand how to provide meaningful analyses to the company. By using the skills in the chapter, you should be able to grow more quickly in your data science career.

What is an analysis, really? An analysis is typically a PowerPoint deck, a PDF or Word file, or an Excel spreadsheet that can be shared with non-data scientists, containing insights from data and visualizations displaying them. Figure 10.1 is an example of a slide that could be found in an analysis. An analysis generally takes on the order of one to four weeks to make, with a data scientist having to collect data, run code for statistical methods on it, and make the final result. When completed, the code is not touched until the analysis must be rerun months later, or possibly never. Example analyses include

- Analyzing customer survey data to see which products have highest satisfaction
- Looking at data on the locations that orders are being made from to pick out the location of a new factory
- Using historical airline industry data to predict which cities will need more routes to them

These examples have varying levels of technical complexity; some require only summarizing and visualizing data, whereas others need optimization methods or machine learning models, but all of them answer a one-time question.

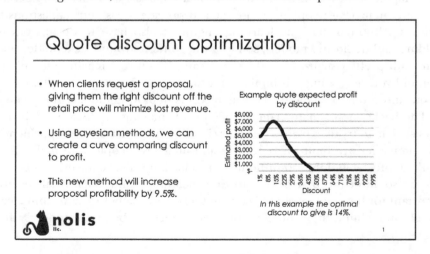

Figure 10.1   An example slide of an analysis PowerPoint deck

Reporting versus making an analysis

A report and an analysis are similar but not the same. A *report* is something that is generated on a recurring basis without much structural change between versions. The monthly financial report, for example, may be a large Excel spreadsheet that updates with new numbers each month. The point of a report is to keep people aware of how metrics are changing. An analysis is something that is done on a one-time basis to answer a deeper question. A customer acquisition analysis may be work done in R on how new customers are purchasing products, with the results put into a PowerPoint presentation. Reports tend to be filled with numbers and metrics, whereas analyses focus on providing a single main result. Most of the traits of a good analysis hold for a good report, so in this chapter, we use analysis to mean both unless explicitly stated otherwise.

So what makes a good analysis? A good analysis has these five traits:

- *It answers the question.* An analysis starts with someone asking a question, so for the analysis to be meaningful, it needs to provide an answer. If the question proposed was "Which of these two websites causes more customers to buy products?", the analysis should show which website causes more sales. That answer could even be "We don't have enough information to tell," but it must be a direct response to the question.
- *It is made quickly.* Answers to business questions will influence decisions that have deadlines. If the analysis takes too long to create, the decision will be made without the analysis. A common expectation is that the analysis will be complete within a month.
- *It can be shared.* The analysis needs to be shared, not only with the person who asked for the analysis to be done, but also with whomever that person wants to share it with. If the analysis involves a plot, for example, the plot can't just live within an R or Python script; it has to be in a format that people can digest, such as PowerPoint.
- *It is self-contained.* Because you can't predict who will see the analysis, it needs to be understandable on its own. Plots and tables have to have clear descriptions, axes should be labeled, explanations in the analysis should be written down, and the analysis should avoid referencing other work if possible.
- *It can be revisited.* Most questions will be asked again in the future. Sometimes, answering them means doing exactly the same work again, such as rerunning a clustering. Sometimes, you have to use the approach somewhere else, such as changing the input data from European customers to Asian customers.

These traits aggregate to the general theme "A good analysis is something that helps non-data scientists do their job."

The rest of this chapter is structured to cover the steps of an analysis chronologically, starting with the initial request for the analysis and ending with the reports being handed over. Although not every analysis will follow these steps, most will (or should). As you become more familiar with making analyses, you may feel inclined to skip some steps, but those shortcuts are the very actions that cause senior data scientists to make mistakes.

> **Analyses for different types of data scientists**
>
> Depending on your role as a data scientist, the situations where you'll be doing analyses will vary greatly:
>
> - *Decision scientist*—For these types of data scientists, making analyses is the core function of the job. Decision scientists are continually diving into the data to answer questions, and those questions need to be communicated to the business. An analysis is the key tool for doing so.
> - *Machine learning engineer*—Although a machine learning engineer focuses on creating and deploying models, analyses are still useful tools for sharing how well the models are performing. Analyses are used to show the value in building a new model or how the models change over time.
> - *Analyst*—Analysts, who are data scientists who focus heavily on metrics and KPIs for the business, usually find themselves making lots of reports. They create a stream of recurring data for the company, often in Excel, SQL, R, or Python. Although these analytics experts will make analyses, they need to think about the maintainability of the work more than the other roles because they have to repeat it so often.

10.1 The request

An analysis starts with a request for an answer to a business question. A person from a different part of the business or your manager will come to you with a question like "Can you look into why widget sales were low in Europe in December?" or "Do our small-business customers behave differently from our larger ones?" Depending on the level of technical expertise of the person asking, you may get an ill-defined request ("Why are sales down?") or a precise one ("What attributes are correlated with a lower average order value?").

The analysis is formed around the business question, but you can't do data science on a business question. Data science questions are things like "How do you cluster these data points?" and "How do we forecast sales?" The data scientist has to do the job of converting that business question into a data science question, answering the data science question, and returning a business answer. This job is a tricky one. Understanding how data science questions and business questions relate requires a combination of experience with the type of problem at hand and an understanding of how the results of different statistical methods could potentially be useful. This workflow of business questions to data science question-and-answer and finally back to a business answer was devised by Renee Teate, who is also interviewed in chapter 14 of this book.

Figure 10.2 shows this process graphically. The business question comes from the stakeholders, who want to know how to target marketing to different customers. The data scientist has to figure out what that request means in mathematical terms—in this example, a clustering of the customer data. When the process is complete, the data scientist has a data science answer (such as a set of three groups of clustered data points). Finally, the data scientist has to convert that answer back into something the business would understand, like groups such as "new customers" or "high spenders."

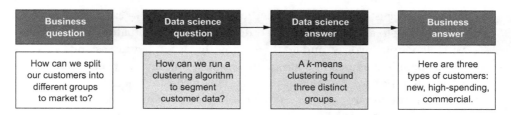

Figure 10.2 The process of answering a business question with data science, devised by Renee Teate

Before you start looking at data and writing code to solve a data science question, you have to do foundational work to best understand the business question. You need to understand what the context is for the analysis so that you can best deliver something helpful. Who is asking for the analysis to be done, and what is their relationship to their team? What is their motive? Do they have a very specific question they want answered or a vague, general idea of a problem and a hope that data could be useful for it? Does it seem like you might even have the data to solve this problem? If not, what would it take to get it? Asking questions not only helps you understand how to solve the problem, but also helps you understand what it will be used for. Many data scientists have spent weeks on analyses only to discover that there was no need for it, because the stakeholder was "just curious."

These questions are generally answered in a 30- to 60-minute kickoff meeting with the person making the request, plus anyone else involved in the work. As the person doing the analysis, you may not be the one to organize a meeting, but if you don't seem to have one on your calendar, scheduling one is worthwhile. If you haven't met the person who's requesting the analysis before, this meeting is a good time to make an introduction and learn about their work.

A hypothetical example set of foundational knowledge would be something like this:

- *Who's requesting the analysis?* Julia from the widget product team requested it.
- *What's the motive?* Widget sales are down 10 percent this month, and the business team doesn't know why.
- *What's the request?* The team wants to use data to see whether the widget-sales dip was focused in one part of the country.

- *What decision will be made?* The decision is whether the widget product should be discontinued or not.
- *Do we have the required data?* Yes, the analysis needs customer orders by shipping zip code, which is available in the order database.

Knowing whether you have data that could plausibly answer the question is *really* important. The last thing you want to do is spend several weeks working on an analysis, only to have to return to the stakeholder without anything they could use.

An example of a situation in which you wouldn't have data would be something like the following: at a retail company, the stakeholder wants to know how many orders each customer made, but because customers pay in cash, there is no way to use existing data to tell who made each order. In this type of situation, it's best to be up-front with all people involved and let them know that what they are asking for isn't possible. Other people may propose alternative ways to use data that may be close enough to what you hoped for, or you may have to explain why the alternatives won't work either. If at all possible, propose a plan that could get the required data someday. In the preceding example, a loyalty program would allow orders to be associated with a particular customer and thereby fix the data problem, although that program would take time to create.

The other questions, such as who the person is and why they are making the request, are useful for creating the analysis plan.

10.2 *The analysis plan*

For data scientists, nothing is more fun than diving right into some data to answer questions. Let's load data! Group it! Summarize it! Fit a model and plot results! Unfortunately, with there being an infinite number of ways to summarize and model data, you can spend weeks working with data only to discover that nothing you've produced answers the business question that was proposed. The realization that you haven't done something relevant is *the worst*. And it happens frequently to data scientists, especially junior ones who haven't been burned too many times.

One solution to this problem is to have a guardrail in place that keeps you on track and doing work that's relevant. An analysis plan is that guardrail. The idea is that before you start looking at data, you write down everything you plan to do with the data. Then, as your analysis progresses, you keep track of how much of the plan you've completed. When you've done everything on the plan, you're done! You not only have a way of knowing whether you're off the plan, but also have a tool for tracking progress and keeping yourself accountable. You can even use it in meetings with your manager to discuss how things are going.

When making an analysis plan, you want to have the work in the plan be actionable. "Make a linear regression on sales by region" is something you can write code to do, whereas "Find out why sales are down" isn't something you can just do; it's the result of doing other things. If the tasks in the plan are actionable, it'll be easy to tell whether you are making progress. It will also make doing the analysis easier, because you won't have to worry about what to do next. Instead, you'll be able to look at the analysis plan and select the next task to do.

For making your first few analysis plans, we strongly recommend using the following template:

- *The top*—List the title of the analysis, who you are (in case the analysis will be shared with others), and the objective of the analysis.
- *Sections*—Each section should be a general topic in the analysis. The analysis work done within each section should be self-contained (not relying on the work of other sections), so it should be possible for a different person to do each section. Each section should have a list of tasks.
- *First level of section lists*—The first level of the section lists should be each question that was posed. This section will help everyone remember why you're doing that specific work, and if all the questions are successfully answered, the topic of the main section should be considered to be understood.
- *Second level of section lists*—The second level of the lists should have the actual tasks to do that can be checked off as the work is being done. These tasks could be types of models to run, for example, and the descriptions should be specific enough so that at any time, you could concretely say whether the work has been completed.

Figure 10.3 shows an example analysis plan, in this case for assessing why customers are leaving in the North American region. At the top are the title, objective, and contact information of the data scientist in case the material is passed around. Each section of the plan covers a different component of the analysis (e.g., either analyzing within North America or comparing to other regions). The subsections (numbered) are questions in the analysis, and the lowest section (lettered) are the specific tasks to be done.

North American Customer Churn Analysis

August McNamara (amcnamara@company.com), May 2020

Objective: to understand why North American customers are joining at a lower rate than in other regions.

Intra-North America analysis

1. Are there attributes within North American customers that relate to new customer acquisition?
   a. Regression model on last month's new North American customers – customer spend and demographic attributes to find importance
   b. Extend part (a) to compare between customers acquired in each month over the past year
2. How much has the acquisition rate been changing over time?
   a. Time series analysis of acquisition rate across the region
   b. Split time series by country / state and look for correlations

Compare North America to other regions

1. How similar are North American customers to other regions?
   a. Generalized linear model with region as an attribute to model acquisition
   b. Create visualization of global map colored by acquisition rate

Figure 10.3   An example analysis plan

When you make your analysis plan, share it with your manager and the stakeholder making the request. They should either give suggestions on how to improve it or approve of the work. An approved analysis plan provides an agreed-upon foundation for the work. If, after you do the analysis, the stakeholder asks why you did things that way, you can refer to the analysis plan and the original goals.

It's likely that as you do the analysis, you'll realize that you left something important out of the analysis plan or have a new idea that you hadn't considered before. That's totally fine; just update the plan and let the stakeholder know that you're making the change. Because you have time constraints, you may have to remove a less-important task from the existing plan. But again, the analysis plan is useful because it creates a conversation around what to remove instead of making you attempt to do an impossible amount of work.

10.3   Doing the analysis

With signoff on the analysis plan, you can get started on the analysis itself! The work starts with importing data so that you can manipulate and clean it. Then you repeatedly transform the data by summarizing, aggregating, modifying, visualizing, and modeling it. When the data is ready, you communicate that work to others.

In the following sections, we briefly cover some of the considerations you should keep in mind while doing an analysis in a work environment. Whole books dedicated to this topic can also teach you the code for conducting the analysis in the language of your choice.

10.3.1   Importing and cleaning data

Before you can tackle the questions on your analysis plan, you need to have the data in a place where you can manipulate it and in a format you can use. That usually means being able to load it in R or Python but could include using SQL or other languages. Almost always, this task will take you more time than you expect. Many surprises can appear in the process. A few of these many horrors are

- Issues with connecting to company databases in your particular integrated development environment (IDE)
- Issues with incorrect datatypes (such as numbers as strings)
- Issues with weird time formats ("year-day-month" instead of "year-month-day")
- Data that requires formatting (perhaps every order id started with "ID-," and you need to remove that)
- Records that are missing in the data

What's worse, none of this work looks productive to nontechnical people; you can't show the stakeholder a compelling graph of how you got a database driver working, nor would they understand that string manipulation helps them with their business problem. So as tedious as this task is, you want to get moving to doing the data exploration quickly.

When working through importing and tidying the data, consider that you have a dual mandate: spend as little time as possible on anything that won't be needed and as much time as possible on work that will help down the line. If you have a column of dates that are stored as strings and doubt that you'll ever need that column, don't spend time changing the strings to the right date and time format. On the other hand, if you do think you'd need that column, definitely do the work as soon as possible, because you want to have a clean set of data for your analysis. It's hard to tell in advance what will be useful, but if you find yourself spending a lot of time on something, ask yourself whether you really need it.

When importing and tidying data, you may find yourself stuck for multiple days on a single issue, such as connecting to a database. If you find yourself in this situation, you have three options: (1) ask for help, (2) find a way to make the problem something you can avoid entirely, or (3) keep trying to fix the issue yourself. Option (1) is great if you can do it: a senior person may be able to find a quick fix, and you can learn from what they did. Option (2) is great too; doing something like using a flat .csv file instead of a database connection will get you going to the analysis, which provides the business value. Option (3)—keep trying and trying—is something you should avoid at all costs. If you spend days and days on a single issue, you'll look like you aren't able to deliver value. If something is insurmountable to you, discuss with your manager what to do; don't just keep trying and hope that somehow the problem will solve itself.

After you've loaded the data and formatted it, you may start using it and find weird data. *Weird data* is anything that is outside basic assumptions. If you were looking at historical airline flight data, for example, and found some flights that landed before they took off, that would be weird, because generally, airplanes take off first! Other weirdness could be anything from a store selling items that have a negative price to manufacturing data showing that one factory made a thousand times more items than an otherwise-similar factory. These sorts of weird artifacts show up all the time in real-world data, and there is no way to predict them until you look at the data yourself.

If you find yourself in a situation in which you have weird data, don't ignore it! The worst thing you can do is assume that the data is fine and then, after weeks of analysis work, find out that the data wasn't fine and have your work go to waste. Instead, talk to either your stakeholder or someone who's responsible for the data you're using and ask whether they are aware of the weirdness. In many cases, they already know about it and suggest that you ignore it. In the airline-data example, you may be able to just remove the data for flights that landed before taking off.

If it turns out that the weirdness was unknown and could jeopardize the analysis, you need to investigate ways to salvage it. If you're going to do an analysis comparing revenue and costs, and weirdly, half of your data is missing costs, you need to see whether you can work with the existing costs alone or with revenue alone. In a way, this approach becomes an analysis within an analysis; you're making a mini-analysis to see whether the original analysis is even feasible.

10.3.2 Data exploration and modeling

During the data exploration and modeling part of the analysis, you go through the analysis plan point by point and try to complete the work. The following sections provide a general framework tackling each point.

USE GENERAL SUMMARIZATION AND TRANSFORMATION

The vast majority of analysis work can be completed by summarizing and transforming data. Questions such as "How many customers did we have each month?" can be answered by taking customer data, grouping it at the month level, and then counting the distinct number of customers in each month. This technique requires no statistical methods or machine learning models—merely transformations.

It is easy to view this as not really data science because it doesn't require anything beyond a lot of arithmetic, but often doing the transformations in the right way is immensely valuable. Most other people in the company don't have access to the data in the first place, don't have the ability to do the transformations effectively, or wouldn't know the right transformations to do.

Depending on the data, you may want to throw in some statistical methods, such as finding values at different percentile levels or computing a standard deviation.

VISUALIZE THE DATA OR CREATE SUMMARY TABLES

After doing the appropriate transformations, create visualizations or summary tables to better see what is happening in the data. Continuing the earlier example, if you had the number of customers each month, you could create a bar plot to see how they have changed. This plot can make it easy to see what patterns are in the data in a way that you couldn't merely by printing a data frame to a screen.

Figure 10.4 shows an example summary visualization showing the overall customer count each month. With this graph, people can easily see that the customer count is trending slightly upward.

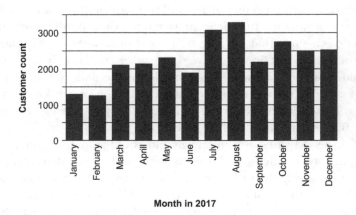

Figure 10.4 An example summary table

The actual visualization you choose depends highly on the data at hand. You may want to use a line graph, a box plot, or any of many other choices. You may also make summary data tables instead of a chart, depending on what you are trying to understand. Consult the resources section at the end of this part of the book for resources that can help you choose the right kind of plot for your data. Note that as you make the visualization, you may realize that you need to change some steps in the transformation. You'll likely go back and forth between steps many times.

Because you'll be iterating through visualizations and continuously transforming the data, you'll have to balance your desire to delete the mediocre ones to keep your code clean with a desire to save everything in case you need it again. The best practice is to save as much as possible, provided that (1) your old code doesn't break after you make further changes, and (2) you can clearly denote which results are "the good ones." Avoid keeping code that doesn't work in your analysis or massive areas of code that are commented out; those situations make maintaining the code enormously difficult. This approach is further enchanced by using version control such as git and GitHub; by continuously making commits every time you add new content to the analysis, you'll be able to keep a log of what you've done and roll back code that suddenly breaks things.

CREATE A MODEL AS NEEDED

If you see patterns in your data that suggest modeling is a good idea, do it! Maybe it makes sense to apply a time-series model to the customer counts to predict next year's customers, for example. When creating models, you'll want to output results and visualize them to understand how accurate or useful the models are. You might create plots that compare the predicted results with the actual values or show metrics such as accuracy scores and feature importance values.

If you create machine learning models that may be used outside the analysis, such as by potentially being put into production (which chapter 11 covers), make sure that you are isolating the code that builds the model from the general analysis work. Because in the future, you'll want to use only the model, you'll need to easily be able to pull that code out from the code that makes the general visualization charts.

REPEAT

You should complete these steps for each point of the analysis plan. During the steps, you may have a new idea about what to analyze or realize that what you thought was a reasonable question doesn't make sense. This is when you should adjust your analysis plan and continue your work.

It's likely that the different analysis plan points are related, so the code you used at one point will be repeated in another. It's worthwhile to put effort into structuring your analysis plan so that you can run the same code repeatedly, and updates to one part of the plan instantly roll out to the others. Your goal is to make a set of code you can maintain; you can easily modify it without spending a ton of time keeping track of complex code.

10.3.3 *Important points for exploring and modeling*

The work of data exploration and modeling is extremely dependent on the problem you are trying to solve. The mathematical and statistical techniques you'd use for trying to cluster data are quite different from those for making a prediction or trying to optimize a decision. That being said, following some broad guidelines can make the difference between an OK analysis and a great one.

FOCUS ON ANSWERING THE QUESTION

As discussed in section 10.2, it's extremely easy to waste time by doing work that doesn't support the goal. If you're analyzing customer orders to see whether you can predict when a customer will never come back, you may get a neural network model working decently and then spend multiple weeks tuning the hyperparameters. If the stakeholder wants only a yes or no answer on whether the model is feasible in the first place, tuning hyperparameters to make the model slightly more efficient doesn't help. The weeks spent on hyperparameter tuning could have instead been spent on something more relevant.

When doing the analysis, it's important to stay focused on the analysis plan and answering the question that the business asked. That means continually asking yourself "Is this relevant?" That question should be something you consider every time you make a plot or table. If you find yourself repeatedly thinking that what you're doing is relevant, that's great. In the much-more-likely instance in which you occasionally find yourself thinking "This plot (or table) isn't useful," you may have to adjust your work. First, try stopping what you're doing and taking a different approach to the problem. If you were trying to group customers by their spend, try doing a clustering instead. By taking a dramatically different approach, you're more likely to succeed than by changing what you're doing only slightly. Second, talk to your manager or the project stakeholder; it could be that the data you are using isn't effective for solving the problem at hand.

Over the course of the weeks in which you do the analysis, you should be steadily building a collection of results that are truly relevant and (ideally) follow the analysis plan.

USE SIMPLE METHODS INSTEAD OF COMPLEX ONES

Complex methods are so exciting! Why use a linear regression when you can use a random forest? Why use a random forest when you can use a neural network? These methods are shown to perform better than a plain ol' regression or k-means clustering, and they're more interesting. So when people ask you to solve business questions with data, surely you should deliver the best methods possible.

Unfortunately, complex methods come with many drawbacks that aren't visible from focusing solely on their accuracy. When you're doing an analysis, the goal isn't to get the best possible accuracy or prediction; it's to answer a question in a way that a businessperson is able to understand. That means you need to explain why you got the result you did. With a simple linear regression, it's easy to provide plots of how much each feature contributed to the result, whereas with other methods, it can be very difficult to describe how the model produced the result, which makes it harder for a businessperson to believe your results. More-complicated methods are also more time-intensive to set up; it takes a while to tune and run a neural network, whereas a linear regression is pretty quick.

So when you're doing your analysis, choose simple methods as often as possible, both in models and in transformations and aggregations. Rather than pruning some percentage of outliers, for example, do a logarithmic transformation or take the median instead of the mean. If a linear regression works reasonably well, don't spend time building a neural network to improve accuracy slightly. Sticking to simple methods whenever possible makes the result much easier for other people to understand and for you to defend and debug.

CONSIDER PLOTS FOR EXPLORATION VS PLOTS FOR SHARING

There are two different reasons why a data scientist would choose to visualize data: for exploration and for sharing. When you're making a plot for exploration, the point is to help the data scientist understand what is happening in the data. Having a complicated and poorly labeled graph is fine so long as the data scientist understands it. When you're making a plot for sharing, the goal is for someone who doesn't know much about the data to get a specific point that a data scientist is trying to make. Here, the plot must be simple and clear to be effective. When making an analysis, you should use lots of exploratory plots, but those plots shouldn't be used for sharing.

Consider an example based on fictional data about pet names in a city: a data scientist wants to understand whether the letter a pet name starts with relates to the species of the pet (cat or dog). The data scientist loads up the data and makes this visualization, showing for each letter the split of cats and dogs whose names start with that letter (figure 10.5).

If you look closely at figure 10.5, you'll notice that the T bar has a much higher number of cats than dogs—a meaningful finding for the data scientist. That being said, this plot isn't something you'd want to show to a stakeholder; a lot is going on in the plot, and it isn't clear what the point is at first glance.

Figure 10.6 shows the same data plotted in a different, more shareable way. In this version, it's clear that cats have a 12% chance of having a name that starts with T, whereas dogs have only a 5% chance. Now this same data is something that could be shared.

CONTINUOUSLY READY TO SHARE

The result of the analysis can take different forms, and which form to choose is typically based on the target audience. If the analysis is to be handed to businesspeople, a slide deck or editable document is often used. PowerPoint or Word (or Google Slides or Google Docs) is a good choice, because anyone can view it (as long as they have the Microsoft Office suite for the first two), and it can include lots of charts, tables, and

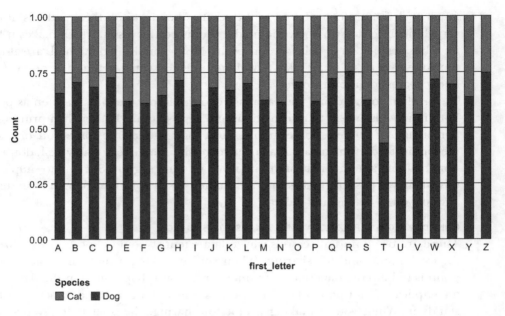

Figure 10.5   Example of a visualization made during an analysis before cleaning

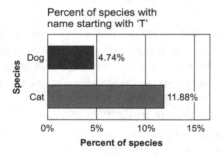

Figure 10.6   The same data as figure 10.5, plotted to highlight the importance of the letter T

text descriptions. If the analysis is for technical people, you could hand over a Jupyter Notebook or R Markdown output HTML file. These methods are good because they usually require less work to polish (that is, you don't need to spend time aligning figures on a slide). If the analysis requires handing over many tables of data to financial people, Excel may be the best choice. Excel is a great tool when the end user needs to take the numbers in the results and do further calculations on them. You should decide early in the analysis-making process what kind of output you expect to deliver to avoid rework later.

Depending on how big the scope of the analysis is, you'll want to check in periodically with the person for whom you are making the analysis and show them your work. This approach prevents the terrible situation in which you spend weeks working on an analysis in isolation, and when it's time to hand it over, the stakeholder points out something that invalidates all your work (such as "You looked at customer sales but forgot to consider returns."). In a situation like this, had that item been pointed out in the beginning, you'd be able to avoid having to throw away lots of work. In addition to avoiding bad situations, the stakeholder can often contribute by suggesting possible areas to focus on or methods to try. In a sense, checking in with your stakeholder throughout the making of the analysis is similar to the software development concept of agile: continuously putting out improvements to the work rather than making one massive software release.

Frequent check-ins with stakeholders are great, but data scientists often neglect to do them. The downside of having a check-in with someone is that the work has to be able to be shown to a non-data scientist; it has to be at a sufficient level of polish that it's not embarrassing to show. Things such as plots with clear labels and meaning, code with minimal errors, and a basic story behind what's happening are all required. So it's easy for a data scientist to think "I'll put off sharing my work until I polish it, and I'll put off polishing it until later." Don't do this! It'll almost always end up being more work in the long run. By continuously maintaining a level of polish so that you can share your code, you end up with a better product.

ONE-BUTTON RUN

Just as it should take running only one script to load and prepare your data, your analysis should take a one-button press to run. In Python, this means having a Jupyter Notebook that automatically loads the data and does the analysis without error. In R, have an R Markdown file that loads the data, analyzes it, and outputs an HTML file, Word document, or PowerPoint deck.

When doing the analysis, you'll want to avoid running too much code outside the script or running your scripts out of order. These practices make it more likely that when you rerun the whole script, it will have an error. It's okay to do a bit of ad-hoc coding, but just make sure that you can rerun your file without errors. This practice will help you keep your results continuously ready to share with other people and ensure that you spend less time fixing the script at the end of the analysis.

10.4 *Wrapping it up*

Depending on the stakeholder for this analysis, the output of your code may be enough to satisfy the request, or you may have to go further and make a final version. If a polished, final version is required, such as a PowerPoint presentation, you may need to do a final level of polishing beyond what you did while making the analysis so that you adhere to company style guidelines. Most importantly, you'll need to craft a narrative for the final document so that people who weren't involved in the work can fully understand the conclusions of the work, what was done, and why.

Making that narrative is the first step in a good final document. What kind of story are you going to tell? How are you going to introduce the problem, explain how your work provides a solution (or doesn't), and discuss the next steps? There are many ways to create a narrative, but one simple way is to think about how you'd explain the work out loud to a person who hasn't seen it before. Think about the story you would tell them, and try to tell that story through your document. Repeatedly ask yourself these questions: "Is what I am showing going to be understandable to my audience?" and "What can I do to improve this?" Eventually, you'll get to a point at which you're happy with your content.

You'll also need to add text to your document—usually to explain the narrative you have or why each graph is worth sharing. Again, try to make it understandable to someone who doesn't have the context you have. Have the text answer the question "How is what I am showing useful for the business?" Different companies have different standards for how much text to include; some want detailed descriptions explaining everything, whereas other companies are happy with a few words. Try to err on the side of overexplaining, because you can cut content later.

When you think your material is ready, you'll want to have some peer review to check for small mistakes before sending it to the stakeholder. Consider having someone on your team who's familiar with the context of the work check it to see whether everything makes sense. Depending on your company, your manager may require you to do this with them so that they can give you a sign-off.

10.4.1 Final presentation

When you have sign-off on your analysis from your manager, you should set up a meeting with the stakeholder to deliver your analysis in person. In this meeting, you'll want to walk them through each component, describing what you did, what you learned, and what you chose not to look into. You will have spent so much time with the data creating the analysis that you should be pretty comfortable explaining it and answering questions.

Depending on the stakeholder, you may find yourself being peppered with questions throughout your presentation, or the person may save questions until the end. Questions may range from calm and curious ("Why did you use dataset X instead of dataset Y?") to critical and concerned ("Why don't these results align with the other team's work? Are there errors in your code?"). How you should handle questions is in many ways the same as answering questions during job interviews (chapter 7): be up-front with what you know and what you don't know. It's okay to say that you need to look into something. As much as possible, be open with your reasoning ("We used dataset X because it covered the time period we cared about"), and when you don't know something ("I'm not sure why they don't align with the other team; I'll look into that"). That being said, most of the time, these meetings are calm and conflict-free!

No matter how good your analysis is, you will inevitably get a question of the form "Well, what about _____?", in which the blank is something you didn't look at in your analysis. Someone might ask "Well, what about if you only use the last month's data in the analysis?" This is a natural thing for people to do because of the nature of data science: you can always find more ways to slice the data and ideas about what might be useful. This is especially common in situations in which the analysis proved to be inconclusive. In these situations, the person making the request often wants to jump in with the hope that something might suddenly prove to be conclusive.

As a data scientist, the best thing you can do in these situations is to try to gently push back against these requests. Although the requests occasionally prove to be useful, they can just as easily end up drawing no new conclusions, causing you to lose days of time trying to work through them. As the data scientist, you should have the best knowledge of what would have a chance of being valuable, and if you don't think something would be useful, you can lean into that conclusion. Often when you're doing an analysis, the business question you're trying to solve is so abstract that you could never give a truly definitive answer. And just like when you were doing the analysis and had to avoid trying method after method to find a result, after the analysis, you have to know when to stop.

10.4.2 *Mothballing your work*

When the final analysis is delivered and approved, you'll be asked to move quickly to the next set of work, such as another analysis. Before you do, however, taking a few small steps will make your life much easier in the future. There is a good chance that at some point down the line, months or years away, you'll be asked to redo the analysis with more-recent data. If you spend some time documenting your work, completing that repeat analysis will be much easier. The steps are

- *Double-check whether you can rerun the whole analysis.* Earlier, we discussed making your analysis a one-button run; at this point, you should do one last check to verify that the analysis still works.
- *Comment your code.* Because you might not look at your code again for years, even light commenting can help you remember how to use or modify your code.
- *Add a README file.* A README file is a simple text document covering what the analysis is for, why it was done, and how to run it.
- *Store your code safely.* If you are using git and GitHub, you've already done this, but if not, consider how someone could access the code a long time from now.
- *Ensure that the data is stored safely.* Check that all data files are stored in a safe place other than your laptop, such as cloud services (OneDrive, a shared network drive, or AWS S3, for example). Also, datasets stored in databases should ideally be checked to ensure that they won't be deleted.
- *Output is stored in a shared location.* The most common way people share analyses are as email attachments, but that's not a good way to archive them. Place your results in a place that other team members and people in other parts of the business can access.

When that work is all done, you can call the analysis truly complete. As you make more and more analyses, you'll find the methods and techniques that work best for you, and you'll get better and faster at making them.

10.5   Interview with Hilary Parker, data scientist at Stitch Fix

Hilary Parker works at Stitch Fix, an online personal styling service, where she creates machine learning models to help suggest clothing to customers. Previously, she was a senior data analyst at Etsy. She has a PhD in biostatistics from the Johns Hopkins Bloomberg School of Public Health.

How does thinking about other people help your analysis?

Just about every analysis I start by trying to understand "who wants what?" For example, was this work requested because the product manager needs to make a decision, and they don't feel they can until they get this analysis of an experiment? Is it that we're trying to drive a strategic vision and in order to get people comfortable with it, we're going to need to show that we believe this would make X dollars over Y years? I make sure to sit down and talk with the eventual consumers of the analysis to understand their context.

When you're presenting, the most important thing is to understand the audience and where they're at and what their goals are. Do they want to understand the nitty-gritty or not? What would be most compelling to them? If they seem eager for more information, you can offer more statistical details, but if they're disengaging, you want to scale that back.

How do you structure your analyses?

I think structuring the analysis in a way where it is approachable is important. I make sure that I have a short summary at the top and that I'm not making complicated graphs, because most people can't absorb them quickly. I also don't do a stream-of-consciousness notebook for an analysis, which I see a lot of people doing in an industry setting. The comments in notebooks look like text, so you add more and more comments and deliver that. You end up delivering something that is "Here's where I started, and here's where I ended." But you actually want to flip that to "Here's the conclusion, and in the appendix, you see where I started." Keep in mind the idea that a human will read it, and what's going to be the easiest to produce quickly may not be the most readable. I focus on the final format so much that it's part of the process. I don't ever have to translate a big notebook and make it pretty; I'm making the pretty thing the whole time.

What kind of polish do you do in the final version?

I think color themes go a really long way. A lot of companies will have their corporate color theme; Stitch Fix has a color theme in our branding. We have ggplot2 templates that import the colors from our color palette. Stuff such as that is really effective because it makes people in the company feel familiar. We have the same thing with Google Slides presentations. There are Google Slides templates that people use because it looks nice when you do it.

I also think "Don't overdo it." One of my early projects at Stitch Fix was launching our plus-size business line. We had some rapid analysis we needed to do in order to understand if we were sending out the right sizes. I spent so much time building my little system for how we were going to deliver the analysis. I got all excited about developing this reproducible website that would dynamically update at every x hours to show what was changing. But ultimately, the people I was working with didn't look at it that much. I got all excited about building the website instead of checking in with the partner. It's easy to go overboard with the aesthetics of the analysis. Do as much as you need, but not too much.

How do you handle people asking for adjustments to an analysis?

I've been reading a lot about design thinking recently, and this happens in a design context all the time. The attitude there is the one that I've taken upon myself: that people are bad at communicating, and they're not going to zoom out and think abstractly. In the design world, the person is going to come to you and say words about what they want, and you can't take them literally. You have to help them frame the problem. That's part of what a designer's value add is: that they're thinking about the problem holistically and systematically framing in different ways until they come up with the frame that makes sense.

I think that data scientists and statisticians are the same way. Someone's going to ask for some feature because they're trying to articulate unease, and that's one way of expressing it. But you have to figure out what the unease is about. Are you saying that you don't want to make this decision? Is this causing hesitancy? What's going to be the end result of this? Almost any time as a data scientist, you're interacting with one of the consumers. You have to constantly be not just doing exactly what they say, but instead figuring out what this person is actually trying to say. What's the root cause of what they're saying? Is that something that it's even appropriate for an analysis to address? There can be a lot going on, and it really pays to have a bird's-eye perspective on the entire situation rather than just iterating until the end of time.

Summary

- Analyses are documents that highlight conclusions and encapsulate important features of an application of data science to solve a business problem. They are critical for data scientists.
- A great analysis requires understanding the business problem and how data can solve it.
- When making the analysis, always think of the end goal, use simple methods with clear visualizations, and be ready to share your work.
- Managing the process of creating the analysis is important to keep the work focused on the goal and to ensure that it has a clear end.

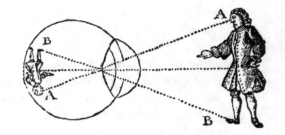

11

Deploying a model into production

This chapter covers

- Building a machine learning model to use in production
- Understanding what APIs are and how they're helpful
- Deploying a machine learning model

This chapter is written to cover the essential concepts of the job of a machine learning engineer—a person who creates machine learning models and deploys them for the business to use. If your work instead involves creating analyses and reports, it's easy to be scared of this material. Don't be! The gap between decision scientist and machine learning engineer is smaller than it seems, and this chapter will be a helpful introduction to the concepts.

Sometimes, the point of a data science project isn't to answer a question with data; it's to create a tool that uses a machine learning model to do something useful. Although you could do an analysis to understand what items people tend to buy together, it's a different task to make a program that recommends the best item to a customer on the website. The work of taking a machine learning model and making it so that it can be used by other parts of the business, such as on the website or in the call center, tends to be complex, and involves data scientists, software engineers, and product managers.

In this chapter, we'll discuss how to think about how to make models that are part of a product and how to get them off your laptop and into a place where they can function.

Two minor notes before we dive into this topic:

- Because the task of creating code that runs in production is fairly technical, this chapter is more technical than the others. Since we want these topics to be easy to understand for people who have less familiarity with the concepts of software development, we'll focus more on the concepts and ideas than the technical specifics.
- Because we are focusing more on the concepts, at times we will make general statements that may not be 100% true. This decision is an intentional one, made to help with readability. If you are already familiar with these topics and can think of a counterexample to something we've written—you're probably right!

11.1 What is deploying to production, anyway?

When people say "deploying into production," what they mean is taking code and putting it on some sort of system that allows it to be run continuously, typically as part of a customer-facing product. Deploying is a verb; it's the act of moving it to a different system. And production is a noun; it's the place where code that is part of a product runs. Code that is in production needs to be able to work with minimal errors or issues because if the code stops working, customers notice.

Although software developers have been putting code into production for decades, it's becoming more and more common for data scientists, specifically machine learning engineers, to train a machine learning model and put it into production as well. Training a machine learning model to be put into production is similar to training a model as part of an analysis, but there are substantially more steps after the model is trained to have it ready for production. Often, the act of building the model for production starts with an analysis. First, you need to understand the data and get business buy-in; then you can think about deploying to production. Thus, the two acts are quite intertwined.

To get a better sense of what deploying to production means, here is a quick example. Suppose that a business stakeholder in a company thinks that too many customers are leaving and asks a data scientist to do an analysis of customer churn. As part of the analysis, the data scientist builds a model and shows that there are several key indicators of churn. The business stakeholder loves the analysis and realizes that if customer care agents working in the call center knew which customers are likely to churn, the agents could offer discounts to try to keep them from leaving.

At this point, the data scientist needs to put the model into production. The model that lived on the data scientist's laptop must somehow run every time a customer calls support to compute the chance of churn. On the laptop, the model took a few minutes to assess many customers at the same time, but in production, this model has to run on a single customer the moment they call in, pulling customer data from other parts of the company and using that data for a rating.

Most production machine learning models are similar: they need to work in near real time to make a prediction or classify something based on provided data. Famous examples are Netflix's movie recommendation model, which predicts which movies a person would like; Facebook's facial-recognition model, which takes an image, finds faces in it, and matches those faces to identities; and Google's Gmail autocomplete model, which takes text as you're writing it and predicts the next word.

Models used for production need to go through several substantial steps. First, the models need to be coded to handle any scenario that might happen when the code is live so that they're less prone to errors. When you're doing an analysis, small amounts of weird data can be filtered out and not fed into the model without disrupting the analysis results. In a production model, the code needs to run regardless of how strange the input data is. It's probably fine for analysis purposes if a natural language processing model crashes when run on an emoji, for example, because you can just ignore input data with emojis. For a production model, if the code breaks when an emoji shows up, that could cause the product the machine learning model supports to break too. Imagine what would happen if the Gmail web page crashed every time you typed an emoji. The production models need to be made to handle weird cases themselves, or code needs to fix special weird cases before they ever get to the model.

Production models must also be maintainable. Because they are being continuously used in products, they occasionally have to be retrained on newer data—or coded in such a way that they automatically retrain themselves. They need ways of monitoring how well they are working so that people in the company can tell whether they are no longer working as well or suddenly stop working altogether. And because they will possibly be running for years, they need to be coded in such a way that they follow the standards of other models and can be updated over time. Coding one model in a long-dead programming language that few people know is bad for an analysis and catastrophic for a production model. Check out figure 11.1 to see an example process of creating and deploying a production machine learning model.

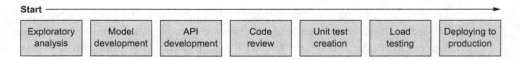

Figure 11.1   Example process of creating a production machine learning product

The rest of this chapter covers three concepts: how to create a machine learning model that is suitable for production, how to deploy it into production, and how to keep it running over time.

Production for different types of data scientists

How much you have to think about production systems varies greatly by the type of data scientist you are:

- *Machine learning engineer*—This is pretty much your whole job. By the time you're comfortable in your role as a machine learning engineer, you should be comfortable with everything discussed in this chapter.
- *Analyst*—An analyst may have to deal with production systems depending on the complexity of their reporting. If the analytics team is creating consistent reporting on a recurring basis, it's best to productionize the reporting systems. By making it so that the reports refresh themselves automatically, the analytics team is free to do other work. This is especially true for dashboards, where the expectation is that the systems are in production, updating themselves.
- *Decision scientist*—Because the work of a decision scientist is mostly ad hoc, there aren't as many opportunities to create production systems. But if models created by decision scientists are handed off to machine learning engineers to productionize, having a better understanding of production systems will help. Decision scientists also can create interactive tools for the business from libraries such as Shiny or Dash that need to be deployed and maintained in production systems.

11.2   *Making the production system*

A production system based on a machine learning model starts with the same steps as making a machine learning model for an analysis; you need to find the appropriate data, do feature selection, train the model, and get business buy-in. When those steps are complete, more work then has to be done:

1 The model needs to be converted to a format that other programs can use. Typically, that's done by creating code that allows the model to be accessed as an API from other systems in the company as though it were a website.

2 The model has to have code added to it to handle many possible inputs that may be fed to it. This ensures that the model won't crash with an unexpected input and has as little downtime as possible. This step requires adding tests to the model to ensure that it's correctly handling all the data it could be expected to process.

3 The model is deployed to a test environment to ensure that it functions correctly. The API is tested to ensure that it works and that it can handle the amount of traffic that will be hitting it when it's live.

When all these steps are complete, the model is finally deployed into a production environment.

11.2.1 *Collecting data*

When you're collecting data to train a model for an analysis, you need to find a suitable set of historical data that contains a good signal. Although this is also necessary for a production model, it's often not enough, because the real-time component of the model needs to be considered. Consider the earlier example in which a company needs a model in production to predict in real time whether a customer is going to leave. If a customer churn model is going to be used for an analysis, a historical collection of customer attributes (number of purchases, years since first purchase, and so on) that was collected a few months ago would be great for a model. Because the production model needs to predict in real time whether a customer will leave, code will need to be written to somehow find out what the customer's attributes are at the time the model is being called upon. If customer #25194 is calling customer support, the code for the model needs to know at that precise moment how many orders the customer has made so that the model can make its determination.

The difference between using historical data to train a model and feeding the model real-time data when running it can be drastic. For technical reasons regarding how the data is collected, there may be a lag of hours or days before data is put into a database or storage location that a data scientist can access. Alternatively, there can be situations in which the data is available in real time but the values aren't stored historically. There may be a way to query whether a customer is located internationally at the moment, for example, but the data on whether the customer was ever international was not stored.

When you're looking for data to create a model for production, consider what data will be needed in real time when the model is run. Will the data be suitably fresh for use? Can it be accessed via a database connection or some other method that someone can set up? It's not uncommon for machine learning projects to fail because of dataset issues.

11.2.2 *Building the model*

When you have a suitable dataset, you can start building a machine learning model. This topic is a broad one; if you want to learn how to build a machine learning model, from feature engineering to model training and validation, lots of books and internet resources are available. That being said, when making a model specifically for production, you want to keep a few things in mind.

PAYING EXTRA ATTENTION TO MODEL PERFORMANCE

Because other systems are going to rely on your model to work effectively on whatever data those systems choose to pass to it, you need to understand how the model will work in all cases. Suppose that you're making a machine learning model as part of an analysis to understand what products customers are interested in, such as a model that predicts the product a customer will buy next. If the model you built correctly predicted 99% of the purchases, but 1% of the time predicted that the customer would order Nicolas Cage temporary tattoos, the model would be a huge success. By understanding the vast majority of customers, you could help the business make an informed marketing decision. If, on the other hand, you were going to deploy that model to show recommended products on the company website, that 1% could be catastrophic and cause you to lose customers (or at least those customers who don't appreciate Nicolas Cage's unmatched charisma). What happens on the margins is really important in production systems, but not in analyses.

BUILDING A SIMPLE MODEL

Once the model is deployed into production and running so that customers interact with it, you'll inevitably run into a situation in which the model does something strange and you want to understand why. If the model is a customer churn model, it could predict that every customer in Alaska is going to churn for some unknown reason. Or a recommendation engine on an outdoor-products website might recommend only kayaks. At this point, you'll need to dig in to try to figure out what is going on and whether the model needs to be changed in some way.

If you use a simple model such as a linear regression, it should be fairly straightforward to trace the computation done to make the prediction. If you use a complex method such as an ensemble or boosted model, it becomes much more difficult to understand what is going on. Although you should use a model that's complex enough to solve your problem, you should use the simplest acceptable model as much as possible, even at the cost of accuracy.

One interesting real-world story involves the Netflix Prize. Netflix ran a contest to see whether a team could create an algorithm that improved its movie recommendation results by 10 percent, and in 2009, the company awarded a $1 million prize for it. As stated in a *Wired* article (https://www.wired.com/2012/04/netflix-prize-costs), Netflix never ended up actually using the winning algorithm. The algorithm was an ensemble method that combined many models, and the engineering complexity of running and debugging it was so high that using it wasn't worth the increase in accuracy. Despite the fact that Netflix paid a high price to have an accurate model, the company realized there are more important things than accuracy. If Netflix, with its army of data scientists and engineers, doesn't maintain a highly complex model, it's hard to say that many companies should.

11.2.3 *Serving models with APIs*

As of the time of the writing of this book, most machine learning models are served as application programming interfaces (APIs). This means that the machine learning model code can run on one computer system and that other systems can connect to it when they need the model to run on their data. If a company has one system that runs the shopping website and wants to add a machine learning model to offer a discount if the customer is predicted to unsubscribe, rather than try to get the machine learning code inside the website code, it could set up a second system that has the machine learning model, and the website could periodically query it.

The concept of breaking up different parts of a system into small microservices is all the rage in software engineering and is covered in beautiful depth in many books. For data scientists, the important concept is setting up one computer system that solely runs the model so that other systems can use it.

Modern APIs are done with web services—colloquially called REST APIs. A REST API is basically a tiny website, but instead of the website returning HTML to render in a browser, it returns data, usually as formatted text. These requests use the HTTP protocol, which is the same protocol that web browsers use (and which is why website addresses start with http:// or https://). A weather API, for example, could be set up so that if you go to the URL http://*exampleweather.com*/seattle_temperature, the site would return the temperature in degrees in Seattle (45). For a machine learning model API, you would want to go to a particular website and get a prediction. In the case of a machine learning model, somewhere in the company network, there could be a site that predicts whether a customer will leave. A site such as http://*internalcompany.com*/predict?customer=1234 would return a number between 0 and 1, representing the probability of that customer's leaving.

Designing the API involves making decisions, such as which URLs return what data and what types of requests to use. Making the design understandable to users is an important part of getting people to actually use it, so often, as much care has to be put into thinking through the interface as into creating the model.

Having a machine learning model run as an API web service is great for a couple of reasons:

- Because it's a web API, anything in the company can use the model, including live systems and other data scientists running analyses. The same churn prediction model being used on the website can be queried for an analysis by a person who's doing decision science.
- Because it works like a website, almost any modern technology can connect the model, regardless of technical platform. If the model is written in R, it can still be used by a website written in Node.js or by another analyst using Python. Also, because it's hosted as its own website, if the model stops working for some reason, it's less likely to take other products down with it. If the company shopping site uses the model and suddenly can't connect, the shopping site should still run.

11.2.4 Building an API

APIs are great for machine learning models, but some additional coding is needed for them. Both R and Python have packages—Plumber and Flask, respectively—that do this coding for you. When you run an R or Python script with these packages, that script takes your function and exposes it to an endpoint on your computer. You could specify that going to the URL http://*yourwebsite.com*/predict will run your machine learning R or Python function and then return whatever the function result is. Then you could go into a web browser to call your code! Assuming that you're running this code on a laptop or desktop computer, if you set your computer to allow outside traffic by adjusting the firewall, other people could hit your API. But the moment you stop running the API hosting program (R or Python), no one will be able to run your model.

Although both R and Python make it easy to serve a model as an API, design decisions need to be made, such as what data will need to be passed as input to the model in an API request. Suppose that you're making a model to predict a customer's likelihood of churning based on their tenure with the company, the amount they've spent with the company, and the number of times they've called customer care. One possible API design would be for a person to do a request with the customer's unique ID in the URL. To look up the customer with ID 1234, for example, you could go to http://*yourwebsite*.*com*/predict?customer_id=1234. Another option would be for users to have to look up all the customer information themselves and then include that information as the body of a request. So for a customer with a tenure of 1.7 years, a total spend of $1,257, and three calls to the contact center, you could send a request to http://*yourwebsite.com*/predict where the request of the body was {"tenure":1.7,"spend":1257,"calls":3}.

Both of these options are valid for an API design, but one requires your API to do all the work of looking up the customer details and the other makes the API user look up the details. It's generally not a good idea to make these decisions alone; the more you can loop in the people who might use your API, the more likely they are to be happy with it.

After you've designed your API, go talk to the people who are going to use it and show them how it works. They should be able to give you feedback on your design. Ideally, you should also share documentation on the API with them.

On plumber: An R package for serving R code as a web API (Jeff Allen)

Jeff Allen works at RStudio and is the creator of the R package plumber, which allows people to create web APIs in R so that machine learning models can be used across an organization.

plumber wasn't started by a company that decided to pour lots of engineers and funding into creating it; it had more humble origins. In 2012, I was working in a biostatistics group at a research center. This group used R for much of their analysis and had brought me in to help them create better software. Primarily, we had three different audiences:

- Other biostatisticians who used R and wanted to leverage or evaluate the methods we had developed
- Nontechnical users, such as clinicians, who just needed the results of our analysis to answer questions like "Which drug would be most effective for this patient?"
- Technical users who wanted to leverage our analysis but weren't interested in or didn't have the computational resources to run our R code

The first audience was the easiest; R comes with a robust packaging system that allows you to bundle your code and data in packages that can be shared and used

(continued)

by others. The second audience was a bit harder to serve at the time. Today, Shiny is the obvious solution to this problem and offers a convenient way for R users to continue working in R to build rich, interactive web applications that can be consumed by a nontechnical audience.

It was this third audience that remained difficult to address. Some users already had an existing application written in another language, like Java, but wanted to invoke some of our R functions from their service. Others had a simple, automated pipeline and wanted to leverage some computationally intensive R function that we had defined. In all of these cases, what they really wanted was something that they could call remotely and rely on us to internally do all of the R processing and then send them the result. In short, they wanted a remote API for R.

It was years later that I actually had the opportunity to start working on the package that would become plumber, but I carried this motivation with me. There is a group of people in most organizations who don't know R but would benefit from the analysis that their data scientists are creating in R. For many, a programmatic and structured interface is required, and web APIs offer an elegant solution. Thankfully, the authors of the Shiny package had already solved all the hard problems around creating a performant web server that could be used by R packages to service HTTP requests. The remaining piece was to create an interface by which users could define the structure and behavior of their API.

My hope is that plumber offers a solution to that technical audience so that these programmatic users can benefit from R just as effectively as the other aforementioned audiences have. As I've watched plumber's growth over the years, both in features and usage, I think it has been able to strike a chord with R users. Because R can be conveniently surfaced over an API, it's now earned a seat alongside other programming languages that are more familiar to traditional IT organizations. It's been fun watching people use plumber to accomplish things that I could never have done.

11.2.5 Documentation

When you have a working API, it's a great time to write documentation for it. The earlier in the process you have documentation, the easier it is to maintain the API over time. In fact, it's a great practice to write your documentation about your API before you write the first line of code. In that case, the documentation is your blueprint for creating the API, and people who will be using your model have plenty of time to prepare for it.

The core of API documentation is the specification for the API requests: what data can be sent to what endpoints, and what is expected back? This documentation allows other people to write the code that will call the API and know what to expect. This documentation should include lots of details, such as

- The endpoint URLs: (http://*www.companywebsite.com*/example)
- What needs to be included in the request
- The format and content of the response

This documentation could live in any text document, but there are also standard templates to store it, such as OpenAPI documents. An *OpenAPI document* is a specification for writing API specification files that can easily be understood by users or computer systems.

Ideally, you won't be the person keeping the API running forever, so you'll also want documentation of what requirements the API has to run on your system and how to install it somewhere else. This documentation will allow the person who takes over to get the code working themselves and make changes as needed.

Finally, you'll want to have some documentation of why the model exists and the basic methods behind it. This documentation is useful when you are no longer working on the product, and knowledge about why it was created is lost.

11.2.6 *Testing*

Before a machine learning model is put into production and customers rely on it, it's important to make sure that the model works. When a machine learning model is trained, part of the process is checking the model output and ensuring accuracy, which is helpful but not fully sufficient to know whether the model will work. Rather, the model needs to be tested to check that it can handle any input that it could receive without failing. If a churn model being put into production has an API that takes a numeric customer ID as input, what happens if the customer ID is blank? Or a negative number? Or the word *customer*? If in these cases the API returns a response that the users don't expect, that can be bad. If the bad input causes the API to crash, it could be catastrophic. Thus, the more issues that can be caught in advance, the better.

There are many types of testing, but for the purposes of creating a production machine learning model, one particularly important type is unit testing—the process of testing each small component of the code to ensure that the system will work in practice. In the case of a machine learning API, that often means testing that each endpoint of the API behaves as expected under different conditions. This testing can include receiving as input enormously large numbers, negative numbers, or strings with weird words in them. Each scenario is turned into a test. For a machine learning model that classifies text as either positive or negative sentiment, the test could be "On input I love you, we expect the API response to be positive." Another test could be that if the input is a number such as 27.5, the code returns a could-not-compute result rather than crashing.

Beyond testing the API endpoints, you can individually test functions within the code. The goal is to have 100% coverage, meaning that every line of code in the API has been tested to function correctly. Each time the model is going to be deployed, the tests are checked, and if any test fails, the issues have to be resolved.

It's easy to brush off testing as something there isn't time for, but it's often the only way to catch major issues before the model is put in front of customers. Writing a bunch of checks feels like busywork compared with the task of building a machine learning model, but it's extremely important and shouldn't be ignored.

11.2.7   *Deploying an API*

If you have a machine learning model coded so that you can run it on your laptop, it's not much work to turn it into an API that runs on your laptop. Unfortunately, sometimes you want to turn your laptop off or use it to watch Netflix, so having an API running on it continuously isn't a long-term strategy. For your API to run continuously in a stable way, it needs to live on a server somewhere so that it'll always run. The process of moving the code to a server to run is what we mean by deploying it. Setting up the server to have the code always running is a bit more work than just creating the API.

The term *server*

When you hear the word *server*, it can be intimidating, like some special computer that normal people don't understand. In practice, a server is just an ordinary computer, such as a laptop, but it runs somewhere without a screen. Instead of walking up to a server and logging in, people connect remotely with other computers, which simulate being in front of it. Servers run almost the same operating systems as computer laptops—Windows or Linux with minor tweaks. If you connect remotely to a server, it should look very familiar, with the same Start menu for Windows or a terminal for Linux.

The advantages of servers are that people usually leave them running and that they tend to live in places safer than a home office. But there is no reason you couldn't take an old home PC, put it in your closet, and treat it like a server; many software engineering hobbyists do just that.

When people talk about using cloud services such as Amazon Web Services (AWS), Microsoft Azure, and Google Cloud Platform (GCP), what they mean is that they're using servers that are rented from Amazon, Microsoft, and Google. But just because you're paying a big company for these services doesn't mean that the computers are different. You can think of them as being expensive sky laptops.

You have two basic ways to deploy an API to a server: run it on a virtual machine or put it in a container.

DEPLOYING TO A VIRTUAL MACHINE

Enterprise servers are generally machines that are both extremely powerful and extremely expensive. It rarely makes sense to have one of these powerful machines devoted to a single task, because for most tasks, that would be overkill. Instead, the server will be doing many tasks at the same time, but it would be catastrophic for one task to crash the computer and then cause unrelated tasks to crash too. Virtual machines are a solution to this problem because they are simulations of computers. The large, expensive computer will run many simulations of other computers at the same time. If one simulation crashes, it's no problem; the other ones keep working. A virtual machine can, in almost all cases, be treated exactly the same as a regular computer; if you log into one, you can't tell that's a virtual machine unless you're looking for it. Every time you use AWS, Azure, or GCP to access a computer, you're connecting to a virtual machine. If you ask your IT department to get a server for you, they'll likely make you an on-premises virtual machine as well.

Virtual machines are great because they're simulations: you can easily turn them on or off. You can also take snapshots so that you can go back to an earlier version or have many copies running at the same time. You can share a snapshot with someone else, and they can run it too. Or you can close your eyes and pretend that the virtual machine is a regular old laptop and generally be fine (assuming that you use your laptop with your eyes closed).

Because a virtual machine is a regular computer, the simplest way to deploy your code to the machine is to install R or Python, install the libraries you need, copy your code to it, and then run your code. These steps are the same ones you'll use to get your API running on your laptop! If you want to make changes to the API, just copy the newer version of the code to the virtual machine and then run your code. It really is the case that you can get a system into production by following only these steps:

1 Start a virtual machine.
2 Install the programs and code you need to run the machine learning model API.
3 Start running your API.

Given how much people talk about the complexity of making production systems, it's shocking how easily you can do it in a bare-bones way.

One major hassle with this simple method of copying and pasting code to a virtual machine and pressing Run is that you have to move the code manually every time you make a change. This process is both laborious and prone to error. It's easy to forget to move the code over or lose track of which version is on the virtual machine.

Continuous Integration (CI) is the practice of having code be recompiled automatically every time it is committed into a repository. CI tools can monitor git repositories, see when changes are made, and then rebuild the software based on that information. If you're using R or Python, recompiling isn't likely to be necessary, but the build process can run steps such as rerunning the unit tests. *Continuous Deployment* (CD) is the practice of taking the output of continuous integration tools and automatically deploying it in production systems. CI/CD refers to using both of these practices together.

Thus, a CI/CD tool will check your repository for changes and, if it finds some, will run your build process (such as check unit tests) and then move the resulting code to a virtual machine. As a data scientist, you don't have to worry about making changes to the virtual machine; the CI/CD tool will do that work for you. Setting up a CI/CD tool yourself isn't an easy task, but if your company has a software development team, it's likely that they already have these tools set up and that you can use them.

Another improvement in using virtual machines is running multiple virtual machines at the same time. If you expect that your API is going to get a lot of traffic, you can make copies of the virtual machine, run all of them at the same time, and assign traffic randomly to a machine. Further, you can monitor how active each virtual machine is and start and stop extra copies of the machine as needed. This technique is called *autoscaling*. Although it's practical for large systems, autoscaling is a bit of a pain to set up, and if you're in a situation in which you need it, you're also likely to be in a situation in which software developers are around to help.

DEPLOYING TO A DOCKER CONTAINER

Setting up and running a virtual machine can be quite a hassle. Because each one is a simulation of a computer, setting it up is as annoying as setting up a regular computer. You have to install each program, change each driver, and get the machine configured just right. It's really difficult to document all the steps needed, and if someone else repeats the process, it's easy to make mistakes. Another problem is that because each virtual machine is a simulation of a computer, the machines take up a lot of space because they have to contain everything that a regular computer does.

Docker is a solution to these problems. To use Mike Coleman's metaphor from the Docker blog (https://www.docker.com/blog/containers-are-not-vms): if a server full of virtual machines is a neighborhood of houses, Docker containers are a set of apartments in a single building. Although each apartment is a fully livable unit, the apartments share services such as a hot-water heater. Compared with virtual machines, Docker containers are much easier to set up and more efficient to run.

Docker allows you to easily specify how a machine is set up, and by having a shared specification across distinct machines, you can share resources. This allows the creation and maintenance of production systems to be far easier than with virtual machines, which is why Docker took the software development world by storm.

To understand Docker, it's important to understand three concepts:

- A *dockerfile* is a text file that contains all the steps required to set up the simulated machine. These steps can include "Install Python 3" or "Copy over the saved model file to the machine." Most of the steps are exactly the same as Linux bash commands, so if you're used to reading those commands, a dockerfile should feel familiar.
- A Docker *image* is the result when Docker follows the steps of a dockerfile to build and store a snapshot of a computer state.
- A *container* is created when Docker takes an image and starts running it. A running container can be connected to and used like a normal physical computer with the programs and data specified in the image.

Docker has lots of advantages over the traditional deployment methods, but using Docker to deploy a machine learning model into production will likely work only if other people in the organization are using Docker containers. If that's the case, the company will have someone who knows how to create a Docker container, deploy it, and monitor it to see whether it's working continuously. If not, there'll likely be pushback for having the machine learning models deployed in a nonstandard way.

Because Docker containers are more complex to get started than virtual machines, if you've never deployed code before, it may be easier to start with virtual machines instead. Even if you can't use Docker for deploying models to production, using Docker for reproducible analyses has lots of benefits. It's definitely worth it to at least gain a little experience in using the tool at some point, even if it's not immediately clear that you have a career need for it.

11.2.8 Load testing

If lots of systems are going to be using your model, or if one system is going to be using your model a lot of times at the same time, you'll want to make sure that the API won't fail under the stress. This failure could happen because the system the API is running on runs out of memory, because the system takes too long to process each request and has a longer and longer queue, or because of any number of other terrible things.

The easiest way to make sure that this doesn't happen is to run a *load test*—a test in which you make a high number of requests to the API at the same time and see how the API does. Usually, you run a number of requests that's at least twice as much as you could ever expect to see. If the API handles these requests gracefully, you're golden. If it crashes, though, you'll know that you need to make your code more efficient, scale your system up, or make other changes.

11.3 Keeping the system running

Even after your API is successfully deployed and being used, that's not enough. (It's never enough.) Either you or someone else in the organization will have the job of continuing to ensure that the API works. Some companies have a development operations (DevOps) team whose charter is to make sure that the APIs are always working. Even if the API is working fine, you still may want to make adjustments for other reasons. The following sections discuss three important considerations for API maintenance over time.

11.3.1 Monitoring the system

It's a good idea to monitor continuously how the model is doing. How many requests is it receiving each hour? Are the model predictions still accurate? Are any errors happening? The easiest way to keep track of these metrics is to have your API include logging and telemetry. *Logging* is recording data on internal issues within the tool—every time the model has an error, for example. *Telemetry* is recording events that occur, such as every time a request or particular prediction is made. Additionally, alerting can be set up for when issues occur.

Logging can be as simple as having your API write information to a file every time an event occurs. Then, to check the logs, you can just enter the Docker container or virtual machine. Telemetry generally involves sending the event information to a remote location (such as a centralized server) so that the telemetry of many systems is located in one place. Then you can make a dashboard so that the telemetry can be viewed and monitored in real time.

Alerting tools are used so that when something is going wrong, people in the company will find out. These alerts can be automatic emails or Slack messages that are sent when a specific set of events occurs. If the model API has a telemetry event for when a request is received, and no requests happen over an entire day, an alert email could be sent out to let someone know that the system isn't receiving traffic but probably should be.

These different monitoring systems are often used in conjunction, and companies try to standardize so that they can monitor all the company APIs in the same way. As in much of this chapter, the more you can work with the standards of your organization, the more useful your tool will be.

11.3.2 *Retraining the model*

It's often the case that at some point after a machine learning model is released into production, it will start to not perform as well. Machine learning models are trained on data, and as time passes, that data becomes less relevant. A machine learning model to predict churn, for example may falter as customers from new regions start to engage with the company. When the model is sufficiently nonperformant, it needs to be retrained.

The simplest solution for retraining is that when the model does badly, repeat the steps you followed to train the model in the first place, but load a newer version of the data. This process likely means loading data in R or Python onto your computer, rerunning the scripts, and then putting the model into production in the same way. This approach is nice because if you did something once, you can do it again. In fact, plenty of important production machine learning systems are handled this way at large, impressive corporations.

One thing you can do to make this process more sophisticated is to create some standard schedule for the work to be done. Instead of trying to keep an eye on the model metrics and using your gut to decide when to retrain it, set a standard practice of doing it every n weeks or months. This practice takes the guesswork out of choosing when to perform an important act.

More critically, doing the retraining on a standard schedule means that you can automate the process. If you have a Python or R script that loads the data, builds the model, and then saves it somewhere, you can set up a system to do those things automatically on schedule. In fact, this retrainer system can be put into production itself so that you don't have to spend time doing the work. Such a system can also test whether the newly retrained model is performing just as well as, or better than, the previous one; if not, it should send an alert to the data scientists. Advanced retraining processes such as these are becoming more common, and cloud tools such as AWS SageMaker have support for them.

Automatic retraining pipelines are sophisticated and in vogue, but at the end of the day, so long as you are retraining your model at all, you're doing great. Data scientists get into trouble when they build a model, deploy it into production, and stop paying attention to it as the model does less and less well over time. By not continuing to monitor performance of a model and fix it if necessary, you run a real risk of doing damage with your work instead of helping. Keep an eye on it.

11.3.3 Making changes

If your model in production is successful for the business, you'll inevitably want to make changes to the model to improve it. You may want to pull in more datasets or change the machine learning method to improve the performance of the API, for example. You'll also hear from people around the business about features that they want in the model or issues that they find with it.

As in the discussion of analyses in chapter 10, these sorts of one-more-thing changes can present real issues. It's not clear that doing this work is necessarily worth the time, even if it's interesting or seems important to someone. If it takes three months to get the model from 84% to 86% accuracy, you'll lose three months that you could have spent on something else. Or a feature that seems important to a particular stakeholder may not actually affect many customers. A successful machine learning model in production will draw the attention of many people, and as the data scientist who helped create it, you should try to ensure that the time spent improving it is well spent.

11.4 Wrapping up

This chapter covers lots of concepts about deploying models, some of which you may have been familiar with and some not. Although not all the topics may be relevant to your work, it's great to have a basic understanding of them in case you need it in the future. You can find lots of good resources in books and online that provide more information about these topics, especially because there is so much overlap with software engineering. As data science continues to change as a field, these topics will stay important and are worth continuing to learn.

11.5 Interview with Heather Nolis, machine learning engineer at T-Mobile

Heather Nolis is a machine learning engineer on the AI @ T-Mobile team, where she helps put into production R and Python models that are hit millions of times a week. She holds a master's degree in computer science and bachelor's degrees in neuroscience and French.

What does "machine learning engineer" mean on your team?

I take the models that data scientists make and engineer them into products that the team maintains. For a long time, T-Mobile had data scientists who would sit around building beautiful models and doing cool analyses that they would then send over to the software engineering department to put it into production. The idea was that this would let the work have a real business impact, but it was really difficult for the engineers to actually use the work because there was a huge language barrier between data scientists and engineers. My goal is to sit in the middle so I can understand all of the things that went into an analysis or are important for a given model and then communicate that to engineers.

What was it like to deploy your first piece of code?

My first deployment was my first week ever as a software developer. It was on an already-existing product, and at first, I didn't understand why it was risky. When you're coding on a computer, it's fine if you run the code 50 times to test it. But in production, if one piece of code has a bug, it can cause a huge problem for your company, so it's not just you on your laptop that you're inconveniencing by running code that doesn't work. In my first release when I thought I was done, I actually had to do three hours of integration testing before it was allowed to release.

If you have things go wrong in production, what happens?

Early on, I built a Twitter-based tool that would recommend you to the nearest T-Mobile store on social media. I wrote it in Node.js, which our team didn't support at all, but I figured, "I will solve it for me and show people that it could be done and then somebody more qualified can engineer it." That's where I learned that "somebody more qualified can engineer it" never actually happens; my code was what was put into production.

We released it, and—me being brand-new to Node—it wasn't beautiful code by any means. It worked and was secure, but having limited production experience, I lacked confidence that it would run in production. Other engineers were nervous because it was a language that we didn't yet support. For the next two months, I got called in every single time any service had a hiccup. I had to be there because I took a risk on releasing something in a different language on a new platform; people assumed that anything weird was from me.

Every single time that I got notified for that entire two months, I felt like it was my problem. But it was never actually my code that broke in production! I think that's something to remember: when you put things in production for the first time, there's a chance that you do break everything, but other people's things don't work too. It's not just your code. You don't have to be scared when things break.

I will also say this about putting things in production: of course I would always like to build the nicest models with all the coolest bells and whistles, but that doesn't always help build the product we want. In the end, we have to sacrifice many of these things to have robust code that will continue to function. My job as a machine learning engineer is to understand these trade-offs and drive the creation of a product.

What's your final piece of advice for data scientists working with engineers?

Two keys to working well together are to understand their language and appreciate what they care about. For understanding their language, consider that things which might seem like a normal sentence to you sound to a machine learning engineer like they walked into your house and you had a big, old console CRT TV. They're wondering "Did I step back in time?" My favorite example of that was when we got our first data scientist on the AI team at T-Mobile. At one point I asked the data scientist, "Can't we just put the R model into production as an API?" She asked, "You want me to run R as a web server?" I had to step back for a second because when I hear the words *web server*, I hear "Hello—I'm coming from the 1980s!" I was completely turned off by that, even though she meant exactly the same thing.

For the latter, at the end of the day, data scientists feel good about their jobs when they're building accurate models. What makes me, an engineer, feel good is putting stuff into production so other people can touch it. The only thing that I really value is working code. If you could go to an engineer and say I designed an API and I created a document that specifies all the inputs and outputs, that shows engineers that you're thinking about the problems that they have too.

Summary

- Deploying to production is the practice of making models run continuously.
- Putting a model in a REST API allows other systems to use it.
- APIs can be deployed to virtual machines or as Docker containers.
- Look closely into how your company manages code, testing, and deployment of production systems.

12

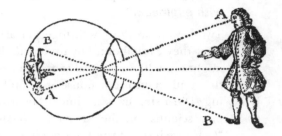

Working with stakeholders

This chapter covers

- Working with different types of stakeholders
- Engaging with people outside the data science team
- Listening so that your work gets best used

It seems like the job of a data scientist would be primarily about data, but much of the work revolves around people. Data scientists spend hours listening to people in their company talk about the problems they have and how data might solve those problems. Data scientists have to present their work to people so they can use the knowledge gained from an analysis or trust a machine learning model. And when problems occur, such as projects being delayed or data not being available, it requires conversations with people to figure out what the next step should be.

Karl Weigers and Joy Betty define the term stakeholder in *Software Requirements* as "a person, group, or organization that is actively involved in a project, is affected by its outcome, or can influence its outcome." For a data scientist, stakeholders can be the businesspeople working in marketing, product development, or other areas of the business who use data science to make decisions. Stakeholders can also be people in engineering who rely on machine learning models created by data scientists to power their software or make sure the data is collected properly. In some situations, stakeholders are high-level executives. Stakeholders can come from across the company, and different stakeholders have different behaviors and needs.

In this chapter, we walk through what to expect from the different types of stakeholders you'll encounter during a data science project. Then we cover how to work with stakeholders effectively and how you should think through communication with people outside the data science team. Lastly, we cover the process of prioritizing the work that stakeholders give you.

12.1 Types of stakeholders

Each stakeholder you may encounter during a data science project has their own background and motivation. Although a stakeholder can be pretty much anyone, depending on how weird your project is, most stakeholders fall into one of four categories: business, engineering, leadership, and your manager (figure 12.1).

Figure 12.1 Types of stakeholders covered in this section

12.1.1 Business stakeholders

Business stakeholders are people from a department such as marketing, customer care, or product who oversee business decisions. These people are the ones who request analyses to help them make better decisions or machine learning models to increase efficiencies. People in these roles have varied backgrounds: a person in marketing could have an MBA degree and come from an ad agency, although a manager in the customer care department could have started as a care agent with a community-college degree and worked their way up. These varied paths to the job will give each person a different perspective on working with you.

Usually, business stakeholders have little technical background. They might be capable in Microsoft Excel, but with a few exceptions, that is the extent of their analytical expertise. Most business stakeholders won't know how to use R or Python, or the merits of different machine learning models. But if they have picked up any news article in the past decade, they've heard over and over the value of data in making decisions and the importance of data science. Thus, business stakeholders are in a tricky situation: they have to rely on data scientists to provide them the critical information they need to make decisions or release machine learning tools, but without technical expertise themselves, they have to trust that what the data scientist is saying is right.

Often, a business stakeholder is highly engaged in a data science project. They're there to help kick it off and define the objective for the project. They are there during the project to look at intermediate results and give feedback from the business. And they are there at the end of the project, when either the final analysis is delivered or the model is deployed. Because they are the ones who ensure that the business gets value from the data science work, they have to be constantly involved.

As a data scientist, it's your job to deliver to them what they need for their part of the business to function, such as an analysis, a dashboard, or (on occasion) a machine learning model. You not only have to do this work for them, but also need to make sure they understand and trust it. If you give them a table with complex statistics and no explanation, they won't understand it and thus won't be able to use it. By being a trusted business partner to them, you're enabling them to use data, and they're giving you avenues for more data science to be done within the organization.

The most difficult situations with business stakeholders tend to be when they don't accept the data science results, such as when a data scientist makes an analysis and the stakeholder responds "Oh, that can't be right." When the facts and premises of the data science work are called into question, there is the possibility of the stakeholder cutting the data scientists out of the loop. In these situations, the best thing you can do is help them understand what you did and how you did it. Usually, a lack of belief comes from a lack of understanding, and by having a discussion about how things were done, you may need to change the assumptions in the analysis.

12.1.2 Engineering stakeholders

The engineering teams are in charge of maintaining the code (and, potentially, physical products) that the company delivers, and when those products require machine learning algorithms or data science analyses, they become stakeholders. In some ways, engineers are easier to work with than other types of stakeholders because culturally, they have many similarities to data scientists. Just like data scientists, they have technical backgrounds that they gained from schools, bootcamps, or online coursework.

Although engineers have extensive technical backgrounds, they often have little experience with key parts of the data science job. Although a software engineer writes code, they usually do it with an extremely specific task in mind, such as creating an API that queries a specific database. The job of a software developer does not have the exploratory component of a data scientist's job, so the idea of spending weeks trying to understand data and gain insights is foreign.

Engineers tend to collaborate with data scientists when a machine learning model is needed as part of an engineering project. This collaboration is most often done as a machine learning model being converted to an API in production that the engineers will use for their work (see chapter 11). The engineers are relying on the data scientists and machine learning engineers to create a product that has clear input and output, is reliable to use, and won't surprise them in production. As a data scientist, it's your job to deliver those things to an engineering stakeholder. You have to think like an engineer and try to understand what would be the best product for their needs.

Engineers also rely on data scientists to do analyses that help power the tools they are building. Data scientists can look at data to help prioritize features, diagnose bugs in the engineering systems, and assess the performance of customer-facing products such as websites. In these situations, engineers are closer to business stakeholders, because they need the data scientists to get them the knowledge to make the right decisions.

Difficulties tend to arise with engineer stakeholders around the uncertainty of data science work. When developing a software product, you generally set out to design an API or process, and you do it. You have clear tasks involved in the design and requirements for what it should do. In data science, on the other hand, you have very little expectations going into creating a product. It's not clear what data you'll end up needing, because you may not know what would be important for the model. It's not clear what the output will be, because output often depends on the model and its performance. And it's not even clear whether the idea will be feasible, because you could find that no model is accurate enough to meet business expectations.

Because of how unknown data science projects are at the start, engineering stakeholders are often taken aback by how little data scientists can promise early on. Thus, as a data scientist, you'll need to take extra care to communicate the process so that engineers will be less surprised as things change. Make sure to communicate early and often about what the data science process is and how you're following it. When you let engineers in on the ambiguities of data science, they'll be less likely to be surprised by them.

12.1.3 *Corporate leadership*

The executives of a company have backgrounds similar to those of business stakeholders (or engineers, if they're leading a technology organization) but far larger spheres of influence. These directors, vice presidents, and chief corporate officers are guiding the organization, and they need data to do it. Data scientists are often tasked with sifting through data to provide the insight that executives need to do their jobs. Data scientists may also be accountable to them if they are involved in a large-scale project of which machine learning is a critical component.

Corporate leaders are extremely busy and have little time to understand details that don't affect them. This fact leads to immense difficulty in getting any time with them, and when that time is granted, it is brief. When you meet with a high-level executive, they generally want to get to the point and understand the implications immediately. This makes sense: they're extremely busy people, and the less work they have to do figuring out what someone is trying to say, the more they can focus on making the decisions.

Corporate leaders tend to work with data scientists when they need data to make a major decision or when they want to have a better understanding of a part of the company. Sometimes, work that is done for business stakeholders or other people is shown to higher-level people in the organization until people at the top are seeing it. In these situations, the analysis and report may be polished again and again as they go higher up. At other times, an executive may request a specific analysis or piece of work to be done, and it's the data scientist's job to create something that someone who's seeing the results for the first time will understand immediately.

Depending on the size and culture of the organization, data scientists may have to do a lot of work before sharing the results with an executive stakeholder. At some organizations, teams of people review results to ensure that they align with business objectives and organizational beliefs. At more relaxed or smaller organizations, data scientists can create work directly for the leader. Regardless of the company, work should always be clean and error-free.

Trouble tends to happen when work is presented that is unclear or incomplete. If the executive can't understand what's being presented to them, they will have no patience to wait for things to become clear on their own. If they ask questions that the data scientist can't answer, they may feel that the work isn't reliable. If collaborating with an executive goes sufficiently badly and the executive is unforgiving, that could be a serious blow to the team.

On the other side of the coin, if the executive likes the results or finds them valuable, that can be a great boon to the data scientists. By becoming a trusted partner to an executive, a data science team can gain leverage in an organization to use data and machine learning in more places and for more reasons.

12.1.4 *Your manager*

Depending on the project at hand, your manager is sometimes a stakeholder. If your manager assigns you a task, continuously checks in on it, and makes suggestions, they effectively are a stakeholder on the project. A manager wants a project to succeed because (1) their job is to make you succeed, (2) it looks good for them if the projects assigned to their team do well, and (3) the project may align with your manager's broader goals for your team.

In general, your manager should be guiding and mentoring you on your project. When you have struggles, you should be able to talk to your manager about them, and your manager should help you find the best course of action. Your manager will take your work and help it go as far as it can in the business—by telling people about it, by helping the work get integrated into existing processes, and by thinking of new opportunities to improve your work.

But a manager is also a stakeholder because they are relying on you to do work. They need you to deliver the best work that you can because your reports, models, and analyses are what your manager shares. So a manager fills a dual role as both a person you can rely on for help and a person for whom you have to do work.

Because of this dual role, everything in the rest of this chapter relates to your manager too. The main difference is that with your manager, you can let your guard down and show more vulnerability. It's reasonable to say something like "Wow, I'm really struggling to finish this analysis" to your manager, but you probably couldn't reveal that information to an executive stakeholder. A manager is able to treat you as more of a human being and provide advice, whereas other stakeholders are purely customers of your work.

Overall, treat managers just as you would the other people you work with: give clear updates, communicate continuously, and deliver presentable work. But when you are having trouble, open up to your manager first, because they want to help you and understand when things need assistance.

12.2 Working with stakeholders

To communicate effectively with stakeholders during your data science projects, there are four core tenets to think about:

- Understand the stakeholder's goals
- Communicate constantly
- Be consistent
- Create a relationship

The following sections go into detail on each of these tenets.

12.2.1 Understanding the stakeholder's goals

Everyone has goals when working a job—objectives they want to achieve when they go to work every day. Those goals are determined both by the job a person has and their personal traits such as ambition and a desire for career-life balance. A lead engineer, for example, may focus on getting their current project complete so that they can get a promotion. Or a senior executive may know that they are going to leave the company soon and want to avoid rocking the boat before then. These goals shape what people do at work and how they respond to other people's actions. A project that takes longer than expected could be terrible for the promotion-oriented engineer but great for the executive who doesn't want to do anything.

When you're working with stakeholders as a data scientist, it's critical that you understand their goals. Exactly the same analysis could be received well or poorly, depending on the stakeholder's perspective. Consider an analysis of the performance of a certain product being sold on the company website. Suppose that the stakeholder is the person who manages that product, and your analysis found that the product was not selling well in South America. If the stakeholder had the goal of making the product seem to be amazing to the company because it was their idea, the analysis could be received very poorly because it shines a light on the problem. On the other hand, if the stakeholder had the goal of keeping an entire portfolio of products performing well, knowing which one may need to be cut is very helpful.

When working with a stakeholder, you should try to understand their goals and motivation as quickly as possible. The faster you can understand those things, the less likely you are to deliver something that is unnecessarily poorly received. You have a few ways to discover a person's motivations:

- *Ask them directly.* By asking a stakeholder "What's important to you?", you're effectively opening a door for them to reveal themselves. What people say openly isn't the whole picture, but you can often pick up the essentials in this way. Also, it's a totally normal question to ask during an introductory meeting.

- *Ask around.* See whether your co-workers have worked with the stakeholder before. Asking someone on your team a question like "So tell me about this stakeholder: what's their deal?" can get co-workers to fill you in. Keep in mind that you want to avoid gossiping; don't take what a co-worker told you in confidence and spread it to others without thought.

- *Infer the stakeholder's motivation from their actions.* Sometimes, it can be pretty clear from what the stakeholder is doing what their motivations are. If you're presenting an analysis that reflects poorly on one of the products they manage, for example, and they get overly defensive, that's a sign that the product is extremely important to them. The downside of this method is that you have to learn through interacting, so you can easily make mistakes, but if you're going to be interacting with them anyway, you might as well spend time learning from those mistakes.

By partaking in these tasks, you should be able to build a mental model of the stakeholder. How will they react to different outcomes of an analysis or delays in a model? If you can think through the outcomes in advance, you can be thoughtful in your communication.

Note that understanding the stakeholder's motivations doesn't mean you have to cater to them. Although understanding their goals helps you predict how they will react, there may be cases in which your goals don't align with your stakeholders' goals, and you have to disregard theirs. If your goal is to be the best data scientist you can, in the example situation in which your analysis shows a product does poorly, it would be in your best interest to be honest in your analysis and not hide your findings. Knowledge of the stakeholder's needs is something that can aid you.

If you find yourself having to deliver news that the stakeholder won't receive well, the first course of action is usually to call in reinforcements. Can your manager or a more senior member of your team help? By having someone help you deliver this message, they'll be able to navigate any political fallout or issues rather than you. A junior data scientist isn't expected to be an expert in the politics of the company and the bigger picture.

When you have to navigate a difficult conversation on your own, it's best to try to frame the conversation as a collaboration. Think about how you can be on the same side as the stakeholder. The news may be hard to hear, but you can try to convince them that you're not intentionally inflicting pain, but trying to see the situation from their side and looking for areas of opportunity to move past the current issue. In this case, the conversation is much more a traditional business negotiation and discussion than a technical one; it's about having different sides come to a shared understanding.

Key Performance Indicators (KPIs)

Key Performance Indicators (KPIs) and Objective Key Results (OKRs) are metrics that a team or organization focuses on because they drive business value. An online retail team, for example, may focus on orders per month as a number they want to raise. KPIs are useful for data scientists because they provide explicit quantification of the goals of the team. If you are able to find out a team's KPIs, you'll be able to frame all of your analyses and other work in terms of how it affects their KPIs. If an analysis or method does not relate to a KPI, the team probably won't be interested.

Not every team has core KPIs, and sometimes, they are constantly changing or are poorly defined, but if you do have a situation in which you are given KPIs, it's best not to ignore them. They're often the easiest way to understand your stakeholder's goals quickly.

12.2.2 Communicating constantly

It's easy for a data scientist to worry that they're either communicating too much or not communicating enough. "Is emailing a stakeholder for the third time in one day too much?" is a thought that may cross your mind as you press Send once again. Or just as easily, you could think "I haven't talked to our stakeholder in a while. I wonder what they're thinking?" Or the worst case of all: you could not put any consideration at all into how you're keeping the stakeholder in the loop and cause your stakeholder to be completely unaware of how the project is doing.

For a data scientist, it is almost always the case that they are not communicating enough. Stakeholders thrive on communication. Emails, meetings, and calls are the only ways that stakeholders can understand what is going on with a project. Without enough communication, stakeholders can believe themselves to be out of the loop and worry that they don't have a good understanding of what is going on. And if there isn't enough communication, by the time a data scientist does talk to a stakeholder, the stakeholder can be taken aback by how different their expectations are from reality.

A data scientist should communicate several messages to stakeholders:

- A data scientist should be keeping a stakeholder in the loop about how the project is meeting the expected timeline. If at the start of the project, it seemed that it would take a month to find and clean the data and then another month to build a model, tell the stakeholder whether that timeline is still the expected one. Ideally, this system will be one in which the data scientist shares changes and delays as they happen. A bad scenario is when the stakeholder is expecting a project to have finished but the data scientist has weeks or months of work ahead and hasn't shared that information. When the stakeholder eventually finds out, they can be upset, and rightly so.

- A data scientist should communicate how the project is progressing, such as findings that the data scientist discovered during the project or areas on which they are finding more difficulty than expected. Something such as being stuck because of access to a database could potentially be resolved with stakeholder help. Sharing where the analysis is going well may help the stakeholder improve the project scope. If the project seems to be faring very poorly, that should be communicated too. (Chapter 13 provides more information about projects that fail.)

- Distinct from how the project is progressing, a data scientist should be continually updating the stakeholder about how the work informs the business and what comes next. Data scientists should have opinions on how what has been done so far should change the project trajectory. If, for example, a data scientist is doing an analysis and finds something totally novel, they should create a set of recommendations to the business on what to do with that finding.

Often, the best way to create this consistent communication is to make it the default way that the project works. Nothing does that better than a recurring meeting on the calendar between the data scientist and the stakeholder. By having a weekly or biweekly meeting, you're ensuring some required communication. This routine is a forcing function: by having it on the calendar, you're forcing yourself to make something to share for each meeting. For each one of these meetings, you should come prepared with a list of updates to the timeline, notes about what is going well or poorly, parts of your work to share, and suggested next steps.

As a data scientist, you should also get into the habit of emailing stakeholders directly as needed. As an aspiring or junior data scientist, you may find it very intimidating to ask questions of senior people in the organization. Most of the time, however, stakeholders are happy to answer questions if that means that your work will be better; that's their role in the organization. If you're worried that the person is so high up that the email needs to be extra-polished, or if you think that the questions sound obvious enough to make them think you don't know much, run the email by your manager first; that's your manager's role. Depending on the stakeholder and the project, you should be emailing them once a week or so.

If things are suddenly changing in your project (perhaps a dataset that you thought existed doesn't) and you need stakeholder input, sometimes, the right route is to set up a call or impromptu meeting with them. These sorts of quick gatherings can be great for getting immediate input when necessary. The only question to ask yourself before getting one of these meetings on the calendar is "Do I actually need stakeholder input on this?" If a change occurs, but you know what to do next, you probably don't need to take up other people's time. If you do require input, go for it. A mistake that junior data scientists tend to make is having a default assumption that other people set up meetings, not them. But the more proactive you can be about keeping the project moving, the better the project will go. Further, this situation is great training for more senior roles in which these actions are expected.

The method and reasons for communication should vary based on stakeholder type. In general, business stakeholders tend to be happy with meetings in which they can provide direction and collaboration. They probably aren't the people who will be able to provide actual data or help with technical blockers. Engineers often have the technical answers for you but will be just as uncertain as you when making decisions about the project or direction of the work. Executives are extremely busy and usually can be in the loop only at the beginning of the project to set broad goals and the end of the project to see the conclusion.

12.2.3 *Being consistent*

Imagine a restaurant down the street from you. One day, you order fajitas there, and they quickly bring out the best fajitas you've ever had. A month later, you order the fajitas again, but this time, they totally forgot to season the meat. You go a third time, and the food was tasty, but it took more than an hour to come out—far longer than you expected. Is this a restaurant you'd want to eat at?

Businesses thrive on delivering a consistent product, and as a data scientist, you are a mini-business within your organization. The stakeholders are your customers, and if you don't serve them well, they will stop asking you for help. One way to deliver consistency in your relationships is through standardization of your work.

In the case of analyses and reports, you can do your stakeholders a great service by creating a consistent framework in which to share them. If you can keep things as much the same from analysis to analysis as possible, the stakeholders will be able to focus on the findings. Here are some things to consider standardizing:

- *How the analysis is structured*—As much as possible, try to have a format for the analysis. Start with the same style of Objective and Data, and end with similar Conclusions and Next Steps. You're training your stakeholders in how to read and think through these materials.
- *How the analysis is delivered*—Although you don't have to stick to it exactly, things tend to go more smoothly if you have one file type for your analyses. These files can be PowerPoint, PDF, HTML, or something else. They should all be stored in the same place each time. You can create a Dropbox, network folder, or other sharing tool for your analyses. Make sure that the tool is something stakeholders can use; a GitHub repository probably won't work, although you could make one for yourself to keep everything under version control.
- *How the analysis is styled*—This point may seem to be small, but consistency in the visuals can go a long way. Use the same colors and templates as much as possible (bonus points for your company's colors).

When you're delivering dashboards, many of the consistency rules for analyses apply here. You want to keep styling and format consistent among multiple dashboards and store all them in a shared location so that people will remember how to access them.

For APIs and machine learning deliverables, the consistency is in the product's design. As a data science team's portfolio of APIs and models grows, it can be extremely hard to keep track of how each one works. The more consistent the APIs are, the easier they are to use. Consistency rules include

- *Consistency in the input*—How your models and APIs take data in should follow the same format as much as possible. All of them can take JSON objects with the same parameter names in them, for example.
- *Consistency in the output*—How the output is structured should make sense with how the input is structured and how the rest of the APIs created by the team work. If the model takes JSON as input, it should return JSON as output.
- *Consistency in authentication*—It is likely that the models and APIs require some form of authentication for security. Whatever method you use use, it should be consistent across as many of the APIs as possible, especially because it's easy to lose track of which credentials are for which API.

In addition to helping your stakeholders, all this consistency will be useful to you! The more you can standardize all of these parts of the data science work, the less you'll have to think about them (and the more you can focus on the interesting parts). The more a data science team can standardize, the easier it is to pass work among different people. Standardization is good for everyone.

> **Elizabeth Hunter, senior vice president of technology strategy implementation at T-Mobile: Managing relationships**
>
> Relationships between people play an important, but sometimes overlooked, part of any business interaction. People subconsciously look for social and emotional cues to establish stability, comfort, and connection, and when they find these cues they tend to be more open to new ideas and experiences. This connectedness to a person provides a welcoming setting for whatever information you want to present to them. How to establish a good relationship with someone is less linear than most work-related tasks. Some people form connections quickly with people based on being generally friendly. Other people take much longer and require numerous interactions with deep personal discussion.
>
> Over the years, I've found that much of my success in my career has depended on the relationships I taken the time to establish, whether it was someone's support in an important meeting, an executive listening to one of my ideas, or someone offering me a new opportunity. A huge part of my career growth was working hard and demonstrating the value of my work, but having established personal connections to people provided them with a lot of context about me, what they could expect, how much leeway they were willing to give me, and how much they would accept from me on belief versus proof.

As an introvert, forming relationships came less naturally to me than to others, and I had to work at how to go about it. Retrospectively, I now realize I conducted a series of small experiments—I formed hypotheses based on what I knew or observed about how I could connect with someone, tested whether that worked, adjusted based on the new information I learned about them, and repeated this in my interactions with them until I figured out what made them tick and could relate to them well. This isn't to say that you should change yourself for others, but some empathy to what makes others comfortable goes a surprisingly long way.

12.3 Prioritizing work

As a data scientist trying to support an organization, you often have to decide what task you should be working on. Although some teams have a project manager who decides what work each data scientist should do, you should still be recommending what the next task should be. These tasks can vary wildly in topic and scope, and each may come from a different stakeholder. You can classify tasks into three buckets:

- *Quick tasks that come directly from stakeholders*—These tasks tend to be small requests such as "Make a graph of sales over time." They are often urgent, and because they don't take much time it's hard to say no. But each one is a distraction from more-important work, and as requests build up, it's harder and harder to do productive work.
- *Long-term projects for the business*—These projects are the core of a data scientist's job. Building dashboards, making long-form analyses, and creating models to put into production all fall into this bucket. These tasks tend to be highly important, but given the fact that they can take weeks or months to complete, they are not always urgent.
- *Ideas that you think have a long-term benefit*—Given the nature of data science, these generally are more technical, such as creating a machine learning model to predict when a customer will call support before they do. This category also includes work that makes you more productive, such as creating functions or even a library to solve common problems faster. If a manual process takes hours each week to run, you can automate the task, providing no direct benefit to the business but indirectly freeing yourself to do more. No one is asking for this work, but it feels important.

It can be difficult to figure out the most important task to be working on and what you can put on the back burner, especially when multiple people are requesting work from you. At the same time, the work that is very important to stakeholders may not be important for the business as a whole. As a data scientist, you rarely have the ability to decline requests from stakeholders, because they usually are the ones who drive the direction of the business. All this creates an environment in which the decision about what you work on can hugely influence the business; it also constrains you in what you can choose to do.

This area is one that many data scientists struggle with. When stakeholders make requests, it's natural to want to please them and not to disappoint them. Also, the requests they make can be intellectually interesting. Trying to fulfill every request is unsustainable, however, because the requests for answers are endless. Further, answering one question with data often leads to new questions, so fulfilling requests often creates additional work rather than lowering the amount of work left to do.

When you're considering possible tasks to work on, it helps to focus on two questions:

- *Will this work have an impact?* Does knowing the result of this analysis materially affect the company? Would any result change decisions? Would this machine learning model increase profit?
- *Will this work do something new?* Would you be applying an existing process over and over, or would you be trying something different?

The answers to these two questions create four combinations of types of work:

- Innovative and impactful
- Not innovative but impactful
- Innovative but not impactful
- Neither innovative nor impactful

In the next few sections, we go into each of these combinations in detail.

12.3.1 *Both innovative and impactful work*

Innovative work that alters the business is what most data scientists want to spend their whole career doing. An example project would be something such as taking inventory data that has never been touched by a data scientist before and using a start-of-the-art machine learning model to optimize ordering product, saving the company millions of dollars. They're the kind of projects that, at their best, get you featured in magazines such as *Harvard Business Review* or *Wired*.

Unfortunately, not many company projects fall into this category. To exist, these projects need to have many things going for them:

- There needs to be enough data for data science methods to be useful.
- There has to be an interesting signal in the data that the models can pick up.
- The part of the business has to be large or important enough that changes can make a difference to the bottom line (so the project probably isn't optimizing dry-erase marker inventory for the office).
- The problem must be complex or unique enough that people haven't tried it before.

The set of problems at a company that fall into all those buckets is exceedingly small.

These projects are great because they create excitement among both stakeholders and data scientists. The stakeholders feel great because they can see the clear value of the project. The data scientists are eager to try new methods on new data and see the results. If you find a project in this category, do everything you can to nurture it. These projects are the sort that can define a career, but because they have so many requirements, they are very rare and don't often succeed.

12.3.2 *Not innovative but still impactful work*

These projects aren't innovative but alter the business, such as very mundane data analysis that persuades a team to launch a product. Often, this persuasion amounts to providing proof of a thing that everyone suspects is true; it's not particularly innovative, but it will help. In engineering, these projects could be taking a model that has already been deployed in one division of the company and redeploying it to another division. Another type of work that falls in this category is streamlining tasks that take lots of time. That kind of work isn't innovative, but it does improve the business.

Although this work isn't glamorous, what's important is that it helps the business. Helping stakeholders see the value of data science work is great for getting buy-in. If you have more buy-in, the next time a project goes over budget or doesn't pan out, people are more likely to keep their faith in you. So as much as possible, try to take on these projects.

At the end of the day, the job of a data scientist is to provide value to the company, not to do the work that's most fascinating to them. A valuable skill for data scientists is to be able to tolerate this kind of valuable-but-not-interesting work. That being said, if a job is entirely full of projects that don't interest you and won't teach you anything, it's entirely appropriate to seek a different job. It's totally valid to consider job satisfaction when you're prioritizing work; just make sure that it's not the only consideration.

12.3.3 *Innovative but not impactful work*

This work is innovative but not useful to the business, such as researching new theoretical data science algorithms and methods that have a low chance of being used. These projects can be ivory towers, in which people spend months or years holed up on work that doesn't interact with other groups and won't end up being used. These projects can be huge time sinks for data science teams and end up costing millions of dollars with little to show for them. Despite these facts, these projects attract data scientists to them like moths to a bright light.

These projects tend to start within the data science team and focus on what is methodologically interesting rather than what is useful for the business. A data scientist could read a research paper outlining a new theoretical technique and persuade the rest of the team that they *must* try using it on their own data. Six months later, it's clear the method isn't as good as the paper suggested, and even if it was, no one in the business has a particular need for the results that the algorithm would have provided. Worse, the data scientist has since moved on to a new paper, and the process repeats.

Often, stakeholders don't even know about these projects. At most, they notice that some of the data scientists on the team seem to be very busy working on something that sounds really hard, but no one has explained what it is. As a data scientist, it's easy to feel that when you complete a project, people will be able to find a use for it. In practice, if you can't see a use for the project immediately, stakeholders probably won't either. As much as possible, don't get stuck working on these projects, which may not be contributing to the business, causing people to question your value.

12.3.4 *Neither innovative nor impactful work*

Unfortunately, plenty of work that data scientists get asked to do is neither innovative nor impactful. The most classic example is a frequently updated report that isn't automated and takes a long time to make, yet no one bothers to read every time it's published. This sort of work takes a ton of time and effort to make, yet if it's delivered to many stakeholders, no one is willing to be the stakeholder who steps up and says that the work no longer needs to be done. As the business collects more and more required reports over time, the time it takes to generate all of them can eventually weigh down a data science team.

Although reporting is one type of work that has the potential to be neither innovative nor impactful, plenty of small one-off requests can fall into this category. Executives who like data and charts can repeatedly make requests of the data science team such as "Make me a chart of sales in Europe by week" or "Find me the product that has the biggest drop in orders in the past 12 weeks." None of these requests may be particularly difficult, but together, they take a lot of bandwidth and probably don't provide very much value to the business.

These sorts of situations are difficult because there are no easy answers. You can try automating reports and processes that take lot of time, but that task itself takes a lot of time, and you may get only limited improvements, depending on the technology being used. If high-level stakeholders are making repeated requests, for example, it's hard to say no without jeopardizing the data science team's standing.

Despite these difficult situations, it's your responsibility as a data scientist to try to advocate for your time being well used. If many of these tasks are going on, you should make it clear to other people that those tasks may not be worth the time by having conversations with your manager or your stakeholders. It's likely that they already know that this work isn't especially useful, but by having continuing discussions about the processes and how you think they should be improved, people will be less willing to accept the status quo. If not, sometimes the best thing you can do is try to make your suggested improvements first and then show them off.

12.4 *Concluding remarks*

Working with stakeholders is a constant process throughout the course of a project. You need to understand their needs and why they are asking for them. A project starts due to a stakeholder request, but what they are requesting will likely change during the project itself, and it's your responsibility to keep up with the changes. The more you can align your project with what the stakeholder is asking for, the less likely the project will be to fail. In chapter 13, we talk about what happens when a data science project fails, such as when stakeholder communication breaks down.

Sam Barrows, data scientist at Airbnb: Turning requests into dialogues

One valuable tool for working with stakeholders is to turn requests into dialogues. You may often have colleagues ask you to complete specific tasks. Rather than immediately accept or reject these requests, start a dialogue about why the request is being made. What business need does the request aim to solve? Is there a better way to achieve the intended outcome? By understanding the motivations behind the requests that you receive, you are more likely to do meaningful work.

This strategy is practicing interest-based negotiation, where the players in a negotiation focus on addressing their underlying interests, rather than just their more immediate needs. In this case, the immediate needs are the requests that you receive, while the underlying interests are the business motivations behind these requests, as well as the objectives of the data science team.

12.5   *Interview with Sade Snowden-Akintunde, data scientist at Etsy*

Sade Snowden-Akintunde works at Etsy, where she specializes in experiment design and analysis to improve purchasing experiences for international consumers. Her areas of expertise include A/B testing and experimentation, implementing reliable data practices, and scaling data infrastructure.

Why is managing stakeholders important?

Unfortunately, it doesn't matter how smart you are if you cannot communicate concepts to non-technical stakeholders. At the end of the day, a lot of these companies are run by people who may not have the same level of technical skill as you. You need to be able to communicate to them in a way that both makes them feel capable and allows you to advocate for yourself if necessary. Managing stakeholders is probably one of the most important aspects of data science, but often, it's highlighted the least.

How did you learn to manage stakeholders?

Trial and error: I've had situations that have worked and situations that did not work, and I paid attention. I think the biggest thing that I've learned is it's really important to communicate early and repeat yourself to make sure that people understand what you're saying. Early in my data science career, I assumed that if I said something once and somebody agreed, then they knew exactly what I was talking about, but people may not even know that they don't understand what you're saying.

Was there a time where you had difficulty with a stakeholder?

Early in my career, I was afraid to advocate for myself and from my perspective as an experiment designer. Other people would make experiments that did not make sense to me, but I didn't say anything. Then I would try to analyze the experiments after they finished, and the results would be difficult to interpret because of the experiment design. I should have been working with the stakeholders from the very beginning to communicate how I could best analyze their work and what they would get from their experiment with proper design. I realized I have to actually say something from the very beginning if I want to be able to do my best work at the end.

What do junior data scientists frequently get wrong?

I think junior data scientists assume people are going to automatically recognize the value in their work. This is especially common among data scientists who come from academic backgrounds. We tend to get really wrapped up in everything being super-thorough and following the scientific method. While this is important in academia, just working hard is not necessarily what's going to get people to recognize the value of your work. The way that you communicate is what gets people to recognize the value of your work.

Do you always try to explain the technical part of the data science?

It depends on how much the stakeholder wants to be involved. I've worked with project managers who did not want to be involved in anything technical. If I just said "This is not working right now," they would take that at face value. I've also worked with project managers who wanted to know every detail, and what I have found is that they do tend to get a little overwhelmed. Some people want you to check in on a regular basis and tell them what's happening, and even if they know that they don't understand, they just want to feel in the loop. So I'll just make sure that they feel in the loop.

What's your final piece of advice for junior or aspiring data scientists?

I think that people tend to want to go into technical careers like data science because they think that you can focus only on the logical element and not deal with the human element. But that's not the case at all. When people are considering a career in data science, they should really think about if they are willing to have a small ego in order to communicate and do their job well. It's really easy to say "I want to learn how to build this model, and I want to learn A/B testing, and I want to learn all these technical things." While that's great, the soft skills are what are going to take you far in your career.

Summary

- Stakeholders come in many forms, with many needs.
- Create relationships with stakeholders so that they can consistently rely on you.
- Have continuous communication, and keep stakeholders in the loop on timelines and difficulties with projects.

Chapters 9–12 resources

Books

Beautiful Evidence, by Eduard Tufte (Graphics Press)

Eduard Tufte is a legend in the field of visualizing data, and his books are filled with detailed guidance on how to think through plots and tables. He has other books as well; you can grab them in a set or, even better, take one of his one-day courses that he does as a traveling tour. A word of caution, though: His advice is sometimes academic. It's pretty much impossible to do everything he suggests and have time to do any other part of your job besides make visualizations.

Fundamentals of Data Visualization: A Primer on Making Informative and Compelling Figures, by Claus O. Wilke (O'Reilly Media)

If Eduard Tufte provides an academic overview of thinking through visualizations, Wilke provides the practical applied version. This text walks though how to think about visualization decisions on a day-to-day basis. When are boxplots good? Are pie charts as bad as people say they are? This book will guide you through those decisions.

The Pyramid Principle: Logic in Writing and Thinking, by Barbara Minto (Trans-Atlantic Publications)

This book is years out of print (although you can find used copies) but still referred to as a foundational work in communicating well. Minto lays out how to think about structuring a report or presentation so that it resonates with the audience, giving critical guidance such as ordering your content in a way that's meaningful, not just in the order in which you created it. Minto is an ex-consultant at the prestigious consulting firm McKinsey, and the book is full of lessons that consultants master.

The Design of Web APIs, by Arnaud Lauret (Manning)

It's common to learn how to design APIs by learning through experience; eventually, you make enough of them that the designs start to be sensible. This book is like a shortcut through that process. It starts by laying out what APIs are and how they are structured; then it goes through the design of them and best practices. It even covers topics such as OpenAPI documentation so that you can write shareable specifications for your APIs.

Amazon Web Services in Action, 2nd ed., by Michael Wittig and Andreas Wittig (Manning)

Azure in Action, by Chris Hay and Brian H. Prince (Manning)

Google Cloud Platform in Action, by JJ Geewax (Manning)

These three books cover how to use Amazon Web Services, Microsoft Azure, and Google Cloud Platform, respectively. As you learn to deploy machine learning models, you'll want a place to host them, and these three cloud providers are the major options. You can pick whichever platform sounds most useful to you and then use the appropriate book to learn the basics.

Difficult Conversations: How to Discuss What Matters Most, by Douglas Stone, et al. (Penguin Publishing)

Communicating is always tricky, but it's even harder when the topic is heated or people are deeply invested. This book is all about having the conversations that people usually avoid. This book provides a great skill set for a data scientist because often, data scientists have to deliver unsatisfying results to the people they work with.

Getting to Yes: Negotiating Agreement Without Giving In, by Roger Fisher, William L. Ury, and Bruce Patton (Penguin Publishing)

Being a data scientist requires a lot of negotiation, from persuading a team to grant you access to data to urging an executive to heed your findings. Being able to successfully convince and negotiate in these moments can be more important to your success than any technical skills. *Getting to Yes* is a great resource for learning how to negotiate with stakeholders and get the results you want.

Software Requirements, Third Edition, by Karl Wiegers and Joy Beatty (Microsoft Press)

Defining what is needed for a project in a way that can be understood by the business is a difficult task. This well-regarded book covers how to create requirements and manage them over the course of the project. While requirements gathering isn't the most glamourous part of data science, it can make or break a project's execution.

Blogs

"R in Production" by Jacqueline Nolis and Heather Nolis

http://mng.bz/YrAA

This three-part series covers creating an API in R with the plumber package, deploying it as a Docker container, and then making it enterprise-ready. The open-source R docker container provided is in use by T-Mobile.

"Advice for new and junior data scientists: what I would have told myself a few years ago," by Robert Chang

http://mng.bz/zlyX

In this popular post, Robert Chang, our chapter 1 interviewee, lays out six core principles that he learned in his journey to becoming a senior data scientist at Airbnb. These important insights could take you years to learn on your own, so take the shortcut and start applying them now instead.

"Data science foundations: know your data. Really, really, know it," by Randy Au

http://mng.bz/07Pl

Randy Au, our chapter 2 interviewee, gives this piece of advice to every new data person: "Know your data, where it comes from, what's in it, what it means. It all starts from there." In this post, he lays out how to get to know your data, from starting at the data layout to knowing the collection decisions being made.

"How to work with stakeholders as a data scientist: what I would have told myself when I started," by Sam Barrows

http://mng.bz/KEPZ

We shared the first of Sam's seven tips for working productively with stakeholders as a sidebar in chapter 12 ("Turning requests into dialogues"), but the other six are well worth reading.

Part 4
Growing in your
data science role

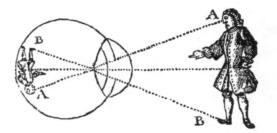

The final part of this book is material to use after you get comfortable in a data science position; it's all about what comes next. The topics in this part eventually affect every data scientist, yet aren't frequently talked about. It's easy to assume that if you have a stable data science job, you've made it, but you always have more to learn. The goal of this final part is to provide materials to help you move from a junior data scientist to a senior data scientist and beyond.

Chapter 13 covers how to handle failed data science projects. This topic is critically important for veteran data scientists, because as your career progresses, you'll certainly run into failures. Chapter 14 is about joining the data science community, from writing blog posts to attending conferences. Although it's not required of data scientists, community involvement can be hugely beneficial for building a network and landing future jobs. Chapter 15 handles the tricky task of leaving a data science position in a way that's best for your career. As the last chapter of this book, Chapter 16 discusses some of the main career paths after senior data scientist, such as becoming a manager or a technical lead.

13

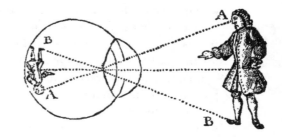

When your data science project fails

This chapter covers

- Why data science projects tend to fail
- What you can do when your project fails
- How to handle the negative emotions from failure

Most data science projects are high-risk ventures. You're trying to predict something no one has predicted before, optimize something no one has optimized before, or understand data that no one has looked at before. No matter what you're doing, you're the first person doing it; the work is almost always exploratory. Because data scientists are continuously doing new things, you will inevitably hit a point where you find out that what you hoped for just isn't possible. We all must grapple with our ideas not succeeding. Failure is heartbreaking and gut-wrenching; you want to stop thinking about data science and daydream about leaving the field altogether.

As an example, consider a company building a machine learning model to recommend products on the website. The likely course of events starts with some set of meetings in which the data science team convinces executives that the project is a good idea. The team believes that by using information about customers and their transactions, they can predict what customers want to buy next. The executives buy into the idea and green-light the project. Many other companies have these models, which seem straightforward, so the project should work.

Unfortunately, once the team starts working, reality sets in. Maybe they find out that because the company recently switched systems, transaction data is available only for the past few months. Or maybe the team runs an experiment and finds that the people who see the recommendation engine don't buy anything more than the people who don't. Problems such as these build up; eventually the team abandons the project, dismayed.

In this chapter, we define a project as a *failure* when it doesn't meet its objective. In the case of an analysis, the project might fail when it doesn't help the stakeholder answer the business question. For a production machine learning problem, a project could fail when it isn't deployed or doesn't work when deployed. Projects can fail in many ways.

Data scientists tend to not talk about projects failing, although it happens extremely often. When a project fails, a data scientist can feel vulnerable. If your project fails, you may think "Had I been a better data scientist, this wouldn't have happened." Few people are comfortable sharing stories about questioning their own abilities.

At its core, data science is research and development. Every day, data scientists take data that has never been analyzed before and search for a trend that may or may not be there. Data scientists set out to build machine learning models on data where there may not be a signal. It's impossible for these tasks to always succeed, because new trends and signals are very rarely found in any field. In a field such as software engineering, however, it's usually possible to complete a task (although it may take more time and resources than planned).

Understanding how data science projects fail and what to do when they fail is important. The better you understand a failed project, the more future failures you can avoid. Failed projects can also give you insights into what will succeed by investigating what parts of the project did work. And you might be able to adjust a failed project with a little work into something that could be useful within the organization.

In this chapter, we cover three topics: why data science projects fail, how to think about project risk, and what to do when a project is failing. We discuss three main reasons why most projects fail, what to do with the project, and how to handle the emotions you may feel.

13.1   Why data science projects fail

It seems that data science projects fail for an endless list of reasons. From budget to technology and tasks that take far longer to complete than expected, there are many reasons for failure. Ultimately, these many types of failures break down into a few core themes.

13.1.1 *The data isn't what you wanted*

You can't look into every possible data source before starting a project. It's imperative to make informed assumptions about what is available based on what you know of the company. When the project starts, you often find out that many of your assumptions don't hold true. Perhaps data doesn't exist, isn't stored in a useful format, or isn't stored in a place you can access. If you're doing an analysis to understand how a customer's age affects their use of a loyalty program, for example, you may find out that customers are never asked their ages when joining the program. That failure can end a project very quickly.

> **Example failure: Analysis of loyalty-program status**
>
> A director in the marketing department of a large restaurant chain wants to understand whether customers spend differently as they increase in status in the company's loyalty program. The program has silver, gold, and platinum levels, and the director wants to know whether someone who hits platinum bought in the same way when they were merely at silver.
>
> The data science team agrees to look into this request because the task should be fairly straightforward and they haven't worked with loyalty data before. They're shocked to find that the antiquated loyalty-program database doesn't keep track of historic program levels—just where customers are now. If a customer is currently at the platinum level, there's no way to know when they used to be silver or gold. Thus, the analysis is impossible to do.
>
> The data science team recommends that the system be adjusted, but changing a loyalty-program database architecture requires millions of dollars, and there's little demand for it in the company, so no changes are made, and the analysis idea is abandoned.

Because you need data before you can do anything, these types of problems are the first major ones that arise. A common reaction to running into this issue is internal bargaining, in which you try to engineer around the holes in your data. You say things like "Well, we don't have a decade of data like we wanted, but maybe a year of data will be sufficient for the model" and hope for the best. Sometimes, this approach can work, but the alternate solutions aren't always adequate to make the project feasible.

When you pitch a project, you don't always have access to the data or even a full understanding of what it is (a special problem in consulting, where you don't get access to the data until the work for the project is sold). Further, the data may exist but have a critical flaw that renders it useless. The data might exist in a database table, but the customer IDs might be corrupted and unusable. There are so many ways a dataset could have problems that it's extremely difficult to check them all before starting a project. For this reason, it's common for data science projects to barely get past the launch phase.

The faster you can get access to the data and explore it, the faster you can mitigate the risk of inadequate data. The best-case scenario for avoiding this error is getting samples of data before starting a project. If that isn't feasible, the next-best scenario is having a project timeline designed around the possibility that the data will be poor. By having an early "go/no go" step in the project at which the stakeholders agree to reassess the project feasibility, there's less of a chance that stakeholders will be surprised that the data could be bad.

If you find yourself struggling with a lack of good data, you have limited options. You can try to find alternative data sources to substitute, for example. Maybe you don't have data on which products were purchased, but you do know what product volume was manufactured, and you can use that instead. The problem usually is that these substitutes are different enough to cause real problems with the analysis.

When you can't find a viable substitute, sometimes all you can do is start a separate project to begin collecting better data. Adding instrumentation and telemetry to websites and apps, creating databases to store data instead of throwing it out, and performing other tasks can help the team take on the task in the future with better data collected.

13.1.2   *The data doesn't have a signal*

Suppose that a gambler hires a data scientist, hoping to use statistics to win a dice game. The gambler rolls a six-sided die 10,000 times and records the rolls; then he pays the data scientist to create a model that will predict the next die roll. Despite the data scientist's having an immense amount of data, there is no way to predict what roll will come next beyond assigning each side a 1/6 probability (if the die is fair). Despite the data scientist having lots of data, there is no signal within that data as to what side will be rolled next.

This problem of not having a signal in the data is extremely common in data science. Suppose that you're running an e-commerce website and want to create a model to predict which customers will order products based on their browser, device, and operating system. There is no way to know before starting a project whether those data points could actually be used to predict whether a customer will order, or whether the data lacks a signal, just like the die-roll data did. The act of creating a machine learning model to make a prediction is testing the data to see whether it has a signal within it, and there very well may not be. In fact, in many situations, it would be more surprising for there to *be* a signal than for there *not* to be a signal.

Example failure: Detecting bugs on a website with sales data

A hypothetical e-commerce company has a problem: the website keeps having errors and bugs. Worse, the errors aren't always detected by DevOps or the software engineering team. Once, the error was detected by the marketing team, which noticed that daily revenue was too low. When marketing notices a bug instead of DevOps or engineering, that's a bad situation.

The data science team sets out to use statistical quality-control techniques on the sales data so that they can have alerts when revenue is so low that there must be a bug on the site. They have a list of days when bugs were detected and historic revenue data. It seems straightforward to use sales to predict bugs.

Unfortunately, the number of reasons why revenue can change on a daily basis makes detecting bugs almost impossible. Revenue could be low because of the day of the week, the point in the year, promotions from marketing, global events, or any number of other things. Although marketing was once able to see a bug, that fact wasn't generalizable because there wasn't a signal for it in the data.

Unfortunately, not having a signal in the data can be the end of the project. If a project is built around trying to find a relationship in the data and make a prediction based on it, and there is no relationship there, the prediction cannot be made. An analysis may turn up nothing new or interesting, or a machine learning model may fail to have any results that are better than random chance.

If you can't seem to find the signal in the noise, you have a couple of possible ways out:

- *Reframe the problem.* You can try to reframe the problem to see whether a different signal exists. Suppose that you have a set of articles, and you're trying to predict the most relevant article to the user. You could frame the problem as a classification problem to try to classify which article in a set of articles is the most relevant.
- *Change the data source.* If nothing seems to pull a signal out of the data, you can try changing the data source. As with the previous failure point of not having good data, adding a new data source to the problem sometimes creates an unexpected signal. Unfortunately, you usually start with the dataset that had the highest chance of being useful, so the odds that this strategy will save you are fairly limited.

It's usual for data scientists who are stuck in this situation to try using a more powerful model to find a signal. If a logistic regression can't make a meaningful prediction, they try a random forest model. If a random forest model doesn't work, they try a neural network. Each method ends up being more time-consuming and more complex. Although these methods can be useful for getting more accurate predictions, they can't make something out of nothing.

Most often, if the simplest method cannot detect any signal, the more complex ones won't be able to either. Thus, it's best to start with simple modeling methods to validate the feasibility of the project and then move to more-complex and time-consuming ones rather than start with the complex ones and go simpler. Don't get lost spending months building increasingly complicated models, hoping that just maybe the next one will be the one that saves the project.

13.1.3 *The customer didn't end up wanting it*

No matter how accurate a model or analysis is, what matters is that it provides value to the stakeholder. An analysis can have findings that are incredibly interesting to the data scientist but not to the businessperson who requested it. A machine learning model can make highly accurate predictions, but if that model isn't deployed and used, it won't provide much value. Many data science projects fail even after the data science work has been done.

Ultimately, a data science analysis, model, or dashboard is a product. Designing and creating a product is a practice that many people have put hundreds of years of collective thought into. Despite all that, every year, billions of dollars are spent creating products that people don't end up wanting. From New Coke to Google Glass, some high-profile products don't land with customers, and some low-profile ones don't either. Just as Microsoft and Nokia can put lots of effort into creating Windows Phone, which customers didn't end up buying, so can a data scientist create products that aren't used.

Example failure: Sales and marketing campaign value prediction

A project at a retail company was started to create a machine learning model to predict how much return on investment (ROI) future advertising campaigns would bring. The data science team decided to build the model after seeing how much the marketing and sales teams struggled with making Excel spreadsheets that predicted the overall value. Suppose that by using machine learning and modeling at the customer level, the data science team created a Python-based model that more accurately predicted the ROI of the campaigns.

Later, the data science team found out that the only reason why the marketing and sales teams created Excel spreadsheets with ROI predictions was to get the finance department to sign off on them. The finance team refused to work with anything but Excel; Python was too much of a black box for them. Thus, the tool wasn't used because the data science team didn't consider the customer's needs. The need wasn't for the most accurate prediction possible; it was for a prediction that would convince the finance team that the campaigns were financially feasible.

The universal guidance on creating products that customers will like is to spend lots of time talking to and working with customers. The more you understand their needs, their desires, and their problems, the more likely you are to make a product that they want. The fields of market research and user experience research are different ways of understanding the customer, through surveys and focus groups in market research or through user stories, personas, and testing in user experience research. Many other fields have come up with their own methods and have been using them for years.

Despite all the good thinking people have done, data science as a field is especially susceptible to failing because of not understanding the customer needs. For whatever reason, data scientists are much more comfortable looking at tables and plots than they are going out and talking to people. Many data science projects have failed because the data scientists didn't put enough effort into talking to customers and stakeholders to understand what their true problems were. Instead, the data scientists jumped into building interesting models and exploring data. In fact, this situation is one of the main reasons why we chose to devote chapter 12 to managing stakeholders. We hope that you already have a better understanding of how to think through stakeholder relationships from reading that chapter, but if you skipped it, maybe you should check it out.

If you find yourself in the situation of having a product that doesn't seem to be landing, the single best thing you can do is talk to your customers. It's never too late to talk to your customers. Whether your customer is a business stakeholder or customers of your company, communication and understanding can be helpful. If your product isn't useful to them, can they tell you why it isn't? Could you potentially fix the problems by adding new features to the product? Maybe you could change an analysis by joining a different dataset to it. Maybe you could improve a machine learning model by adjusting the format of the output or how quickly it runs. You'll never know until you talk to people.

This also feeds into the concept of a minimally viable product (MVP), which is used heavily in software development. The idea is that the more quickly you can get a product working and to market, the more quickly you can get feedback on what works or doesn't and then iterate on that feedback. In data science, the faster you have any model working or any analysis done, the faster you can show it to customers or stakeholders and get their feedback. Spending months iterating on a model prevents you from getting that feedback.

The better you understand customers throughout the design and build processes of your work, the less likely you are to get a failure from a customer not wanting the product. And if you end up failing in this way, the best way forward is to start communicating to try to find a solution.

13.2 Managing risk

Some projects are riskier than others. Taking data the team has worked with before and making a standard dashboard in a standard way is pretty likely to succeed. Finding a new dataset in the company, building a machine learning model around it that will run in real time, and displaying it to the customer in a pleasant user interface is a riskier project. As a data scientist, you have some control of the amount of risk you have at any time.

One big consideration with risk is how many projects you are working on at the same time. If you are working on a single risky project, and that project fails, it can be quite difficult to handle that failure careerwise. If, however, you are able to work on several projects at the same time, you will be able to mitigate the risk. If one of those projects fails, you have other projects to fall back on. If one project is an extremely complex machine learning model that has a limited chance of success, you could simultaneously be working on simpler dashboarding and reporting; then, if the machine learning project fails, your stakeholders may still be happy with the reports.

Having multiple projects can also be beneficial from a utilization standpoint. Data science projects have many starts and stops, from waiting for data to waiting for stakeholders to respond and even waiting for models to fit. If you find yourself stuck on one project for some reason, you'll have an opening to make progress on another. This can even help with mental blocks; distracting yourself when you're stuck can be a great way to refresh your thinking.

Another way to mitigate risk is to bake early stopping points into a project. Ideally, a project that seems like it may fail should be designed with the expectation that if by a certain point it isn't successful, it'll be cut off. In a project in which it's unclear whether the data exists, for example, the project can be scoped so that if, after a month of searching, good data can't be found, it's considered to be infeasible and scuttled. If the expectation that it might not work out is presented early, ending the project is less surprising and less costly.

In a sense, having the project end early codifies the fact that data science is research and development. Because data science is filled with so many unknowns, it makes sense to plan in the possibility that as more is learned through exploratory work, the idea may not pan out.

Although it's worthwhile to minimize the risk in a project portfolio, you don't want to remove it entirely. Data science is all about taking risks: almost any sufficiently interesting project is going to have plenty of uncertainty and unknowns. Those risky unknowns can occur because no one has used a new dataset before, no one in a company has tried a certain methodology before, or the stakeholder is from a part of the company that has never used data science before. Plenty of valuable data science contributions at companies have come from people trying something new, and if as a data scientist you try to avoid projects that could fail, you're also avoiding potentially big successes.

Although this chapter covers many ways that data science projects have failed, data science teams can eventually fail in aggregate by not taking enough risks. Consider a data science team that comes up with some new project ideas and reports, finds them successful, and then stagnates by only updating and refreshing the previous work. Although those projects might not fail in that they are delivering work to the company, that team would miss potential new areas for data science.

13.3   *What you can do when your projects fail*

If your data science project has failed, that doesn't mean all the time you spent working on it was wasted. In section 13.2, we outlined some potential actions you can take to turn the project around. But even if there's no way the project can succeed, there are still steps you can take to get the most out what's left of it. In the following sections, we give you some strategies for handling your emotions when a project fails.

13.3.1 *What to do with the project*

Although the project may have failed, there likely is still a lot that can be gained from the project, both in knowledge and technology. The following steps can help you retain many of those gains.

DOCUMENT LESSONS LEARNED

The first thing to do with a project that failed is assess what you can learn from it. Some important questions to ask yourself and the team are

- *Why did it fail?* This question seems almost obvious, yet it's often the case that you can't understand why a project failed until you step back and look at the bigger picture. By having a discussion with all the people involved in the project, you can better diagnose what went wrong. The company Etsy popularized the concept of a *blameless postmortem*—a discussion held after something failed in which a team can diagnose the problem without blaming a person. By thinking of a problem as being caused by a flaw in the way the team works (instead of a person's mistakes), you're more likely to find a solution. Without the fear of punishment, people will be more willing to talk openly about what happened.
- *What could have been done to prevent the failure?* When you understand the factors that contributed to the failure, you can understand how to avoid similar situations in the future. If the data wasn't good enough for the project to work, for example, the failure could have been prevented by a longer exploratory phase. These sorts of lessons help your team grow and mature.
- *What did you learn about the data and the problem?* Even if the project is a failure, you often learn things that will be valuable in the future. Maybe the data didn't have a signal in it, but to get to that point, you still had to join a bunch of new datasets; now you can do those same joins more easily in other projects. These questions can help you brainstorm possible things that can be salvaged from the project and help you come up with alternative project ideas.

By having a meeting in which the team works through these questions and then saving the results in a shared location, you'll get a lot more value out of the failed project.

CONSIDER PIVOTING THE PROJECT

Although the project itself may have been a failure, there may be ways to pivot it into something useful. If you're trying to build a tool to detect anomalies in company revenue, for example, and it fails, you may still be able to use that same model as a pretty decent forecasting tool. Whole companies have been built on taking an idea that was a failure and repurposing it into something successful.

Pivoting a product requires a lot of communication with stakeholders and customers. You're essentially back at the beginning of the product design process, trying to figure out a good use for your work. By talking to stakeholders and customers, you can understand their problems and see whether your work is useful for anything new.

END THE PROJECT (CUT AND RUN)

If you can't pivot the project, the best thing you can do is end it. By definitively cancelling the project, you allow yourself and the team to move onto new, more promising work. It's extremely easy for a data scientist to want to keep working on a project forever in the hope that someday it'll work. (There are thousands of algorithms out there; eventually one will work, right?) But if you get stuck trying to get something to work, you end up spending unnecessary effort. Also, it's not fun to work on the same thing until the end of time! Although cutting a project is hard, as it requires you to admit that it's no longer worth the effort, it pays off in the long run.

COMMUNICATE WITH YOUR STAKEHOLDERS

A data scientist should be communicating with their stakeholders throughout the course of a data science project (see chapter 12), but they should increase the amount of communication if the project is failing. Although it may feel comfortable to hide risks and troubles from stakeholders to avoid disappointing them, running into the situation where a stakeholder is surprised to find that the project has failed can be catastrophic for a career. By letting the stakeholders know that problems are occurring or that the project can no longer move forward, you're being transparent with the stakeholders and inspiring trust. After helping them understand the project state, you can work together to decide the next steps.

If you're uncertain how to communicate the problems with a stakeholder, your manager should be a good resource. They can either brainstorm an approach to delivering the message or potentially take the lead in delivering it themselves. Different people and organizations like to have messages delivered in different ways, from spreadsheets that lay out the issues with green/yellow/red color coding to conversations over coffee. Your manager or other people on your team should have insight into what works best.

It's common for you, as a data scientist, to feel anxious when communicating that a project is failing; you feel very emotionally vulnerable and think that you're in a position of weakness. Although there are occasions when the news is received poorly, other people are often willing to help work with you to resolve issues and decide next steps. After communicating the project failure, you may feel relief, not suffering.

13.3.2 *Handling negative emotions*

Forget the project and the company for a bit: you also need to think about your own well-being. Having a project fail is emotionally difficult! It's the worst! If you're not careful, a failed project can be a real drain and haunt you long after the project is over. By being thoughtful about how you react to the failure and the story you craft about it, you can set yourself up for more long-term success.

A natural internal monologue at the end of a failed project is "If I were only a better data scientist, the project wouldn't have failed." This thought is a fallacy: most data science projects fail because data science is inherently based on trying things that could never work. Most great data scientists have been involved with, or even led, projects that haven't succeeded. By placing the blame for the failed project on yourself and possible data science deficiencies, you're putting the weight of the whole project on yourself. But as discussed earlier in this chapter, there are many reasons why data science projects fail, and it's very rare that the issue is the competency of the data scientist. It's very common to be anxious that the project is failing because of you, but that anxiety is in your head and isn't a reflection of reality.

If you allow yourself to fail and accept that failure isn't a sign of a weakness, you'll be more able to learn from the experience. Being confident about yourself and your skills makes it easier to think about the failure and what contributed to it, because it won't hurt as much. That being said, the ability to be confident and own a failure is one that takes time, patience, and practice to gain, so don't be surprised if you're struggling to have confidence. It's okay!

The key point here is that the best thing you can do for yourself when a project fails is understand that failure is not a reflection on your skills. Projects fail for reasons outside your control, and you'll be able to move on from failure. The more you're able to hold those things close, the easier the failure will be to accept.

We'll end this chapter with a metaphor for data science. It's common for aspiring and junior data scientists to think of a professional data scientist as being like an architect of buildings. A novice architect may design simple homes, and an experienced architect can build skyscrapers, but if either of them has a building collapse, it's a career-ending failure. Similarly, one way to view a data scientist is that they build more and more complex models, but if one fails, their career is jeopardized. After you read this chapter, we hope that you recognize that *this isn't an accurate model of a professional data scientist.*

A better metaphor is that a data scientist is like a treasure hunter (figure 13.1). A treasure hunter sets out looking for lost valuables, and if they're lucky, they'll find some! A novice treasure hunter may look for standard goods, but an experienced hunter finds the most legendary of treasure. A data scientist is much more like a treasure hunter; they seek out successful models, and once in a while, their models and analyses work! Although a senior data scientist may work on more complicated or tricky projects, everyone is continuously failing, and that's just part of the job.

Figure 13.1 Two metaphors for data science: architecture and treasure-hunting

13.4   *Interview with Michelle Keim, head of data science and machine learning at Pluralsight*

Michelle Keim leads the Data Science and Machine learning team at Pluralsight, an enterprise-technology learning platform with a mission to democratize technology skills. Having previously grown and led a data science team at a range of companies including Boeing, T-Mobile, and Bridgepoint Education, she has a deep understanding of why data science projects can fail and how to handle failure.

When was a time you experienced a failure in your career?

I got pulled in to lead a project to build a set of customer retention models. I thought I had talked with all the right stakeholders and understood the business need, how the team worked, and why the models were necessary. We built the models but soon learned that there was no interest in them. The problem was we hadn't sat down with the customer care agents who would actually be using the output; I had only ever talked to the leaders. We delivered a list of probabilities of whether a customer would leave, but the care agents didn't know what to do with that. They needed to know what they should do when a customer is at risk of leaving, which is a very different problem than the one we had tackled. The biggest lesson learned for me was that you really have to get down into the weeds and understand the use case of the problem. What's the problem being solved by the people who will use the output?

Are there red flags you can see before a project starts?

I think partly it's an instinct that you gain from experience. The more things you see that go wrong and the more you take the opportunity to learn from the failures, the more you know what red flags to look for. The key is keeping your cycle short so that you have a chance to see them sooner; you need to bring feedback in at a frequent rate.

Data scientists tend to get excited about their work and forget to pull their heads up. It's really important to have not only an understanding of where you want to go at the end of the day, but also what success looks like at different points along the way. That way, you can check your work against that, get feedback, and be able to pivot if necessary. Checkpoints let you quickly know when you've missed or misunderstood something and correct course, rather than learning that at the end and having to backtrack.

How does the way a failure is handled differ between companies?

It's highly tied to the culture of the company. I would advise folks when job searching to try to find out if the company has a culture of learning and ongoing feedback. When you're interviewing, you have an opportunity to ask the interviewer: What are you learning yourself? How did that opportunity arise for you? If I were to take this role, how would I get feedback? Is it something that you have to seek out, or is it formalized? Getting the feel for how employees respond to these questions is very, very telling.

When you're already at a company, there are questions you can try to answer for yourself to see if there's a healthy culture. After a project is finished, is there an opportunity to pause and look back? Do you try to retrospectively learn at the end of projects? Do you see the leadership use open communication and taking ownership for failures at various levels in the company? You get a sense for fear too when a strong culture isn't there. You start to see behaviors that are more self-serving than mission-serving, and that unhealthy behavior kind of just hits you.

How can you tell if a project you're on is failing?

You can't know if you're failing if you haven't from the outset defined what success is. What are the objectives that you're trying to attain, and what do checkpoints along the way towards that success look like? If you don't know this, you're just taking a stab at whether the project is going well or not. To set yourself up for success, you have to make sure you've collaborated with your stakeholders to have a well-defined answer to those questions. You need to know why you're doing this project and what problem you're trying to solve, or you won't know the value of what you're delivering and if your approach is correct. Part of the role of a data scientist is to bring your expertise to the table and help frame the problem and define the success metrics.

How can you get over a fear of failing?

You need to remember that you actually want some failures; if everything went perfectly, you'd never learn anything. How would you ever grow? Those experiences are necessary, as there's no replacement for dealing with failure and becoming okay with it. It's true that failure can be painful, and you may ask "Oh, my gosh, what am I going to do?" But after you see yourself bounce back, learn from it, and turn it into the next thing, that resiliency you gain will snowball into confidence. If you know to expect some things to go wrong, that makes it easier the next time around. And if you make sure you're frequently getting feedback, you're going to catch your failures before they become devastating. No one expects perfection. What is expected is for you to be honest about what you don't know and to keep learning by asking questions and looking for feedback.

Summary

- Data science projects usually fail because of inadequate data, a lack of signal, or not being right for the customer.
- After a project fails, catalog why and consider pivoting or ending it.
- A project failure isn't a reflection on the quality of the data scientist.
- A data scientist isn't solely responsible for a project failure.

14

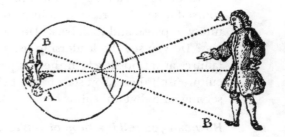

Joining the data science community

This chapter covers
- Growing your portfolio of projects and blog posts
- Finding and getting the most out of conferences
- Giving a great data science talk at a meetup or conference
- Contributing to open source

When you're in a data science job, doing well at it can feel like the only way to advance your career. But there are many other ways to grow your skills, especially by engaging with the data science community. Spending time outside work doing activities such as presenting talks or contributing to open source can be enormously beneficial for your career.

In this chapter, we go over four ways you can join the community: growing your portfolio, attending conferences, giving talks, and contributing to open source. We present four activities so that you may choose the ones you like best; very few people have the time and energy to do them all. Although these things will take time outside your normal day job, that doesn't mean they should take over your life. Throughout this chapter, we give advice about using your time effectively with tactics such as reusing talks, turning a blog post into a talk, and writing a blog post about your first open source contribution.

Writing blog posts   Attending conferences   Giving talks   Contributing to open source

Figure 14.1 Some ways to join the community that are covered in this chapter

Although these activities can be helpful and immensely rewarding, you don't have to do them to have a fulfilling data science career. Plenty of data scientists, including those in senior positions at top companies, don't do any of them. But both of us (the authors) feel that being part of the community has helped us at numerous times during our careers, including in getting job offers and getting promoted. Public work is an area in which the time you invest can pay back twice over.

We see four main benefits of joining the broader data science community (figure 14.1):

- *Gaining skills*—By engaging with the community, you learn new techniques that you wouldn't be exposed to if you only relied upon your day job. Creating an open source project is the activity that most directly develops your technical skills because you'll be writing code for others to use and working collaboratively on a technical project. But every activity has benefits. Blogging is a great way to realize gaps in your knowledge and get feedback. Giving talks helps you hone your presentation skills, which may help you convince a stakeholder that you need funding or that they should back your project. Hearing the right talk at a conference could unblock an important project and save you hours of work.

- *Growing your network*—Connecting with the community is a great way to find a supportive group of peers who understand your struggles. Even if you have peers at your company, you may be lacking expertise in a certain niche that can be filled with advice from a community member. You can also learn what's it like to work in data science at different companies.

- *Gaining opportunities*—The more involved you are in the community, the more you'll be asked to help on projects, give talks, or speak on a podcast. You may even land your next job thanks to someone finding you through your online work or meeting you at a conference. This is a large positive feedback loop: talks lead to more talks, and projects lead to more projects. These opportunities can be informative, interesting, and fun.

- *Giving back*—This is less a direct benefit to yourself but more integral to the well-being of the community. When you ask a mentor how you can pay them back for their support, many will say, "Pay it forward. Help others, and become a mentor to them." Being part of the community can make a data science job much more fulfilling. By doing tasks that help others, you'll feel valuable, like you're doing work for more than just a paycheck.

14.1   *Growing your portfolio*

Just because you have a job now doesn't mean that you can forget all the excellent habits you developed to get it. In chapter 4, you learned about writing blog posts and building a portfolio. Being employed doesn't mean that there's no value in continuing to maintain and expand them. Working on a blog or side project doesn't have to be burdensome; in this chapter, we discuss new topics and ways to recycle your work to get multiple uses from the same effort.

14.1.1   *More blog posts*

We hope that you're learning a lot of new things in your job as a data scientist. How can you optimize SQL queries on a 30-billion row table? How do you work effectively with marketers? What are some strategies to start navigating hundreds of tables?

If you're at a company that employs other data scientists, you'll be learning directly from them, whether by reading their code or pair-programming. It's a good idea to take notes during this process, as you'll be getting a lot of new information, and it's unlikely that you'll remember it all in a few months. When you're doing that, why not share your notes with the class (in this case, the entire internet)? Strangers on the internet aren't the only ones who will benefit; writing a blog post is a great way to consolidate your learning. You may even find yourself years later referring to an earlier tutorial you wrote.

If you followed our advice in chapter 4, you should already have a blog that is up and running with a few posts. If you didn't, but you're interested in starting one, we recommend going back to that chapter and following the steps there. Everything we wrote there still applies; the same strategies that made effective blog posts when you were looking for your first data science job hold up even after you're working in the field. The only major change is that you need to make sure, if you're writing about projects that you've done at work (versus general programming, statistical, or people management skills you've learned), that you aren't sharing any confidential or proprietary information, and that you follow any other rules your company has for employees' personal blogs (such as running posts by the communications department first).

If you don't want to have your own blog, see whether your company has a tech blog. Even if past posts have been engineering-centric, you can do a data science post. It might take time to get approval, but a bonus of going this route is that you can write up your thoughts during work time. Even if your company doesn't have a public blog, it should have some internal documentation and training. If you find that you had to learn something by asking multiple people or wading through outdated instructions, create or update a resource with clear instructions for future new hires. If the topic is something that will be helpful to people outside the company (not on a proprietary internal tool or description of your data, for example), you can later turn it into a blog post or talk.

14.1.2 *More projects*

Data science projects (which we also went over in chapter 4) are ones in which you pick or create a dataset and analyze it to answer a question. You could use the Twitter API to make a network analysis of the users tweeting about a data science conference, for example. In some cases, a project doesn't even have to be an analysis; maybe you show off your engineering skills by building a Slack bot to allow users to give each other "points," keeping track of the totals in a database you set up.

Projects can be much harder than blog posts to keep up with. Depending on your industry, your company may be open to or even encouraging of writing in broad strokes about your work. Even if it's not, you can write nontechnical posts about how to deal with business stakeholders or your experience in the job market. Very few companies, however, share their data publicly, so even if you could share the code of an awesome analysis you did, it wouldn't make much sense, because you couldn't share the data or the results. If you want to share analyses you do, you'll have to do it as a side project strictly on your own time.

That said, it's good to do a side project occasionally. For one thing, when you want to move to your next job, companies may ask for an example of a data analysis you've done. If you've been working at your company for a few years, you don't want to show a project you did while in a bootcamp or enrolled in a MOOC, as you want to showcase how your skills have evolved while working as a data scientist. That said, the principles of finding a topic and writing a good analysis remain the same as in chapter 4.

The good news is that a project doesn't have to take a lot of time. David Robinson, whom we interviewed in chapter 4, does a weekly screencast in which he records himself doing an analysis on a dataset he's never seen before (from the Tidy Tuesday project https://github.com/rfordatascience/tidytuesday/). This analysis takes him about an hour, as he does no preparation, but when the code is uploaded to GitHub, it could serve as an example analysis project. Now, it does take a pretty experienced data scientist to make a good analysis so quickly, but anyone can try setting a time limit on their analysis to help them stay focused on sharing results (and not spend 14 hours on a project they never show anyone).

14.2 Attending conferences

Sometimes, being part of the community means having to get out of your home. For the most part, this means going to conferences, where people who are in (or want to be in) similar industries or fields come together to talk about their work.

Conferences are usually annual events that take place all over the country and the world. The field of data science has many conferences. Strata, rstudio::conf, PyData, EARL, and Open Data Science Conference are just a few of the larger ones, and many of them have regional offshoots. You may also be interested in more general technology conferences that overlap with data science, such as Write/Speak/Code, PyCon, Grace Hopper, and SciPy.

Conferences tend to range from two to four days and have programming from early in the morning until the evening, plus social activities after. They may be single-track (only one talk happening at a given time) or multitrack, but they all have multiple speakers. They also can be very expensive—usually between $300 and $700 per day just for the ticket. Some conferences also have half-day to two-day workshops beforehand for an extra fee, usually around $750 a day.

One reason why we're giving approximate prices is that there are many ways to pay less than full price for a ticket. If you're a member of an under-represented group, look for scholarships or discount codes that are offered to all members of a group such as R-Ladies or PyLadies. If you work at a not-for-profit organization or in academia, you may also pay less, and many major conferences give discounts for purchasing in advance. Another great way to lower the expense is to give a talk, as conferences should give you a free ticket. Finally, some conferences have scholarships you can apply to that will cover the cost of your ticket and potentially your entire cost, including transportation and accommodations.

Given this potential steep price, why should you spend your time and money (or your employer's money) to attend, especially if the conference records and puts the talks online? Here, we return to one of the primary benefits we talked about at the top of the chapter: networking. Networking can have a negative connotation: someone going around a room, glad-handing everyone in hopes of meeting an important person and gaining something from them. But networking at its best is about finding a community of people who support you. That support may come in very tangible ways, such as someone introducing you to a person who works at a company you're applying to, or intangible, such as the feeling of finally being in a room of technologists in which the vast majority are women.

Building a network is best done over the long term, so even if you don't have anything you think you need help with now, it's great to lay that groundwork before you're looking for a new job or a partner for an open source project.

DRESS CODE A common question for first-time attendees is what to wear. In general, conferences are casual-dress. For a specific conference, see whether you can find pictures of the conference on Twitter or the conference website. One thing to keep in mind, though, is that the speakers may be more formally dressed than the audience; just because all speakers are in business casual doesn't mean that the audience is too. If you're really stuck, bring things that can fall in the middle, such as a casual dress or a polo shirt and dark jeans. It's rare for a conference to be so extreme that you need to be in either a suit or a T-shirt and shorts to fit in, and there usually will be at least some range in people's dress, so it's unlikely that you'll be an outlier!

With so many conferences to choose from, how do you figure out which ones are worth attending? Conferences vary, but here are a few axes to consider:

- *Academic*—Some conferences, such as useR!, NeurIPS, and JSM, have a large number of attendees in academia or in research-heavy industry jobs. At the extreme end, there are conferences at which essentially everyone is a graduate student or professor. If you're in industry, you may not find as many of the talks to be applicable; although people in industry may be presenting, the presentations may be on a cutting-edge machine learning algorithm that's useful only if you're at a giant e-commerce company.

- *Size*—Conferences can range anywhere from 150 to tens of thousands of people. We recommend starting with a small to medium-size conference—between 200 and 1,500 people. The smaller size means that it's less intimidating to navigate and you're more likely to run into people multiple times, leading to stronger connections.
- *Hiring companies*—On the other hand, you may want to go to a large conference because you're looking for a job. Although you can meet someone who's hiring at any conference, some larger conferences have job fairs, where employers pay specifically to set up a booth and talk to potential employees.
- *Level of talks*—Most conferences are generally for people who are working or studying in the field. If you don't know any R, for example, you probably wouldn't get much out of rstudio::conf, a conference run by the company that develops the primary interactive development environment (IDE) for R. Conference talks are generally aimed at an intermediate level of general knowledge but vary in the level of specific knowledge expected. rstudio::conf, for example, could have a talk introducing a package for time series. You'd need to know some R to understand the talk, but the speaker wouldn't expect you to have much experience working with time series. Or a talk at a conference about online experimentation might be an introduction to how qualitive research can complement quantitative methods.
- *Diversity and inclusivity*—Unfortunately, not all organizers are concerned about making sure that their conferences are welcoming to all. If you see that all 45 speakers are men, you can make a good guess that the attendee population is going to look similar. Besides the speaker lineup, look on the website to see whether there's a code of conduct. If you need certain accommodations, such as a wheelchair-accessible venue, look for an email address on the conference website, and send an email to ask.
- *Specialty*—Just as data science has many specialties, so do conferences. Whether you're looking for a specific language or domain, there's probably a conference that's right for you.

When you've decided what type of conference you're interested in, look for reviews of conferences before you commit to going to one. If you don't know anyone personally who has been to one, ask on Twitter or LinkedIn. Also look at the schedule for the conference or, if it's not available yet, the schedule from the previous year. If there are recordings of a talk, watch a few of them. You want to make sure that your investment is worthwhile. Unfortunately, some conferences do not have many good speakers.

Going to these conferences can be helpful for your career and also for your employer, which gets to have you representing it and learning things that can help you do your job better. As a result, you may be able to persuade your company to pay for the conference in full or in part. Some companies have a formal conference or training budget, which is great in that money is earmarked for your purpose, but if you want to exceed that budget, it will be difficult to get the company to make an exception for you.

Beyond the cost, most conferences happen at least partially during the week, so you'll have to take a day or two off work. You don't want that coming out of your vacation days, right? You need to make the case to your manager that it's worthwhile for you to spend the day at the conference rather than do your normal work. Some companies have a policy, which may or may not be formal, about how many conference days you can take. At tech companies, it's pretty normal to attend at least one conference, but other industries may not have that system.

If you need to make the case for conferences to your manager, here are some benefits to focus on:

- *Recruiting*—It costs thousands or even tens of thousands of dollars to recruit a data scientist. One of the biggest problems is getting good candidates to apply in the first place. Huge tech companies such as Google and Amazon and hot startups may have great candidates knocking down their door, but most companies don't have that name recognition. If you meet people at conferences, you put your company's name out there. This publicity is magnified a lot if you're speaking, which we cover in section 14.3.
- *Knowledge*—Your manager wants to know what you'll be able to do after a conference that you couldn't do before. It's even better if you share that knowledge with the team by writing an article (which can also become a blog post!) or presentation. Start by looking at the conference schedule and reporting to your manager the talks that will be immediately applicable to solving your problems. But keep in mind that conferences also have the hallway track: informal conversations happening outside the presentations. You may find someone there who has the solution to a problem you're facing! Five or ten minutes of the right person's time can pay for the cost of your ticket.

If you live in or near a big city, look for a conference there so that you won't have to pay for travel or accommodations. Overall, the best strategy when requesting money from your company is to show how what you learn from the conference will help you realize business wins or impact.

14.2.1 *Dealing with social anxiety*

It's a cliché that engineers and scientists are socially awkward introverts, but most people struggle with social anxiety at some point. Even the most confident people don't walk into a roomful of strangers and feel totally comfortable. What should you do if you're so nervous that you get to a conference and hide in the corner looking at your phone the whole time?

Fortunately, the advantage of attending a conference is you have something built in to talk about! In general, a solid strategy is to ask questions; people love to talk about themselves. You can ask why they're at the talk, how long they've been programming in X, or whether they've been to this conference before. Remember that many people are feeling awkward, not just you. If you're nervous, a nice time to try talking to people is the few minutes before a talk, when you're in your seat. Sit next to someone, and strike up a conversation. If your fears of a bad conversation are realized, you know that the conversation can last only a few minutes, because the talk is about to start!

When you're in a room with a lot of people, look for those standing in a Pac-Man shape: a circle with an opening. Head over to stand in the opening, and try to shift around so an opening reemerges for more people to join. You don't need to introduce yourself as soon as you arrive; you can wait for a break in the conversation or even join in the conversation without an introduction, especially if the group is large.

We talked about impostor syndrome in chapter 8, and this is another area in which it can strike. You might end up at a talk that goes way over your head. The most important thing to remember is that you shouldn't be made to feel like an impostor. If people treat you as though you're not worth their time or act shocked if you don't know a term, or if they make a belittling comment, that's on them. Some other conferences will be welcoming. Many people love helping others and remember what it was like to be new. If you end up at a conference that you don't enjoy, try not to let that experience dissuade you from ever going to one again.

Although we've covered some strategies for meeting people in this chapter, it's totally normal to take personal time during the conference. Several days of socializing with strangers can be exhausting. It's a common mistake to feel that you need to be doing something productive every moment of the conference, whether that's attending a talk or networking. But you absolutely don't! Don't feel bad about taking a walk by yourself instead of attending a talk during one session; you'll get more out of a conference overall if you take time to recharge.

14.3 Giving talks

Giving talks can offer you a lot of opportunities for growth, and also give you leverage to go to more talks and conferences. One fight that you may have is to get enough time to go to conferences to improve your skills and network, but giving talks is a great way to represent your company (in addition to the monetary benefits of talking, which make it less burdensome to your employer). Although it may seem that you need to be an industry expert, a spectacular orator, or a social butterfly to give a talk, that's not the case. Giving talks is actually a great strategy for an introvert. After your talk, people will come up to you to pay compliments, ask follow-up questions, or just introduce themselves. Having your talk be a conversation topic is an enhanced version of the general advantage of talking about the topic of the conference.

This section could be a whole book in itself, and in fact, in the resources section for chapters 13–16 we recommend a book about public speaking. We want to emphasize that the bar for giving a good talk is lower than you may think. You're not giving a TED talk here or keynoting a huge conference. Those folks have tons of experience and have likely hired speaking coaches. We believe that if you want to give a good talk, you should focus on two things: entertaining people and motivating them. If people aren't interested when you're speaking, it will be very hard to teach them anything. Additionally, people can get a limited number of takeaways from a 20-, 30-, or even 60-minute talk. But if you can fan the desire to learn more and equip the audience with the tools to get started, you'll have delivered a lot of value.

14.3.1 *Getting an opportunity*

How do you find opportunities to speak? The best place to start is looking for conferences that have calls for proposals (CFPs). You can submit a short summary of your talk, called an *abstract,* and the conference organizers will choose speakers from among the submitted abstracts. Some conferences do blind reviews, in which they pick abstracts without knowing anything about the speakers, although others ask to know more about you.

When you're looking for conferences to speak at, apply similar criteria to those you use when you're looking for conferences to attend. If going to a conference with 10,000 people sounds like your nightmare, you probably don't want to apply to speak there. Moreover, speaking is a great way to lower the cost of attending a conference, so why not get that benefit for one at which you really want to hear the other talks? Make sure to ask people you've met online or at meetups what conferences they recommend; great smaller conferences are easy to lose under the radar.

The first part of a good abstract is paying attention to what the conference is asking for. Even if you write the best 500-word abstract, you're not going to get in if the organizers were asking for a 150-word one. The same applies if you submit a talk on data engineering to a conference that focuses on statistics.

Overall, a good abstract has a first sentence that's a hook: it draws the reader in to learn more. Then you should explain the problem you're solving and give an overview of what the audience will learn. Here's an example from one of Jacqueline's talks:

> *Deep learning sounds complicated and difficult, but it's really not. Thanks to packages such as Keras, you can get started with only a few lines of code. Once you understand the basic concepts, you will be able to use deep learning to make AI-generated humorous content! In this talk I'll give an introduction to deep learning by showing how you can use it to make a model that generates weird pet names such as Shurper, Tunkin Pike, and Jack Odins. If you understand how to do a linear regression, you can understand how to create fun deep learning projects.*

When you're coming up with an abstract idea, a great way to start is to think about who you were three months, six months, or a year ago. What do you know now that you wish you knew then? It's easy to feel like everyone already knows these things, but even for stuff that you consider to be basic, such as how to use git and GitHub or how to do web scraping, thousands of people out there don't know it and would benefit from it. You can also choose to go into your subfield if that would be interesting to a broad audience. Maybe you can teach how to make interactive maps, use a package tailored to fast data analysis, or explain what a generalized linear model is. You don't need to be an expert in the field; in fact, people who've just learned something are often the best teachers. Those who learned something a long time ago forget what it was like to struggle and what misconceptions they had.

Another great way to start giving talks is to speak at local meetups. See whether any are hosting lightning-talk events, which are a series of short (often five-minute) talks. These events are a lot less pressure to prepare for, as they'll have anywhere from five to a dozen speakers in one evening. The events usually are explicitly welcoming to first-time speakers. If no lightning-talk evenings are planned, but you faithfully attend a local meetup, recommend a lightning-talk event to the organizers!

Gabriela de Queiroz: Starting R-Ladies

When I moved to San Francisco from Brazil in 2012, I was amazed by the number of resources I found. I quickly discovered the meetup scene, and for a few months, I would go to meetups every night. Learn and eat for free: it was a perfect combination, especially for a student who didn't have much money. But the majority of meetups didn't have a diverse audience. I didn't see anyone like me and couldn't feel welcome, so I would end up in a corner, not interacting much.

After a while, I decided that it was time to give back to the community and start my own meetup. I was passionate about R, but I didn't want to create a regular R group; I wanted a group where I (and the attendees) could feel safe and welcome, with no judgment, and we could see ourselves in the audience. That's how R-Ladies was born. In October of 2012, I hosted the first event, an introduction to R (http://bit.ly/rladies-first), and only eight people showed up. I was a little disappointed, but I was happy to be creating this space and for being brave enough to teach a programming language in a foreign language.

For four years, I was the only person behind R-Ladies. I was organizing, hosting, teaching, advertising, running the website, and looking for places and sponsors. I would go to conferences and events, and talk about the group. I was active in social networks, trying to make as many connections as I could. Unfortunately, most of my employers would not sponsor my work, so R-Ladies was my side project, which means I would spend nights and weekends working on it.

Leading R-Ladies gave me the opportunity to meet numerous people, some of whom I would never have dreamed of meeting in real life. And because I had to teach in the events, I became more comfortable speaking in front of people.

For people wanting to start their own communities, I would suggest a few things:

- *Define a purpose, and create a mission statement.* What is the goal of this community? What are you trying to achieve? Why are you creating it? What is the

(continued)

mission of the community? Who will be the audience? Thinking about these questions will help your future members understand the reason why they should care and why they should join. It also helps influence decisions like whether you want to focus on a specific subgroup, such as R-Ladies did with women and gender minorities, or whether you want to reach everyone interested in the topic.

- *Set up social channels, a website, and an email.* Set up a Twitter account, Facebook page, LinkedIn group, Instagram profile, and any other social channel that has a big userbase. You'll also want to have a website and email so people can easily contact you and find out more about the group.
- *Create a logo.* Having a logo brings awareness of your brand and therefore your community. Some people have a better visual memory, and they will remember your logo. With a logo, you can make laptop stickers, for example. Laptop stickers are a way to express yourself, your beliefs, and the communities you are part of. It is a big hit!
- *Think about the format.* Is this going to be mainly talks or workshops? Will it all be in person, or will you be an online community with live-streamed events or coffee chats? If your community is a tech community where you want to empower your audience, a workshop would be a great format. Active learning is the best way to learn something.
- *Use a platform* (meetup.com or eventbrite.com, for example). You want to make it easy for people to find and register for your events. A centralized website such as www.meetup.com or www.eventbrite.com will allow for some organic traffic when people are searching for the topic and help keep track of your expected attendance.

Building a community requires time and effort. You will probably need to work after hours and on the weekends, so make sure it is something that you are passionate about and whose mission you believe in. Despite the work, it is worth it. Hearing the success stories, seeing how your community changed local communities around the world, especially in underserved places, is very rewarding and a source of great joy. You feel that you are doing something to change the world for the better. Good luck in your journey!

Finally, you may be able to get people to come to you through your blog. For conferences that have invited speakers, if one of the organizers reads a blog post that fits perfectly with the theme of the conference, they may reach out to you to see whether you could design a talk on the same topic. Even if this doesn't happen, blog posts are great ways to show conference organizers that you are effective at communicating when you don't have previous talks to point to.

Just like first data science jobs, first speaking gigs are the hardest to get. After that, you'll often experience a snowball effect, especially if your talk was recorded. A recording is great because people may see your talk and reach out to you, but also because some CFPs ask for a recording of a previous talk.

14.3.2 *Preparing*

When you've got a speaking engagement, you'll want to spend a lot of time preparing your talk. If you've never given a public talk before, it's easy to underestimate how much time it takes. Yes, you could throw together a talk at the last minute by making every slide five bullet points that are just your thoughts on the subject matter and wing it the day of the event, but this is disrespectful to your audience and not showcasing you at your best. It's also not the road to building a successful speaking side gig.

You want to practice giving the talk to a live person, not just reading the slides to yourself. Find someone whose criticism you trust, and give the talk to them. Unless you are giving a very technical talk, it probably doesn't matter whether your reviewer has a background in your subject. They can suggest general things that will make your talk better, such as using fewer filler words or not moving your arms around as much.

You will generally be given a time frame for your talk, but the time frame can be complicated based on whether there will be a question-and-answer session afterward. To calculate how long you need to prepare for, you generally should budget five minutes for questions and work backward, but it's a good idea to time yourself giving the talk. Be careful, as there is a temptation to speed up when giving a talk in front of people. You may also want to add some extra slides at the back in the event of extra time, as you may find that you hurried a little too much through the main talk. If you're under by a few minutes, though, that generally is fine; there will just be a slightly longer break before the next talk. The worst outcome is that your talk is way too long and you either get cut off before finishing or finish over time, disrupting the next speaker's slot.

Because of all the work that goes into any talk, we highly recommend reusing talks. It's very unlikely that there will be overlap in the audience, especially if the talks are in different cities or given at a multitrack conference (where attendees could choose to go to another talk that's happening at the same time). Although it would be flattering to think that everyone has watched the recording of your talk, most people won't have.

The day of the talk, gather your supporters. This group doesn't need to be limited to your friends and colleagues in the data science space; invite your family members, your partner, and that friendly person in your building. If the event is a paid event, see whether the organizers will give a pass to a family member or partner to attend your talk. Emily's grandfather has been to several of her talks for free (much to the delight of the other audience members). It's nice to know that at least part of the audience is definitely in your corner.

14.4 *Contributing to open source*

For those of you who like the idea of being part of a community but dislike the thought of standing in a room with other people in that community, open source can meet that need. Contributing to open source allows the sharing of ideas and develops a sense of community among people with the same passion. Creating a project in open source can generate lots of interest, as people will push in new directions that you possibly hadn't considered. Similarly, you might be able to expand upon someone else's work to generate an entirely new project.

R and Python thrive because volunteers continually expand and refine them. In the following sections, we discuss how you can become one of those volunteers; you can also contribute financially to the organizations that sponsor some of the core development. Although R and Python may be free to use, they're not free to maintain and develop. The R Foundation, the Python Software Foundation, and NumFOCUS are three organizations (the latter two are registered U.S. charities) to which you can donate to support the continued development of the languages.

14.4.1 *Contributing to other people's work*

Hopping on to an open source project can feel like peeking into someone else's closet. It's their space, and you feel like an intruder, but open source was built for exactly this purpose, and you have to get past this feeling. Instead, imagine that open source projects are like throwing a giant dinner party. You probably don't want to be responsible for making the main course just yet, but lots of jobs need to be done; you can help set the table, make sure that everyone has water, or put the dishes away afterward. If you're respectful and enthusiastic, most creators and maintainers will welcome your help.

A great place to start contributing is documentation. See how fleshed-out the documentation is for a package you like. You may see something that is incomplete, unclear, or misleading. Even a typo fix is worth making a pull request on GitHub for. The creators of packages and libraries love to get more work written on them. This work saves them time, and as someone who recently learned how to use these tools, you'll have a better perspective about what will motivate and teach new users.

If you want to contribute code, don't jump right in and start rewriting things or submitting a new function. If the project is large, it may have a guide on how to contribute or a code of conduct. If it doesn't, watch the repository for a while to understand the flow. Watching the repository will also tell you whether the project is actively maintained or dormant for long periods. If you decide that you do want to start contributing code, start by making an issue sharing what you'd like to add or change. This way, you can get feedback from the maintainers before you've done a lot of work.

Working in open source is one of the best ways to grow your technical skills, especially if nothing at work requires you to cooperate with a large group of people. Maybe on your work GitHub repositories, you don't use branches, informative commit messages, or tagging. That's okay, but when you enter a project with hundreds of issues and dozens of people working on it at the same time, that extra work starts to make more sense. These types of practices do add extra constraints, whether you're working within a style guide or the maintainers don't add a feature you created because it's not performant enough. Ultimately, they'll be the final decision-makers until you create a project of your own. Although this can be frustrating, you'll learn a lot of best practices that you can apply to your own work.

> ### Reshama Shaikh: Hackathons
>
> Contributing to open source can seem enigmatic and daunting. Open source sprints, sometimes referred to as *hackathons*, are structured events that provide a welcoming space for beginners. Sprints are typically one- or two-day events where participants work on open issues submitted to the GitHub repository of a Python or R library. These issues could be related to documentation, bug fixes, tests, feature requests, and more.
>
> The benefits of participating in open source sprints are many:
>
> - The majority of open source contributors are volunteers, so community involvement is essential and welcome.
> - It is an active, hands-on event which builds engineering and coding skills.
> - Contributing to open source is an excellent learning opportunity which advances your data science skills and builds your portfolio.
> - It provides a valuable networking opportunity with other data scientists and experienced contributors.
>
> A well-organized sprint will utilize people's time effectively. The preparation ensures that beginner contributors are able to leave the sprint having accomplished something. Look for an available central repository of resources and preparation work, which includes the contributing documentation, R or Python installation instructions, tools to sign up for prior to the event (such as a GitHub account or messaging platform), and a curated list of open issues specially prepared for the sprint participants. Keep in mind that people who organize these sprints are volunteers; if you find that some of these items are lacking, offer to help. Organizing open source sprints is also contributing to open source.
>
> The goal of an open source sprint is to submit pull requests (PRs) that resolve open issues. Submitting a PR is a back-and-forth process, and it is common for it to take several weeks to be merged in. Allocate some time post-sprint (typically, 5 to 10 hours) to follow up on work and see a PR through to merged status, which is represented in the GitHub repo as a beautiful purple icon.
>
> If you're interested in organizing a sprint yourself, I wrote a detailed guide on my blog at https://reshamas.github.io/how-to-organize-a-scikit-learn-sprint.

14.4.2 Making your own package or library

When you find yourself copying functions between projects or messaging them to your co-workers, it may be time to make a package or library. A package allows you to store functions in one place, easily share them, and enforce best practices such as testing the code. Many companies have internal packages with functions to make the color of your plots the corporate color, access data, or solve common problems. If you think others may be facing the same problem, you can share your package on GitHub so that other people can download and use it.

Before you try to get the public to use something, you need to make sure that all your code is in order. Just because something has worked well for you running one task doesn't mean that it will hold up under the stress of public consumption. If your code is something that you just cobbled together, but you're not sure how it works, don't invite people to use it just yet. Making your package more broadly useful may require more-advanced programming as you refine or adapt the package to fit a generalized case. Make sure your underlying work has been read by someone you trust. Users won't look under the hood, so if you tell them it's a Ferrari, they'll be upset when it turns out to be a golf cart half the time.

When you've tested your code and had it reviewed, you still have to do work to get people to find out about it. You can market it on social media or your blog, but even then, it might be slow going. Don't expect to be a star overnight; it's better to put in work early with fewer users than to be immediately successful and then realize that you made an error in your underlying code. It can take a while for something to be adopted, if it ever is, but even attempting to spread good work is a good deed. The reward of success is also a curse, of course: if people start relying on your project, it becomes very hard to stop developing it. You'll get bug reports and feature requests, and you'll have to seriously consider whether you're going to make a change that will break reports that used the old version of a function.

> **TOXICITY IN OPEN SOURCE** Open source communities can be toxic. People have had negative experiences in which they're discriminated against, harassed, belittled, or just made to feel unwelcome because of their race, gender, ethnicity, or sexuality. Fortunately, many communities are recognizing this fact and actively working to make the environment more inclusive. Guido van Rossum, the creator of Python, has committed to mentoring only women and underrepresented minorities (http://mng.bz/9wPo). Some project creators tag issues "beginner-friendly" or "first-time" to encourage those who are new to open source to contribute. While you should always prioritize your mental and emotional health, many people, including those from underrepresented groups, have had only positive experiences in open source; a bad one is not inevitable.

14.5 *Recognizing and avoiding burnout*

We're not health experts, so we defer to the World Health Organization's definition of *burnout*: a "syndrome conceptualized as resulting from chronic workplace stress that has not been successfully managed." It lists the three symptoms as "feelings of energy depletion or exhaustion," "increased mental distance from one's job or feelings of negativism or cynicism related to one's job," and "reduced professional productivity" (https://www.who.int/mental_health/evidence/burn-out/en). For now, we're focusing on stress that doesn't come from your full-time job but from the extra career-related work you do on the side.

Writing this book was something we both did completely separate from our full-time jobs (and, for Jacqueline, separate from raising a toddler). We certainly get jealous sometimes when colleagues go home and do nothing related to data science.

For us, it helps to go back to why we decided to take on this extra work and see whether we're still working toward our goals. With this book, it's never been about making money. (Spending those writing hours consulting instead would have been much more lucrative.) Rather, we wanted to write this book to help aspiring and junior data scientists, and that mission has kept us motivated. It was especially helpful to see positive impact along the way as we released chapters.

If you feel like you are burning out, start by asking yourself whether there are ways to cut back. Something that's helpful to remember is that once you've created something, you don't have to remain as active. If you keep a blog, you may want to write a new post occasionally, but you don't have to write as frequently as you did at the beginning. Someone who's visiting is more likely to say "Oh, wow, those six posts are really helpful to me" than "Oh, she now posts only every six months."

In today's culture of side hustles and the praise of busyness, it can feel like any time not spent being productive is time wasted. This is very damaging! We all need time to reset. Things like going to the gym and hanging out with friends are good for this purpose, but it's also okay to take time to watch television or otherwise veg out. Continue to make time for hobbies that have nothing to do with data science or making money so that you don't feel like your whole life revolves around work.

You can add a lot of stress by trying to keep up with people. It's a common saying that social media is someone else's highlight reel, and you shouldn't compare that with your full life. Similarly, just because someone is a prolific maker of packages or blog posts doesn't mean that you need to keep up with that person. For some people, creating packages, giving talks, or writing blog posts is part of or even the full mandate of their job! The best thing you can do for your career is make sure you're working sustainably enough to stay in it for the long term.

14.6 Interview with Renee Teate, director of data science at HelioCampus

Renee Teate is known on Twitter by her 50,000-plus followers as Data Science Renee at @becomingdatasci. She's also created a podcast, blog (www.becomingadatascientist .com), and www.datasciguide.com, an online data science learning directory. She regularly speaks at and organizes conferences.

What are the main benefits of being on social media?

Twitter has benefited me in so many ways. All of the guests that are on my podcast are actually people that I met through Twitter. I found people I thought were tweeting about interesting things and figured if they can tweet about interesting things, they could also talk about interesting things. I made a list and sent a bunch of direct messages all at once, thinking maybe half of them might be interested, and I could schedule in the future. Well, every single one of them said yes!

I'm regularly asked to speak at conferences and meetups through Twitter. When I put out content, I know there's an audience for it and it will get engagement. I've met so many cool people. Besides the networking, I also use it to learn. I actually wrote a blog post early on about how I use Twitter to learn things, and it's mostly focused on picking up the lingo of the industry. If you start following people in a certain industry and reading the articles that they're linking to, you pick up all that terminology. If somebody said something I didn't know, I would just go look it up and figure out what that thing was. Often, there would be a link to a tutorial or paper on the topic, so it really helped with learning as well.

What would you say to people who say they don't have the time to engage with the community?

I really understand that, especially for people that have responsibilities outside of work, such as caring for a child or other relative. When I was in my master's program and working full-time, I didn't do anything else. In those cases, I would advise to find an online community that you can engage with asynchronously. Whenever you have a little bit of time, like you're in a waiting room somewhere, you can read and respond to some tweets or bookmark interesting articles to read later. Even if you can only make it to one event a year, pick a conference that's related to data science or your particular industry, and make an effort to squeeze it in. You can keep up with the people that you meet there afterwards on LinkedIn or other social media, and eventually they can be a small group where you can hold each other accountable for your learning and share resources.

Is there value in producing only a small amount of content?

Absolutely. I think even if you put one blog post out there, it will help solidify the topic in your mind because you learn by helping other people understand something. I have referenced some of my old blog posts for years. When I blog, I try to make it something that's very generally applicable and beneficial to learners, so I can refer back to it multiple times without it quickly becoming outdated. For my podcast, I've only recorded two episodes in the last year and a half. I got busy with life and had started my job at HelioCampus and set the podcast aside, and it was really hard to get back to it once I committed to other things. It's still out there, and I still plan to make more episodes. But I have stopped feeling guilty about taking a long break. I realize that the episodes that are out there are still helpful to people, and I can always pick it back up later.

Were you worried the first time you published a blog post or gave a talk?

Yes, I was anxious about putting something out there for the first time because when people look up your name, they're going to find it and associate it with you. Of course it is a little bit nerve-wracking. But one thing that I realized is that the kind of blog posts that were already out there that I got value from weren't always the most technically advanced, perfectly written pieces. I would read blogs that described something that I wanted to learn in a slightly different way than I had heard before, and suddenly, the material clicked. There's always going to be somebody that benefits from what you put out there.

I've also learned not to care too much about naysayers. They're going to be out there no matter what. I've seen people make negative comments to people that have been doing data science for years. There are lots of ways to approach an analysis, and maybe one way is better than another for some reasons, but it doesn't mean that your way is not a good way. Sometimes, you just have to stop listening to detractors.

Summary

- There are four ways we recommend for getting involved with the data science community: building your blog and data science portfolio, attending conferences, giving talks, and contributing to open source.
- Remember that you don't have to do any community activities to have a successful career; choose what works for you, and don't worry about keeping up with other people.

15

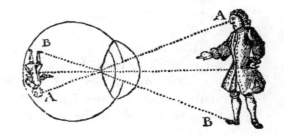

Leaving your job gracefully

This chapter covers

- Deciding when to leave a job
- Understanding how the job search differs from your first data science job
- Giving notice and managing the transition

The days of spending 40 years at one company and retiring with a golden watch and a pension are over. In most fields, it's now common to switch companies at least a few times in your career, and in tech, people may switch jobs as often as every couple of years. There are many good reasons for leaving a job: you could be looking for a compensation bump, different responsibilities, accelerated learning, or simply something novel. Deciding that you might be interested in a new job is the first step, but you have additional mental hurdles to overcome between that step and actually doing something about it.

There's always going to be uncertainty about leaving something you know for a new role. No matter how much research you do or how many questions you ask in the interview, you can never know what it will truly be like until you start the job. You can understand the big things—the salary, the company size, and the structure of the data team—but you won't know how you'll feel day to day until you're living

246

it. Moreover, it's likely that your current job isn't completely horrible. (If it is, we recommend going back to chapter 9, where we discuss what to do if the work is terrible or the environment is toxic.) You probably like some of your co-workers, know where to get help, and are comfortable navigating the data. You can think of some things that might be better. But what's the guarantee that a new job that you think will be better actually will be—or that it won't be something even worse? Is it really worth the risk and time to find a new job?

These nagging doubts can slow your job-hunt progress even after you decide that you want to leave. You're probably also dealing with a lot of uncertainty. How should you approach your second data science job search? If you get an offer that you want to take, how do you tell your manager? Do you meet individually with every co-worker you've worked on a project with to tell them you're leaving? If you're given a counteroffer, should you accept? What should you do in those last few weeks after you've given notice? But your search for a second (or third, or fourth) job doesn't have to be intimidating if you know that simply looking for greener pastures doesn't stop you from changing your mind.

We've raised lots of questions that we asked ourselves when we considered looking for new jobs. The sheer volume of uncertainty can paralyze all but the hardiest of job seekers, but fear not: we're here to turn you into one of these.

In this chapter, we divide leaving gracefully into three parts: deciding to leave, starting the job search, and giving notice. Some of this guidance applies to any job, but we also discuss some things that are more unique to data science. Changing data science jobs is a common and usually rewarding experience; many people change jobs every one to three years, which allows them to try new areas of data science and dramatically increase their salaries and other benefits. This chapter will help you make that transition as easy and stress-free as possible.

15.1 Deciding to leave

Unfortunately, most of the time you won't know when it's right to leave with 100% certainly. There's no Magic 8 Ball that will tell you what to do or even a set of questions you can answer that helps you reach a definitive decision. In chapter 8, we discussed choosing between two good life choices when deciding between offers, and that same style of reasoning applies here. At the end of the day, you can only do the best you can with the information that you have, and very few decisions are completely irreversible. You can always switch from the new place, too; you're not signing a 100-year contract.

15.1.1 Take stock of your learning progress

What should signal that it's time to look for a new job? Our biggest piece of advice is to make sure you're always learning. Unfortunately, it can be common for your learning to slow when you stay in one role. When you're in your first few months, you're drinking from the firehose. It's pretty much impossible to *not* learn anything; at the very least, you're learning about the company's data, gaining new technical skills from colleagues, and working with business stakeholders. But if you keep doing the same thing after a year or two, you might plateau.

As you get more comfortable with the day-to-day aspects of your job, see what you can do to find ways to improve your nontechnical skills. See whether you can take charge of a team (or at least an intern) and work on your management ability. Although the work that the company needs you to do may be limiting, as you get experience in it, you can usually find more time to broaden your portfolio. Maybe you could collaborate with the data engineering team to learn how to build some of the pipeline yourself instead of relying solely on the engineers. Taking the initiative to push yourself in this way isn't for everyone, though; sometimes, people need to be externally motivated by their company to take on new challenges. If you find yourself in a rut and unable to get out of it, that's a sign that it may be time for a change of scenery.

An exciting thing about data science is that there's always more to learn, but that fact also makes the work challenging. If you don't grow, finding your next position will be harder. It's also expected of a senior data scientist to have noticeably different skills from those of a junior data scientist, both in breadth and depth. We've emphasized throughout this book that you don't need and can't know everything under the umbrella of data science, but you're expected to know more as you gain experience.

15.1.2   *Check your alignment with your manager*

Before you cut ties and run, make sure that you've done what you can to tell your manager what you'd like to change. What may seem to you to be an unsolvable problem might actually have a solution. Maybe you're bogged down with doing rote tasks that can't be automated but aren't challenging anymore. Your manager may say that you can hire an intern who can do that work. That intern gets a learning experience, and you get the work somewhat off of your plate and gain mentoring experience. Or maybe the data science team does mostly analytics work, and you really want to start doing production machine learning. Your manager may set you up to "bootcamp" with an engineering team for a few months; you can learn some fundamentals of engineering while contributing your analytical knowledge.

Another question to ask yourself is how aligned your goals are with your manager's. Philip Guo, an assistant professor of cognitive sciences at the University of California–San Diego, wrote a blog post called "Whose critical path are you on?" (http://www.pgbovine.net/critical-path.htm), in which he discusses the importance of knowing your boss's (or mentor's) critical path and whether it aligns with yours. *Critical path* means "the path of work that's critical for their career advancement or fulfillment at the given moment in time." It's about their success being tied to yours. Managers have limited time and energy, and if your critical paths overlap, they'll be more likely to focus on you.

Knowing how well you're aligned with your manager's goals requires knowing what your own career goals are. We're not talking about a ten- or even five-year plan; in such a new and quickly developing field, it's impossible to know what opportunities will be available that far in the future. But how do you want to spend the next few years? We hope that you've thought a lot about this question during your first job search, but maybe things have changed. You may have wanted to be on a large data science team, but now you find a few years in that you'd like to be able to work on different types of projects rather than being siloed. Or you could be focusing on your family and looking for a job that allows you to do more 9-to-5 rather than a job at a startup that will demand a lot of hours.

In summary, some key factors to consider in thinking about finding a new job are

- Are you learning in your current role?
- Have you tried to improve your day-to-day experience by discussing your issues with your manager?
- Is your manager focused on your needs and advancing your career?
- Have you spent time thinking about what you do and do not want in your next job?

Leaving your job without another one lined up

You may want to take a significant amount of time off between jobs. Most new employers will want you to start as soon as possible; although you can generally get a week or two weeks between leaving your current job and starting a new one (especially if you already have a vacation planned), it's unlikely that you'll get more. If you've been dreaming of a three-month backpacking trip through Asia, you'll probably need to leave your job without something else lined up.

Leaving without another job is risky. There's the financial risk that you won't have enough savings for an indeterminate amount of time without income. Are you willing to (or able to) rely on short-term loans from family members or money from a partner's income? The other part is that it's easier to find a job when you're currently employed. One reason for that is unfair prejudice among hiring managers against those who are unemployed. Another is that your negotiating position is weaker: whatever the new employer is offering will be more than you're making, so it's harder to ask for higher compensation. Yet another reason is that if you've taken months off, you may not have kept your skills up and could be rusty for technical interviews.

If you do want to take time off, it's hugely helpful to have a strong data science network: people who are familiar with your work and can get you in the door and talking to a hiring manager. You also want to plan for some time before interviewing to brush up on your technical skills. Overall, unless you're in a toxic work environment, we recommend not leaving a job without having another one unless you have a plan for the possibly extensive time off between jobs that you're excited about.

15.2   How the job search differs after your first job

Many of the basics of finding your second data science job are the same as the first. But you do have some significant advantages now that you have experience working in data science:

- You'll get more (any) recruiters coming to you. To increase recruiter interest, you can go to your LinkedIn profile and select it to show recruiters that you're open to job opportunities (and don't worry—LinkedIn takes steps to ensure that your employers don't see this).

- You've learned more about what aspects of your job you like and those you don't. It's early enough in your career to pivot your specialty: if you did a lot of data engineering work but didn't enjoy it, you could go to a bigger company that has data engineers to do that work.

- It will be easier to get to the first hiring screen. Many employers use whether someone has held the same title (or something very similar before) as a quick screening tool.

- Ideally, your network in data science is more developed. (If not, go back to chapter 14.)

- If you're still employed, you likely don't want to post on LinkedIn or Twitter that you're looking for a new job, but you can start quietly putting out feelers and letting a few trusted folks know that you're looking. They may be able to refer you to a job at their companies, or they could connect you with someone they know is hiring.

Don't be afraid to apply for jobs, even if you are reasonably happy at your current one. There are plenty of reasons you can talk yourself out of a change. Maybe you worry that you might not have the skills that you think everyone else has ("What if I have years of experience, and I don't pass the technical take-home case study?") This is just impostor syndrome talking (and if you've learned anything from this book, let it be to fight the nagging voice telling you that you aren't as good as everyone else). If you don't pass a technical screen, that doesn't mean that you're a failure or a "fake" data scientist. Plenty of bad interview questions out there don't accurately judge ability. Also, data science is so broad that maybe the questions were in an area you haven't worked in before.

You may also be worried about the repercussions on your social life with your work friends or the possibility that a new job could take you farther from home. But whatever your concerns, you'll be doing a disservice to yourself to not be open to an application process that could improve your career.

15.2.1   Deciding what you want

The first step in your job search is making a list of what you've enjoyed in your current job. *Designing Your Life: How to Build a Well-Lived, Joyful Life,* by Bill Burnett and Dave Evans (Knopf, 2016), suggests that for a week, you make a note before and after every activity about how much you thought you would enjoy it and how much you actually did. Do you hate having meetings for a couple hours each day, or do you actually like meetings because they bring structure to your day? If you're in a distributed data science team, do you wish that you reported to a data science manager? You can use this list to design your search. Find a company that values the same things as you or has the structure you're looking for. You don't want to apply to a company in which you'd face the same issues that are causing you unhappiness now.

In your search, you may run into the title issue. In chapter 5, we talk about not concerning yourself with titles. Data scientists have a lot of different titles, including data analyst, research scientist, machine learning engineer, and product analyst. Data analyst is the most common title and can be seen as a junior role. If you're a data scientist, should you be willing to accept a senior data analyst title? If you're a data analyst, should you concentrate on moving up to the data scientist title in your new role?

Learning is still the most important factor in your search. What would you be doing in your new role? Think in terms of five years, not the next two. What will set you up for success in the long term? Is it possible to join as a senior data analyst and then transition to a data scientist role, for example? Will working at a smaller technology company let you learn how to work with web data, setting you up to go on to a large tech company?

When you're considering your options, you have to protect your market value. Fairly or not, data scientist is still usually viewed as being a more prestigious title than data analyst, and a senior data analyst's role may pay less than a data scientist's. You'll want to balance these considerations as you think about your next role.

15.2.2 *Interviewing*

After you start applying to companies and getting interviews, you'll have to answer the question "Why are you leaving your job?" If you got your current job out of school or a bootcamp, you didn't get asked that question at all.

A good answer is that you're looking for challenges. Another good strategy is to pretend that the question is "Why do you want to work for us?" If you imagine that, your answer will be positive ("I've heard amazing things about your machine-learning team and am eager to learn") rather than negative ("My past boss insisted on displaying our experiment results in pie charts"). If you give a more specific answer, make sure that it fits the new employer. You don't want to say "I'm looking for a team with senior data scientists I can work with" if the interviewing company doesn't have any! Avoid bad-mouthing your current job at all costs; some employers view this behavior as disqualifying, no matter how poorly you are treated at your current company.

Just because you are leaving your company doesn't mean that you shouldn't be proud of the work you've done there. You should absolutely talk about projects that you've worked on or skills you've learned. You are likely to be bound by certain confidentiality agreements, so you can't literally show your code or talk about the parameters of the recommendation algorithm you built, but you should discuss your contributions in a general way. A fine nonspecific answer is "I created a chatbot in Python that generated responses to frequent client questions, decreasing the average time a customer service representative needed to spend with each client by five minutes and increasing customer satisfaction by 20%." On the other hand, if you work at a private company, "I conducted A/B tests that brought the company's total revenue from $20 million to $23 million" is a bad answer, as you're disclosing private financial information.

You may be looking at jobs that use different technologies, whether those are different cloud providers, SQL dialects, or main programming languages. In this case, you want to use the strategies similar to those you used when you framed your work experiences in terms of skills that are transferrable to data science. Suppose that you've been working in R, and the company uses Python. You could say something like "I know it will take a little time for me to get up to speed on the syntax in Python, which I've already started doing with an online course. But in my four years of programming in R, I've developed web applications, built packages, and analyzed large datasets, all of which will make me a strong Python programmer quickly."

We mentioned impostor syndrome earlier in this chapter, but you really do have to be careful of it when preparing for interviews. When you're looking for your first job out of college or transitioning to a new career in data science, it's easy to say "I haven't learned that yet." (At least, it's easy if you convince yourself that it's easy.) When you've established yourself a little, however, it can be embarrassing to not know something. If you don't know something in an interview, don't be afraid to admit it. You can say that you haven't found a chance to use it or that you hope to learn more about it, but it hasn't been a part of your job yet. Suppose that you're quizzed on machine learning algorithms, but you've been working on statistical modeling, SQL, data cleaning, and working with stakeholders, because the data is on such a scale that machine learning is done by dedicated machine learning engineers. No one knows everything, and we hope that you've been doing a pretty good job as a data scientist so far; have faith in that. You can show the work you've done, and if you've studied a particular topic before, even if you haven't been using that knowledge recently, you'll be able to get up to speed more quickly. It's always better to demonstrate willingness to learn than to try to fake your way through.

15.3 *Finding a new job while employed*

If your path to becoming a data scientist included doing a bootcamp, you were probably doing your job search while unemployed. If you were at school, it was expected you might need to take time off for interviews and that you'd be spending time preparing your résumé or cover letter (chapter 6). If you're employed full-time, though, your manager generally doesn't want to hear that you need time off because you're looking for a new job. So how do you make the time to do that?

Things that can be done anytime—such as updating your résumé and cover letter, researching jobs, sending in applications, and working on take-home assignments—you should do on your own time. You don't want people to see what you're doing, and you owe it to your current company to continue to do your job well. But interviews almost always happen during your normal working hours. If interviews are conducted over the phone, we recommend taking the call in a phone booth, meeting room, or somewhere else you won't be overheard.

Later-round interviews, however, generally need to be done onsite. If an interview is an hour or two long and near your office, you can claim a doctor's appointment. If it's longer, and your company allows you to work from home, you can do that and work only part of the day (or try to work a little more later), but you need to ensure that you won't be expected to take a call or respond quickly while you're in an interview. You also can try to schedule the interview toward the end of the day and work a half-day in the morning.

Scheduling interviews is certainly easier to do if you're looking within your city. If you're looking to move, most companies will fly you in for an in-person day of interviewing on a weekday. In this situation, it's hard to avoid taking a full day off, and most people will usually call in sick that day. But as you can imagine, this is hard to do if you have lots of final-round interviews.

That's one of the reasons why we recommend applying to jobs strategically. If you have a dozen phone interviews and two onsites in a week, it's hard to take that time without people noticing, and your job performance will almost certainly be affected negatively. You should be selective in two stages: applying in the first place and advancing after the initial phone call. If you're at a startup and you want to work at a larger company, don't apply to other startups, even if the job descriptions look great. If, during the initial phone screen, you find out that the position is more data engineering, and you want to do analysis work, it's OK to stop the process even if the interviewer wants to continue.

Although you can use interviews for positions you wouldn't take as practice, you don't want to do too many of them. Experienced data scientists are highly sought-after, which means that you may get a bunch of interest from recruiters and managers when you announce that you are looking for a new job. This is a great feeling: people like you! Although it's fine to enjoy that feeling, don't allow yourself to spend time in the interview process with a company that you know isn't a good fit. It's not a good use of your time, even though it is flattering.

When you're job-hunting, it's easy to let your current work slip. To feel OK about moving on to the next thing, you're often thinking about what you don't like about your job, which can sap motivation. But try to continue to do good work; you may need a recommendation from your manager one day, and the company is still paying you.

It's possible that during your job search, you realize that the grass is not always greener on the other side. In other words, you're not finding anything you'd rather do than your current job, or everything pays much less and offers worse benefits, or the jobs won't give you the flexibility you currently enjoy. It's OK to decide to call off your job search! It wasn't a waste of time if it gave you a newfound appreciation of your current job. If you decide to stay, we recommend returning to our advice in section 15.1.2: make sure that you've tried to solve any problems you can at your current job.

> ### Going to graduate school
>
> After working in data science, you may decide that you want to go back to school to get more formal academic training, either while continuing to work full-time and going to school evenings and weekends or switching to working full-time on a degree. If this is something you're thinking about, we recommend that you go back to chapter 3, where we discuss how to find a good program.
>
> We do want to caution you to think carefully about whether the investment of time and money will be worth it, however, given that you've already proved that you can get a data science job. Some reasons why going back to school might make sense: you've decided that you want to do a very research-heavy position that requires a PhD, you've gotten explicit feedback from companies you want to work for that you need a master's degree (not just that you've seen it listed in the job description), or you've found your progress hampered by a lack of certain skills (such as in-depth knowledge of algorithms) and free online options aren't working for you.
>
> If you decide that you want to go back to school full-time, you can usually be more open with your manager about that than about leaving for another job. If you work at a larger firm, your company might even pay for part of your degree if you study part-time while continuing to work full-time or if you agree to come back after earning a full-time degree. Even if not, your manager could write a great letter of recommendation. A good manager knows that school offers you something completely different from a job and should be supportive of your choices.

15.4   Giving notice

If you've decided to leave your job and have accepted an offer, you'll need to let your manager know. Generally, you should give at least two weeks' notice unless the situation is dire. Though unlikely, it's possible that as soon as you give your notice, your manager will tell you that your last day is today. You should be prepared for that possibility and make sure that you've forwarded anything personal on your work computer to yourself.

Your boss should be the first person to know that you've leaving. Schedule a meeting with them (call it "career discussion," not "my two weeks' notice"), or use your weekly one-on-one time. You want to give notice in person if you're co-located with them or by phone or video call if you're not; don't give notice by email. Start the conversation by expressing gratitude for how they've helped you and the opportunities you had at the company. Assure them that you'll do all you can to help with the transition; you can list a few ideas you have, such as commenting your code or suggesting someone to take over a share of your work, but figuring that out will require collaboration with your manager. It's normal to feel anxious about telling your manager that you're leaving, but remember that changing jobs is a normal part of a career.

15.4.1 *Considering a counteroffer*

It's possible that your manager will try to convince you to stay by making a counteroffer, as it's expensive and risky to hire a new person. They may ask you to meet with your skip-level manager, who has the authority to give you a raise, extra stock options, a one-time bonus, an accelerated review, or other incentives to stay.

There are mixed opinions about whether you should ever take a counteroffer from your current company. On the one hand, the company now knows that you're a flight risk and may be reluctant to give you serious responsibilities. The situation may also strain your relationship with your manager. On the other hand, the company may be willing to address the main reason why you're leaving. The solution could be monetary, or it could be switching you to work with a different team.

We hope that we've impressed upon you the importance of having open communication with your managers. If you've been open with your manager and still felt the need to move to a new job, it's unlikely that the change you desire can be brought about in a counteroffer. Although we don't love the idea of moving to a new job as a last resort and feel that you should make the decision to leave well before that point, we've stressed the importance of communicating your desires before your dissatisfaction grows. If you've done that, you should know that last-minute changes aren't likely to change the overall job environment.

Your manager may try to stress how valuable you are to the team and how difficult it will be for team members if you leave. This can make you feel guilty, especially if your boss or team has generally been good to you. But remember that you're not betraying them by leaving. At the end of the day, a job is a job, and despite the rhetoric of some startups, a company is not your family. Although you should always be respectful and do your best at your job, you don't have a responsibility to work at that company indefinitely. And you're just leaving a company, not dying! If you've grown close to your co-workers, you can still see them socially and maybe even work together again one day.

15.4.2 *Telling your team*

Talk to your manager about how they would like to let the rest of the team know. They may ask you to wait a few days while they figure out a transition plan so that they can share that information with the team when you tell them you're leaving. They may ask whether you prefer to tell everyone in a regular team meeting or want to meet with people one-on-one. We recommend considering the size of your team when thinking about this issue. If you've worked with the same five people consistently over the years, you may want to tell them individually. On the other hand, if you're on a 20-person data scientist team and have worked with a dozen stakeholders, it would be emotionally exhausting to meet with all of them individually for half an hour each.

One mistake to avoid is scheduling meetings with people before talking to your manager, even if you schedule those meetings for after your manager conversation. If your co-workers become suspicious about why you suddenly want to meet with them and ask whether it's because you're leaving, it will be really awkward: you'll either have to lie or tell them before your manager knows.

Most people will ask why you're leaving. Make sure that you have something to say, and try to keep it positive, focusing on the new opportunity and what you're grateful for at your current company. Even if you've become friends with a co-worker, be wary of being negative just the same. Remember that you may desire to come back at some point, and you don't want a reputation as someone who trashed the place on the way out. Some people have very close relationships with their managers, but even if that's the case, you don't want to talk too much about the negative aspects of your current job, as this can damage your friendship and usually is also unnecessary. Among the other good reasons for exiting gracefully is that keeping a good relationship with your past co-workers and managers can be invaluable careerwise, as you may run into them again or need recommendations from them later.

As you say your goodbyes, give people a way to contact you after you leave (email, LinkedIn, Twitter, and so on). It's nice for co-workers to be able to stay in touch, and it's also a good way to ensure that you're part of a functional network for yourself and for others.

Checklist for before you leave

Before you head out, you'll want to make sure that you have a few administrative items:

- The contact information for human resources in case you need something later, such as information on your stock options.
- Any personal pictures, passwords, or files that you have only on your company computer.
- Benefits and stock compensation portal log-in information.
- Copies of employee agreements, offer letters, and termination agreements.
- Information about how your vacation time will be paid out if you have any left.
- If you're not starting a new job immediately, your options for continuing your health insurance.
- If you contributed to a flexible savings account for health or dependent care, what the last day you can spend it is (generally your last day or the last day of your last month of employment). These funds are "use it or lose it" funds, so if you don't spend them, they'll be gone.

15.4.3 *Making the transition easier*

The best way to leave on a good note is to make the transition as easy as possible. You may not be able to find a replacement, but you can set the team up for success while they're backfilling the role (if they choose to). Make a transition document for your manager, listing your responsibilities, which ones you can wrap up, which ones need to be transferred (and suggestions about who could pick it up), and which ones will have to wait until someone new is in the role. Beyond informing the person who's taking over that project, you may need to make introductions to outside partners or clients, or let them know that you will not be handling the project any longer.

Try to clean up any loose ends. If you have work that may be useful for others but is only on your computer, add it to a git repository or share the Google Doc with someone else. You'll probably be given little work in those last few weeks, because people will know you won't be around long. This gives you time to do things that you may have been too bogged down to do before, such as documenting all of the processes you've created. Other things you could do include

- *Adding tutorials*—Have you been the "go to" person for a certain topic, such as how the finance data is organized or best practices for A/B testing? There's no way to replace your being there, but by making presentations, internal posts, or documentation, you can help fill some of the gaps you'll leave.

- *Organizing your files*—Even if you add everything to GitHub, that's not going to help anyone if "everything" is 100 files with names such as random_stuff and misc_analyses. Although you may end up needing to dump a few files in an extras folder, try to make the files easy to navigate, and add explanations where necessary.

- *Adding comments and explanations to analyses*—Ideally, for any impactful analyses, you've already written up the findings, linking to commented code. If you didn't have time to finish some findings, though, and you think it would be valuable for someone to continue the work, you can flesh your comments out. Although you don't need to comment every piece of code, it can be helpful to explain some surprises in the data (and how you worked around them), what you've already tried, and explanations of why you chose analytical methods.

The worst thing you can do is forget that you are the only person who knows how to do *x* at the company and leave it unassigned. If you do, you may get frantic calls and emails about how to do the work while you are trying to adjust to your new job. Forgetting that you own the only password to a particular system is a good way to get into trouble even after leaving. Some employers don't know how to say "Goodbye and good luck" and may call you about projects you were working on. For your sanity, it's best to be able to refer them to your exit documentation until they get the hint that you no longer work there. Even if they don't follow up, you won't find much value in the network you built there if you left a huge mess for them to deal with.

We hope that this chapter made it clear that although the uncertainty about leaving your job may be stressful, the process is normal, and there are ways to approach it to make it smoother. As we've discussed many times in this book, few decisions that you make are final. Just because you start looking for jobs doesn't mean that you have to leave, and even when you leave a company, you may end up coming back in a few years. The most important thing to do throughout this process is make sure that you focus on how to make your job best fit your career goals.

15.5 Interview with Amanda Casari, engineering manager at Google

Amanda Casari is an engineering manager at Google on the Google Cloud Developers Relations team. Previously, she was a principal product manager and data scientist at SAP Concur. She also served five years in the U.S. Navy and holds a master's degree in electrical engineering.

How do you know it's time to start looking for a new job?

My advice for people is to understand what kind of work they want to be doing and if that fits with the role and where the product, team, and company is at. For me, I do very well in times of high change. I enjoy working on projects at their start during the ideation phase, but I also enjoy sunsetting products. A data science job where I was spending the majority of my time optimizing models for single-digit-percentage increases or doing hyperparameter tuning, on the other hand, wouldn't work very well. I also think about the stage of the team cohesion. Do you want to join a team that has a strong bond and culture already, or do you want to join one that's just forming? Overall, my role, where the product is in this product life cycle, and where the team is in forming versus conforming to a culture, all influence whether or not a role is still a good fit for me or if I should look for something more challenging.

Have you ever started a job search and decided to stay instead?

All the time. When I'm looking at other roles, I may identify things I could actually be doing at my current company. It's kind of a kick to go out and find those opportunities as opposed to waiting for somebody to give them to me. This fits into my broader philosophy that your current job responsibilities should be a conversation you're having with your manager. For the engineers I manage, I try to have open and honest conversations where they let me know what opportunities they're looking for. I can then figure out whether that exists within the current team or, if not, whether we can find them a 20% project outside of our team. This way, they can explore it to see whether or not that's actually what they want to be doing.

Do you see people staying in the same job for too long?

Oh, yeah. I've seen some people get a kind of hero complex, where they feel like nobody else could possibly do their job. And the real answer is nobody else is going to execute your job exactly like you do, but that doesn't mean that no one else can do it. Sometimes, somebody sticking around teams can be very harmful because they remember all the problems and small decisions the team has ever made. They may point out "We tried that idea two years ago and it didn't work, so you shouldn't possibly try it." But that can hold the team back by not focusing on what's currently possible—just decisions made in the past.

I've also seen folks who have become fairly jaded about management, where they spend a lot of their time just complaining. They'll always have an open door when there's gossip for how things are going, and that's really negative for a company. You don't want people who are going to be taking their discontent and turning it into something that infects the rest of the team.

Finally, I've seen folks who are not being challenged by their current roles and are simply doing what's asked of them and no more. This can be fine when you're newer, but for experienced people and those in leadership, I expect something more than that. I want to see experienced people having larger kinds of impact and change. If you see a problem, you should think about addressing it in a way that scales, is repeatable, and solves an organizational problem, not just something that is a one-off fix.

Can you change jobs too quickly?

When I'm looking at job applicants, I might question if somebody has had a job for less than a year. As a hiring manager, what you're trying to understand by looking at people's job tenures is if they're going to leave in a few months, because hiring and onboarding someone is a long and expensive process. But although in other industries, you may see two to three years as the minimum, in technology, I see that as a long time. Two to three years is multiple projects with multiple cycles in technology, so leaving by then makes sense to me; really, anything more than a year does. If you have to leave earlier than a year for your mental or emotional health, that makes sense too; it's not worth any job to jeopardize those.

What's your final piece of advice for aspiring and new data scientists?

Find your community and people who can help you. I have benefitted so much from having a dear friend who's sponsored me by recommending me for speaking opportunities and talking me through job offers. Having a person with experience to talk through those details is invaluable and has really helped me understand my worth and feel confident walking into a new position. For finding community, there are so many places that you can belong, but there may be some where you don't feel that sense of belonging. You don't have to stay in a place where you feel uncomfortable, whether it's because of the language, the people who are gathered there, or the focus of the group. And if you can't find a space you feel comfortable, look for someone who you would want to be in that kind of group, and ask them if they can help you form one.

Summary

- When deciding whether you should look for a new job, four questions to ask yourself are whether you're still learning, whether you've talked to your manager to see if your responsibilities could change, whether your manager's career goals are aligned with yours, and whether you've thought about what you're looking for (and not looking for) in your next role.
- Although many principles of having a successful first data science job search (which you can find in part 2 of this book) still apply, for your second job, you should also reflect on what you liked (and didn't like) in your first. Prepare to share your experience in a positive way that respects confidentiality, and plan how to juggle interviews with your full-time role.
- After you've given two weeks' notice to your manager, focus on how to make the transition as easy as possible for your teammates by tying up any loose ends, documenting anything that currently lives only in your head, and sharing any helpful code.

16

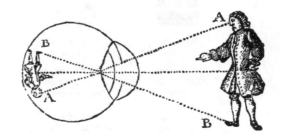

Moving up the ladder

This chapter covers

- Different paths beyond senior data scientist
- The opportunities and risks of possible career trajectories

Through the last part of this book, we've covered how to flesh out your career: learning to cope with failure, joining the community, and switching jobs. As your career strengthens, you'll eventually want to decide where that career is heading. It's not obvious what options data scientists will have as they progress upward; becoming a manager is one possibility, but it's not the only one.

In this chapter, we cover three common career trajectories for a data scientist—moving into management, becoming a technical leader, and switching to independent consulting—as well as the benefits and drawbacks of each.

The management option is what most people think of when they think about career growth. *Managers* are the people who lead teams, including hiring and promoting, setting strategy, and giving career mentoring. *Principal data scientists* are people who are masters of their field, and companies rely on them to solve difficult technical problems. *Independent consultants* are data scientists who have enough skills and a large-enough network to be able to freelance for a living. See figure 16.1 for an extremely high-level summary of the paths in this chapter.

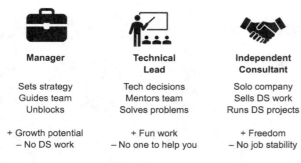

Manager	Technical Lead	Independent Consultant
Sets strategy	Tech decisions	Solo company
Guides team	Mentors team	Sells DS work
Unblocks	Solves problems	Runs DS projects
+ Growth potential	+ Fun work	+ Freedom
– No DS work	– No one to help you	– No job stability

Figure 16.1   The paths in this chapter

As you continue to build your career, you will want to focus on taking one of these paths. By having a clear goal, you are more likely to achieve want you want. That being said, the closer you get to achieving an opportunity you want, the more you may realize that it isn't something you want after all. Fortunately, making changes such as becoming a manager and then deciding that you don't like it, or going from industry to consulting and then back to industry, is not unusual. And although reversing decisions you've made can be difficult, learning from your missteps is a fast way to grow as a person!

Knowing what level you are

As you grow as a data scientist, you'll gain valuable skills (as the preceding 15 chapters discussed). But as your skill set and professional maturity grow, at some point you'll no longer be working like a junior data scientist. It's difficult to know exactly when that transition happens, which makes deciding the right time to advocate for a promotion or new job title difficult. Keep in mind that each company has its own levels and expectations, so the same title may mean very different things at two different companies. Within a company, there may even be a skills matrix describing exactly how the levels differ, but people may interpret the matrix differently, and there is always ambiguity. To help you, here is our high-level guide to the different expectations for levels of data scientists:

- *Junior data scientist*—A person who can complete a data science task given clear direction on what that task should be. If told to use a clustering algorithm to segment new customers by their purchasing attributes, a junior data scientist should be able to do this with guidance from a manager. If technical problems occur, such as bugs in code or data systems not connecting, they may need to consult other team members to solve them.
- *Senior data scientist*—A person who can not only complete a data science task, but also figure out what other tasks are needed. They not only could do the example segmentation through clustering (described earlier), but also would realize things like the fact that the same algorithm could be used for existing customers too (and then do that). They're skilled at solving technical issues and are the people who are brought in when others have problems.

- *Above senior data scientist*—At levels higher than senior data scientist, the role becomes more about helping others. Thus, a person usually moves beyond senior data scientist when they are consistently mentoring others, creating strategies, and seeing the bigger picture.

16.1 The management track

Going into management can seem to be the default option for data scientists as they go further into their careers. It makes sense due to exposure: everyone has a person they report to. Despite this fact, the day-to-day tasks of a manager can still be mysterious.

A manager is a person who is responsible for a team of people successfully performing their objectives. These five basic tasks are usually, but not always, the job of a data science manager:

- *Determining the team's work*—This work can be done at a strategic level, such as deciding what large projects should be taken on. It can also be done at a more tactical level, such as deciding what features should be included in a product.
- *Determining who should be on the team*—A manager usually chooses who to hire and who to let go, with the approval of human resources and other parties. They coordinate the interview process and weigh in during it.
- *Mentoring team members*—Everyone on a team has unique challenges to work through, and a manager helps them meet those challenges. A manager regularly checks in on each person and provides advice and recommendations to help them solve their problems.
- *Resolving team issues*—If the team is having issues that prevent work from being done (for example, if another team is unwilling to provide necessary access to data), it's the job of the manager to find a solution so that the team can continue.
- *Managing projects*—A manager has to keep track of the work going on within the team and ensure that things are on schedule. Although many teams have a project manager specifically assigned to this task, the manager still needs to maintain oversight of the work.

Together, these tasks cover a wide range of work and involve a high amount of responsibility. A manager has to communicate continuously with people inside and outside their team. They need to be aware of how team members are doing, how projects are doing, and what is on the horizon. These tasks add up to an immense amount of work, and if any of these tasks isn't done well, the whole team will suffer.

It's important to note that the basic tasks of a manager aren't technical; a manager generally isn't creating machine learning models or providing analyses that help the company make decisions. A manager doesn't have time to do that sort of work—and even if they did, it would be better for a data scientist who reports to the manager to do it. Becoming a manager involves giving up much of what drives people to become data scientists in the first place: a desire to use data to solve interesting problems. Instead, the job becomes supporting other people who do that work.

16.1.1 Benefits of being a manager

Being a manager has a bunch of perks. First, if you're a person who hates it when other people do work that you think is silly, being a manager means that you get to influence situations so less silly work is done. If you think a particular machine learning model would be helpful for the company, for example, you can assign the team to make it, and if you think it's not a good idea, you could make sure the team avoids it. It's incredibly fulfilling to get to choose the direction of the team and then see the team succeed. Although you don't have total control—sometimes, people higher up demand that something be done, or people on your team strongly recommend doing something—you have a large say.

Moving up into management often gives you an initial pay raise from being an independent contributor. Management also opens the door to further roles: senior manager, director, or vice president. Each of these roles comes with higher pay and broader leadership across the company. You may even get to a level where you oversee more fields than just data science, such as customer research or software development. You may eventually transition out of data science entirely and lead in other areas.

If you like teaching and helping others, management is a great role for you. Much of your job is helping people on your team succeed by working with them, teaching them what you've learned in your career, and helping them with their struggles. A great manager is like a business therapist: they sit down with a person for 60 minutes and help them work through their problems.

Finally, you can have an immense sphere of influence as a manager. Being the person who makes the final decisions about whether to build a new product or expand to a new country is really fun! As you go higher up in the company, you'll be able to influence more and more. If you follow this path, you have the possibility of someday running a company.

16.1.2 Drawbacks of being a manager

The biggest downside of management is that you don't have time to do data science. Your job will be filled with things like talking about data science, mentoring data scientists, and thinking about data science strategies, but you won't be doing data science yourself. Your day may be filled with 30-minute meetings ranging from deciding team strategy to buttering up stakeholders to get funding to one-on-one meetings to help underperforming employees learn how to improve.

No longer doing data science as your job is a drawback for two reasons:

- You probably became a data scientist because you like working with data, so you are giving up the job you trained so long to have.

- When you're not doing data science, over time you'll become out of practice and disconnected from the latest changes. If you decide that you don't like management and want to go back to being an individual contributor, you may find that your data science skills have atrophied.

Another downside is that you are still limited by the management above you. You may have great ideas for your team's strategy that get shot down by your boss. Then you have to lead your team down the path your boss set, even though you don't agree with it. Having to keep a positive attitude about work you don't agree with for the benefit of the people on your team can be extremely frustrating. If you let the people below you feel your frustrations, you may lower their job satisfaction.

Being a manager gives you a lot more things to worry about. You have to worry about your own performance, just as you did when you were an individual contributor, but you also have to worry about the performance of the rest of your team. You have to worry about their career satisfaction, and you have to worry about what's happening politically at levels above you. You have to worry whether the team will have funding and whether a project that's going too slowly will be canceled. Having this many worries, most of them not directly in your control, can be extremely stressful for people with certain personality types. If you have trouble not taking work home, management may not be for you.

Finally, managing people requires a totally different set of skills from being a data scientist. When you switch to being a manager, you'll have to learn these new skills and return to being a beginner at your job. Switching from being great at your job to being a novice can be stressful and miserable. Although you'll eventually get the hang of it, the journey to becoming a good manager is a long one.

16.1.3 *How to become a manager*

If you are an independent contributor and want to be a manager, you need to find opportunities to develop and practice leadership skills. These skills include working well with others, both more junior and senior than you, seeing the bigger picture, and managing a timeline for a project.

Unfortunately, there isn't a single course you can take to learn these skills; the best you can do is find situations within your current work where you can grow. One example is a small initiative within your team that someone needs to take charge of, such as setting up a new software stack or coordinating the rollout of a new model. The important component of these situations is that you're the one leading them and making the decisions. This may feel extremely unnatural at first; that feeling is totally normal and will fade. Books about management and business can be somewhat helpful, but only if you have opportunities to use what you learn.

When you feel that you have grown the skills be a manager, the next step is finding a role.

EARNING A PROMOTION WITHIN THE COMPANY

Often, the most straightforward way to become a manager is to get promoted within your company. This way can be easiest because the people who will decide to put you in the role of manager are the ones who have watched your skills grow in your current job. The difficulty with this route is that the company has to need a new manager: either your current manager has to quit or be promoted, or a manager role needs to open up on a related team. Depending on your company, these situations may rarely, if ever, occur.

GROWING A NEW TEAM YOURSELF

Another route is to become a manager by growing a team yourself. You might start a project in your current company that ends up requiring more people or become the first data scientist at a new company and then grow a team there. This route can be extremely fulfilling, because by growing the team yourself, you have a strong hand in who is on it and how it functions. The work requires you to be in the right place at the right time and to be a strong-enough leader that you can quickly grow the whole team infrastructure. Sometimes, the people who take this approach are called player–coaches because they are both functioning as the team's first independent contributor and becoming a coach for others. Unfortunately, the opportunities to create your own team are even rarer than the previously mentioned path.

GETTING A MANAGER ROLE AT A NEW COMPANY

The last approach is getting hired in an open manager position at a different company. This route relies on being able to show that you have management skills without having technically been a manager before. In your cover letter and when interviewing, you'll need to talk about all the projects you've been leading and people you've been mentoring as an independent contributor. You should be able to tell by the amount of attention your résumé is getting when you share it whether you have a chance with this route; companies are desperate for good data science managers, so if your résumé looks good, you should get responses.

> ## Rob Stamm, director overseeing the AI @ T-Mobile team: Learning to manage
>
> I learned a lot about being a manager during my first experience in a full-time managerial role. Before that, I had been a product manager, which meant guiding the direction and development of a product (but not people). Then, as a newly hired senior manager, I had to oversee several different product managers and help them do their jobs. I ended up failing miserably in this role. I wanted to be a senior manager and lead a team, but I wouldn't stop doing the product management role too. I wasn't letting the team do their jobs; I kept doing it for them.
>
> Four months into the job, one of the product managers walked into the office and told me they were going to quit, and how I was acting was the reason why. That was a huge realization for me that you can't both be a manager and continue to try to be an individual contributor. It was the first time someone pointed out that a manager has to enable their team to make decisions, and that stuck with me.

Eventually, I learned and grew from that experience and started leading bigger teams and larger projects. Being a leader is incredibly rewarding: I have the job of helping my team be their best, and I feel gratified when I see the results. One particular project at T-Mobile that was especially fulfilling was getting to help the AI team start from just an idea and a few dollars into funding for a large-scale team. While I wasn't designing the product or writing the code, I got to help the team when they were stuck or needed resources like money or people. That's rewarding in its own way.

16.2 *Principal data scientist track*

A principal data scientist (or staff, chief, data scientist V, technical lead, or other title, depending on the company) is a person in an organization whose job is to be an expert in data science and help others with technical tasks. Becoming a manager involves steadily doing less and less data science, although being a principal data scientist allows you to do more and more of it. But instead of doing data science on your own (although you'll do plenty of that), you'll also be tasked with helping other data scientists with their jobs.

Principal data scientists generally start as junior data scientist, get promoted to senior data scientists, and continue to grow beyond those roles. As they grow in their data science careers, they become more experienced and more mature in their ability to understand problems and how to solve them. Soon, they know so much that when other people are struggling, they are able to go in and quickly assist. People throughout the company come up to them asking for suggestions about how to handle problems and what is likely to work (or not).

A principal data scientist job involves multiple responsibilities:

- *Influencing data science strategy*—A principal data scientist has to lay out the plan for tackling data science problems. Is modeling payment fraud feasible? Should a neural network be used? The manager is responsible for the idea and business plan; the principal is on the hook for how it should work.
- *Mentoring junior data scientists*—Because a principal data scientist has so much experience, it's their obligation to share what they know with more-junior employees. Their growth is as important as the principal data scientists' own work.
- *Finding solutions to difficult problems*—When the data science team is plagued by a difficult technical problem, the principal data scientist is the person who's on the hook to devise a solution—or declare it impossible to solve.

Compared with a manager, a principal is still very much doing data science work. Thus, this role is great for people who love being a data scientist. If all you can think about is data science, and you love going to conferences, being part of the community, and learning more about techniques and methods, you'll get to keep doing those things as a principal data scientist. Because of how critical a principal data scientist can be to a team, the role requires a person with maturity, responsibility, and enough experience in data science to ramp up quickly in new areas as needed.

Although the work of a principal data scientist is related to data science, it's rare for a principal to do individual-contributor work such as making a single analysis or creating a machine learning model. Those tasks require a lot of time and unified focus, and a principal data scientist has to split their work across many projects and areas. Data science projects tend to fall on junior and senior data scientists, although the principal coordinates and oversees them.

Asking for a promotion

At some point, you'll likely feel ready to be at a higher level, but you won't have been promoted. This situation can be frustrating (you can see why you're ready; why can't everyone else!?), but it's not hopeless. The best thing you can do to help move the process along is advocate for yourself. Let your manager know that you're interested in moving to a higher-level position and that you want to work with your manager to create a plan to get there. If your manager is good, they should be happy with this: by being clear that you are ready to make changes to achieve the next position, you're opening the conversation about how that can happen. Try to set a goal that has a specific date, such as the next performance review cycle, to be promoted. The goals should be as specific possible, such as "Perform three technical presentations in the company" or "Create and deploy an entire machine learning API on my own." By having clear goals with a timeline, you'll be able to have ongoing discussions about whether you're making progress.

If your manager is giving you feedback as to why you aren't ready, listen to it. Although it's hard to hear negative feedback, your manager has a perspective that you don't on what you need for the promotion. If your manager is telling you that they think you're ready and want to advocate for you in the promotion process, try to give them as much documentation as possible about what you've been doing and why you're capable of taking the new job. That documentation can help your manager move you on.

If it seems like no matter what you do, you still can't get the promotion you seek, that may be a sign that it's time to switch to a different company. There are plenty of occasions when people are so used to seeing someone in a particular role that they're unwilling to risk putting that person in a new one. By changing companies, you'll get to work with a group of people who don't have expectations about what you can do and may give you more opportunities.

16.2.1 *Benefits of being a principal data scientist*

A principal data scientist often gets the most interesting problems. If the team has an idea for a totally new data science approach no one has tried before, you're going to be involved in trying it for the first time. If a complex technical stack needs to be integrated, you're going to be there. If a project is supposed to be launching, but the team just can't get the model to work, you'll be there too. Getting to be in the middle of the action can be enormously fulfilling. It's interesting on the technical side, and you get to feel validated as you prove yourself to be useful over and over. The team will be aware that simple, menial data science projects aren't worth your limited time, which means that you'll have to do less of those than most data scientists.

Your manager will also understand just how important it is for you to keep up with technology, which means that you'll likely have funding to go to conferences and the time to toy around with new technology. Depending on your manager, you may be expected to present at conferences to promote your company, but because you've been working on interesting problems, you'll likely have done work that's worth sharing. If you ask your manager for resources, such as money to try out a new cloud service, you'll usually get them. Your manager will trust you to use your time and budget effectively and not be wasteful with it, which is not something that every data scientist gets.

You'll also get to talk about data science all the time. Because you'll be mentoring junior data scientists, you'll get to tell them about different approaches, work with them to hone their ideas, and point out areas where data science approaches could have problems. For a person who likes data science, this role can be quite fun.

Making data science plans can be very empowering. By being the person who decides what types of models to use, how to structure data, and how to scope a project, you're more likely to see projects done the way you want them done. And because you're an expert in data science, the projects should be more likely to succeed! More-junior data scientists don't always get to devise a data science approach, execute it, and see the results themselves without having someone else make key decisions about it.

16.2.2 *Drawbacks of being a principal data scientist*

The biggest problem with being a principal data scientist is that you won't have someone to turn to for help when you're stuck. A junior data scientist usually has a mentor or senior data scientist to ask questions of, or they can even do Google searches to find answers to their problems. As a principal data scientist, you probably won't have data scientists more senior than you in your team. The problems you'll face will often be so unusual or unique that no one has faced them before, so no Google search will provide an answer. Thus, you'll need to be able to work in environments in which you don't have help, which can be crushing for many data scientists.

Although you'll get to be involved in the most interesting data science problems, you may also face the most annoying ones. If, for example, a dataset is stored as terabytes of poorly formatted .csv files on a server no one has touched in years and with a schema no one knows, you'll be called in to figure out how to use the data. That problem isn't really interesting; it's just a minefield that no one else can navigate. You'll face many problems such as this, and you probably won't be able to delegate the solutions to other people.

Because your knowledge is so vast, you'll be in high demand—and be very busy. You'll frequently find yourself with more work than time to do it, and you'll have to let interesting projects go because you don't have the bandwidth for them. It's easy to fall into the habit of working more hours than you should and still not feeling like you've done enough. Because so many people rely on you, having only a 40-hour work week or weeklong vacations without your laptop are a lot harder to pull off. If you want a nice, relaxing job, principal data scientist probably isn't it.

16.2.3 *How to become a principal data scientist*

If you work as a data scientist and continue to grow your career, you default into becoming a principal data scientist. The role is the natural progression from senior data scientist; it's an expanded version of that role. Unfortunately, many senior data scientists struggle to get promoted to the next level. To be qualified to be a principal data scientist, you need to be a strong-enough data scientist to work independently effectively and to lead others. Then you need to draw attention to your abilities and contributions, and find other people in the company to champion you so that you're well-known as a critical part of the team. With those qualifications, you can advocate for promotion to this higher role.

To work independently as a data scientist, you need to be able to handle full projects without outside guidance. If your manager gives you a task such as "Create an analysis on where we should place our next retail store," they need to be able to trust that you can do the work without the help of others and without getting stuck and not telling anyone. As you grow as a data scientist, the ability to work independently should come somewhat naturally as you become more practiced in the work. To speed this growth, try to pay attention to when you get stuck and what you do in those situations. If you ask for help, what does that help provide that you couldn't do on your own? The more you can maximize the times when you can solve the problem yourself, the better.

As you gain experience, you should also pay attention to the data scientists around you. What are their problems, and are you able to help them? If you're a more senior data scientist, it's likely that junior employees are dealing with issues you've faced and solved in the past. The more opportunities you can find for technical mentorship, the stronger you'll be at helping others—which is great for a principal role.

Finally, as new ideas are thrown out, look for situations in which you can create the approach. If the company wants to find the locations of retail stores, for example, you could come up with the idea of using location-optimization techniques. Your ideas may or may not work, but if they work, you'll look great, and if they don't, you'll learn more about coming up with ideas. It's easy to rely on other data scientists to formulate an approach, but it's hard to be a principal data scientist without this skill.

16.3   *Switching to independent consulting*

It's a common dream to be your own boss and have your own company. In the case of data science, that usually means being an independent consultant: having a business that companies hire to work on specialized data science projects. In theory, companies want to hire an outside consultant only if they need a special set of skills for an important problem. If you're running your own company, you get to keep all the revenue for yourself, so no money is lost on the fat-cat executives above you. People will hire you because they believe that you're a great data scientist, so you'll be valued for your expertise.

As an independent consultant, you have to be an entire company, which means that you have to do many different things, such as

- *Marketing your business*—You won't be able to get new clients for your company unless people know about you. That may mean going to conferences, having meetings with old colleagues, or creating promotional materials such as blog posts.
- *Doing sales*—When you find a company that's interested in hiring your company for a data science project, you'll need to meet with people from that company and make a proposal for the work. If you can't get them interested in this proposal, you won't get the work.
- *Executing the project*—This work is the data science work you were hired for. It also includes project management to keep things on track and deal with any situations that may arise (such as bad data).
- *Delivering the results*—When you've created the model or done the analysis, you need to present what you've done to the client and get them on board with it. If they like it, you may get a follow-on project, and if they don't, you may lose them as a client.
- *Managing the business*—Businesses need to do things like pay taxes, create legal documents, keep track of accounts and cash flow, and perform lots of other small tasks that add up over time.

You need skills to complete all those tasks, which go far beyond those of a data scientist, to be effective as a consultant.

Depending on the type of clients you get as a consultant, your job is likely to be half data science and half all the other work to keep the business going. The work will have a certain flow: you'll be working on one project for a client company, and as the project nears its end, you'll be close to sealing the deal on another project for a different company. Also, the work will come in at a chaotic rate: you may find that in one month, you have three companies asking for your time, and the next month, no one has work available.

Finding clients is often the hardest part of being an independent consultant, requiring dedication and a strong network. Most clients tend to come from recommendations by former colleagues or clients. The more people who know a consultant and can vouch for their work, the more work will come in. Thus, for a consultant to be successful, many people (ideally, those with the authority to hire a consultant) have to know about the consultant's expertise. The more diverse the network of connections is across different companies and industries, the more likely it is that work will come in at different times. Having such a strong network requires a consultant to have worked with many different companies before, either by having changed jobs a lot earlier in their career or by having been a consultant at a larger firm.

If you're successful as an independent consultant, you have the opportunity to start hiring more people and grow the business. The company can go from just you to a team of 5 to an organization of 100. As the CEO and founder of the organization, you'll get to lead it in the direction you want with the culture you want. By taking a cut of the money that all the other consultants bring in, you may find yourself wealthy. Although this outcome is rare, being an independent consultant can be by far the most profitable of all the paths covered in this chapter.

16.3.1 Benefits of independent consulting

As an independent consultant, you get to be your own boss, which means you get to choose whether to accept possible data science projects, what approach to take, and how to present the results. You don't have to rely on anyone else, which for some people can be incredibly liberating. If you can keep your expenses down, keep your rates high, and keep a consistent set of clients, your business could potentially be quite lucrative. You have the opportunity to make twice as much as or more than you would working for a company. If you want to work from home or take a day off, you have the power to do that without having to argue with anyone.

You have ownership of what you make, too. If you come up with an interesting method of solving a problem, you can decide to patent it or market it as your company's product. No one has the ability to take away your work, whereas if you work for someone else's company, the company can claim your ideas as its intellectual property. If you are able to come up with a portfolio of useful products, that portfolio can sustain you for years.

Consulting can be fun! There's a certain thrill factor to flying around the country, helping people with your ideas, and doing all that under your own company's name. It can be incredibly validating to have many people wanting to pay money for your time. It can also feel great to deliver a solution that the client likes and to know you did the work yourself.

16.3.2 Drawbacks of independent consulting

The drawbacks of being an independent consultant are staggering (so onerous, in fact, that we'll use a bold font liberally in this section):

- **Independent consulting is wildly stressful.** Whether you get paid in a month is entirely dependent on whether people decide to hire you, which is often due to factors outside your control (such as company budgets). Conversely, you may find yourself with more work than you can handle, and you have to figure out which project you're going to let slide. You often have to sell consulting projects before getting full access to the data to see whether the project would even be feasible, and you have to figure out what to do if it isn't. There are a thousand ways that being a consultant can keep you up at night.

- **Independent consulting can make you broke.** If you become a full-time independent consultant and can't find opportunities, you'll lose money—fast. Even if you can sign a contract to do consulting, large companies often won't pay until 90 or 120 days after the work is done, which can be a half a year after you started. If you aren't able to handle those wild swings in cash flow, you won't be able to be a consultant.

- **You won't have anyone to turn to.** If you're working on your own as a consultant, people are bringing you on because they have a problem they can't solve, so there probably won't be people to bounce ideas off. You're on your own. If you're having trouble performing an analysis or getting a model to work, you'll be forced to find a solution yourself; otherwise, you'll have to tell the client that you failed.

- **Your work won't be much data science.** The amount of time you'll spend doing marketing, negotiating sales, writing contracts, and keeping up with accounting will feel immense compared with the time you spend doing data science. Being a strong data scientist is not enough; all that other work is necessary for your consulting company to survive.

16.3.3 How to become an independent consultant

To become an independent consultant, you need to have a strong set of data science skills and a track record of solving problems independently on the job. You'll also need a network of people who know your abilities, either from working at multiple companies or (even better) by working at a large consulting firm.

You can test the waters by doing freelance data science work in your free time. Put up a website, post on LinkedIn, and let people know that you're available to help. If you're able to get clients, you'll learn more about consulting as you do freelance work in the evenings. If you find that you don't have the energy to do work in the evenings, you probably won't like being a consultant. If you aren't able to get freelance clients, that's a sign that your network isn't big enough, and you should focus on that first.

If you find that you have so much freelance work that it's difficult to continue with your full-time job, that's a sign that now is a good time to transition to full-time independent consultant. At this point, you can start focusing heavily on consulting, and if you can find a core set of clients to start with, you can quit your job and move to full-time consulting.

Leaving data science

One last route is leaving data science altogether. Maybe you find that the work is no longer interesting. Maybe the workload doesn't align with your work/life balance needs. Maybe you've found yourself in a position where you have to use data science for unethical purposes, and you can't bring yourself to do it anymore. There are plenty of reasons why data science isn't the right field for everyone, and there is no shame in that.

It's difficult to give suggestions about how to leave the field because your method of leaving is so dependent on your next field. A data science résumé is an easy hire for related fields such as software development or engineering. Other fields may be harder to transition to. But just as you can make previous roles sound as much like data science as possible (chapter 6), you can try to make data science roles sound as much like another field as you can.

If you do leave, you may find yourself wanting to return later. After you've left data science, as long as you do a small project periodically or try to keep up with the field, it should be feasible to catch up with what you missed when you're ready to return. In that case, it'll be like starting at the beginning of this book again, only with a much stronger background.

Although data science has lots of marketing and buzz right now as a hot field, don't let that make you feel that you have to stay; your happiness is the most important thing. Do what's right for you.

16.4   Choosing your path

In this chapter, we've presented three paths to growing in data science, but you have many other choices too. All these choices can be overwhelming, and for the most part, you can't try a path before making a heavy commitment to go down it. How can you know which career path is right for you?

The raw truth is that you can't know. You can't know which choice is "right" because there is no right choice. These decisions are dependent on the companies you're working with, the people around you, and your personal interests at that point in your life. You can only make the choice that feels best for you and not worry too much about missed opportunities.

This lesson has shown up over and over in this book. Just as there is no right way to learn data science skills or one right type of company to take a job with, there's no best way to navigate the senior parts of your career. You can only do what's best for you with the knowledge you have. We hope that this chapter provided you enough knowledge to make navigating these career choices a bit easier.

16.5   *Interview with Angela Bassa, head of data science, data engineering, and machine learning at iRobot*

Angela Bassa is a director at iRobot, where she oversees data engineering, data science, and machine learning work across the organization. She previously worked as a consultant and as a senior manager and director of analytics, and holds a bachelor's degree in math.

What's the day-to-day life as a manager like?

It really depends on the complexity of the organization, which is often a function of its size. When you have three people, you have three edges that connect them; when you have seven people, you need exponentially more edges to still connect everyone to each other. If I need to coordinate across different products, teams, objectives, and timelines, then it's going to take a lot of meetings. I spend about a third of my day on that strategic coordination to make sure we're working on the right things in the right way for the right reason. Another third is spent working with my team, generally by being a sounding board and helping to give them context or feedback. The final third is administrative. For example, is the budget in line? Does everybody have the money for their training and development that they signed up for? If there's a really interesting women's conference coming up, and I have a bunch of openings in my team, do I want to sponsor that conference?

What are the signs you should move on from being an independent contributor?

Deciding to become a manager takes a lot of introspection, self-awareness, and being open-minded. Finding the point at which becoming a manager is most likely to succeed has a lot to do with being at a place (both professionally and personally) to make such a large transition. Management is a different profession: it has a different skill set and a different risk profile. If you mess up as an individual contributor, you're really only in charge of your own destiny. When you're managing other people, the responsibility that you're dealing with is somebody else's access to health care or somebody else's ability to pay for their rent. But I do think anyone can be a manager, and if you're worried about being a manager, then you're probably a great candidate.

Do you have to eventually transition out of being an independent contributor?

Data science as a profession is so new that there's still a heavy self-selection of who chooses to go into this profession. A lot of us are ambitious go-getters: we're paving a brand-new career because we're the kind of people who do that with our lives. But if you look at other career paths, like accounting, they're not up and out; you can absolutely be a senior accountant for a very long time. What can happen is that you may hit a limit to compensation growth or growth in your knowledge. If that is something that meets your career objectives, I see no problem with somebody who likes what they have staying right where they are. Still, there are so many talented professionals flooding data science as a career that if I find somebody who is eager and gunning for it, then I am more likely to be biased towards that personality type when deciding who to bring in.

What advice do you have for someone who wants to be a technical lead but isn't quite ready for it?

Find a sounding-board person that you can have a frank and open conversation with so that you're not just in your head. That can help you get concrete feedback and understand the things that you need to get better at. Having a person who has already been successful in a technical lead role can also be helpful in getting you to understand what they needed to get to and succeed in that position. You'll see your blind spots when you investigate your own skill set. It's funny: we accept that it takes a lot of communication and collaboration to grow and that it takes a village to raise a family, but professionally, we expect that that everyone is just supposed to be able to do it all on their own. The best way to grow is to find people who have your back and to be willing to hear their feedback.

What's your final piece of advice to aspiring and junior data scientist?

My first piece of advice is to be *humble*. It's easy to believe that we are the kings and queens of the hill since data science is the "sexiest" profession and that any employer should be sprinkling rose petals at our feet when we walk. It's so important to remember that it takes many people to make a product successful and that just because data science is in the limelight doesn't mean that it's better or special.

The second piece of advice is to be *kind*. It's easy to be hard on ourselves, especially because data science is so broad and can mean so many things. If you are great at analysis but not as much at machine learning engineering, you might feel that means you're not a "real" data scientist. But you are! There are so many ways to shine.

Summary

- Management is a great track for people who want to help others but are willing to give up doing data science. Following this track can eventually lead to being high up in the company.
- A principal data scientist gets to lead on the technical side and has to be responsible for others. This role is a great option for staying technical while helping others.
- Independent consulting is highly stressful and risky, but also potentially rewarding. You'll need a strong network of connections to find work consistently.

Chapters 13–16 resources

Books

The Design of Everyday Things, by Don Norman (Basic Books)

This classic book introduces ideas from the field of design and discusses how to think about design in any type of work. Being able to understand a user and how a design influences what they do is critical to a product's success. By reading this book, you'll get better at understanding your stakeholders' needs and lowering the chance that your data science project will fail because it's not what the customer wants.

Self-Compassion: The Proven Power of Being Kind to Yourself, by Kristin Neff, PhD (Harper-Collins Publishers)

If the part of chapter 13 that discussed how people mentally beat themselves up when they fail resonated with you, you'll want to read this book. It goes deep into the author's struggle with self-criticism and her journey to being kind to herself. This journey is one that many data scientists should go on, and this book is a great guide to it.

Demystifying Public Speaking, by Lara Hogan (A Book Apart)

Lara Hogan is a popular public speaker in engineering leadership who wrote this book to give practical advice to help people get started speaking. In this short and engaging book, she covers tactics for everything from choosing a topic to making the presentation to handling your nerves.

R Packages, 2nd ed., by Jennifer Bryan and Hadley Wickham (O'Reilly Media)

This book covers the details of how to create an R package, a great way to improve your own workflow, and how to give back to the community. As of January 2020, this book was still under development, but you can find the work-in-progress copy at https://r-pkgs.org.

Resilient Management, by Lara Hogan (A Book Apart)

This book is a great, short guide for any new manager, with advice and templates for getting to know your teammates, mentoring, setting expectations, and handling challenges. Even if you're not planning to be a people manager, this book will be very helpful if you're starting to lead projects or have struggled with communicating with your teammates.

The Manager's Path: A Guide for Tech Leaders Navigating Growth and Change, by Camille Fournier (O'Reilly Media)

If you're thinking about shifting from a data scientist to a technical lead or manager, this book is perfectly targeted to you. Written by Camille Fournier, the former CTO of

Rent the Runway, the book walks through how to think about the work of a manager and get out of the mindset of being an independent contributor. Reading this book will help you understand ideas that may take years to figure out on your own.

The E-Myth Revisited, by Michael E. Gerber (HarperCollins Publishers)

Although it's totally unrelated to data science, this book is a great resource for people who are considering working as independent consultants or starting their own businesses in another way. It discusses how the framework of thinking about your work needs to change as you run a business. You need to go from a person who's focused on completing tasks to someone who has to systemize everything they do to keep the business running continually.

High Output Management, by Andrew S. Grove (Vintage)

Running a business well is a complex ordeal that requires an immense amount of strategic thinking. *High Output Management* breaks down the concepts, using easy-to-understand cases such as delivering breakfast, and is a useful resource for people who want to understand more about managing a business. The book was written in 1983 but has since been updated and has aged well.

Blogs

"Making peace with personal branding," by Rachel Thomas

https://www.fast.ai/2017/12/18/personal-brand

Rachel Thomas does an excellent job of branding herself in the field of data science and on social media, and this blog post provides perspective on how to do it while still feeling comfortable with yourself.

Lara Hogan's blog

https://larahogan.me/blog

We recommend two of Lara Hogan's books in the preceding section, and her blog is similarly full of great advice about the soft skills you need to succeed. Although many of her posts focus on managers, she also gives advice that is applicable to anyone, including what to do if your manager isn't supporting you, how to give feedback, and handling your emotions when you're thinking "Why can't leadership just . . . ?"

"The art of slide design," by Melinda Seckington

https://missgeeky.com/2017/08/04/the-art-of-slide-design

This five-part series (each subsequent post is linked at the bottom) is a master class on making effective slides. Seckington shares the principles of slide design—maximize signal, minimize noise, make important information stand out, show and tell, and be consistent—and illustrates them with many examples and counterexamples.

"Overcoming social anxiety to attend user groups," by Steph Locke

https://itsalocke.com/blog/overcoming-social-anxiety-to-attend-user-groups

If social anxiety has been holding you back from attending meetups or conferences, check out this post by Steph Locke. She addresses common concerns such as "I won't know anyone" or "How do I talk to people?" with short, practical advice.

"How to ask for a promotion," by Rebecca Knight

https://hbr.org/2018/01/how-to-ask-for-a-promotion

This article shares tips from two leadership coaches on how to ask for a promotion. Each tip, such as "Plant the seed" and "Do some research," comes with a paragraph of specific examples.

Epilogue

Well, we've sure covered a lot. We started with defining data science and what skills you need to do it, walked through how to prepare for and get a data science job, and then discussed how to grow and flourish in the field. Over 16 chapters, we went from understanding different types of companies to making unit testing for production models to becoming a manager.

When you look at the book holistically, a few trends seem to flow through it. These lessons apply to all points of a data scientist's journey in different forms. For us, these three ideals have kept our careers continuously moving forward:

- *A data scientist needs to be able to communicate.* Over and over, people we interviewed for the book mentioned that their success came from communicating their work effectively. Whether effective communication is making a report for an executive, collaborating with an engineering team on a model, or being able to speak in a way that non-data scientists understand, it can help you through the process of finding a job and working with other people in that job.
- *A data scientist needs to be proactive.* It's exceedingly rare for a data scientist to be handed a perfectly well-formed problem and the tools to solve the problem. Instead, data scientists need to proactively try to find data, create new ideas for models, and try experiments. Being proactive and doing things like making a portfolio will also help you get a job. The more you can take initiative and find solutions to problems, the better.
- *A data scientist needs community.* No one makes it in any career without help from others, but as members of a new and fast-growing field, data scientists especially benefit from developing strong professional relationships. These relationships can take many forms. A sponsor can recommend you as a speaker for a meetup that leads, two years later, to keynoting an international conference. A mentor can give you feedback on your résumé and refer you to a position at their company. A manager can help bridge the gap with stakeholders and suggest areas for personal growth. Or a peer can simply commiserate with

you and lift your spirits after a tough day at work. It's worth spending time building these relationships to tackle the many challenges you'll face in your career.

We hope that you've enjoyed reading the book; we certainly enjoyed writing it. In creating the book, we found that many of our own experiences poured into it. At multiple times during the writing process, we even reread it ourselves to better think through our own career decisions. We wish you the best of luck in your data science career journey!

appendix
Interview questions

Often, the most helpful thing in preparing for an interview is getting into the mindset of what it will be like. Being comfortable answering questions and thinking in a way that is well suited to the fast-paced thinking of an interview can mean the difference between getting the job and not. Thus, we've provided example interview questions for you to think about and understand. You should view these questions in conjunction with chapter 7, which discusses how to view the interview process as a whole.

The questions in this appendix fall into five categories:

- Coding and software development
- SQL and databases
- Statistics and machine learning
- Behavioral
- Brain teasers

This is a wide range of topics, and it's impossible to study for the thousands of questions that could be asked. One company may ask you to invert a binary tree while the other asks only Python and behavioral questions. That's why we recommend asking before your onsite interviews what types of questions to expect. You won't get the exact questions, of course, but the hiring manager or recruiter should give you a general idea so you can focus your preparation. They might say, for example, "In your first interview, you'll answer some SQL questions on a whiteboard. Then you'll have two behavioral interviews in a row, one with an engineer and one with a data scientist. Finally, one of our machine learning engineers will ask you about your previous data science projects."

It's extremely unlikely that you'll only see questions covered in this appendix during your job search process. That's why we've not only provided answers for each question (with the text we'd say out loud and any code we'd write on the whiteboard), but also notes on what we think makes an effective answer. All the answers are given from the first-person viewpoint of a hypothetical data scientist who has a combination of experiences similar to those of the authors of this book. For some of the questions, we drew on experiences we had at past jobs; you should try to come up with your own examples for these questions.

Some of the questions come from our shared experiences going through many interviews; others were provided by fellow data scientists. Thanks so much to everyone who helped make this appendix much more useful!

A.1   Coding and software development

A.1.1   FizzBuzz

Write a program that prints the numbers 1 to 100. But for multiples of 3, print "Fizz" *instead of the number, and for the multiples of 5, print* "Buzz". *For numbers that are multiples of both 3 and 5, print* "FizzBuzz".

EXAMPLE ANSWER

Here is pseudocode for one solution to the problem:

```
for (i in 1 to 100) {
    if (i mod 15) {
        print("FizzBuzz")
    } else if (i mod 5) {
        print("Buzz")
    } else if (i mod 3) {
        print("Fizz")
    } else {
        print(i)
    }
}
```

The program iterates through the numbers 1 to 100. For each iteration, it first checks whether the number is divisible by 15, and if so, it prints "FizzBuzz". If not, it checks whether the number is divisible by 5 and, if so, prints "Buzz". If not, it checks whether the number is divisible by 3 and prints "Fizz" if it is, and if none of those are true, it prints the number.

NOTES

This problem is an extremely famous interview question in software development, having been created by Imran Ghory and popularized by Jeff Atwood (https://blog.codinghorror.com/why-cant-programmers-program), so it's common to get this exact question as part of a data science interview. The two main tasks within it are figuring out how to iterate over the set of all numbers (in the example, we used a for loop) and how to check what should be printed at each number. A common mistake is to check whether the number is divisible by 3 or 5 before checking whether it's divisible by 15, but any number that is divisible by 15 is also divisible by 3 or 5. Thus, if 3 or 5 is checked first, "Fizz" or "Buzz" might be printed in cases where "FizzBuzz" should be.

Although our proposed solution is straightforward, there are ways to improve on it. In some languages, including R and Python, you can take a cleaner functional programming approach by using purrr in R or list comprehensions in Python. You could also make a generalized function that as input takes the list of multiples to check and words to print at those multiples and outputs any list. Depending on how the interview is going, you may want to talk about ways you would want to improve the answer.

For fun, check out FizzBuzz Enterprise Edition (https://github.com/Enterprise-QualityCoding/FizzBuzzEnterpriseEdition) or a FizzBuzz TensorFlow machine learning model (https://joelgrus.com/2016/05/23/fizz-buzz-in-tensorflow).

A.1.2 *Tell whether a number is prime*

Write a function that, given a number, returns true *if it's a prime number and* false *otherwise. Assume there is no built-in function to check whether a number is prime.*

EXAMPLE ANSWER
Here is the pseudocode for one solution to the problem:

```
is_prime = function(n){
    for (i in 2 to n / 2) {
        if ((n mod i) == 0) {
            return FALSE
        }
    }
    return TRUE
}
```

A *prime number* is one that is not divisible by anything except 1 and itself. The program iterates through all the numbers from 2 to the half of the number given and checks whether the given number is divisible by them. If it is, the function returns false and stops. If it goes through the whole for loop without stopping, the function returns true.

NOTES
Similarly to FizzBuzz, this problem tests whether you can write a for loop and a function. You also need to know how to stop iterating when a condition is reached so that you can safely return true at the end if the for loop completes. You can add small tricks like realizing that you don't have to check whether the number is divisible by all numbers lower than it or half of it—just those lower than its square root. But the main point of the problem is simply to test whether you can write a function that works.

A.1.3   **Working with Git**

Can you talk about a time when you used Git to collaborate on a project?

—Alex Hayes

EXAMPLE ANSWER

At my last job, I created an R package, funneljoin, with two co-workers during an afternoon hackathon, using Git from the beginning. We spent the first hour pair-programming on one computer and then made a list of tasks to split among ourselves. Each of us created a different branch to work on our tasks, which enabled us to easily merge them back together in the end. Using Git ensured that we never accidentally overwrote someone else's work. By committing early and often as we progressed, we knew that we could always go back if we decided that a previous way of implementing a feature was better. Finally, using GitHub meant that afterward, anyone in the company could download the package and start using it right away.

Since that initial afternoon, I've remained the maintainer of the package. I continue to use Git features like branches so that I can prototype features without merging them in until they've been thoroughly tested.

NOTES

If you're asked this question and haven't collaborated using Git on a project before, you can talk instead about how you've used Git for a personal project. One thing this question is testing is whether you've used Git, and you can explain that you've used different features (such as branches or forking), even if just by yourself. You might add how you would adapt your practices if you were collaborating with other people—by using branches more, for example, or by sticking to a consistent commit message structure.

If you haven't used Git before, be honest about that in the interview. But we do recommend trying to learn it before having too many more interviews.

A.1.4   **Technology decisions**

Given a totally blank slate, how do you pick your tech stack?

—Heather Nolis

EXAMPLE ANSWER

This question is interesting to answer because it really depends on the project at hand. My decision for a tech stack relies primarily on balancing what would be the most straightforward for me to implement with what would be easiest for everyone else to work with. Let me give two examples of how I picked technical stacks and what I learned from them.

On one project earlier in my career, I had to develop a new product entirely from scratch, and I was the only data scientist on my team. I chose to use the .NET stack and F# because I was very familiar with them, and because I was so familiar, we were able to get a working product out the door quickly. The downside was that because the F# language is so uncommon, when it came time to hire a data scientist to take it over, we couldn't find anyone who already had the required knowledge. In retrospect, using .NET and F# was not the right decision.

On a more recent project, I was tasked with creating a machine learning API. I was in the middle of an engineering team that worked with microservices, so I decided to create a REST API in R as a Docker container. Although I hadn't used Docker containers before, I chose it because I knew that it would be easiest for the team to maintain. From that project, I learned a lot about Docker and containers, and the work I created was able to integrate well.

NOTES

When interviewing candidates at T-Mobile, Heather Nolis usually has a person pick a project and describe the decisions they made; the decisions other people made; and how they would do things differently, knowing what they know now. Your interviewer may not ask you those things directly, but they're all worth including anyway.

Whatever answer you give, you'll want to include plenty of references to decisions you've had to make in work you've done before (which can include side projects or coursework). The point of this question is to see how much thought you have put into choosing the right technology for the right project. Having chosen technological stacks that ended up being problematic is fine as long as you learned from the problem. In fact, having learned from things is even better than getting everything right the first time, because it shows that you can change.

A.1.5 *Frequently used package/library*

> *What's an R package or Python library you use frequently, and why?*

EXAMPLE ANSWER

It's not one package, but I really love the suite of packages that make up the tidyverse in R. The packages get you all the way from reading in the data to cleaning it to transforming and visualizing and modeling it.

I especially enjoy working in dplyr because, thanks to the connected package dbplyr, I can write the same code whether I'm working with a local or remote table as dbplyr translates dplyr code to SQL. Using dbplyr at my last job meant I could stay in RStudio for my entire workflow, even though all our data was stored in Amazon Redshift and required SQL queries to access. I would use dbplyr to do summaries and filtering and then pull the data down locally if I needed to do more complicated operations or visualizations.

Overall, I really like the philosophy of Hadley Wickham, a core tidyverse developer: that the bottleneck when coding is often thinking time, not computational time, and that you should build tools that work seamlessly together and let you translate your thoughts into code quickly.

NOTES

The interviewer shouldn't be looking for a specific answer here. Rather, they're looking to see whether you (a) program enough in either language to have a frequently used package and (b) can explain how and why you use that package. This answer also gives the interviewer a sense of what kind of work you do day to day. Don't forget to explain what the package does, especially if it's a niche package. If another package is more widely used for the task, you may want to explain your reasoning for why you choose this package, as that shows your broader awareness of what alternatives are out there. Finally, don't worry about picking the most "advanced" library, such as a deep learning library, to impress the interviewer. Ideally, this question is one of the easiest and (potentially) most fun to answer, so don't overthink it.

A.1.6   *R Markdown or Jupyter Notebooks*

What is an R Markdown file or Jupyter Notebook? Why would you use an R Markdown file or Jupyter Notebook over an R or Python script? When is a script better?

EXAMPLE ANSWER

I'm going to answer this in the case of R and R Markdown, but the basic idea is the same for Python and Jupyter Notebooks. R Markdown files are ways of writing R code that allow you to put text and formatting around the code. In a sense, they merge the code and results of an analysis with the narration and ideas of the analysis. By using an R Markdown file, you can have an analysis that is easier to reproduce than raw R code, with separate documentation on what the analysis was. Ideally, your R Markdown would be formatted so clearly that when you render the output file, you could hand the resulting HTML output, Word document, or PDF to a stakeholder.

R Markdown files are great for reproducible analysis, but they're less useful when you're writing code that you're going to deploy or use in other places. Say you have a list of functions that you want to use in multiple other places (such as one to load the data from a file). It might make sense to write an R script that creates all the functions and keep the script separate from an individual analysis. Or, if you wanted to use R with the plumber package to create a web API, you wouldn't want an R Markdown file for that.

NOTES

This question is a check by the interviewer to see whether you have experience in doing reproducible analysis. Many people who use R or Python write scripts in ad hoc ways and don't think about how they will share the results with others. By showing that you understand the point of R Markdown and Jupyter Notebooks, you show that you're thinking about how to make your code more usable. If you haven't used either R Markdown files or Jupyter Notebooks, definitely go try one of them out.

Don't worry about understanding both R and Python versions; either should be fine.

A.1.7   When should you write functions or packages/libraries?

At what point should you make your code into a function? When should you turn it into a package or library?

EXAMPLE ANSWER

In general, if I notice that I'm ever copying and pasting code, it's probably a sign that I should make a function out of it. If I need to run code on three different datasets, for example, I should make a function and apply it to each one rather than copy the code three times. The library purrr in R or list comprehensions in Python make it easy to apply a function many times.

I have found that packages and libraries are best when you have code that spans multiple distinct projects on the team. At my current job, we have a lot of data that we store in S3 but want to analyze locally. Rather than copying and pasting functions to access the code in each project, I created a library that could be called from all of them. The downside of libraries is that if you change them, you have to change all the projects that use the library, but for core functions, this approach is often worthwhile.

NOTES

This question is somewhat of a softball question because it has a right answer: "as much as possible." Generally, copying and pasting code over and over is a bad practice; a data scientist should make functions in such a way that the code is easier to read and understand. For that reason, as much as you can, add examples that show you understand the value of reusing code as functions or packages. Was there a time you made a function and reused it a lot? What about a library? Talk about those situations as much as possible.

A.1.8   Example manipulating data in R/Python

Here's a table, called tweets. The data has the account that sent the tweet, the text, the number of likes, and the date sent. Write a script to get a table with one row per person with a column that's the minimum number of likes they got, called min_likes, and a column of the total number of tweets, called nb_tweets. This should be only for tweets sent after September 1, 2019. You also need to eliminate any duplicates in the table first.

account_name	text	nb_likes	date
@vboykis	Data science is…	50	2019-10-01
@Randy_Au	It's hard when…	23	2019-05-01
@rchang	Some news…	35	2019-01-01
@vboykis	My newsletter…	42	2019-11-23
@drob	My best advice…	62	2019-11-01
…	…	…	…

EXAMPLE ANSWER IN R

```
tweets %>%
  filter(date > "2019-09-01") %>%
  distinct() %>%
  group_by(account_name) %>%
  summarize(nb_tweets = n(), min_likes = min(nb_likes))
```

EXAMPLE ANSWER IN PYTHON

```
tweets = tweets[tweets.date > "2019-09-01"].
drop_duplicates().
groupby("account_name")

tweets['nb_likes'].agg(nb_tweets="count", min_likes="min")
```

NOTES

This type of question is a mix between the FizzBuzz and prime-number questions (knowing how to do something in R/Python) and SQL queries (analyzing data). This specific question should be relatively easy for someone who has done data analysis before, but you may face one that has tricks (such as needing to convert a character column to a date column or change it from long to wide format) that you can't remember at the moment. If you don't remember how to do something, just say "I don't remember the exact syntax for *X*, so I'm going to put some pseudocode in there now as a placeholder," and move on. You don't want to spend too much time getting stuck on one part. If the question does include something that's more unusual, it's likely that the interviewer considers that part to be a bonus rather than a requirement for going on to the next stage.

A.2 SQL and databases

A.2.1 Types of joins

Explain the difference between a left join and an inner join.

—Ludamila Janda and Ayanthi G.

EXAMPLE ANSWER

Joins are ways of combining data from two different tables—a left table and a right table—into a new one. Joins work by connecting rows between the two tables; a set of key columns is used to find data in the two tables that are the same and should be connected. In the case of a left join, every row from the left table appears in the resulting table, but rows from the right table appear only if the values in their key columns show up in the left table. In an inner join, however, both rows from the left table and the right table appear only if there is a matching row in the other table.

In practice, you can think of a left join as attaching data from the right table to the left, if it exists (such as using the right table as a lookup). An inner join is more like finding all the shared data and making a new table from only the pairs.

NOTES

Janda likes this question as an early screener for more-junior roles because it isn't a
trick question and is important knowledge for a candidate to have. She finds that you
can learn a lot from how the candidate chooses to answer. There are plenty of valid
answers, from ones that are textbook-correct but not easy to understand to very sim-
ple-to-understand ones that miss edge cases.

Notice that in our answer, we didn't talk about any complexities from duplicate
rows appearing in the data. It might be worthwhile to mention these complexities
because they can affect the results, but more likely, they're a distraction from the
point you're trying to get across.

A.2.2   *Loading data into SQL*

*What are some different ways you can load data into a database in the first place, and
what are the advantages and disadvantages of each?*

—Ayanthi G.

EXAMPLE ANSWER

There are many ways to load data into a database, primarily depending on where the
data exists in the first place. If the data is in a flat file such as a CSV file, many SQL versions have programs to import the data. SQL Server 2017, for example, has an Import
and Export wizard. These tools are easy to use but do not allow for much customiza-
tion and are not easily reproducible. If the data is coming from a different environment, such as R or Python, there are drivers that allow for passing the data into SQL.
An ODBC driver, for example, can be used along with the DBI package in R to move
data from R into SQL. These methods are more reproducible and programmatic to
implement, but they require you to get the data into R or Python.

NOTES

This question is really a test of whether you've had to load data into a database before.
If you've done it before, it shouldn't be too difficult to describe how you did it. If you
haven't loaded data into a database before, that may signal to the interviewer that you
don't have enough experience.

The part of the question about advantages and disadvantages checks whether
you understand that different tools are better in different situations. Sometimes,
using a GUI to upload data is a nice, easy solution when you have a single file. At
other times, you'll want to set up a whole automated script to load the data continuously. The more you can show that you understand the nuances of what to use when,
the better.

A.2.3 Example SQL query

Here is TABLE_A from a school, containing grades from 0 to 100 earned by students across multiple classes. How would you calculate the highest grade in each class?

Class	Student	Grade
Math	Nolis, Amber	100
Math	Berkowitz, Mike	90
Literature	Liston, Amanda	97
Spanish	Betancourt, Laura	93
Literature	Robinson, Abby	93
...	...	...

EXAMPLE ANSWER

Here is a query to find the highest grade in each class:

```
SELECT CLASS, MAX(GRADE)
INTO TABLE_B
FROM TABLE_A
GROUP BY CLASS
```

This query groups the data into each class and then finds the max from it. It additionally saves the result into a new table (TABLE_B) so that the results can be queried later.

NOTES

This question is almost as simple as you can get for a SQL question; it's testing whether you have basic understanding of grouping in SQL. The reasons why people typically mess this question up include not seeing what to group (in this case, the class variable), or they find the question to be so easy that they overcomplicate it and miss the simple solution. If you are in an interview and a question seems to be too easy, it very well may be as easy as it seems.

If that solution doesn't seem to be obvious to you, now would be a good time to review how grouping variables work in SQL.

Finally, the INTO TABLE_B line was totally optional, but it sets you up well for the next question.

A.2.4 Example SQL query continued

Consider the table from the previous question. What if we wanted to not only find the highest grade in each class, but also the student who earned that grade?

EXAMPLE ANSWER

Assuming that we have the result from the previous question stored in TABLE_B, we can use it in this solution:

```
SELECT a.CLASS, a.GRADE, a.STUDENT
FROM TABLE_A a
INNER JOIN TABLE_B b ON a.CLASS = b.CLASS AND a.GRADE = b.GRADE
```

This query selects all the students and their grades from the original TABLE_A that have classes with grades that show up in the table of maxes, TABLE_B. The inner join acts as a filter to keep only the class/grade combinations that are the maxes, because only in that case does the grade appear in TABLE_B. Alternatively, we could use a subquery to do the same thing without calling TABLE_B:

```
SELECT a.CLASS, a.GRADE, a.STUDENT
FROM TABLE_A a
INNER JOIN (
  SELECT CLASS, MAX(GRADE)
  FROM TABLE_A GROUP BY CLASS) b
ON a.CLASS = b.CLASS AND a.GRADE = b.GRADE
```

NOTES

Although this problem has multiple solutions, any solution almost certainly requires more than a single query off TABLE_A, and for that reason, this question can easily trip people up. The solution may appear to be straightforward on paper, but being able to think of it during an interview may be hard. If you get this kind of question wrong, it'll still be possible to pass the interview.

The solution doesn't make any special case for a tie for the max. In the example solution, multiple students would be returned. It might be worth pointing this fact out to the interviewer because it shows that you're paying attention to edge cases.

A.2.5   *Data types*

> *What disadvantages are there to storing a column of dates as strings in a database? In SQL, for example, what if we stored a column of dates as a* VARCHAR(MAX) *instead of* DATE*?*

EXAMPLE ANSWER

Having dates stored as strings instead of dates (such as storing March 20, 2019 as the string "03/20/2019") is a common situation in databases. Although you may not lose any information, depending on how you do it, you may experience performance hits. First, if the data isn't stored as a DATE type, we couldn't use the MONTH() function on it. We also couldn't do things like find the differences between two dates or find the minimum date in the column.

This problem tends to happen a lot when you're loading data into a database or cleaning it. The earlier you can correctly format the data, the easier the analysis will be. You can fix these sorts of situations by using functions like CAST. That being said, if you're loading in data with hundreds of columns and there are plenty you'll never use, it may not be worth the time to fix all these issues.

NOTES
The problem of having data stored in an incorrect type is an extremely frequent occurrence. It doesn't happen just in databases; it can also happen in flat files or in tables within environments such as R and Python. This question is checking whether you understand that when this happens, it's generally bad, and when you see these situations, you generally should fix them. Being able to answer questions like this one should come naturally from doing data cleaning as part of data science projects that start with messy data.

A.3   *Statistics and machine learning*

A.3.1   *Statistics terms*

> *Explain the terms* mean, median, *and* mode *to an eight-year old.*
>
> —Allan Butler

EXAMPLE ANSWER
Mean, *median*, and *mode* are three different types of averages. Averages let us understand something about a whole set of numbers with just one number that summarizes something about the whole set.

Suppose that we did a poll of your class to see how many siblings each person has. You have five people in your class, and let's say you find that one person has no siblings, one has one, one has two, and two have five.

The *mode* is the most common number of siblings. In this case, that's 5, as two people have five siblings compared with only one person who has every other number.

To get the mean, you get the total number of siblings and divide that by the number of people. In this case, we add $0 + 1*1 + 1*2 + 5*2 = 13$. You have five people in the class, so the mean is $13/5 = 2.6$.

The *median* is the number in the middle if you line them up from smallest to largest. We'd make the line 0, 1, 2, 5, 5. The third number is in the middle, and in our case, that means the median is two.

We see that the three types of averages come up with different numbers. When do you want to use one instead of the other? The mean is the most common, but the median is helpful if you have outliers. Suppose that one person had 1,000 siblings! Suddenly, your mean gets much bigger, but it doesn't really represent the number of siblings most people have. On the other hand, the median stays the same.

NOTES
It's unlikely that someone interviewing for a data science position won't know about the different types of averages, so this question is really testing your communication skills rather than whether you get the definitions right (although if you get them wrong, that's a red flag). In our example, we used a simple example that an eight-year

old might encounter in real life. We recommend keeping the number of subjects simple; you don't want to get tripped up doing the math for the mean or median because you're trying to calculate them for 50 data points. If there's a whiteboard in the room, it might be helpful to write out the numbers to keep track of them. As a bonus, you can add as we did when you might want to use one type of average instead of another.

A.3.2   *Explain p-value*

> *Can you explain to me what a p-value is and how it's used?*

EXAMPLE ANSWER

Imagine that you were flipping a coin and got 26 heads out of 50. Would you conclude that the coin wasn't fair because you didn't get exactly 25 heads? No! You understand that randomness is at play. But what if the coin came up heads 33 times? How do we decide what the threshold is for concluding that it's not a fair coin?

This is where the *p*-value comes in. A *p*-value is the probability that, if the null hypothesis is true, we'd see a result as or more extreme than the one we got. A null hypothesis is our default assumption coming in, such as no differences between two groups, that we're trying to disprove. In our case, the null hypothesis is that the coin is fair.

Because a *p*-value is a probability, it's always between 0 and 1. The *p*-value is essentially a representation of how shocked we would be by a result if our null hypothesis is true. We can use a statistical test to calculate the probability that, if we were flipping a fair coin, we would get 33 or more heads or tails (both being results that are as extreme as the one we got). It turns out that probability, the *p*-value, is .034. By convention, people use .05 as the threshold for rejecting the null hypothesis. In this case, we would reject the hypothesis that the coin is fair.

With a *p*-value threshold of .05, we're accepting that 5% of the time, when the null hypothesis is true, we're still going to reject it. This is our false-positive rate: the rate of rejecting the null hypothesis when it's actually true.

NOTES

This question is testing whether you both understand what a p-value is and can communicate the definition effectively. There are common misconceptions about the *p*-value, such as that it's the probability that a result is a false positive. Unlike the averages question in the preceding section, it's possible for someone to get this wrong. On the communication side, we recommend using an example to guide the explanation. Data scientists need to be able to communicate with a wide variety of stakeholders, some of whom have never heard of *p*-values and some who think that they understand what they are but don't. You want to show that you both understand *p*-values and can share that understanding with others.

A.3.3 Explain a confusion matrix

What's a confusion matrix? What might you use it for?

EXAMPLE ANSWER

A *confusion matrix* lets you see for a given model how your predictions compare with the actual results. It's a 2x2 grid that has four parts: the number of true positives, false positives, true negatives, and false negatives. From a confusion matrix, you can calculate different metrics, such as accuracy (the percentage classified correctly as true positive or true negative) and sensitivity, otherwise known as the true positive rate, as well as the percentage of positives correctly classified as such. Confusion matrixes are used in supervised learning problems in which you're classifying or predicting an outcome, such as whether a flight will be late or whether a picture is of a cat or a dog. Let me draw an example one for the flight outcomes.

	Actual late	Actual on-time
Predicted Late	60	15
Predicted on-time	30	120

In this case, 60 flights that were predicted to be late actually were, but 30 predicted to be on time were actually late. That means our true positive rate is 60 / (60 + 30) = 2/3.

Seeing the confusion matrix instead of a single metric can help you understand your model performance better. Let's say that for a different problem you just calculated the accuracy, for example, and found that you have 97% accuracy. That sounds great, but it could turn out that 97% of flights are on time. If the model simply predicted that every flight is on time, it would have 97% accuracy, as all the on-time ones are classified correctly, but the model would be totally useless!

NOTES

This question tests whether you're familiar with supervised learning models. It also tests whether you know different ways of evaluating the performance of models. In our answer, we shared two metrics that you could calculate from a confusion matrix, showing that you understand how it could be used, as well as a case in which seeing the whole matrix instead of just one metric is useful.

A.3.4 Interpreting regression models

How would you interpret these two regression model outputs, given the input data and model? This model is on a dataset of 150 observations of 3 species of flowers: setosa, versicolor, and virginica. For each flower, the sepal length, sepal width, petal length, and petal width are recorded. The model is a linear regression predicting the sepal length from the other four variables.

INPUT DATA TO THE MODEL

	Sepal.Length	Sepal.Width	Petal.Length	Petal.Width	Species
	<dbl>	<dbl>	<dbl>	<dbl>	<fct>
1	5.1	3.5	1.4	0.2	setosa
2	4.9	3	1.4	0.2	setosa
3	4.7	3.2	1.3	0.2	setosa
4	4.6	3.1	1.5	0.2	setosa
5	5	3.6	1.4	0.2	setosa

MODEL CALL

```
model <- lm(Sepal.Length ~ ., iris)
```

OUTPUT 1

term	estimate	std.error	statistic	p.value
<chr>	<dbl>	<dbl>	<dbl>	<dbl>
(Intercept)	2.17	0.280	7.76	1.43e-12
Sepal.Width	0.496	0.0861	5.76	4.87e- 8
Petal.Length	0.829	0.0685	12.1	1.07e-23
Petal.Width	-0.315	0.151	-2.08	3.89e- 2
Speciesversicolor	-0.724	0.240	-3.01	3.06e- 3
Speciesvirginica	-1.02	0.334	-3.07	2.58e- 3

OUTPUT 2

variable	value
<chr>	<dbl>
r.squared	0.867
adj.r.squared	0.863
sigma	0.307
statistic	188
p.value	2.67e-61
df	6
logLik	-32.6
AIC	79.1
BIC	100
deviance	13.6
df.residual	144

EXAMPLE ANSWER

Looking at the model summary results, it looks like a very good model; the R-squared is 0.867, meaning that the predictors explain 86.7 percent of the variance in sepal length. The predictors are all significant at the *p* less than .05 level. I see that the wider the sepal and the longer the petal, the longer the sepal, whereas wider petals actually are associated with shorter sepals. Both the versicolor and virginica species have negative coefficients, which means that we'd predict those species to have a smaller sepal length than the setosa species.

Suppose that we found a new flower, with a sepal width of 1, petal length of 2, petal width of 1, and that it was the virginica species. Our model would predict the sepal length to be the following: 2.17 + .496 * 1 + .829 * 2 – .315 * 1 – 1.02, which is about 3. Before using this model, though, I'd want to look at a few more diagnostics, such as whether the residuals are normally distributed, and I'd want to find a test set to see how it performs out of sample to make sure it's not overfitting.

NOTES

The interviewer is looking for multiple things, and you can get points depending on how many you get right. In this case, the interviewer is checking whether you under-stand the model statistics (such as R-squared), as well as the estimates and their associ-ated *p*-values. Although this information wasn't explicitly asked for, in our answer, we added how we would use this model to predict the sepal length of a new flower. Finally, we added some information about the model we'd want to know before we started using it. This type of open-ended question is a good opportunity to hit what the interviewer is probably looking for and to add bonus information. Avoid trying too hard and ending up spending 20 minutes on a single question; show that you understand as many concepts as you can and then move on.

A.3.5 *What is boosting?*

What does the term boosting *mean when referring to machine learning algorithms?*

EXAMPLE ANSWER

Boosting refers to a whole class of machine learning algorithms that are built on taking a weak model and reusing it enough times so that it becomes a strong one. The idea is to train a weak model on data, look for areas where the model had errors, and train a second model of the same type that weights the data points where there were errors more heavily, hoping that the second model will fix some of the mistakes of the first. You repeat this process again and again until you hit some limit to the number of models. Then you use all of these models together to make the prediction. By having a large set of models, you'll get a more accurate result than if you'd used a single model.

One very popular implementation of a boosting method is XGBoost, which is used heavily in both R and Python.

NOTES

Boosting is an uncommon-enough term that it's entirely possible someone with a basic data science background may not know exactly what it means. Thus, this question is more a test of being senior than of having any data science expertise. The question is also a little bit academic; you can imagine someone using XGBoost successfully in their code for years without thinking too deeply about how it works. This question is more "It's nice to get it right, but not the end of the world if you don't" than "If you don't get this question right, you're unlikely to get the job."

A.3.6   *Favorite algorithm*

What's your favorite machine learning algorithm? All right, can you explain it to me?

—Jeroen Janssens

EXAMPLE ANSWER

My favorite machine learning algorithm is a recurrent neural network. I have been doing a lot of work with natural language processing lately, and recurrent neural networks are great models for classifying text quickly.

Do you know a linear regression? A neural network is like a linear regression except that you have groups of linear regressions and the output of one group of linear regressions is the input to the next group. By tying all these linear regressions together into layers of models, you can make predictions much more accurately.

A recurrent neural network is a special case of a neural network that's tuned for data that falls in sequences. In the case of natural language processing a block of text, the output part of the way through a sequence of words is the input for the model of the next words.

NOTES

This question is one of the many you might get during an interview that are designed to see whether you can explain a complex idea in a simple way. What algorithm you choose for your answer isn't nearly as important as being able to express how it works clearly. That said, this question is a great opportunity to highlight interesting past work you've done by expressing an algorithm that relates to the work and talking about it.

A.3.7   *Training vs. test data*

What is training data, and what is test data? What is your general strategy for creating these datasets?

EXAMPLE ANSWER

Training data is data that is used to train a machine learning model. Test data is data that is not used in training a machine learning model; instead, it is used to validate how well the model works. These datasets need to be separate because if data is used to train a model, the model can learn the correct result for the data and will be artificially good at fitting to it.

There are many ways to split training data and test data. My general approach is to take a small random sample, such as 10%, at the beginning of an analysis and use that as my test data for all my models while the other 90% is training data. When I've found a model I like that performs well enough, I retrain the model on all the data (both training and test) to get the most accurate model to deploy to production.

NOTES

It's really important to have a good explanation of the difference between training and test data, because understanding the distinction and how to think about it is a fundamental part of creating a machine learning model. That being said, there are many valid strategies for splitting your data. Besides random sampling, for example, you could use cross-validation to avoid biasing your model while training it on more data. So long as you have a logical explanation of why you chose a method, you should be good.

A.3.8 *Feature selection*

How would you do feature selection if you had 1,000 covariates and had to reduce them to 20?

—Alex Hayes

EXAMPLE ANSWER

There are several different ways to do this. One possible solution in the case of a prediction problem is to use a lasso regression. A lasso regression is a special type of linear regression that applies a penalty to increasing the value of the coefficients. By increasing the penalty term in the regression, you can make the model have fewer and fewer coefficients until it uses only the 20 most important covariates. In this way, the model selects what the coefficients should be in the model. Although a lasso regression has a lower accuracy score than a linear regression with all the covariates on the training data, it has the benefit of using only a small number of them and may perform better on the test data, as lasso reduces the likelihood of overfitting.

You could also use dimensional reduction techniques like Principal Components Analysis (PCA) to reduce the dimensionality of the problem from 1,000 to 20. The lasso approach will choose 20 features out of the existing 1,000. Methods like principal components analysis will create 20 new features that try to capture as much of the data from the 1,000 as they can.

NOTES

There are many possible solutions to this question. One more solution is to try to use a stepping function to remove covariates over and over until you're down to 20. You could even take many samples of sets of 20 features and choose the set that works best. Think of this question as less of a test of knowing the right approach to a problem and more a test of being able to show that you could find a solution if you faced this problem. This question is a test to make sure you won't get stuck on the job. Can you think of anything you'd want to try? If so, great; you can go try it. If not, you may struggle when working on your own.

If you give multiple answers, be prepared to answer the follow-up question: when would you use one instead of the other? This question is a way to check whether you understand the techniques or just picked them because someone told you to use them. In this case, you could answer that there's a trade-off between interpretability and capturing variability: lasso is easily interpretable, but PCA captures as much variability as possible. Which one you choose depends on what you're looking to achieve with the analysis.

A.3.9   *Deploying a new model*

> *You developed a new model that performs better than your old model currently in production. How do you determine whether you should switch the model in production? How do you go about it?*

—Emily Spahn

EXAMPLE ANSWER

For me, the answer depends on a couple of factors in the environment. First, by what metric does the new model do better? Assuming that it's overall accuracy, I'd check whether the model is sufficiently better that it's worth swapping out the old model. If it's only a percentage point better in accuracy, it may not be worth the effort of changing, because the effect might be negligible. Next, is there a risk to disrupting the current model? If the model was deployed using a well-maintained pipeline with clear logging and testing, I'd probably make the swap, but if the model was deployed by manually moving a model into a production system by a person who is no longer at the company, I'd probably hold off.

Finally, is there a way to A/B test the model first? Ideally, I'd like to have the old and new models run in parallel so that I could test for any problems with the new model or edge cases missed by it. No test system can cover everything from production, so being able to have it running for a select set of customers or inputs first would be ideal.

NOTES

Deploying a model is often a labor-intensive and risky proposition for a company. This question determines whether you understand what that's like and how you would approach the situation. A more-junior data scientist or machine learning engineer may feel that the right choice is to deploy the most accurate model as quickly as possible, but there are risks that need to be managed. If you have any experiences you can draw on (such as model deployments failing), this question is a great place to mention them. If you haven't, that's totally fine; just try to describe what you think might go wrong.

A.3.10   *Model behavior*

> *Given a model you developed, how would you design a metric to evaluate it from the end user's perspective? How would you decide what errors are acceptable?*

—Tereza Iofciu and Bertil Hatt

EXAMPLE ANSWER

Standard model metrics like R-squared or accuracy can miss the end-user or business perspective. A classification model could be right 99% of the time, but the 1% of the time it's wrong, it's such a problem for the business that the model would never be used.

I find that the best way to evaluate a model is to try running an experiment with it. If I'm creating a model to cluster customers into segments, for example, I would present the clusters to marketing and have them try to do a test run of custom marketing to a sample set of customers from the different segments. I would compare how well the marketing performs with and without the customers segmented, and if there is a meaningful improvement, the model is a success. That's totally different from using metrics about the model itself, such as how effectively it performs the segmentation, because those sorts of measures analyze only the model. Here, I'm actually analyzing how it performs compared with no model at all.

The downside of running an experiment with the model is that it's often difficult to set up the experiment. Sometimes, you can't split your customers into ones who get the model and ones who don't. At other times, the effect of the model is so small that it wouldn't show up in any KPIs that are easy to measure. But despite these difficulties, if it's possible to run an experiment, that's almost always the best approach.

NOTES

This question is tricky because it's very general, but to answer it, you need to talk about specifics. Your answer could vary dramatically for a predictive model versus an unsupervised model or, if you're working with marketing, versus the operations department. You'll want to talk a lot about the idea that the statistical measures aren't the same as the measures that the business cares about; junior data scientists can get overly focused on maximizing the statistical measures and ignoring the business ones. But how you end up talking about these ideas is very open. As with many answers, if you can bring examples from your experiences, you can add a lot of depth.

A.3.11 *Experimental design*

(Question, answer, and notes by Ryan Williams)

> *You're developing an app and want to determine whether a newly designed layout would be better than your current one. How would you structure a test to pick the better app layout?*

EXAMPLE ANSWER

There are lots of different ways to answer the specifics of this question, but A/B tests generally follow this type of flow:

1 Define what *better* means by picking the metric(s) you care about improving: active users, button clicks, impressions, and so on.
2 Choose a null hypothesis based around your success metric, such as "Button clicks will be the same for all groups." Use that hypothesis to run a power calculation, which will tell you how long you need to run the test for to detect a change of a certain size.
3 Randomly split your population of app users into groups, and provide each group a different version of the app.

4   After you've run the test for the length of time you decided on in step 2, evaluate whether you see a statistically significant difference between the two groups by using an appropriate statistical test (like a t-test).

NOTES

Questions like this one are common for data science roles on teams that are heavily involved in media measurement, app/web development, and so on. The interviewer usually just wants to know that you understand the purpose and general principles of A/B testing, especially for more-junior roles. Rather than getting bogged down in the specifics of stat testing (such as when to use a chi-square test instead of a t-test), we recommend sticking to a clear high-level approach when answering to demonstrate that you know how to design an experiment and determine causality.

A.3.12 *Flaws in experimental design*

(Question, answer, and notes by Ryan Williams)

> *Assume that you've done an A/B test to select a better app layout; what is a case in which you might not want to implement the new layout despite seeing a statistically significant improvement in the metric you're testing?*

EXAMPLE ANSWER

You wouldn't want to implement the layout if you see it negatively affecting other important metrics (guardrail, or do-no-harm, metrics). An example might be a situation in which the metric you're testing for is user click-throughs, and although you do see a significant improvement in click-throughs for users exposed to the new layout, you also see pages in the app taking longer to load in that layout. In this case, the degradation in app performance may not be worth the increase in click-throughs, because over time, the worse in-app experience may drive users away.

NOTES

This question is very open-ended. What the interviewer wants to see is your recognition that just finding a low *p*-value isn't always a good-enough reason to consider an experiment successful. It's risky for a company to make changes to a live product like an app or website, and a single statistical test usually doesn't encapsulate all the information needed to make the right decision. Some other reasonable answers to this type of question include seeing too small an improvement relative to the cost and risk of changing the app or bias in the sampling/splitting methodology.

A.3.13 *Bias in sampled data*

(Question, answer, and notes by Ryan Williams)

> *What types of biases should you be aware of when using sample data? How can you tell whether a sample is biased?*

EXAMPLE ANSWER

Many types of bias can affect sampled data. One of the most common biases in practical data science applications is selection bias (selecting your sample incorrectly). Selection bias can happen in scenarios such as selecting a random group of customers from of a transaction-level table, which overrepresents customers with multiple transactions. Other types of common bias include survivorship bias (the sample overrepresents a group that made it past some preselection process) and voluntary response bias (the sample overrepresents a group that was more likely to volunteer information about themselves).

There are statistical methods that you can use to identify bias in a sample, like comparing the mean value from your sample with a known or expected mean of the population. You should also think rationally about the sampling process to identify biases, trying to answer this question: is there something about the way we've sampled this group that might make it different from the population we care about?

NOTES

This question is meant to test your understanding of limitations in working with data and drawing conclusions. It's less important to understand specific terms, like *selection bias* and *survivorship bias*, than to understand the ways in which data can be limited or misinforming. The interviewer wants to see that you understand the nuances of working with real-world data—all of which is biased in one way or another—and all the messiness that this data entails. Using data from an optional survey, for example, has a clear voluntary response bias. This doesn't mean that the data is unusable, but it does mean that you should be aware of the bias, think about the consequences it has on your analysis, and take it into account in any conclusions you make.

A.4   Behavioral

A.4.1   Project that had the most impact

What's the project you worked on that had the biggest impact?

EXAMPLE ANSWER

In my last job, I was brought in to build an online experimentation, or A/B testing, analytics system. The company was interested in starting to run experiments and had an engineer who could implement them, two growth marketers who could come up with the ideas and lay out the changes, and a manager, but they needed a way to understand what the results of the experiment were.

When I started, I analyzed each experiment individually in R. But I knew that this wasn't the best system: it meant that the team needed me to run the scripts to see the results and that I was duplicating work across analyses.

That's what led me to build an internal dashboard to monitor experiments. This dashboard included not only the results of each experiment, such as the percentage of people who registered or subscribed in the control versus the treatment group, but also health checks to make sure that the experiment was running as expected and that the results could be trusted. With this dashboard, anyone at the company could see the most up-to-date results.

By the time I left, this dashboard was being used for all the experiments being run across five teams. Thanks to the work I did with the rest of the experimentation team, almost every feature the company launches now is first tested as an experiment to measure whether it has any positive impact.

NOTES

For this answer, if you have done any data science projects for a company, you want to use one of those instead of a non-data science project. On the other hand, if you've done data science projects only for personal use or class assignments, you can highlight another project. The biggest thing here is to focus on the impact on the business. Saying "I built a model with 90% accuracy!" is not what they're looking for; they want to understand how someone used the model, tool, or analysis you built and why it mattered.

A.4.2   *Data surprises*

Can you tell me about a time you found something in the data that surprised you?

EXAMPLE ANSWER

My previous job was at a company that made money with subscriptions. I worked on experiments there, and when I started, I would calculate the subscription rate in an experiment as the percentage of people who entered who later subscribed. Although that sounds good, it turned out that people had subscriptions starting in the future!

After talking with the data scientist who owned the subscription data, I found out that these subscriptions with future start dates were subscriptions that someone had paused. Take a user with a monthly subscription starting in September. She could choose instead of renewing or canceling her subscription in October to pause it, not paying and losing access for two months, but then having the subscription start again in December. In this case, she'd have two rows in the subscription table: one for the September-to-October subscription and then starting in December.

For my use case, I didn't want to count those subscriptions that would start because they would become unpaused; I wanted only subscriptions that someone was actively choosing!

I learned two lessons: that I should never make assumptions about the data and that I may need to customize a data source for my needs. I'd assumed that it would be impossible for subscriptions to start in the future, so I hadn't checked for that. When I realized this issue, I didn't overwrite the original data, because other people still needed to know about subscriptions that had been set to start in the future. Instead, I made my own table that counted only new subscriptions.

NOTES

In this answer, we used an example in which we were surprised by what is essentially a data quality issue for our use case. But you could talk instead about a time your intuition just didn't match the results, for example, an exploratory data analysis you did of the Reddit subthread on data science, when you thought the word count of posts would correlate positively to the number of comments, but it turned out that there was a negative correlation. You also want to make sure that you explain why you held your initial assumption.

This question is testing whether you think about your data before simply diving into it. It's also testing that you don't just try to confirm your initial hypothesis but let yourself be surprised by results and adapt to the new information.

A.4.3 *Previous job reflections*

What is the thing that you wanted to change most in your previous job that you couldn't?

—Bertil Hatt

EXAMPLE ANSWER

I found that at my last company, there were real struggles with communication. The leadership team was constantly asking people to be more open and express their concerns, but it wouldn't happen. My theory is that it was due to the leaders themselves not being open; they would constantly tell us everything was going great when we knew that there were problems.

The thing I wanted to change the most was to have the leadership open up to us. If they would express their own struggles and concerns more, it would have made it easier for the more-junior employees to open up and made for a better working environment.

NOTES

This question is *tricky*. You need to show that you understood your previous working environment well enough to have a proposed improvement for it, but you need to do it while making it sound as though you had a good relationship with your previous employer.

You could list lots of different types of changes, such as technical changes, team dynamic changes, and product changes. The more meaningful a change you can list, the better (so not "I wish we had free soda"). It's also great if you can reflect on why that change didn't happen ("I wish we had been using a modern language like R or Python, but we were using SAS because of all the legacy products we maintained"). Explaining why the change hadn't happened shows that you put thought into the limitations of the environment.

Avoid insulting your previous employer ("Can you believe they were unintelligent enough to use FORTRAN!?"). You don't want to give the impression that someday, you'll leave your next company and insult them too. Be respectful of the work your past employer has done, even if it's ultimately lacking.

A.4.4   *Senior person making a mistake based on data*

> *What would you do if you had calculations or results that conflicted with the previous results of a senior person in the company? Would you try to convince them that you were right, and if so, how?*

—Hlynur Hallgrímsson and Heather Nolis

EXAMPLE ANSWER

First, I'd ask myself whether this result is important enough to bring up. If it was off by a small percentage, but we'd still make the same decision with the new results, or if the previous results were never used for anything, I might let it go.

If not, I'd start by trying to understand the motivations and goals of the other person. Suppose that this person was the vice president of sales and they had done an analysis showing that each salesperson they hired brought in more than twice their salary in sales. Then they used this analysis to justify hiring five more people for the team. If I show that each salesperson actually brings in less than their salary, that could jeopardize the whole sales department. People would have a lot riding on the outcome so it would be important to be careful.

I'd set up a meeting with them. By understanding the situation, I could make an educated guess about how they would react. If the results conflicted because they had an error in their analysis or if the result was fundamental to their business, I'd expect that they might be defensive and try to find flaws in my analysis, so I'd prepare emotionally and triple-check my results. I'd try to find a solution that lets them save face, pivot their strategy, and put the business in the right direction.

In the worst case—they didn't listen or offer any valid reasons why the new results were wrong, and I think the new results are vital to the business—I'd work with my manager to come up with a strategy to have the new results shared and acted on. Unfortunately, sometimes people won't end up agreeing with your new analysis, and the focus needs to shift from convincing them to finding a way to accomplish your goals and limit the impact of a wrong analysis.

NOTES

This question seeks to understand how'd you handle conflict with someone more senior. Although many answers exist, some like "I would email everyone in the company to publicly talk about how wrong they were" or "I'd always handle it this way no matter the situation because the only thing that matters is the data" would definitely be an issue. Academics especially can struggle with handling conflict in businesses; in academia, talks can be a contest of who in the audience can find the most flaws in the research and tear down the arguments. In industry, on the other hand, you need to be able to share your viewpoint and help the business make right decisions while balancing other factors and understanding the nuances of different situations. The interviewer is looking for signs that you've successfully resolved disagreements before, so exhibit that experience as much as you can.

A.4.5   *Disagreements with teammates*

Tell me about a time you disagreed with a teammate. What was it about, and what did you do?

EXAMPLE ANSWER

One time, I was working with a product manager on an experiment in which we'd set a run time of two weeks based on a power calculation. Four days in, they wanted to stop the experiment early and fully launch it because the p-value was .04 on the main success metric. But I knew this could be an artifact of peeking: by checking your results every day to see whether the p-value dips below .05 and stopping if it does, you greatly increase your false-positive rate. I also knew that the product manager was highly incentivized to have a successful experiment: one of the main metrics they were evaluated on was the incremental revenue gained through successful experiments.

In this case, I focused on making sure that I knew where they were coming from and asking questions. I brought us back to our shared goals: making the company as successful as possible. I walked them through a simple example from the webcomic xkcd to help them develop the intuition about why stopping early could be a problem: that if you check whether 20 different colors of jelly beans were associated with acne, even if none was, by chance a statistical test would likely "find" that one of them was. (Here is a link to the comic, for reference: https://xkcd.com/882/.) In the same way, we were chasing statistical ghosts and were liable to trick ourselves into thinking that we had a positive impact when we didn't. In the end, they agreed to keep the experiment running for the planned two weeks.

This situation also led me to think more about how I could improve the experimentation tool to make it easier for people to do the right thing. One experimentation platform I know has a little circle that fills up more every day and turns in to a check mark at the end of seven days. This helped people run their experiments for at least a week, which is best practice.

NOTES

This answer uses the STAR (situation, task, approach, result) approach. STAR is a classic framework for answering behavioral interview questions, as it provides a structure for the answer that is easy to follow. When thinking of a good example for this question, you want to find a situation that had a positive result, not "And then we never spoke again" or "I got him fired." You also want the disagreement to be business-related, not "We disagreed about how to load the office dishwasher." Interviewers are looking to see whether you can empathize with someone you disagree with and avoid bad-mouthing them or blaming them for your problem.

APPENDIX *Interview questions*

A.4.6 Difficult problems

What do you do when you don't know how to solve a data science–related problem?

EXAMPLE ANSWER

For coding questions, Google is my friend. Often, an answer in the Stack Overflow question is the first result if I Google an error message or something like "How do I do Latent Dirichlet allocation in R?" If I know what the function or package I want to use is, but I'm not sure exactly how it works, I'll check for any documentation.

But sometimes, I don't know how to approach a problem. In those cases, I usually start breaking down the problem, sometimes by writing the different components on the whiteboard. This helps me get down to the core issues, which may be ones I know how to tackle, even if initially the whole problem seemed daunting.

I also like the rule of spending 15 or 30 minutes on the problem myself (depending on whether I feel that I'm making any headway) and then asking another data scientist at my company for help. It's my responsibility to try to figure it out on my own first, but it's also on me not to be stuck on something for a whole day when a colleague could have helped me in a few minutes. When I reach out, I'll share what I've tried along with a small, reproducible example to make it easier for the other person to see the issue (rather than send them hundreds of lines of code to parse).

NOTES

Data science is a field in which you'll continually be learning and challenged by problems you've never seen before, so it's important to develop a few strategies for getting unstuck. One thing this question is looking for is that you've developed strategies for outside the classroom setting, where you had an answer sheet, classmates, and a professor there to help you. You'll potentially need to tailor this answer to the company you're talking to. If you say that your main strategy is asking your data scientist colleagues, and you're interviewing to be the first data scientist, that answer will be a red flag.

A.5 Brain teasers

A.5.1 Estimation

What's an estimate for how many mini shampoo bottles are used by all the hotels in the United States in a year?

EXAMPLE ANSWER

I estimate the number of bottles by using the following formula:

```
number of hotels in the US * average number of rooms per hotel * 1 shampoo
bottle per occupied room per night * average room utilization * 365 days per
year = number of shampoo bottles per year
```

Then I estimate the numbers in the formula:

- *Number of hotels in the United States*—If I assume that there is a hotel for every 5,000 people in the country, and there are around 300 million people in the country, that's 60,000 hotels.
- *Number of rooms per hotel*—Fifty seems like a decent guess for the average number of rooms in a hotel from the hotels I've stayed in.
- *Average room utilization*—Because hotels need to be profitable, I'll guess that each night, a room has an 80 percent chance of being occupied.

This makes the formula `60,000 * 50 * 1 * 0.8 * 365 = 876 million bottles`.

NOTES

The solution to this question is to come up with a formula for the number you're trying to estimate and take a guess at the numbers to put in the formula. There are many, many versions of this question, from "How many ping-pong balls can fit into a Boeing 747 airplane?" to "How many pianos are there in France?" The interviewer is looking to see whether you can come up with a formula that makes some sense and that your logic for guessing each of the numbers in the formula makes sense. There's almost no chance that you'll get the number close to right during the interview (we have no idea whether 50 is a good guess for the average number of hotel rooms, for example), but that's not important.

There isn't much you can do to prepare for these questions except practice the improvisational component of coming up with formulas and estimates on the fly.

A.5.2   *Combinatorics*

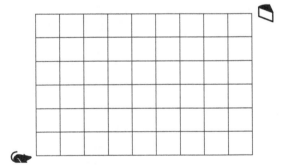

Imagine a grid like the one pictured above, with a mouse at the bottom-left corner of the grid. At the top-right corner is a piece of cheese. The mouse can travel only along the lines in the grid and would never move away from it. How many paths are there from the mouse to the cheese?

EXAMPLE ANSWER

To get to the cheese, the mouse has to move one space alone a horizontal line in the grid nine times and then move one space along a vertical line in the grid six times (because the grid is 9x6). Let's call a horizontal move H and a vertical move V. Then any string with 9 Hs and Vs is a valid path from the start to the end. Going straight up and then to the right, for example, would be VVVVVVHHHHHHHHHH. There are 15 factorial (15!) ways to arrange 15 distinct characters, which are called *permutations*, but because 6 of them are the same letter (V) and 9 of them are the same letter (H), we have to remove all the duplicate arrangements. We can remove them by counting how many duplicates there are of each. The Vs are duplicated 6! times (the number of ways they can be arranged), and the Hs are duplicated 9! times. That means that the answer is 15!/(6!)/(9!), or 5,005 paths.

NOTES

This question is a really hard one to answer. First, it's hard to know the right answer. If you've somehow studied the field of combinatorics, you may know it; otherwise, it's hard to suddenly realize that you can think of the problem as arranging paths. Even if you see that way of formulating the problem, you may not know how to count the number of solutions.

Second, even if you know the answer, it's hard to give it in a way that clearly explains the problem and solution without being verbose. You can't assume that everyone knows terms such as *permutation*, yet if you were to explain it all, you'd spend too much time on it.

Finally, there really is no way to study for this question. There are so many combinatorics questions that you can't have answers for all of them prepared in advance. Your best bet for questions like these is to explain your thought process and how you might approach the problem. If the interviewer is putting a lot of weight on questions like this one, that's a red flag.

index

jobs *(continued)*
    referrals 97–98
    résumés 86–94
  finding new employment while employed 252–254
  interviewing for 251–252
  past, on résumés 88–89
  searching for 73–74, 81–84
    attending meetups 79–80
    decoding descriptions 75–77
    different after first job 250–252
    pitfalls 77
    setting expectations 77–78
    social media for 80–81
joins, types of 289–290
junior data scientist, defined 262
Junior positions 75
Jupyter Notebooks 168–169, 287

K

Kaggle 57, 78
Kehrer, Kristen 99–100, 133
Keim, Michelle 226–227
keywords, in résumés 96
Knight, Rebecca 279
KPIs (Key Performance Indicators) 199

L

Lamott, Anne 69
Lander, Jared 68
large organizations 34–36, 138–139
lasso regression 299
late-stage startups 28–30
  pros and cons of 29–30
  team culture 28–29
  tech used by 29
Lauret, Arnaud 209
leaders in data science organization 16, 151
leadership interviews 104
learning
  at conferences 234
  at early-stage startups 25–26
  at giant government contractors 33
  at late-stage, successful tech startups 30
  by self-teaching 23
  comparison between types of companies 34
  from bad jobs 150–151
  from mentors 147
  necessity of 248
  to manage 266
  via books 50
  whether part of company culture 226
  See also skills

letters of recommendation, for graduate program 42
libraries
  creating in open source 241–242
  frequently used 286–287
linear regressions 166, 179
LinkedIn 80, 88
  bootcamp graduates on 45–46
  referrals via 97
  setting to show openess to recruiters 250
load testing 187
Locke, Steph 279
logging 187–188
logistics, questions asked about during interviews 110
logos, for communities 238
long-form analyses 203
long-term projects 203
loyalty program analysis example 217

M

machine learning
  interview with Nolis, Heather 189–191
  questions during job interviews 109, 293–303
    boosting 297
    confusion matrix 295
    deploying new models 300
    favorite algorithm 298
    feature selection 299–300
    model behavior 300–301
    training vs. test data 298–299
  taught at bootcamps 44
machine learning engineers 74
  experience of 190
  making analyses 158
  production for 177
Madubuonwu, Brooke Watson 129–133
management role 263–266
  benefits of 264
  drawbacks of 264–265
  how to obtain 265–266
    earning promotions within company 266
    growing new teams 266
  with new company 266
Manager's Path, The (Fournier) 277
managers
  as stakeholders 196–197
  resolving issues with 248–249
master résumés 96
master's degree programs 38
mathematics 6–7
McDowell, Gayle Laakmann 132
median 293